DISCREPANT SOLACE

Discrepant Solace

Contemporary Literature and the Work of Consolation

DAVID JAMES

UNIVERSITY PRESS

Great Clarendon Street, Oxford, OX2 6DP,
United Kingdom

Oxford University Press is a department of the University of Oxford.
It furthers the University's objective of excellence in research, scholarship,
and education by publishing worldwide. Oxford is a registered trade mark of
Oxford University Press in the UK and in certain other countries

© David James 2019

The moral rights of the author have been asserted

First Edition published in 2019

Impression: 1

All rights reserved. No part of this publication may be reproduced, stored in
a retrieval system, or transmitted, in any form or by any means, without the
prior permission in writing of Oxford University Press, or as expressly permitted
by law, by licence or under terms agreed with the appropriate reprographics
rights organization. Enquiries concerning reproduction outside the scope of the
above should be sent to the Rights Department, Oxford University Press, at the
address above

You must not circulate this work in any other form
and you must impose this same condition on any acquirer

Published in the United States of America by Oxford University Press
198 Madison Avenue, New York, NY 10016, United States of America

British Library Cataloguing in Publication Data

Data available

Library of Congress Control Number: 2019933241

ISBN 978–0–19–878975–8

Printed and bound by
CPI Group (UK) Ltd, Croydon, CR0 4YY

Links to third party websites are provided by Oxford in good faith and
for information only. Oxford disclaims any responsibility for the materials
contained in any third party website referenced in this work.

For María and William

Acknowledgements

This book started life a decade ago at the University of Nottingham, began to mature at Queen Mary, University of London, before then coming to fruition many years later at the University of Birmingham. In these successive professional homes, I've had the fortune of working alongside encouraging, patient, and inspiring colleagues. I also feel fortunate to have had the chance to contribute to institutions where the Humanities have received support and investment, throughout what continues to be a challenging moment—understatement—for higher education in Britain. Nor do I take for granted how lucky I've been to work under the exemplary leadership (and in some cases the valuable mentorship too) of Michèle Barrett, Warren Boutcher, David Colclough, Mark Currie, Markman Ellis, Paul Hamilton, Dominic Head, Andrzej Gasiorek, Deborah Longworth, and Julie Sanders.

Being awarded the Philip Leverhulme Prize as this project began to emerge from its chrysalis was an exceptional honour. I thank the School of English and Drama at Queen Mary for supporting my application for the scheme and for so convivially accommodating my subsequent leave from teaching and administrative roles in the department. This Leverhulme Trust grant facilitated a transformative period of research and reflection—a rare, privileged opportunity. I thank the Trust not only for the resources themselves, but for continuing to encourage and foster the kinds of humanistic inquiry that take risks.

Over the past decade, the conception and development of this book has benefitted immeasurably from an international community of academic friends, collaborators, and correspondents. It has been an absolute pleasure to work with Rebecca L. Walkowitz and Matthew Hart on a book series for Columbia University Press that has genuinely transformed my sense of contemporary literature studies as a field. This editorial partnership has also revamped my understanding of what can be done with a monograph, and hopefully this book bears some trace of the many things I've learned from our labours on Literature Now. I'm also grateful to Michèle Barrett, Tim Bewes, Kevin Brazil, Joe Brooker, Santanu Das, Robert Eaglestone, Jane Elliott, Ben Etherington, Patrick Flanery, Jonathan Flatley, Finn Fordham, Yogita Goyal, Patrick Hayes, Andrew Hoberek, Suzanne Hobson, Chris Holmes, Rachael Gilmour, Eric Langley, Michael LeMahieu, John Lurz, Molly Macdonald, Doug Mao, Huw Marsh, Nicky Marsh, Jesse Matz, Peter D. McDonald, David McAllister, Sam McBean, kitt price, Jacqueline Rose, Matthew Rubery, Paul Saint-Amour, Charlotta Salmi, and Urmila Seshagiri for generous and invigorating reflections on the ideas surrounding this book. Gerard Aching, Derek Attridge, Elleke Boehmer, Mrinalini Chakravorty, Rita Felski, Peter Howarth, Katherine Ibbett, Michelle Kelly, Heather Love, Laura Marcus, Scott McCracken, Deborah Longworth, Ankhi Mukerjee, Graham Riach, Nadia Valman, and Jarad Zimbler invited me to consider unforeseen implications that turned out to be genuinely significant as this book began to take shape. Neal Alexander, Mark Currie,

David Dwan, Andrzej Gasiorek, Matthew Hart, Dominic Head, Heather Houser, Julia Jordan, Peter Middleton, Paige Reynolds, Andrew van der Vlies, Nathan Waddell, and Rebecca Walkowitz all went well beyond the call of friendship by tackling quite sizeable portions of the manuscript with great insight and thoroughness. I'm deeply fortunate to have benefitted from the wisdom of these brilliant scholars—who effortlessly combine intellectual companionship with rigorously unbiased advice—and of course any remaining kinks in the following pages are wholly mine.

Audiences attending symposiums and research seminars at Cambridge, Cornell, Frankfurt, Keele, London's Institute of English Studies, Oxford, Portsmouth, Queen's Belfast, Queen Mary, Virginia, Sussex, York, and Zurich, as well as those attending panels at MLA conventions and Society for Novel Studies conferences (in Austin and Philadelphia, and in Pittsburgh and Ithaca, respectively), all provided memorable discussions and provocative suggestions that helped to strengthen the sinew of my arguments. In recalling such occasions, I feel especially indebted to Elizabeth Anker, Nancy Armstrong, Harriet Baker, Nick Bentley, Peter Boxall, Alicia Broggi, Angus Brown, Stuart Burrows, Robert Caserio, Jonathan Culler, Ben Davies, Jim English, Grant Farred, Paraic Finnerty, Jonathan Grossman, Nathan Hensley, Adam Kelly, Alexandra Kingston-Reese, Elizabeth Kollmann, Michael Levenson, Caroline Levine, Alex Murray, Christopher Nealon, Kent Puckett, Bryan Radley, Jahan Ramazani, Gayle Rogers, Ellen Rooney, Antony Rowland, Martin Ryle, Melissa Schuh, Pam Thurschwell, Sara Upstone, Johannes Voelz, and Hope Wolf.

This book contains, on purpose, a good deal of close reading, some of which is directed at works in translation. As such, I'm tremendously grateful to David Grossman's English-language translator, Jessica Cohen, for finding the time to meet and talk about his work. She tolerated my queries about tiny details, appeased my nagging worries about working on translated text, and generously commented on what would become a crucial chapter in this book's critical story.

The anonymous readers for Oxford University Press offered superb advice and compelled me to think well beyond my comfort zone about this book's larger conceptual and historical purposes. The editorial and production teams at the Press itself are exemplary and it has been so reassuring to be in their safe hands. From the outset, Jacqueline Norton astutely recognized what this book was trying to do. I've benefitted in equal measure from both her advice and her patience, doubtlessly exploiting the latter a little too much as the manuscript entered its (seemingly interminable) final approach.

Like countless scholars who are drawn to the riches of the Harry Ransom Center in Austin, I have enjoyed the care and guidance of the Center's infinitely helpful staff. They enabled me to navigate J. M. Coetzee's voluminous archive, along with the more recently catalogued papers of Ian McEwan and Kazuo Ishiguro. I would especially like to thank Rick Watson, Head of Reference and Research Services at the HRC, for speedily sorting out numerous practicalities. I've been able to incorporate these archival materials with the permission of the HRC and with the direct consent of John Coetzee, Kazuo Ishiguro, and Ian McEwan, to each of whom I extend my gratitude here. For Ishiguro and McEwan, quotations from their respective papers are reproduced by permission of these authors c/o Rogers, Coleridge & White Ltd, 20 Powis Mews, London W11 1JN.

Finally, I'm grateful to a number of presses and editors for being able to include material here that, in rather different form, appeared in essays of various kinds. Portions of 'Critical Solace', *New Literary History*, 47.4 (Autumn 2016): 481–504, reprinted with permission of Johns Hopkins University Press, allowed me to test-drive contentions that were subsequently developed more extensively in Chapters 2 and 6. Chapter 7 integrates material from a review of David Grossman's *Falling Out of Time* in *Public Books* (1 November 2014): special thanks to Sharon Marcus for her assiduous and generative editorial advice. Chapter 7 also includes revised sections from 'In Defense of Lyrical Realism', an article that first appeared in *Diacritics* 45.4 (2017): 69–91copyright © 2018 Cornell University. Elements of critical and archive material from Chapter 4 have been reworked for the essay 'Styles', in *The Cambridge Companion to J. M. Coetzee*, ed. Jarad Zimbler (Cambridge University Press, 2019), reprinted with permission of Cambridge University Press.

I knew this book was never going to be straightforward to conceive, research, and write, revolving as its pages do around losses of all magnitudes. María del Pilar Blanco has accompanied me through all the twists and turns of that process: reading and rereading the fruits of my labours along the way, she tolerated their embryonic arguments while tolerating too their knock-on effects for our daily rhythms at home. Somehow, she found the patience and energy to remain my most razor-sharp reader from start to finish. Midway through my time spent drafting commentaries on the unconsoled, our life was given over to the beautifully exhausting commotion that only a newborn can bring. Every day since, my son has offered up his own rascally consolations, memories of which would no doubt have been consumed by the mists of sleep deprivation without a smartphone's handy and now invaluable archive of snaps. He has brought immeasurable joy to families on both sides of the Atlantic, not least by bringing them closer. If this book turned out in part to be about the powers of description, I make no pretences to felicity when it comes to finding words that might capture how precious the gifts are that flow from William and his mum. Together they've helped me to learn how to read emotion differently.

Contents

Introduction: Consolation's Discrepant Forms	1
1. Fetched from Oblivion	41
2. Description as Redress	65
3. Elegy Unrestored	88
4. The Religion of Style	114
5. Life-Righting and Magical Thinking	148
6. Apprehensive Alleviation	175
7. Walking with the Unconsoled	193
Epilogue: Bribes of Aesthetic Pleasure?	213
Notes	227
Bibliography	259
Index	271

Introduction
Consolation's Discrepant Forms

Taking solace. A commonplace for comforters, the phrase is no less consequential for being so reusable. As instructions go, it sounds benign, tactful, virtually straightforward. Yet when we try to console we also, however delicately, try to counsel and the advice we bestow can present an emotional feat—a virtual leap from what's lost. For solace recommends the prospect of feeling otherwise, a rather speculative prospect that may seem like a betrayal of the damage for which consolation is designed. Accepting solace in turn means conceding what cannot be repaired, facing what escapes easy mitigation. Unlike effortless distraction, solace only brings into greater focus the wound it targets, more often exposing than dispelling the desolation it promises to offset. On this score consolation rarely guarantees lasting comfort, let alone augurs a cure. As a countervailing phenomenon that closely tracks the distance we travel from loss, consolation also maps the affectively rocky ground we may yet need to cross.

What has literature to say about these things? *Words of solace*. Another commonplace, perhaps. But how do consolation's verbal lineaments actually work in literary expression? Do writers seek to approximate the potencies of solace—unwanted or welcomed, unsuitable if nevertheless expected—we glean from words of compassionate reassurance or uplifting alleviation in life? Or do they in fact do something quite different, something we can only grasp when the emotional approximation of consolatory effects isn't the text's only possible or indeed desirable goal? Lingering on the implications of that last question, this book examines what's at stake in contemporary literature's extension of consolation's critical and creative conditions of possibility. In orientation, my inquiry moves beyond the issue of whether or not literature tangibly consoles readers in order to consider the contexts and consequences for writers who negotiate solace as a problem—a source of equivocation rather than a placating solution. Granted, consolation isn't typically regarded as a conundrum in this sense; earmarking instead the prospect of relief, it carries hints of revival and eventual endurance. For this very reason, we also know that consolation isn't always condoned by the bereaved or harrowed, for whom remedial stories might feel intolerable. It's not difficult to imagine situations where the impulse to console would seem inappropriate and disrespectful, even insolent or obscene. And one could imagine in turn how a book's impulse to console, to redress the scars it describes, only diminishes rather than magnifies the emotional costs of the turmoil it plots. In critical discourse, this sort of aesthetic treachery is well documented and easily indicted. But in creative practice, is the work of solace really that uncomplicated or ethically unsound?

Sonali Deraniyagala doesn't think so. In late December 2004 she was visiting Yala national park in Sri Lanka with her husband, Steve, and two sons, accompanied by her parents from Colombo. At dawn on 26 December Deraniyagala first glimpsed a 'foamy wave' rising rather higher than usual along the shore next to her hotel; although one 'never saw water on that stretch of sand', she 'thought nothing of it'.[1] Moments later, as 'more white froth' appeared, 'not receding or dissolving', suddenly 'charging, churning', she fled with Steve and the boys with such terror that they 'didn't stop' even to alert her parents (5). Their ensuing attempt to escape the tsunami in a friend's jeep lasted only minutes, as the wave swamped and overturned them. Deraniyagala herself was flung clear into 'unknown chaos' from which she somehow emerged alive (9). Found staggering deliriously in circles she began to make out a wasteland of annihilation, a 'knocked-down world' left by the receding waters her family did not survive (11).

Wave is Deraniyagala's 2013 memoir of that horrific day and the months and years of extreme grief that followed. It's also a book about formidable challenges of assembling in prose the particularities of such an unspeakable loss. 'When I began writing', she notes, 'I was terribly afraid of details',[2] a fear that turns into a temporary source of endurance, enabling her to withstand the void that remains: 'I must stop remembering', we're told in *Wave*'s first part, since the 'more I remember, the greater my agony' (44). But as she later recalls, 'gradually with the writing I began to reach for details and recover them'.[3] As a chronological whole, the memoir testifies to Deraniyagala's arduous progression from her fear of verbalizing what's gone, of affirming the family's absence by describing them with any detail at all ('They are my world. How do I make them dead? My mind toppled' [34]), towards a desire instead 'to get right into those details', where her impulse 'to write well allowed [her] to access the memory as closely as [she] could'.[4] Readers of *Wave* would doubtlessly find this most dreadful of losses irremediable. But in between the book's searing accounts of heartache, tenderly narrated recollections reanimate the loved ones they both capture and mourn. 'Remembering has been the huge consolation', attests Deraniyagala, 'making' bereavement 'tolerable, even more than tolerable'.[5]

This sense of finding consolation in agonized retrospection is reciprocated at the level of form. *Wave*'s forensic approach to memories, distressing and cherished alike, suggests that descriptive specificity can itself be restorative, if also avoidably painful. Deraniyagala seems determined to appreciate past experiences in a language of vigorous precision. To 'recover all the details and in the process recover myself', became 'my way of keeping them with me', she reflects. Facing recollection with such exactitude 'was agony'—but 'a better quality of agony' than 'try[ing] to keep it out'.[6] One stylistic consequence of this shift from rejecting details to seeking them out is the book's movement from ferocious restraint to elegiac lyricism. Descriptions evolve from spare, shard-like glimpses throughout *Wave*'s catastrophic exposition to incrementally prolonged, lusciously recounted moments of everyday family life as the years pass. Expanding, increasingly scrupulous depictions release the prose from the clutches of sorrow. Deraniyagala's register and syntax thus double the mental effect she favours more than once of being slowly *unclenched*, as immediate calamity makes way over time for the possibility of reconstructing the habits, routines, and fascinations she shared with Steve and their sons, Vikram and Malli. In the opening sections, for instance, her clipped, declarative syntax simulates not only the tsunami's physical horror but also those ensuing weeks of psychic devastation and self-destruction that led her to research reliable methods of suicide: 'All that they were missing, I desperately shut out. I was terrified of everything because everything was from that life. Anything that excited them, I wanted destroyed' (35). Four years later, in the London home she always assumed would be unbearable to revisit, she finds herself 'clinging to its familiarity, which soothes me somehow' (94). Just as 'the descriptions of nature' in Peter Matthiessen's *The Snow Leopard*—the 1978 book that consoled and inspired her while writing *Wave*—proved to be 'a painkiller',[7] so here, in Deraniyagala's all-too-empty home, naturalistic observations offer their own consolatory elevation.

The uplift accompanying those observations syncs *Wave*'s style with Deraniyagala's discovery that recollections, though periodically torturous, keep her 'buoyant' with the details they recover.[8] While this domestic setting couldn't be more unremarkable, the affective swell it causes couldn't be less so: her cautious, granular appreciation of a frosty garden at dawn both acknowledges and audits the scene's percolating solace. Since the picture she forms cannot be disarticulated from the violent absence of the children who could be sharing it, Deraniyagala's assiduous work of description initiates and fosters a variety of vigilant consolation.

> And there is a lovely web on the climbing rose this morning, very showy and intricate. But they can't see it. So is it because I am hazy from sleep that I still feel a stab of wonder when I do? My desolation of last night is now dissolving, but is this just the cheer of the early sun? I wonder, but I am also certain that, for some time at least, I will keep returning to this house and to its warmth and comfort. There is a small snail edging across the table on the patio. The heat from its tiny body is thawing out the beads of frost that have studded the table overnight. It leaves a watery trail. They would be so stirred by this. (94–5)

Note the emotional alternations. Though wary at first of the way 'wonder' attenuates 'desolation', Deraniyagala then acknowledges her wonderment's affinity with the 'stirred' response she imagines in her sons, a response whose studied fascination, whose close-up enchantment with the frosted snail-trail, is enacted by the scene's pictorial devotion to the fauna of an otherwise ordinary morning. While her paired questions temporarily confirm her initial caution—watchful as she seems of her own surrender to the appealing 'cheer' of what she sees—this momentary segue into self-scrutiny is surpassed by the descriptions that follow. From interiorizing worry, from the shame implied by delight escaping for an instant the mesh of grief, she turns in the end to the garden, captivated again, just as she resolves to 'keep returning to this house' notwithstanding the loss it monumentalizes. The solace yielded by this episode is staged yet also examined with a language that accepts yet also inspects the 'warmth and comfort' Deraniyagala identifies in spite of herself—and in spite of whatever limits we as readers would impose upon the very idea of consolation in this shattering book.

Nothing seems more indiscreet than evaluating a narrative about scales of grief that few of us are ever likely to experience. But if it's not for us to judge whether *Wave* offers any tangible solace in the end—just as Deraniyagala herself has insisted that despite the letters of gratitude she receives from bereaved readers she is 'not in a position to give advice or to console'[9]—then the line of affective inquiry needs adjusting. For Deraniyagala invites more than respectful appreciation, however awed we are by the extremity of what she recalls. Doing justice to this book therefore means doing justice to what its very style makes possible when we are confronted with experiences that might appear inexpressible. With great rhetorical dexterity, Deraniyagala imparts emotions at once fierce and poignant, macabre and mundane, finding a vocabulary for the convulsions and convolutions of grief that refuses to sanctify sorrow as ineffable. A work of reconstruction that's as formally innovative as it is emotionally courageous, the memoir confronts preconceptions about what consolation amid inconsolable loss means for literature and indeed for life.

Wave movingly proves that 'figurative language', as Christina Crosby attests, 'helps us approach what's otherwise unapproachable or incommunicable'.[10] Crosby had her own harrowing reasons to discover that '[w]riting offers, not a way out, but a way into the impossible dilemmas of not-knowing' (200). A literature professor of gender and sexuality studies, Crosby was at the peak of her career in 2003; a keen cyclist, she was also at peak fitness, aiming to clock 1,000 miles over the season. In September of that year she celebrated her fiftieth birthday. A month later, she caught a branch in her spokes at the brow of a hill, slamming her chin-first onto the pavement with a force that left her instantly paralyzed. *A Body, Undone: Living on After Great Pain* is Crosby's 2016 record of confronting and adapting to a new life of profound physical disability and chronic neurological pain. She maintains that 'living *in extremis* can clarify what is often obscure, in this case the fragility of our beautiful bodies and the dependencies of all human beings' (10). The book itself allows her to dramatize the struggle of reconciling two selves in time, before and after paralysis, in much the same way as Deraniyagala embarked upon *Wave* 'to re-enter each aspect of my life, of before, and recover all the details and in the process recover myself'.[11] For her part, Crosby 'started writing this book to create something from an otherwise confounded life. Only through writing have I arrived at the life I now lead, the body I now am' (12). Finding 'solace in tropes' (12), she shares with her friend, the writer Maggie Nelson, a conviction that 'language' is 'the most likely medium for addressing the imponderable' (8), just as Deraniyagala gradually hones in writing the means for 'absorb[ing]' memory's 'findings free from the fear of always colliding with the too familiar' (206). Indeed, Nelson's poems 'were a second gift' for Crosby: composed while bearing witness to her agonizing hospitalization, they focus on 'a time that left a deep, confused, and overwhelmingly painful impress' on her; yet they also 'suspend' Crosby's 'life in the richness of poetic language' (9). *A Body, Undone* reprises this consolatory metaphor of preservation towards the close:

> Tropes transport memories and transform them, as resin is transformed under pressure into amber, sometimes with a small, ancient bit of life suspended inside. Amber can be remarkably clear, but the piece that conserves a suspended life is often more valuable. Writing works on memory, compressing and doubtless distorting the past, and offers bodies for the inspection of reader and writer alike. (201)

Crosby concedes that literature cannot entirely recapture the fullness of past experience. Depiction itself may even damage what's recalled. But she also suggests that although the 'intricacies of bodymind interactions defy certainties and confound representation' (21), finding a form to communicate experience's resistance to expression, to work through the very paradox of describing affects that escape signification, affords its own consolation. Literary creation, in this account, is an emotional incentive that's also an epistemological imperative: 'I see no other way to go on – how else will I understand? How will you?' (21).

When works like Deraniyagala's and Crosby's eloquently delineate feelings that seem to defy description and stable comprehension, they present creative possibilities and solicit critical opportunities. Because these texts further our understanding of how narrative figuratively captures and transmutes seemingly opaque or indecipherable feelings, they also provoke alternative ways of reading *for* emotion's literary registration. By supplying a language for states that struggle for inarticulacy, *Wave* and *A Body, Undone* also test and extend our analytical literacies for approaching affective depiction. Like many of the works in chapters to come—fiction and memoir alike—these narratives involve us in the fraught process by which emotional and physical devastations achieve legibility, even dramatic immediacy, a process they announce rather that conceal when using the difficulty of expression as a spur to creation. Pain that seems to 'confound representation', to recall Crosby's terms, pushes the envelope of style in contemporary writing in ways that warrant further examination. And throughout this book, writers will 'transport' us into formidably affecting worlds where we're invited to ascertain literature's capacity to 'transform' the ravages it so adeptly describes—and to gauge the ethics of associating that transformation with what literary consolation might now entail.

'Discrepant solace' refers to these contentious operations, which present us with stylistic, ethical, and affective destinations for textual analysis. Consolation in works that seem all about inconsolability will invite us to notice how the very language of fiction and memoir countenances solace in emotionally forbidding climates. These texts don't simply communicate experiences that are patently extreme but also challenge the suspicion that the very depiction of such experiences serves to prosecute form as a balm for what otherwise cannot be faced or enunciated. In this way, the contemporary figures I consider unseat conventional wisdom about what consolation might consist of in critical encounters with ferocious situations that their writing animates. While pursuing this story of solace in works where it doesn't comfortably belong, I acknowledge that the very 'question of what does or does not console', as Angela Leighton shrewdly reminds us, 'involves some fixing of the emotional stakes'. Consider that 'most bleak and "anti-sentimental" of elegies, Larkin's "Aubade",' a poem, reflects Leighton, that 'might also be grimly, even upliftingly, consoling'.

By contrast, an overtly 'consolatory ending' (Tennyson's from 'In Memoriam', for instance) 'may only depress with triteness'.[12] These observations point not merely to the capriciousness or sheer variety of responses that any given text may elicit—responses that may not always fit hand in glove with the emotional terrain a book crosses—but also to the way that language solicits our participation, as Derek Attridge has described it, in the very 'medium itself as it reveals some of its powers and possibilities'.[13]

Part of what's revealed will also include the capacity of literary style to work aslant the stirring action it conveys (the ethical repercussions of which I'll consider later in this introduction). The very different texts this book brings together elaborate the way style frequently 'complicates the direct emotional effect of the represented scene'.[14] Contemporary writers thereby unsettle the premise that for literature to be tangibly consoling—and, by extension, for consolation to be an object worth analysing—it must ultimately replicate some direct semblance of solace in its audience. My corpus suggests that we are in a historical moment when novelists and memoirists are confronting consolation's contested legitimacy not by producing 'just some mental simulacrum of affect', as Attridge puts it,[15] but by locating that contestation in the anatomy of *form*—a term I invoke capaciously in practice to include stylistic tenor and texture, idioms of diction, syntactical and rhythmic connotations, as well as the overarching organization of a given narrative. Over the following chapters, writers raise the critical stakes of discovering what it means to read for consolation as a paradoxical affordance of the formal operations of texts that may seem virtually antithetical to comfort. Consequently, the byword *discrepancy* will be as applicable to interpretive method as to the conflictive elements and implications intrinsic to those creative works under discussion.

Counterintuitive though such an approach sounds—foraging for consolation's ingredients in textual habitats renowned for its scarcity—we are not unaccustomed to reading like this as a matter of course. Mostly it happens the other way around: we exalt texts that refuse to console us, applauding their responsible prudence in leaving damage uncompensated. One corollary of this habit is that disconsolate art becomes synonymous with adventurous art. When novelist Colum McCann warns that a noticeable amount of contemporary writing has been 'devalued in favour of comfort', his concern dovetails with the tendency in literary and cultural studies to view such comfort as a hindrance to criticism's task of identifying what he calls 'more dangerous' prose. 'Good sentences', insists McCann, 'have the ability to shock, seduce, and drag us out of our stupor'—the opposite, one would assume, of leaving the reader consoled. Such are the sentences we're inclined to celebrate in works that lead readers 'beyond coercion, intimidation, cruelty, duress', even though this mission, as McCann pictures it, of defying aesthetic comfort in order to defend 'the freedom to articulate yourself against power' sounds like a consolingly dignified one for contemporary writers to pursue.[16] Indeed, as novelists and memoirists in this book will reveal, reckoning with consolation by no means inhibits the sort of oppositional creativity McCann holds in high regard. But where criticism is concerned, the assumptions underlying his complaints about comfort are true enough: we don't expect writing that we politically or ethically admire to alleviate the strenuousness of reading about history's ravages, whether at the personal or global scale.

And you will find few soothers in this book. *Discrepant Solace* is concerned with something different, something that has less to do with whether literature today fortifies or assuages readers more effectively than at other points in its history or with the supposed disservice done to contemporary culture by writers who are deemed insufficiently combative because they swap antagonism 'in favour of comfort'. For what would literary consolation now look like if we approached it not as a calmative but as an agent of contestation, one that signals rather than mitigates the implications of traumatic eloquence, implications that surface in renditions of acute, all but incommunicable feeling? And could we unveil an alternative picture of consolation's conceptual, experiential, and political richness in contemporary literature if we deemphasize hypotheses about audience response as the principal foundation for defining writing's consolatory operations? What might it mean, in other words, to think of solace not only as a phenomenon we estimate with rough calculations of how readers emotionally react to diegetic illustrations of consolation (or its privation and inadequacy), but as an affective state *staged by* the formal components of literary works themselves? In the chapters to come, writers perform this staging of solace for different ends: in some instances, to scrutinize how tenable or unattainable consolation becomes at a characterological level; in other cases, to offset crushing events against the very language that conveys them. Writers may thus bring solace dramatically into play over the course of events, where consolation's agitated viability emerges in the milieu of characters' sorrows, longings, and atonements; and they may also manifest it linguistically, in the torsion of sentences that contend with, at times tonally counterpoint, the very experience of loss, shame, or fear that they so vividly communicate. By drawing the work of form into critical contact with dramas of devastation (at scales ranging from the personal to the environmental and world-historical), the phenomenon of discrepant solace brings together narratives that twin the aesthetic conundrum surrounding how writing consoles with the ethical one of whether consolation is desirable at all.

In memoir's case the stakes of identifying consolation in hostile moments couldn't be higher, of course: not only for the memoirists themselves, trying to do justice to the experiences they redescribe, but also for readers, especially sceptical ones. Reading for solace in contemporary literature ignites methodological arguments about how we approach and appraise literary works that innovatively engage ethically testing and emotionally forbidding material. *Wave* and *A Body, Undone* offer a flavour of what several memoirs in the coming pages do: answering back to critical misgivings about consolation as commensurate with reckless denial, placid acceptance, or soothing escapism, they also refuse to privilege devastation's impenetrability or presuppose that the grammar of loss is inexplicable. As these defiant works would imply, *Discrepant Solace* is concerned with what narrative *can* do in overcoming the intractability of formidable emotional states, and its chapters select writers for how they debate solace amid the sorts of physical and psychological devastation, dereliction, or threat that allegedly evade representation. By these lights, consolation's contemporary conditions of possibility become historically apparent: twenty-first-century novels and auto/biographical texts not only thematize but also formally embody in their construction (and for personal memoir, in the lived turbulence of their creation), the recognition that solace, like suffering, 'demands the continued existence of the very art it forbids'.[17]

That, in any case, was Adorno's prescient verdict, from his 1962 reflection on literary commitment. He goes on to add that 'hardly anywhere else' than in art 'does suffering still find its own voice, a consolation that does not immediately betray it'.[18] Conveying some sense of the variety and texture of such a voice defines one major mission for this book. But I set about this task in the thick of considerable doubt over a phenomenon that's easily merged with the very impression of betrayal Adorno suggests we should correct. For we don't tend to think of solace as performing good work, especially not the kind of work that would enable 'someone to have an unmystified, angry view of large and genuinely systemic oppressions', in Eve Sedgwick's influential account, even though the resistance to reparative thought or ameliorative art such a view normally entails 'does not intrinsically or necessarily enjoin that person to any specific train of epistemological or narrative consequences'.[19] Neither does consolation typically figure among those maligned or neglected structures of feeling that affect theorists and historians of emotion have encouraged us to comprehend anew.[20]

Perhaps this is not surprising. After all, few emotional promises would seem at once so desirable and dubious as solace. Though seldom ranked among our most forbidden pleasures, it can nonetheless feel distinctly illicit: a temporary patch in times of sorrow; an indulgent diversion from pressing iniquity; an expedient sedative that blunts compulsions to rebel, that invites us to acquiesce, to be content with what we have. Consolation can be charged with all these misdemeanours. Contemporary writers know its impeachments well, knowing too that they can do more than merely satisfy our assumptions about consolation's impediments, since that would be to comfort us by confirming our own cherished misgivings. What could be more consoling than a gratifying consensus over consolation's suspect ploys? Self-validated objections to solace are themselves irresistibly soothing, and in recent years writers have offered striking counterarguments that don't always fulfil readymade expectations about an affective condition that seems both trusty and mercurial—or about the critical work contemporary literature itself can perform when evoking consolation's experiential and representational complexities. Those counterarguments are the subject of this book.

READING FOR SOLACE

When we consider what consolation means for literary experience the temptation is to focus on claims about the salubrious profits of reading. According to this trend, consolation is a variety of vicarious escape: we enter fictional realms of distress from which we're relieved, in reality, to be spared; we find respite in imagined lives thanks to the compelling diversions they afford. From the Latin *consolari*, consolation shares with solace the same root, *solari*, 'to soothe', an affinity that not simply justifies their interchangeability—though they will indeed be transposable over the pages to come—but that also signals semantic foundations which tend to prompt reservations. Being soothed by a book may be a common enough reward. But the palliative perks of one's immersion in literary worlds are not what professional criticism is trained to appreciate, still less to endorse. Hence consolation's hazy reputation in life as in art: for companions, a mollifying gesture can reconcile intimates to behaviours or beliefs that they really shouldn't tolerate; for culture, the uplifting experience reading or spectating might momentarily allay material need, insinuating solutions to social contradictions that one ought to oppose. According to such allegations, solace should be seen as a fiction in itself—a fable recasting what cannot be put right as something that might still be overcome. To be consoled in this way is to betray the very losses that dispose us to distraction. To allow oneself to be soothed in the eye of grief's storm is to diminish distress by self-deception. To seek refuge in visualizing how blighted events could otherwise have transpired is to entertain stories of speculation that deceive rather than edify, that threaten to attenuate the love for what we have lost, that coax us to retreat from the inexorable turbulence of experience altogether.

'Change always solaces' loss, observed Michel de Montaigne; by diverting us from the wrenching fact of what we cannot recover, change 'dissolves' loss and consequently 'dispels it'. Reading, following his account, becomes one of several mechanisms by which we can 'escape' distress 'into the crowd of other pastimes and cogitations'.[21] To postmillennial ears, this may sound downright irresponsible. Yet there's nothing wrong with regarding literature as an affective amenity. Indeed, the dismissal of writing's palliative or therapeutic potential suggests that criticism may be most hubristic and uncharitable when it invokes a notional reader all too susceptible to solace, a reader who bears little resemblance to how and why audiences find support in the cultural works they consume. What's more, literature may not need to be comforting or dangerously distracting for it to be tangibly consoling. Traumatic scenarios can leave us feeling fortunate, buoyed up by our recognition that we're in the custody of tranquillity—possessing the very security that's chimerical for characters whose fates we follow. Along these lines, reading not only transports us beyond immediate worry, but does so, curiously, despite what we read *about*. One might come away from a text consoled, regardless of the subject matter at hand. Whether distressing or elating, reading can be a welcome detour, a mental getaway that's no less fortifying for being so temporary.

Again, this is likely to carry a whiff of irresponsibility, even though refusing to indulge literature's aesthetic compensations doesn't guarantee the critic a passport to effective resistance. Warning readers of the hazards of diversion or pointing out a work's bewitchments isn't an intrinsically progressive mandate, even if the variously curative and ameliorative effects of reading have often been greeted with 'almost embarrassment or disdain', as Timothy Aubry has shown, as though such benefits were 'indicative of a dangerously self-centred worldview's inescapable influence'.[22] In any case, it's feasible to imagine a book leaving us consoled *and* productively incensed. Uplifted by the creative radiance and singularity of a work, we can still find its content enraging. There's no reason why aesthetic consolation should necessarily inhibit our incentive to act upon the outrage provoked by reading stories of injustice, trauma, or heart-rending deprivation. And yet, simply restoring this kind of complexity to consolation in relation to how we experience the form and content of literary worlds doesn't altogether shield it from certain stock reputes. Because solace is readily equated with inactive or compliant forms of response, it tends to be regarded as the gift from literature that any ideologically vigilant and sufficiently suspicious reader should refuse—the epitome of a naïveté that's easy to see through.

This disapproval of solace has become a dutiful habit that's hard to shake off, and the following sections outline some of the advantages of giving it up. To make that case, I unpick the assumption that consolation remains a close ally of aesthetic therapy. It's not that there aren't circumstances in which the specifically therapeutic assets of the solace people cherish in literary reading aren't worth defending. What could be more sanctimonious, surely, than exhorting some purportedly better—that is, more politically virtuous, self-consciously responsible, or allegedly urgent—way of admiring literature for audiences who may genuinely want to gain some respite or encouragement from what they read, without being accused of carefree passivity or ideological complicity. However, by shifting beyond a reception-model of solace as the primary means of analysing its textual effects, we have a better chance of noticing how consolation has as much to do with the work that style does as with what implied readers supposedly feel. Sometimes emotionally complementing narrative content, at other times conflicting with it, solace leads a provocative life in discreet elements of rhythm and syntax—including the micro-inflections of lexical register and acoustic connotation—as well as in larger-scale units of structural progression (or stasis), motivic patterning, and manipulations of genre.

From this perspective, what often makes consolation 'discrepant' in contemporary writing is the restive interplay between the solace afforded rhetorically or structurally by a text and the affective repercussions of its wrenching outcomes. My critical story of solace hopes therefore to be as attuned to consolation's formal triggers and manipulations as to the variety of reactions its dramatic presence or absence can provoke. To do so, I observe that important 'difference', as Steven Mullaney helpfully clarifies it, 'between narrative *representations* of emotional states—whether descriptions, depictions, or enactments—and the narrative process and phenomenology' of the reader's participation in affecting plots. 'In the one', explains Mullaney, a reader may be 'presented with an example, a model, or an illustration of an affective state'; whereas in the second process, the reader 'is being modelled or shaped or reconfigured as much by his or her own reading...as by a represented state of being, capable of imitation'.[23] With these distinctions in mind, I disaggregate—without of course disconnecting—the stylistic and diegetic lives solace leads *in* representation, the role it plays compositionally for some writers (especially in the case of memoirs where the writing process itself is also one of grappling with whether creativity surmounts or perpetuates the very inflictions that are the writer's inspiration), and the myriad responses that consolation (including its unacceptability) may arouse in readers. With the help of these analytic tiers, we can infer more precisely what solace does at different levels in literary works today that make consolation's experiential breadth and aesthetic diversity seem impossible to overlook.

If solace presents a formally and ethically animating problematic for contemporary literature, it also invites us to reconsider the critical values we might associate with its effects—values that are tricky to compile, less easy still to defend. One probably wouldn't shortlist consolation as a prime candidate for helping literature 'to be a site of agitation', in the words of activist poet Cathy Park Hong, 'where the audience is not a receptacle of conditioned responses but is unsettled and provoked into participatory response'.[24] But as we'll discover, the kind of participation Hong is advocating here is precisely what consolation in contemporary writing solicits. Recent works of life-writing and fiction dislodge solace from its etymological ancestry as a soothing remedy, attentive as they are to the ethical and emotional costs of propping up cushions between word and world. Contemporary works considered throughout *Discrepant Solace* allow us to understand solace less as a beneficent yet typically censured emotional residue of consuming books than as an active, often volatile ingredient in how they are made.

And what's made is by no means conventionally consoling. Providing few lasting tranquillizers, the contemporary writers considered in coming chapters test and vex the traditional connotations of solace through character, action, and form. From this tripartite perspective, solace will have as much to do with what literature enacts (inadvertently or purposefully) and with the affective consequences of what it compositionally performs, as with our vicarious or sympathetic reaction to how characters feel. Complementing Sianne Ngai's compelling work on 'tone', I thus see consolatory effects as 'never entirely reducible to a reader's emotional response to a text', nor 'reducible to the text's internal representations of feeling (though it can amplify and be amplified by both)'. When consolation is entertained as an identifiable affordance of the interaction—and, as we'll see, often the friction—between elements such as grammar, diction, and focalizing register, its implications as an 'objectifiable emotion' become critically useful. Even in palpably traumatic, poignant, or ethically disturbing works, consolation can present us with what Ngai calls an 'unfelt but perceived feeling'. When framed in this way, consolation is not simply a by-product of our 'sympathetic identification with the feelings of characters', but rather a phenomenon whose various states of impermanence or contestability are embodied in and animated by specific formal techniques.[25] To be sure, the nature of readerly identification and immersion is hardly irrelevant, particularly if we are to account for the ways in which becoming empathically or sentimentally absorbed in a text is not always synonymous with being consoled. To shift consolation beyond what Katherine Ibbett has termed 'the therapeutic model' of textual affect 'by attending to formal devices and structures' is not to sideline our reactions to literal descriptions of feeling in favour of taxonomizing solace in purely narratological features. Rather, it is to recognize how we can enrich accounts of literary consolation by examining the shifting dynamics—sometimes reciprocal, sometimes discrepant—between one's aesthetic experience of a text and the emotive tensions or orientations it formally engenders.[26]

Reading for solace by reading for form in this sense provides a tempting shortcut to plurality, skirting consolation's definitional stodginess. Its dynamic presence in contemporary writing as something prosaically attractive yet potentially duplicitous—defended in some works, dreaded in others—contrasts consolation's staid meanings over time. Certain denotations and self-evident characteristics stick, notwithstanding how historically and culturally contingent accounts of public and private emotion remain. According to the 1822 edition of Johnson's *Dictionary*, for instance, the substantive *consolation* (along with its numerous, though nowadays rarer, derivations: *consoler* and *consolator*) is firmly synonymous with giving 'comfort', with the 'alleviation of misery'. In turn the idea that someone or something (an artwork, a piece of rhetoric) can be *consolatory* is explained along the same lines, and indeed the word not only functions in an adjectival sense but is also given as a substantive category (*conso'latory*), naming a 'speech or writing containing topics of comfort'.[27] Meanwhile, *solace* too is associated with comfort yet also with 'pleasure', even 'recreation'—a connotation Johnson draws from Milton. In this historical usage, to solace someone means therefore 'to cheer' and 'amuse' them.[28] So what has changed?

In one sense, not much. The homology of consolation and comfort survives today mostly untouched: it isn't hard to envisage how one might delicately opt for amusement when trying to ease a friend's sorrow; nor is it uncommon to hear of recreation being proposed as a physical antidote to immobilizing dejection. Levity may still be a potent remedy in our time as in Johnson's, however ticklish amusement seems as a stratagem for cheering someone up. It turns out that solace—a calculated action and a felt condition, denoting available treatment as well as charity received—can appear as consistent in the realm of everyday gesture as it is contentious in aesthetic thought, even though we know consolation, like any affect, is unfathomably variable across centuries and continents. That being the case, equally satisfying—if equally imperfect—options present themselves. One would be to preserve consolation in literary-historical amber, so that it's readily available for analysis irrespective of contextual permutations. Another would be to admit defeat by assuming one's perspective on solace will always be just that—perspectival, temporally relative, partial, even distorted by one's present interests. Neither solution will do, but they offer undoubtedly appealing ways for the critic to deal with consolation's aesthetic and historical heterogeneity. Foreswearing the analysis of what solace means for literature on the grounds of sheer diversity over time is just as self-reassuring as anchoring consolation to formulaic modes of feeling justified by the diachronic persistence of its definitions.

In this book, I try to avoid such solutions, without presuming to catalogue the archive of contemporary literary solace in its entirety. Whether consolation is positioned as a facet of representation, as a psychological asset of reading, or as one chapter in the bewilderingly long history of emotions, there is no superior platform from which to view it correctly. Instead, solace asks that we 'face the porousness of our knowledge', in Stanley Cavell's phrase, so that we may recognize that there's no definitively authoritative '*place* from which we can see the past'—including our more immediate past.²⁹ If consolation provides opportunities to reflect on how literature solicits new ways of critically attending to affect, then it also invites us to acknowledge that our own interpretive 'position' towards consolation's historicity is 'to be discovered' rather than nailed down, in Cavell's words, 'in the painful way it is always done, in piecing it out totally'. While I can't pretend to offer a theory of literary solace in its transcultural totality, what I do hope to show, adapting Cavell, is how we can 'put ourselves in' consolation's textual *'present'*. This can be a risky move, especially if it results in 'the repudiation of our perception altogether', when literary solace answers back to embedded assumptions about its inefficacy.³⁰ But when it generates this kind of epistemic turbulence, consolation also motivates us to ask how we might do better justice to what it does in the literary imagination—not least for narratives that would seem inimical to consolation's feasibility. Discerning in the formal quiddities of those narratives the conceptual, emotional, ethical problems that revolve around solace is one way of thinking *with* contemporary literature as it models its own distinctive modes of affective inquiry and insight.

That consolation might be a custodian of critical and creative value isn't a prospect that enjoys much support in contemporary literary studies. And yet it's not at all obvious that the 'impulse to see fiction as a form of redemption', as the late Carol Shields put it, a consoling resource that can recuperate and 'redeem what otherwise might be lost', is inherently misguided, philosophically bovine, or politically suspect.³¹ Literary succour of all generic stripes cannot be so easily dismissed. However, if the figures at the centre of this book refuse to affirm expectations about consolation's own long-lasting definitions, they also complicate its links to appeasement, alleviation, progressive adjustment, and—again—redemption (a term to which the following section turns). Uncoupled from such kinships, consolation in these works coincides with the examination rather than dissipation of sorrow and apprehension. Whether the privations in question are foregoing or anticipated, several of the writers I consider achieve this by putting style and structure in argumentative relation to 'topics of comfort' (to recall Johnson's meaning of *consolatory*), helping us to see how literature formally collides with as much as it reciprocates the emotions it plots. Works in this vein refuse the typical suspicion towards consolation's reputedly placating side-effects, especially since they often boycott that epitome of structural solace: the reparative ending, or what Reta—Shields's writer of 'light fiction' in *Unless* (2002)—ruefully calls 'the calculated curving upward into inevitability'. These manipulations of circumstance could be seen as epitomizing the consolations of structure, where the 'corruption of cause and effect' contrives, in Reta's words, the 'gathering together of all the characters into a framed operatic circle of consolation and ecstasy'. Alas, readers will be disappointed if they hope to see this compensatory 'architecture' exposed for indictment in *Discrepant Solace*, with its disentangling denouements, its 'lovely slope of predicament'.³² Instead, the works we'll encounter arrive at affectively disruptive conclusions that deflect gratifying repair—often deflecting too some of the interpretive gratifications of critique. Throwing the conflation of consolation and resolution out of joint, they also thwart the critical satisfactions of calling to account the complicities of works that cultivate solace in the first place.

THE PROBLEM WITH FEELING REDEEMED

Nowhere do these satisfactions seem more tangible than in the indictment of aesthetic redemption, the very goal of complicit or placating art in which consolation is regarded as a likely accomplice. In contrast to work in other periods, modern literature's consolatory elements have usually met opposition from critics upholding the virtues of unswerving ideological decipherment.[33] An influential critique of this kind is expressed in Leo Bersani's 1990 polemic, *The Culture of Redemption*, where he declares that modernist '[a]rt redeems the catastrophes of experience – of individual and collective histories – by the violence of its symbolic reconstructions of experience'.[34] Although consolation as such isn't his prime target, Bersani's opposition to 'an *aesthetic* of redemption' implies that solace would be the sort of equivocal asset of modernism that might loom in his sights.[35] As I show in Chapter 1, modernist writers actually developed a self-examining, ethically vigilant stance on both the consolations of aesthetic form (the purported redemptions of elegantly wrought designs that attempt to sublimate the wounds of history) and the solace afforded by aesthetic engagement and judgment (the presumably cushioning rewards of analyzing and admiring those reconstructions in literature of otherwise forbidding aspects of traumatic experience). This stance, I will argue, has crucial legacies for reading the poetics of consolation in contemporary writing, whose affective-aesthetic sinews cannot be productively traced if we associate modernist redemptions with the art of superficial compensation—supplying the 'beneficently reconstructive function' of 'patching' historical lesions.[36] Modernist works purportedly reach through aesthetic totality and virtuosity for 'a correction of life', in Bersani's account, resulting in a 'transformation of things into signs', thereby delivering an illusory yet comforting 'negation of the reality of pain'.[37] Fiction's salving effects here are put on a par with the immensities of traumatizing history as a premise for then construing formal mitigations for real-world 'catastrophes' as gestures of 'trivializing nobility'.[38]

Audacious, maximalist modernists are the most conspicuous cultivators of aesthetic redemption in this sense. With their intense perspectivism, lush psychological descriptions, and encyclopaedic scale (compositional conceits that conspire to restore some sense of wholeness, purpose, and integrity to selfhood), Joyce and Proust conjure what Bersani calls a 'redemptive alchemy' that tends to 'force the reader to perform the central operation of art—the operation of corrective vision'.[39] Their technical innovations, on this model, confirm modernism's mission to possess 'the authority to master the presumed raw material of experience in a manner that uniquely gives value to, perhaps even redeems, that material'.[40] But such oppositions to art's assuaging embrace of historical devastation are underpinned by certain suppositions about the temperament of implied audiences. For who, ultimately, is salved or corrected by 'redemptive' writing? Can literature actually seduce readers to such an extent that it pacifies them, shielding them from historical harm with the deceptive pleasures of reading about the (potentially worse) fates of fictional figures in the grip of modernity? Do aesthetic forms—by their affectingly sumptuous manoeuvres, by their lures to intellectual inquiry, or simply by provoking the reader's astonishment with stylistic experimentation alone—really sponsor our tolerance of social injustices, blinding us to their historically contingent causes? Are readers so easily duped as to find readily ameliorative the world's transfiguration into linguistic beauty? And if they're not, then why should the figurative vistas of enthralling fiction be considered tantamount to violence? Can literature and history be set on the same plane—the former competing against and correcting the latter's brute 'reality of pain'—when writers may have no intention of converting trauma into palatable symbolism or buffering its impact with layers of allusion or obfuscating irony?

In light of these questions, one might reasonably ask to what extent the projected witness of aesthetic redemption also remains something of a monolithic fiction, a fiction that depends upon the portrait of a reader who allegedly conflates the promise of material repair with the recuperative force of representational ingenuity. Whatever we feel about consolation's politics, there is something uncomfortably condescending about assuming that readers are incapable of recognizing the imaginative refuge of art for what it is, without romanticizing it as a cure, and without assuming that their embrace of an enchanting text will durably appease either the material costs of social dispossession or the mental costs of psychic deterioration. If consolation is to have any explanatory power for criticism, we need a different notional reader in mind, one for whom captivation and peril, immersion and alarm, seduction and scepticism, relief and aggravation, or redemption and despair in practice coincide to produce a complicated, perpetually sliding scale of multitiered responses to a given work. Throughout this book, I try to be mindful of this scale of possible reactions in the course of grasping what solace does to the linguistic fibres of contemporary writing. This in turn means entertaining consolation, as I have suggested, not only as an emotional element of a work's dramatic impact, but also as a more affectively unpredictable phenomenon unleashed by the syntax of that work. It is 'through formed language', suggests Derek Attridge, 'that we're invited to participate in its emotion-arousing capacities'; if, as readers, we end up feeling consoled after engaging with a striking representation of loss (one familiar upshot of elegy, say), then we certainly 'feel the emotions, but always as performances of language's powers'. Attridge goes further by reminding us that '[i]f art produced the emotions it enacts directly, in a completely unmediated manner, we would be very tentative about exposing ourselves to it'.[41] I agree. But I would add that what distinguishes consolation as an object of literary inquiry, what makes it somewhat tricky to analyse, is the way it requires us to apprehend form's affective potential without also surmising that readers will naturally be comforted by consolation's linguistic enactment. In fact, quite the opposite may be true, even when a text dramatizes solace (or its conspicuous absence) in events of intense pathos, '*as if* to provide an experience', in Attridge's words, 'that replicates modes of thinking and feeling in the non-literary domain'.[42]

How might this model of reading consolation—where the simulation of solace by no means coincides with, still less satisfies, any hunger for amelioration, still less redemption—operate for emotional states whose indescribability seems inescapable, their resistance to aesthetic redress indisputable? To answer that, we need to turn for a moment to what's generally considered to be representation's ostensible limit.

SIMULATING THE UNSPEAKABLE

Commendable trauma fictions are often valued precisely for the way they vividly embody, or attempt to embody, the seemingly ineffable experiences they narrate, etching the imprint of trauma's irresolvable syndromes upon the reader. Consolation's direct opposite, trauma is honoured by literary critics and by historians of cultural memory as a condition of extremity: a visceral, unspeakable, often unmanageable state whose symptoms resist the symbolic repair of narrativization, let alone explanation. Set into motion by humanity's most atrocious crimes, trauma makes the very prospect of solace comparable to a moral obscenity. In turn, this position has strongly influenced the ethical judgments about literature's capabilities—or, more pointedly, responsibilities—in representing traumatized persons. Work in this area understandably privileges textuality that, like trauma itself, 'resonates beyond what we can know and understand', as Cathy Caruth describes it, because for this model 'it is in the event of this incomprehension and in our departure from sense and understanding that our own witnessing may indeed begin to take place'.[43] Even the narrativization of that incomprehension may not be adequate to its volatile experience, especially if *narration* implies some level of progression from opacity to gradual assimilation. For 'victims themselves', argues Dominick LaCapra, 'trauma, instead of calling for processes of working-over and working-through, may be valorized as a limit experience or as stigmata demanding endless melancholy or grieving, whose mitigating or rendering in narrative is perceived as objectionably consoling'.[44]

At its most prescriptive, such a perspective would suggest that even artistically modest attempts to write about the effects of psychic damage are inherently questionable, indeed unacceptable. If so much remains unassimilable inside the psychic precincts of trauma, literary representation will always entail some level of compression or distortion. Accordingly, the more a text exerts itself to incorporate harm and enunciate its effects, the more it lays bare the duplicity of recuperative expression. To deal with this potential impasse, literary critics have been drawn to modes of writing that are explicitly self-conscious about the strategies they employ. Structural fissures and temporal involutions are regarded as permissible successes of fictions that grapple with trauma's enigmatic ontology. In keeping with this broad consent, Beverley Southgate suggests that 'it might be that narrative disruptions – breaks in narrative and gaps in history – could represent what happened more convincingly than that even flow that seems to take everything so comfortably and comfortingly into its embrace'.[45] Note the doubleness of *comfort* here, pointing both at what narrative 'flow' performs so effortlessly and what form delivers to the reader who finds its 'embrace' appeasing. This dual—and purportedly dubious—function reinforces an opposition between (usually postmodern) writers committed to self-referential fractures and (presumably realist) writers who rely on continuity and the pretence of similitude. As a qualitative scheme, it also rehearses a common presupposition, which rests on speculation: the presupposition is that disruption ought to be inherently more convincing for narrating trauma than non-experimental description; and the speculation in turn is that readers find less adventurous forms of expression more comforting, with detrimental consequences. Adopting a similar line, Anne Whitehead observes that 'novelists have frequently found that the impact of trauma can only adequately be represented by mimicking its forms and symptoms, so that temporality and chronology collapse, and narratives are characterized by repetition and indirection'.[46] Likewise, such tactics can potentially amount to an ethical practice, providing writers forestall their own desire to redress what they depict: in essence pre-empting any 'notion of art', recalling Bersani, 'as making over or repairing failed experience'.[47]

Coming from literary studies, approaches that emphasize (however cautiously) textual tactics that capture trauma's symptoms do not always sit easily with historians of trauma, for whom narrative's attempted rendition of devastating events and their emotional scars inevitably falls short and may even be unethical. Hence, in some critical models of traumatic representation, it's not that literary narrative by definition fails in the presence of incomprehensible violence so much as its success depends on whether it can formally emulate the psychic disintegration associated with trauma as something that cannot be processed. Certain categories of aesthetic invention may be endorsed, from this perspective, providing they mime psychological damage rather than mitigate its effects. Accordingly, stylistic incarnations of trauma's mental commotions have been celebrated in recent literary encounters with anguish: Eimear McBride's 2013 debut *A Girl is a Half-Formed Thing* is perhaps the most compositionally radical and disturbing example of a novel that tries to reproduce through splintered, heterodox syntax the devastating mental toll taken by chronic sexual abuse.[48] And in more oblique fashion, W. G. Sebald's entire oeuvre now occupies a canonical place in trauma studies. In episodic, genre-defying books, Sebald captures the disarming apparitions of memory across historically distinct experiences, his pseudo-biographical vignettes spanning a 'significant gap', in Adam Phillips's terms, between 'the written and the spoken in the telling of lives'.[49]

But although criticism in recent times has tended to laud such strategies— partly, perhaps, because they enable us to recognize how adept literature is at conveying psychic injury—in practice the opposite can also obtain. For the ethical promise of contemporary narrative may be most apparent when writers refuse that mantle of mimicry, outperforming rather than simply imitating symptoms of desperation and dissolution. Instead of following in the footprints of loss or emulating the recursions of harrowing memory, the works I examine hazard through their forms salient ways of contending with the upheavals to which solace is conventionally drawn. Thanks to style itself—and thanks too to the way style doesn't self-evidently mirror emotional content—consolation becomes more volatile and unresolved than remedial or climactic.

As we will come to know it in this book, solace therefore shares some traits with what LaCapra and other trauma theorists have associated with 'working through': namely 'an open, self-questioning process that never attains closure and counteracts acting-out (or the repetition compulsion) without entirely transcending it'.⁵⁰ Finding consolation uncommonly in tune with this process, Chapters 1 and 2 further the work of adjusting relations between suffering and style, by considering how Ian McEwan and Sebald himself extend modernist efforts to challenge what has arguably become an orthodox sacralization of suffering's unrepresentability. In a refreshingly broad-minded survey that cuts across disciplinary boundaries, Roger Luckhurst has suggested that contemporary literary and filmic 'narratives have developed a repertoire of plots that explore both traumatic disruption and the possibility of release into narrative,' even though for some this may seem 'at odds with some of the most influential cultural theories of trauma', which posit the term '*in opposition* to narrative'. As a result, there's now 'a flat contradiction', notes Luckhurst, 'between cultural theory that regards narrative as betraying traumatic singularity and various therapeutic discourses that see narrative as a means of productive transformation or even final resolution of trauma'.⁵¹ Complicating the standard line on trauma's intractability, research both in medical humanities and among practising therapists provides a more usefully counterintuitive sense of how narrating psychic distress might console with no pretence of repair. Drawing on the findings of psychologists like James Pennebaker, poet David Watts observes that '[w]riting of the kind that attacks difficult issues with ruthless honesty has the power to soothe psychological disturbances, to preserve or reinforce healthy states', while also helping victims in a therapeutic setting 'to speak' through narrativization, in Judith Lewis Herman's words, 'of the unspeakable'.⁵² Far from disclosing 'a dubious departure from, or distortion of, historical reality', or betraying the comforts of 'unproblematic closure',⁵³ these narratives testify to how the affective work of writing might be exercised without aspiring to complete restoration—without assuming that trauma's verbal rendition is thereby a ruse to implant illusions of rehabilitation.

In contrast to these therapeutic applications, cultural theory's evolving paradigms of trauma haven't always been amenable to the notion that writers may find aesthetic incentives in dealing with psychological or social catastrophe.⁵⁴ Whether distress or sorrow can be formally generative without ethically compromising the writer herself is a question especially pertinent to memoir, a genre central to this book. Contemporary life-writing has provided 'a powerful form of scriptotherapy', as Suzette Henke observes, whereby the work's 'artistic replication of a coherent subject-position...generates a healing narrative that temporarily restores the fragmented self to an empowered position of psychological agency'.⁵⁵ Yet what if the disruption of that restorative process was precisely life-writing's topic and occasion? And what if, moreover, the work of capturing that disruption presented opportunities for writers to engage, even contest, solace through the very description of incoherence, with the dramatization of agency's refusal or dissolution proving more formally generative than any claim to 'healing' self-consolidation?

Such are the questions candidly posed by Julian Barnes, a novelist whose latest memoir occupies me in Chapter 3. Faced with selecting either hope or despair,

Barnes has said that he 'would definitely situate' his work 'on desolation if that's the choice'. Nonetheless, he 'maintain[s] that writing what George Sand would consider desolating literature is and can be consoling. Describing things as they are rather than as we would like them to be can have a consoling effect. Bleak truths can be purging.'[56] Barnes suggests another way of thinking about consolation that's not solely based on the perception of it as the antidote to unresolved trauma but rather as an upshot of articulating raw, unsentimental 'truths' of experience. Some six years after these observations, Barnes puts them to the ultimate test in *Levels of Life* (2013). This elegy for his late wife, Pat Kavanagh, is also, more implicitly, a deliberation on the whole issue of whether loss can ever be given explanatory shape in narrative, let alone redeemed by the ritual experience of re-encountering one's loss in written form. Barnes seems adamantly watchful of supposing that writing can afford the grieving writer solace; all the same, as an artefact of feeling, a performance of self-scrutinizing solace, *Levels of Life* still poses the question of whether literature can afford bereavement's unpredictability some degree of articulation, redressing the despair of grief's silencing aftermath. Barnes provokes this debate in crystalline reflections on the difficulties of adequately expressing not only the brute effects of Kavanagh's death but also what his lifelong love represented for the very life they shared.

Rhetorically, *Levels of Life*'s eloquence counterpoints even as it helps readers to appreciate the barbed undergrowth of Barnes's grief; yet thematically, the book does everything to confirm Freud's rather beautiful insistence on what can never be consoled. Writing to Ludwig Binswager in April 1929, Freud shifts mid-letter to recount how he had deciphered from Binswager's 'enigmatic' handwriting that his friend had lost a son. If the ensuing bereavement amounts to a sensation beyond repair, observes Freud, that's precisely how it ought to feel. In itself, this knowledge seems to be implicitly reassuring: a state that we might all expect at some point, implies Freud, that may even be valuable in some way, providing we don't attempt to solve its opacity or replenish its signature void. Only a pain that refuses to be replaced can do justice to the magnitude of what feels irrevocable:

> Although we know that after such a loss the acute state of mourning will subside, we also know we shall remain inconsolable and will never find a substitute. No matter what may fill the gap, even if it be filled completely, it nevertheless remains something else. And actually this is how it should be. It is the only way of perpetuating that love which we do not want to relinquish.[57]

Literature inhabits that space of 'something else', even as the experience of reading it can make the grace of loss's depiction seem like an attempt to 'fill the gap'. If solace seems discrepant in works evoking situations that 'remain inconsolable', it is also because those works advance rather than mend the 'perpetuating' process Freud commends—never quite making it easy for their forms to 'find a substitute' and thereby to soothe. That chasms of loss cannot, indeed should not, 'be filled completely' is a conviction animated both dramatically and stylistically by writers we'll soon encounter. Analysing this process allows us to discover something of the critical potential of consolation's most discrepant forms.

CONSOLATORY FORM

It would be tempting to assert that this double act of formally instantiating and ethically investigating solace is an exclusively contemporary development or 'turn'. I don't necessarily believe it is, as my effort to historicize its modernist development in Chapter 1 makes clear. However, the twinned stylistic performance and critical deliberation of solace has intensified for writers whose work comes face to face with such emotional conditions as grief, disappointment, threat, or dread, without succumbing to their psychic obliterations; writers who vandalize convenient escapism without altogether renouncing the chance in and through language to accost mute despair. Set within these coordinates, consolation also reveals how contemporary life-writing and fiction animate the very temporality of affect. By this I mean that writers chronicling the duration and durability of pain address it not only as an emotional aftermath to be worked through but also as the anticipation of perishability (Chapter 4), of oncoming damage to lives that feel already undone and for now are held in the balance (Chapter 7). Although they seem temporally divergent, retrospective and prospective orientations for solace often coincide: when recollection captures the vision of alternative yet impossible fortunes, compressing solace between disarming retrospection and alarming apprehension (Chapters 2 and 5); when trepidation conspires with memories of what might have been (Chapter 6), provoking readers to consider whether consolation is even desirable when there's seemingly no way of avoiding the future onset of harm.

Connoisseurs of hypothetical outcomes, novels and memoirs have become peculiarly adept at showing how these volatile experiences of time shape consolation's expression. And expression, as we'll see, is all. That solace might somehow inform the very composition of works that thematically pursue consolation's antitheses is nothing new. Poet and translator David Constantine points out that across history 'sorrow in itself' has become 'a maker of the beauty' of literature. Such works 'are not beautiful by virtue of their subject's sadness', but rather 'by the way the poet shapes that sadness'—'which is to say by their form, their words in rhythm'.[58] Although I pay close attention to the consoling potential of form through this book (including microelements of rhythm, sound, and syntax), I also take the paradox Constantine highlights a step further. If consolation has always played a dissident part in the literary history of loss, in recent decades its most generative discrepancies seem to arise in the most forbidding genres: shattering voyages into traumatic recollection (W. G. Sebald), along with elegies that confront solace head on when meditating on grief's longevity (Julian Barnes, Helen Macdonald, Colm Tóibín); bereavement memoirs that refuse to posit any timescale for recovery (Joan Didion), burrowing between resilience and recuperation to show that they are not one and the same; novels that anticipate oblivion and tackle the very legitimacy of solace in reckoning with impending ends (J. M. Coetzee, Marilynne Robinson); counterfactual biographies that rewrite blighted family fortunes (Doris Lessing), together with renditions of atonement that revolve around rather than resolve irreversible actions, plotting experiences that can never be mended by their transcription into art (Ian McEwan); and finally, narratives that movingly pitch solace against acute apprehensiveness (Kazuo Ishiguro, David Grossman), featuring persons who would flinch from consolation because the very anticipation of receiving it presages something macabre, and who try thus to pre-empt the moment when condolences may be required—pre-emptions that prove how solace can feel at once imminent yet undesired.

These scenarios attract their own distinctive tactics of representation, scenarios that also plot the broad arc of this book. Its chapters are organized around readings of works that share affective orientations in their taxing navigations of solace, opening up for analysis formal operations that yield fruitful comparisons. The works I consider illustrate how consolation frequently resides in genres where we might least expect to find it. Set alongside each other, this sizeable group of seemingly unrelated novelists and life-writers present us with a spectrum of formal innovations that accompany consolation's difficult coexistence with grief, remorse, longing, and dread—the typical nemeses of emotional wellbeing that solace is supposed to foil. Each chapter identifies formal features in fiction and memoir which posit shared preoccupations between apparently contrasting figures who lead us beyond national paradigms. Elaborated incrementally, my formal categories for consolation's literary manifestations are therefore both pragmatic and performative: they enable, in a practical sense, coherent groupings of salient texts to coalesce in comparative discussions; and they elaborate, by virtue of such illustrative comparisons, facets of consolation across writers read in conjuncture that would otherwise remain inconspicuous in isolation.

Connecting solace to specific elements of writing and at different scales—from the architectonics of genre to the micro-inflections of syntax—gives it some interpretive traction. For much like neighbouring feelings such as pity, sympathy, and compassion, as Katherine Ibbett has incisively shown, so solace has arguably been embroiled in a 'lexically eclectic' and 'synonymically sticky cluster of terms', even though some unfavourable associations have clung to it over time.[59] In one sense, this terminological murk offers opportunities of its own, especially if one heeds the advice of scholars working on queer archives of affect who, like Ann Cvetkovich, prefer a term like 'feeling in part because it is intentionally imprecise', preserving the 'ambiguity' between sensory embodiment and 'psychic or cognitive experiences'. For Cvetkovich, concepts 'such as *affect, emotion*, and *feeling* are more like keywords, points of departure for discussion rather than definition'.[60] Such a position is undoubtedly liberating. And it would be appealing to salvage consolation with this mandate of permissiveness, were it not for the fact that solace tends to fare worse as an object of critical inquiry when it becomes more definitionally capacious and historically mobile. If negative portraits of consolation are susceptible to straw man propositions (just as its recuperation can be equally prone to turning consolation's detractors into straw figures), then the universalization of solace only increases such risks. For this reason, consolation warrants a short diachronic detour, before I set out in more detail the precise route taken by this book.

Historians of Renaissance humanism and theologians concerned with medieval 'doctrines of suffering' have connected the emotive, spiritual, and social meanings of solace with specific genres of writing and thought—genres emerging from philosophical, rhetorical, and lyric engagements with 'psychological care' or 'mortal existence'.[61] George W. McClure contextualizes the Christian reception of classical precepts for solace by observing that using 'the letter, the dialogue, the oration, the elegy, and the manual, classical philosophers, rhetors, and poets established a diverse canon of consolatory genres'. At first glance, he suggests, the insistence that faithful subjects ought to regard death as 'a welcome deliverance' from their 'ephemeral earthly state' might imply that the 'tenor and parameters of Christian solace must necessarily differ from those of classical consolation'. In fact, continuities emerged between these traditions, when the Christian adaptation of 'classical genres of the funeral oration, the letter, the treatise or dialogue on death' became integral to liturgical 'genres of the sermon, the congregational letter, and the theological treatise'.[62] Similarly, Ronald K. Rittgers's work on the afterlives of pagan consolation literature in the Middle Ages recalls that '[b]oth Jerome and Augustine read [Cicero's] *Consolatio*' and that 'the *Tusculan Disputations* directly influenced the important works of consolation by Boethius and Isidore of Seville'.[63] In these accounts, northern Europe witnessed a flourishing of 'consolatory and therapeutic genres', speaking to the commitments of 'lay and clerical figures alike'. Such genres burgeoned in tandem with increasing literacy at a moment when '[r]itual was yielding to rhetoric'. As private reading supplemented collective prayer, 'early modern pastoral care was inspired by humanist thought to become more responsive to the problems of grief and sorrow', concludes McClure, 'sometimes harvesting classical consolation and sometimes competing with it'.[64]

Now, elaborating consolation's forms through the discursive practices it has inhabited offers an invitingly transferrable framework for literary histories of affect. Consolation's temporal fluidity comes with a few hazards, though, posing hermeneutic glitches that might make us pause before wholeheartedly embracing the attractions of consolation's portability. In her compelling and wide-ranging work on nineteenth- and twentieth-century elegy, for instance, Melissa F. Zeiger quotes a Renaissance scholar (G. W. Pigman III) who notes that 'the major purpose of consolation is to induce the bereaved to suppress grief'. Although Pigman is speaking about sixteenth-century consolation manuals, Zeiger sees that 'the point' applies to 'modern culture and elegy as well', the affects she interrogates surpassing periodicity.[65] To be clear, that is her professed remit: to pursue the *longue durée* of elegy's reinforcements and challenges to gendered codes and social orders of grieving. What's more, generic kinships between eras are undoubtedly useful in helping us to connect artistic purposes and their emotional consequences that are separated in history. My book by no means insists that we ought to historicize consolation's subjective and cultural meanings down to the last degree, as though the only proper way to read solace is to assume it changes incrementally from one era to the next due to an unfathomable array of psychic and material variables. Nevertheless, it's worth recognizing how the transferability of solace can assist negative accounts of it. Licensed anachronisms help to reinforce consolation's adverse connotations by telescoping its idiosyncratic collective and private manifestations, while literature's dealings with solace become linked over time by the same undertow of complaisance. Understanding consolation as historically untethered can thus be interpretively appealing; but we run the risk of inadvertently colluding in its normative conflation with acquiescence.

Work on late medieval and early modern discourses of suffering usefully reminds us that what 'consolation literature' means, including what it means to achieve, are at once more culturally variegated and more specific than consolation's portability implies. Via numerous channels of communication, lessons in consolatory practice in the later Middle Ages were likely 'passed on by word of mouth from senior to junior clerics', notes Rittgers, producing 'a truly impressive array of literary resources' that would have 'a profound influence on the actual care of suffering souls'. Viewed theologically, consolation's utility and application appear in epochal terms quite distinct. Early Christianity posited the effort 'to try to make sense out of sorrow' as a 'common project', in Rittgers's words—one that continues as a pastoral duty to this day. But when viewed through the lens of genre, consolation's implications in spiritual practice have closer affinities with creative discourse. For when seen 'as a whole, the medieval consolation literature set out to accomplish a very ambitious goal', which was 'to persuade human beings that suffering was good for them, indeed, that suffering was actually "sweet" – or that it produced desirable effects'.[66] This goal is generically echoed in the time-honoured ethical dilemma of tragedy, where spectators witnessing fate dealing its cruel hand can somehow find themselves edified, even uplifted. Mounted on a history of ideas too vast in its span from Aristotle to Nietzsche to survey here, the conundrum is summarized in Henry Ansgar Kelly's broad (if perhaps somewhat presumptuous) claim that 'the best-expressed tragedies have given us much solace and comfort'.[67] What these otherwise very different intellectual and theological traditions have in common, it seems, is the conception of solace as a mellowing agent in the wake of loss, an unbreachable safeguard against further onsets of despair—the received notion of a temperate and tempering affect that contemporary writers in this book confront.

By attending to the poetics of that confrontation, the following chapters recognize that beyond their scope is an encyclopaedic account of what 'consolation literature' might now constitute around the globe, across religious and secular situations of emotional support. Beyond their remit too is a systematic analysis of how cultural practices of solace in the late twentieth- and twenty-first centuries have either relinquished theological assuagements for suffering or else departed from the more ascetic, ancient meaning of consolation as 'the combating of grief through rational argument'.[68] What I do hope to show, within more manageable parameters, is how the very troubling of consolation's claims generates possibilities in contemporary literature—for writers who are giving loss or its anticipation expression, and for readers attentive to how consolation works in multi-dimensional ways, both thematically within a text and formally through particular strategies of affective representation. Over the course of this study, I consider writers who operate at the threshold between unflinching stories of desolation, fear, or contrition and their luminous description, a threshold where they are alert to the saccharine decorations of metaphor and the siren-call enticements of choreographed resolutions. Reminding us of emotion's own 'older connotations' of 'disturbance', as historian Rachel Hewitt calls them, these writers invite us to consider that when literature reflects on its own capacity for consolation it reflects too on the disruptive comportments of style itself.[69] Articulating states of mind that seem *in*expressible, they raise the ethical stakes of felicitously evoking spheres of harm, while compelling us as readers to recognize the repercussions of seeing in such eloquence some lasting, compensatory value.

How peculiar is this phenomenon to our contemporary moment, and what might its historical determinants be? My reader will need to wait for the Epilogue for responses to that dual-pronged question of periodization and causality, because the matter of how contemporary literature coincides with and responds to a specific set of historical situations for consolation can only be sufficiently and concretely addressed in light of the contexts my central chapters cover. For now, on a more *literary*-historical note, I want to admit that it has been important for this project to discover that discrepant consolations can't easily be ring-fenced in time, despite the temptation to see the heightened reflexivity of their articulation as a recent strategy belonging to texts that are working through postmodernism's numerous afterlives. As a result, I use the opening chapter to elaborate on a genealogy for consolation's discrepancies that stems from literary modernism. I tap into a dialogue spanning the twentieth century between modernist aesthetics and contemporary fiction, a dialogue that suggests how writers like Virginia Woolf, who at times have been seen as practitioners of aesthetic redemption, probed in virtually self-contesting fashion the consolations of experimental form. The work—the necessity, even—of testing out form's own compensatory relation to the traumatic commotions of plot is one of modernism's most potent bequests for contemporary writing, a legacy that surfaces even in novels that maintain a combative stance towards the perceived values that modernism engendered. Ian McEwan's *Atonement* (2001) is one such text, a genre-medley of wartime romance and high-modernist pastiche, which mounts an inquest into the resuscitation of devastated individuals through hypothetical futures they would never in reality live to see. *Atonement* dissects the moral ramifications of solace as a contentious subplot of reparation, especially when that reparative impulse also turns out to be an ethically compromised stimulus for artistic creativity. It also enables us to see how reading for discrepant consolation's early twentieth-century genesis and postmillennial reprise can in turn advance our reading of modernism's own fraught contemporaneity.

Consolation for modernism, as we might expect, is often most legible—and controversial—in works whose ruptured forms draw energy and articulacy from traumatic, sorrowful, or foreboding situations that seem beyond textual representation, let alone recovery. Of all genres, elegy has perhaps made the longest-standing contribution to this problematic opportunity, where loss itself becomes formal nourishment. Showing how elegy thrives as vibrantly in contemporary narrative as in its natural habitat of poetry, Chapter 3 reads two grief-memoirs—Julian Barnes's *Levels of Life* and Helen Macdonald's *H is for Hawk* (2014)—alongside Colm Tóibín's 2014 historical (and implicitly autobiographical) novel, *Nora Webster*.[70] Together they ask not only whether grief's intricacies can ever be captured in language but also whether the quest for such a language reaches for aesthetic consolations of its own, setting up an internal competition in these works between bereavement's ingenious description and the proviso of inexpressibility that elegies often thematize. Loss thus becomes both an occasion and incentive for literary invention—even if that sense of invention is oriented around scrupulous restraint, as it certainly is for Tóibín. Conscious of this tension without seeing it as an artistic double bind, these writers instantiate through elegy the principle that if literature can 'tell us how best to live' in the wake of grief, in Barnes's phrase, 'it does so most effectively when appearing not to do so'.[71] Far from equating elegy, as some critics have been too quick to do, with 'the notion of commemorative form as a permanent replacement' or superficial 'substitute for human life',[72] Barnes, Macdonald, and Tóibín enlarge its generic coordinates to resist the simplification of consolation itself as a flimsy remedy bent on resolution. In this we may discern another of contemporary elegy's paradoxical offerings: when style's agility appears most consoling precisely in its animation of bereavement's mercurial unravelling.

What if the unravelling, though, begins in advance of what's lost? Chapter 4 pursues this question and in doing so tilts the book's temporal axis from retrospection to expectation, bringing together two strikingly different novels that exhibit comparable modes of anticipatory mourning: Marilynne Robinson's *Gilead* (2004) and J. M. Coetzee's *Age of Iron* (1990). Their plots sketch poignant preparations for mortality, testing consolation's sufficiency without stripping its contribution to the role fiction can 'play' in what Paul Ricoeur calls 'the apprenticeship of dying'.[73] Testaments to what writing itself might conserve in advance of what physically cannot be altered, these diary-like fictions elaborate Ricoeur's hunch that a 'fruitful exchange can be established between literature and being-toward-death'. They confirm too his shrewd warning that when 'consolation' emerges in this exchange 'one must not cry self-delusion too hastily',[74] even if the unpicking of self-delusion is part of a novel's economy of affect, as *Disgrace* (1999), my third selection in that chapter, powerfully exemplifies—a work that subjects solace to scrutiny at a juncture for South African culture 'replete', as Andrew van der Vlies has observed, with 'disappointment' and political disconsolation.[75]

Which isn't to say that alternative, if not virtually illusive visions of the way life might have turned out aren't tempting or creatively propulsive. In Chapter 5 parallel or potential fortunes become the emotive subject and aesthetic trigger for texts that enter the consolatory scene of magical thinking. There I return to the genre of grief-memoir—Joan Didion's now-iconic account of her husband's death in *The Year of Magical Thinking* (2005)—but also to a hybrid of autobiography and historical fiction in Doris Lessing's final book, *Alfred & Emily* (2008). To frame the chapter, I connect a type of behaviour to a mode of narrative redress: magical thinking that speculates on rectifying the circumstances of losses that generate it; and compensatory attempts to rewrite irreparable pasts, which re-envision alternative fortunes for damaged lives. Taken together, Didion and Lessing present us with works of 'life-righting', revealing how the prospect of rewriting what cannot ultimately be rectified is inescapably seductive and formally energizing. Simultaneously conjuring and questioning consolatory counterlives, their narratives draw rhetorical and structural impetus from existential speculation, while confronting the dilemmas of recreating the dead. Lessing and Didion simulate only to rescind the hypothetical amelioration of scarred fortunes and the compensations of magical thought, respectively, consciously unsettling intimations of reparation while, in the very process of doing so, mobilizing affective self-examination as a trigger of contemporary memoir's formal development.

Genres in this central cluster of chapters thus travel from elegy's animated debates with the salving properties of retrospection towards fantasies of resuscitation. Along the way, I step deliberately into turbulent events where solace seems not only improbable but no doubt taboo, precisely with the view to throwing the critical suppleness of consolation into relief. But when would the idea of consolation not only be unexpected but undesired? Forestalling the very reason for emotional aid, what might it mean to resist the occasion when solace is required? Bringing the question of consolation's desirability to bear on its legitimacy, my closing two chapters address novels with explicitly distinct scenarios by writers from different literary-cultural traditions: Kazuo Ishiguro's *Never Let Me Go* (2005) and David Grossman's *To the End of the Land* (trans. Jessica Cohen, 2010). What has seemed to many readers an unequivocally bleak work, offering a stark forewarning of the perils of biotechnology, *Never Let Me Go* is for Ishiguro curiously hopeful: a chronicle of how 'people can find the energy', he suggests, 'to create little pockets of happiness and decency while we're here'.[76] I turn to this speculative novel about state-authorized cloning to show how, through his depiction of what some critics have deemed futile, institutionalized forms of care, Ishiguro provokes readers to reflect on their own parameters of sympathy and judgment—most notably, on our grounds for subjecting to critique what his characters utilize to console. Examining the obscene distortions of institutional care in a world defined by imminent loss, *Never Let Me Go* disturbingly models the way solace survives in the face of dread, tracking its characterological work in adaptable and often wishful techniques of endurance amid circumstances where bodily comfort alone is no longer the horizon of relief.

And relief itself becomes the disagreeable opponent to the determined heroine of *To the End of the Land*. Grossman's epic anti-war novel dramatizes the trepidation surrounding solace, focalized as it is by an Israeli mother, Ora, for whom intimations of respite are shot through with jeopardy. Consolation for her is nothing less than an oracle of the worst-case scenario for a son who has willingly returned to the army after completing his military service. From Ora's pre-emptive stance on solace, we learn just how differently consolation applies to situations facing persons who fear for those who are very much living (but whose lives could be cut short), in contrast to the compensations available to persons who know they are dwindling and who become the eulogizing subjects of their own conciliations. In contrast, then, to many of the works that precede it in this book, *To the End of the Land* strives not for angry settlement with mortality (Barnes), for belated reparation and the release of confession (Lessing, McEwan), or for the personal amelioration of preparing journals of wisdom as a legacy for one's children (Coetzee, Robinson). Rather, Grossman's Ora mounts a lyrical defence against death's imminence, writing to repel the oncoming moment when elegy will undoubtedly be the most fitting mode of address. Horrifically for Grossman's own family, reality meshed with fiction.

A novel he hoped—in a knowing gesture of magical thinking—would 'protect' his son became through its resemblance with appalling events an apprenticeship for precisely that outcome Ora tries to avert. Out of this tragic congruence emerged the narrative-verses of Grossman's *Falling Out of Time* (trans. Jessica Cohen, 2014), an enigmatic book of collective memorialization with which I close.

Together these writers will redefine what we mean by the consolations of literary form. For them, form is not an aesthetic sanctuary where a work's architectural cohesion or shapelessness offer reconciliation; it is the organ of consolation's simultaneous emergence and examination, even in narratives that affirm the artistic solace of evocatively articulating experiences that seem otherwise indescribable. In this way, we'll find that consolation depends precisely on form's own motility rather than on any tranquilizing illusion of permanence. 'In its apparent fixity', observes Ali Smith, 'form is all about change'. And writers across *Discrepant Solace* share her sense that despite its reputation for 'fixity, form is all about the relationship of change to continuance, even when the continuance is itself precarious'.[77] Still, ethical questions abound when writers' expressive vigour gives the appearance of form parrying the traumas they dramatize—turning the pathetic consolations of precarious continuity into the aesthetically thrilling consolations of linguistic redress.

Pathos often stems from the vivid consciousness of what ultimately cannot be repaired, of course, more so than from our intimations of renewal. Yet as we shall discover, the rendition of poignant moments frequently mediates sorrow with militant grace of the sort that insinuates its own varieties of rejuvenation. Which poses questions central to Chapter 2—and my discussion there of the affective energy language draws from catastrophe in the work of Cormac McCarthy and W. G. Sebald—questions that also posit some of this book's principal interpretive coordinates. Namely, can style compensate for plot? What ethical implications does the brilliant description of devastation magnify, when athletic acts of depiction counterweigh the material or mental damage they elegantly convey? Behaving as such, is it possible for literary style to probe as much as it furnishes its own consolatory affordances?

LITERARY STYLE AND THE ETHICS OF SOLACE

Setting this much store by style is not to turn away from the complex politics of solace by any means. Even so, pursuing a poetics of consolation is likely to be grist for suspicion's mill. And not only for wary critics, either. Novelists themselves have been distrustful of what J. M. Coetzee calls the 'religion of style', which propagates the belief in style's redemptive potential as it modifies—even attenuates and counteracts—irreducibly disconsolate material. As Chapter 4 examines, the 'temptations' inherent to this faith in form stem, in Coetzee's view, from Flaubert's bid for formal autonomy in a work like *Madame Bovary* and extend forward to the bleakest registers of late modernism. Solace is imputed to style because it entices writers to indulge aesthetic ornamentation and the 'grace of language' as creative buffers against the fears, losses, and futilities they plot.[78]

Seen by these lights, style is an artful dodger, lending the novel crafty solutions for confronting harsh worlds from which it simultaneously desires aesthetic immunity. Modernists of various persuasions lampooned and rejected such charms, as we know, with Beckett emerging as the most iconic among the dissectors of form's charisma. But even in his case, stylistic facility survives the combination of dissolution and disillusionment that some critics have seen as characteristic of late modernism's rejection of formal integrity, which marked too a rejection of high modernism's perceived quest for redemptive design.[79] For Beckett practised his own 'religion' of lexical repetition, grammatical dissent, and phenomenological estrangement, strategies whose recurrent subversions of the consolations of form echoes in a question posed rather knowingly by *Company*: 'Why duplicate this particular solace'?[80] Beckett's overturning of—among many other things—the conventions of setting and characterization curiously enough re-energizes style in the athletic negation of its allure. The sheer technical 'energy of Beckett's repudiation', admits Coetzee, is itself 'a measure of the potency of the seductions of Style', as though that daring resistance to any compositional standards were itself a thoroughly incentivizing consolation.[81]

The novelist and translator Tim Parks would no doubt concur. In his combative take on the novel as a genre of coercion against which 'we must defend ourselves', Parks too reaches for the somewhat extreme example of Beckett. In this account, Beckett's formidable attempts to 'draw attention to the dangerous consolations of literature' might ultimately be seen as 'mocking the consolation to be found from writing', while nonetheless 'then finding consolation in this superior awareness that no consolation is to be had'.[82] Shouldering this superiority can be comforting for critics too, a pay-off that they may utilize to their advantage. Parks himself, for instance, exhibits a self-affirming sense of diagnostic 'awareness' when he brings the reader into his portrayal of consolation, pinpointing the all-too 'reassuring emotions' that arise in our 'adulation and reverence' towards novels we consume.[83] Solace is, predictably enough, among such emotions. Isolating its source and side effects, Parks wonders 'whether the process of fiction writing offers resolution, greater ease, to the writer or the reader, or whether it is a way of rendering an unhappy situation chronic, by allowing just sufficient consolation and reward from the expression of unhappiness to prevent us from making big changes'.[84] After rehearsing this familiar equation of consolation with pacification, Parks then considers the rather more paradoxical work of style: 'When we read Colm Tóibín's silver prose'—as I'll be doing in Chapter 3—especially 'the fine cadences with which emotional suffering is described, it really does seem that art might somehow make up for, or *almost* make up for, a lost love, an empty life'.[85] Parks's qualifying '*almost*' happens to be one of the key concerns of *Discrepant Solace*. An adverb that seems well aware of the ambiguity it insinuates, *almost* captures the provisional, often fleeting, yet nevertheless analysable attempt—an attempt enabled and embodied by style itself—to hold out the promise of consolation without necessarily fulfilling it, to draw affective blueprints for solace without underwriting their success, to tender options for redress without blithely endorsing them.

The qualification borne by *almost* also applies to the thorny issue of authorial motivation. For consolation, under my watch, isn't necessarily driven by or somehow measurable against writers' intentions—how could it be, in records of inconsolable grief as penetrating as those by Deraniyagala or Didion? That's not to say implied motives or circumstances of composition are entirely irrelevant. In some instances—Coetzee, Grossman, Lessing, Macdonald, Tóibín himself—the biographical backdrops to writing are unavoidable, even if they don't always prove to be sustainable foundations for discussion. At times, we will need to pause over the issue of how consolation's explicit thematic matrix (the prominent part it plays in the course of events) relates to its formally inadvertent or seemingly discrepant presence (those apparently unintended, surprising effects of language that offset emotional content, complicating the presumed knit between action and description). We will also need to do the opposite, when writers invite us to scrutinize style's compensatory efficacy (as Sebald and Ishiguro so movingly do), especially when worlds of irremediable damage host countervailing modes of expressive energy.

And it's those modes that invariably ring alarm bells. Do they not epitomize the nostrums of literary style, as Adorno might have warned? The danger with art's 'aesthetic stylistic principle', in his phrase, is that it can 'make the unthinkable appear to have had some meaning'; thanks to style's cosmetic enhancements, catastrophe 'becomes transfigured, something of its horror removed'.[86] Two decades later, Fredric Jameson would reach a similar conclusion about the propensity for literary impressionism to deflect modernity's violence into the compensations of linguistic profusion, resulting in a mitigating 'transformation' of social 'realities into style'. Modernism here ends up transmuting if not beautifying sorrow 'for consumption', in Jameson's phrase, 'on some purely aesthetic level', while the political contradictions that instigate collective harm are veiled by linguistic virtuosity.[87] These critical positions have proven to be pretty durable, and they continue to be felt in scholarship that draws attention to the acute moral dilemmas of representing abomination. John Whittier Treat, for instance, discusses what it means to put 'atrocity into words' by insisting that 'a belief in the human instinct for form may make us think that the well-executed lyric or novel can restore coherence, through its own internal order, to even a disintegrating world'. What all these accounts appear to have in common is the premise that style is 'to be distrusted'.[88]

It is not unreasonable to wonder, though, why one should think literature behaves like this at all. For how, exactly, might aesthetically absorbing elements of style dispose us to expect that the catastrophic wounds of world history will be sutured by their deft depiction? Does an 'instinct for form'—whether that applies to innovative writers or to avid readers—really precipitate our incapacity to notice what happens to individual or collective pain when it becomes the substance of literary art? And do the emotional worlds that style mediates coerce us through 'the microscopic experience of words', in Jameson's memorable warning, into thinking that, 'sheltered from the omnipresence of history and the implacable influence of the social, there already exists a realm of freedom', an ultimately deceptive realm that only goes to prove how literature can harbour the false consolation 'of a purely individual, merely psychological, project of salvation'?[89] The assumption that engrossing structures of expression might equate to the alleviation of material oppression, remorse, or dread will be a target for several writers in this book—notably Sebald, Coetzee, Ishiguro, and Grossman. In their work, our emotional captivation in elaborately described individual lives is not 'merely psychological' or soothingly insulated from the social. Rather, style is the very mechanism by which that captivation becomes critical, as these writers engage with consolation as a stimulus for ethical and political argument rather than as a facilitator of readerly appeasement.

If style can serve as a pressure gauge for solace, then recent fiction of historical atrocity has put it to the ultimate test. In his devastating novel of slavery, *The Underground Railroad* (2016), Colson Whitehead draws attention to the agonizing pathos of brief moments of respite. One of the novel's main focalizing centres of consciousness, the young Cora is watchful of such moments because of what they fleetingly trace yet forever deny by offering slivers of how freedom might feel. A birthday celebration on her Georgia plantation sets Cora on guard, 'wary' of the moment 'when the music tugged'.[90] Fellow slaves form 'a circle of themselves that separated the human spirits within from the degradation without' (28). Producing a verbal analogue for this separation, Whitehead disarticulates style from the setting's 'shared tension', temporarily offsetting the 'communal apprehension' that besets the cotton fields' black inhabitants (28). As a result, style seems to intervene in the novel's predominantly hellish focus on 'the routine facts of their bondage' (28), while confronting the potential mitigations of its own eloquence. The moment of musical immersion contains a nanosecond of linguistic uplift that concedes its own evanescence, bearing witness to a consolatory lyricism that dissipates as quickly as it takes hold among players 'in servitude to the song' (28):

> The music stopped. The circle broke. Sometimes a slave will be lost in a brief eddy of liberation. In the sway of a sudden reverie among the furrows or while untangling the mysteries of an early morning dream. In the middle of a song on a warm Sunday night. Then it comes, always—the overseer's cry, the call to work, the shadow of the master, the reminder that she is only a human being for a tiny moment across the eternity of her servitude. (29)

All the more crushingly poignant for being so 'tiny', the moment enacts the impossible solace it briefly tenders. Whitehead captures through the scene's sudden phrasal swell the perilous respite of 'reverie', whose 'brief eddy' affords a tangible glimpse of 'liberation', the unattainability of which is only reaffirmed by the way his final sentence here grammatically recedes to a stark catalogue of servitude's reminders.

The Underground Railroad makes shattering use of such ephemeral events, fragile episodes of adjournment that arc from abated toil to the grim anticipation of their own extinction, when the 'call to work' resumes. For Whitehead, moments of consolation are thus all the more painful for betraying through their impermanent rescue the slave's imminent return to abjection. Towards the end of the novel, this kind of moment recurs in its most pathetically extended form. We learn that Cora's mother, Mabel, did not intend to abandon her daughter (as Cora is left to assume) after she embarked on her own solitary escape. Before planning her return, one that would be cut short by a fatal snakebite, Mabel struggles through bogs and comes to rest amid 'noises of the swamp' (294). What ensues is a tranquil enumeration of naturalistic detail that seems like the stuff of reverie; but the episode swerves into a more purposeful moment of recognition, as she details the nascent sensation of freedom:

> Above—through the leaves and branches of the black-water trees—the sky scrolled before her, new constellations wheeling in the darkness as she relaxed. No patrollers, no bosses, no cries of anguish to induct her into another's despair. No cabin walls shuttling her through the night seas like the hold of a slave ship. Sandhill cranes and warblers, otters splashing. On the bed of damp earth, her breathing slowed and that which separated herself from the swamp disappeared. She was free.
>   This moment.
>   She had to go back. The girl was waiting on her. This would have to do for now. Her hopelessness had gotten the best of her, speaking under her thoughts like a demon. She would keep this moment close, her own treasure. When she found the words to share it with Cora, the girl would understand there was something beyond the plantation, past all that she knew. That one day if she stayed strong, the girl could have it for herself.
>   The world may be mean, but people don't have to be, not if they refuse. (294)

This late scene's searing tragedy is that we know full well the effect Mabel's absence has had on Cora, who (in her mind) is still 'waiting on her'. We know too by this point how slim Cora's prospects are for thriving 'beyond the plantation'. The very fact that Whitehead offers 'this moment' as resilient 'treasure' just pages before the novel ends stands as a discrepant kind of structural compensation, a wrenchingly brief interval between the aftershock and onrush of incessant horrors. Just as the consolatory realization that Mabel 'was free' seems to buckle under the weight of convulsive events we have just read, so she never survives the return journey from this moment 'to share it with Cora'. And yet, that message lingers in extra-diegetic form: it's as though Whitehead's decision to insert this standalone episode before the book's denouement gifts his reader the very 'words' to 'keep this moment close', to foster all that it briefly and sincerely yields, words that are still felt even though never fully verbalized by the moment's focalizing character. After *Railroad*'s preceding journey through unspeakable violence it seems, irrefutably, difficult to construe this episode's translucence as anything other than transient. Even as 'anguish' and 'despair' disperse into an unfettered ecology of sights and sounds, readers may nonetheless sense that the counteractive impulse of such naturalistically lush description is evanescent—dissipating, as this scene itself will soon do, back into desolation.

Yet at the same time, the solicitations of Whitehead's agile style are multifarious: he draws attention to what moments snatch back from misery, yet without diminishing the prescient indictment of harrowing inhumanity that *Railroad* achieves in showing how the 'labor of struggle', as Anna Kornbluh notes, 'the work to survive against the work of the nation, is not historical fiction in the past but searingly ongoing reality in the present'.[91] As Whitehead squares up in this novel to the twenty-first century's escalating racism and resurgent nationalism, his shimmering rendition of an instant that counterpoints oppression produces a stylistic correlative to what Kornbluh calls that 'grace of striving'. *This moment*, typographically isolated from its surrounding text, thus invites the reader to cradle its significance, to mourn its passing after the devastation of the novel's foregoing barbarities, yet to notice too how that same moment may, dialectically, also 'furnish the projective synthesis of a utopian pole'.[92] Such an otherwise fragile, fleeting moment thereby provokes readers to participate in the consoling message Mabel then manages to assert, if only for herself in this tragically foreshortened life—a conviction whose militant uplift reads more like an authorial interjection by the lights of populism's surge in the year of *Railroad*'s release, which saw the aggressive rise of patriotic isolationism in the United Kingdom and United States—an assertion that's paragraphically offset as well, distinguished in its apparent simplicity as a germ of redress even as it echoes as a call to action: 'The world may be mean, but people don't have to be, not if they refuse.'

While these late pages in *The Underground Railroad* 'are almost unbearably poignant', as Alex Preston points out, they thus 'seem to offer a model of resistance, a small gleam of hope'. By the same token, the consoling prospect of opposition amid devastation 'not only shines a bright light on one of the darkest periods of history, but also opens up thrilling new vistas for the form of the novel itself'.[93] Such are the ways in which the consolations of style can be as artistically generative as they are ethically contentious, especially when they enable unexpected modes of political projection to be articulated so lyrically—if also vulnerably and impermanently—amid the ravages of systemic violence. Hardly an aesthetic poultice for suffering, Whitehead's lyricism invites us to look again at the emotional latitude of solace itself as well as the suppleness with which it pervades vividly arresting narrative situations. Far from 'allowing just sufficient consolation and reward from the expression of unhappiness to prevent us from making big changes' (to recall Parks's phrase), Whitehead's novel orbits style's consolations rather than simply dispensing them. While doing so, *Railroad* requests the reader's participation in a narrative that angles across history—making the work of envisioning political transformation, in a current era of nationalist division and emboldened xenophobia, seem irrefutably urgent.

What writers like Whitehead emphasize, and what critics like Parks perhaps underestimate, is the affective *agency* of style: its nimble and undoubtedly ambivalent habit of diverging from plot's principal emotional pathways; its scope for countering rather than always complementing a narrative's prevailing currents of sorrow or threatened fortune. Moreover, if there's a useful lesson to be gleaned from Parks's bristling encounter with consolation, then it applies to the treatment of one's hypothetical reader. By and large, his discussion prioritizes the writer—including, unfashionably perhaps, authorial biography—and he insists on 'a continuity of atmosphere between everything that writing means for the writer and everything that happens in his writing'.[94] But when it comes to conceptualizing the reputed dangers of consolation, Parks pictures a reader who seems effortlessly manipulated. Only then can he recommend, rather melodramatically, that we should 'defend' ourselves from fiction's placating 'cadences' and anaesthetizing finesse. Only then can he imply that feeling 'pleasantly sad' while reading a novel is a disincentive to political and moral action.[95] One wonders what sort of easily beguiled reader Parks has in mind. We might also wonder, as I do throughout this book, whether in fact literature is most consoling when it doesn't entirely depend upon the reader's consolation.

CONSOLATION IN CRITICAL PRACTICE

While pursuing this hunch, I acknowledge that the ensuing account exposes my own visible manoeuvres *as* a reader. My inclinations will be made all the more conspicuous not only by my decision to read solace against the grain of its customary definitions and generic operations, but also by my effort to navigate between consolation's objectifiable analysis as an effect of language (legible in discrete units of style or structure) and its more subjectively discerned presence as an effect of aesthetic absorption. I see no necessary tension in offering close readings that rely on my own interpretive moves in order to shift beyond conceptions of solace that rely on conjectures about how readers might be comforted and about which narrative strategies comfort them most. Throughout this book, I privilege a mode of analytical proximity that does nothing to hide its priorities, advocating an attention to form that's conscious, I hope, of how close reading itself carries certain gratifications that can in themselves be consoling. Consequently, my own presence, perhaps too my own mood, as a reader will be everywhere apparent, even as I work to release the very concept of consolation from the cordons of imagined audiences and their approximated reactions.

To emphasize consolation's role in affectively surprising and disruptive properties of form is by no means to devalue the relevance of how readers respond to specific diegetic situations in ways that they may find consoling. Neither should it forestall the discussion of *how* particular formal features furnish immersive and unpredictable experiences of solace for readers—a narratology, so to speak, of how consolation occurs in our intimate encounters with texts. Therefore, if I situate solace throughout this book among 'the contradictions of form', in Ellen Rooney's phrase, then I also regard those contradictions as an 'enabling condition and product of reading' *for* consolation. When viewed this way, consolation is no longer the result of form's imposition of coherence and resolution on a text's otherwise difficult portrayal of messy, refractory realities of personal or social life; no longer the affective equivalent of those stylistic or structural guarantors of what Rooney calls 'the peculiar contentments of literature'. Instead, as we'll discover, the forms solace takes—together with the formal properties that enact the contestability *of* solace—are often integral to 'the contrariness of the text', whose implications are 'revealed only in the act of reading'. Examining the ethical consequences of close reading moments in contemporary writing where solace invigorates our sense of what form can affectively do will be a key metacritical task for this book. By doing so, I hope to free up an account of consolation's figurations that forgoes its conventional association with 'a dulling of ideology critique', with the acceptance of the status quo, or indeed with 'anything else that is constitutively "easy" '.[96]

This emphasis on the *poiesis* of solace, of course, signals one of the book's limitations. Empirically contextualized and sociological explanations of the reasons why certain audiences value affecting experiences in the literature they read demand very different modes of inquiry. Likewise, the question of whether solace is culturally specific, perpetually altering across time according to the volatilities of social existence, would warrant a separate study in its own right.[97] Given the immense, transdisciplinary opportunities presented by working conceptually and historically on emotion, together with its political affordances and affective representations, I ought to manage expectations upfront. This book by no means offers a sociocultural history of solace in the present or an extensively diachronic account of the term's evolving medical or philosophical transactions. Nor does it provide a comprehensive typology of consolation's transcultural variegation, one that might catalogue its sources and uses across diverse experiences of political conflict, racial injustice, economic disenfranchisement, mass-migration, or domestic hardship within specific regions of the global North and South. Like all other emotions, life-enhancing or injurious alike, what solace personally and communally means is contingent upon the discrete 'emotional regimes' within specific social and religious systems, reflecting complex variations in customs across different continents.[98] A robustly ethnographic and sedulously transnational report on consolation's psychotherapeutic, theological, and artistic manifestations in the twenty-first century is well beyond the purview of this book.

But while *Discrepant Solace* makes no attempt to offer a globally systematic, materialist diagnosis of consolation's contemporaneity, what it does try to do is examine the presence of consolation as it is performed by—and shapes the innovative forms of—contemporary writing, in ways that both demonstrate and test literature's potential for assaying disputable affects. The readings it offers take seriously the possibility of evaluating the feeling of encountering and inhabiting literary works in terms that are not confined to a historicism that would look to contemporary writing primarily for its reflections of consolation's social determinations and ideological sublimations. Consequently, I also take seriously the opportunities for regarding literature as a conceptual resource: a fellow interlocutor with whom to engage consolation's challenges as they manifest for characters or narrators, challenges that coincide with the connotative tensions of style. The textual instantiations of solace I cover, therefore, are by no means intended to provide a definitive index of consolation's discrete historical causes or twenty-first-century symptoms. Rather, they serve to demonstrate how we might address literature as an act of thought that makes consolation legible—including its undesirability, its misplacement, its absence—and that sharpens the critical implications of distinguishing represented experiences of consolation from the aesthetic consolations of representation.

Exploring this relation requires some comparative work, bringing writers into conversation who might not otherwise be considered together. And working comparatively also means moving between seemingly dissimilar styles with a fluency that crosses cultural and generic thresholds, creating points of analytical contact between writers' contrasting artistic projects and sensibilities. As Judith Brown has suggested, 'style as a methodological entry point offers an unlimited horizon not tied, at least in determining ways, to a historical moment, nation, or political framework'. This book means to say something fruitful about discrepant solace as a peculiarly prevalent phenomenon for contemporary writing, without assuming that its claims can be effortlessly transposed to other moments in time. By the same token, my approach to linguistic affects is very much in keeping with Brown's notion of style as an adjustable lens that can be 'freed' from positivistic contextualism and through which 'we can observe a text's other languages, other loves, and other means of expression'. In making style one of the gateways to reinterpreting consolation's contemporary potencies and provocations, I thus share the sense that '[s]tyle will always be embedded in discursive networks, will always be shaped by its critical moment, yet we should attend to its evasions, its alternative, even unlikely visions'.[99]

If, as recent work in the history of emotions indicates, it 'is the *language* in which emotion is clothed that opens the clearest view of how cultural attitudes shape our personal experiences of feeling', then a closer look at how literature now tailors the cloth seems warranted.[100] Drawn to the complex and often contradictory lives that solace leads in the properties of language as well as in the emotive scenarios that contemporary narratives represent, the story this book tells not only avoids guesswork about why and how readers might find certain works consoling, but also assesses motivations for rethinking literary solace at all.

That story takes on greater urgency in view of the default wariness towards solace in literary and cultural studies, which itself threatens to become as comforting as it is predictable. How expedient would it be to ensure consolation's conceptual dilution and ethical deprecation in the interests of turning our attention to more unequivocally progressive or politically serviceable subjects for discussion? Refusing this convenience, the following pages afford the consolatory dynamics of contemporary writing something of an analytical amnesty. In so doing, I'm mindful of giving the appearance of a methodological alliance with some strands of what commentators have dubbed our 'post-critical' turn.[101] But these affinities are matched by my departures. For instance, the chapters to come will indeed share at times 'the slow pace, receptiveness and fixed attention' of 'surface reading', as Sharon Marcus and Stephen Best so influentially characterized it in 2009, sharing too some of their 'refus[al] to celebrate or condemn' literary works as 'objects of study' for instrumental ends.[102] However, my own readings certainly don't stop at the surface. Examining a work's internal contradictions, granular antinomies, or uncalculated connotations, as I do through this book, need not mean overlooking that work's particularity nor forgoing some respect for how it is made by dissecting what it deliberately or unconsciously conceals.

Illuminating tensions or discrepancies between a narrative's affective consequences and its formal operations shouldn't have to be in league with the inquisitional circumspection and hawk-eyed paranoia that have in the past propelled the diagnoses of ideology-critique. While I agree with Elizabeth Anker and Rita Felski that a 'concern with drawing out shadowy, concealed, or counterintuitive meanings can lead to a neglect of the formal qualities of art and the sensual dimensions of aesthetic experience',[103] this disregard of form is by no means inevitable: the watchful investigation of a work's contradictions and a stylistic appreciation of its sensuous impact can productively coincide as analytical aims without compromising each other. What's more, although contemporary postcritical approaches display an apparent 'refusal of depth', to borrow Jennifer L. Fleissner's phrase, often giving primacy instead to critical procedures based around appreciation, description, and evaluation, these alternative priorities shouldn't '*necessarily* entail a lack of interest in allegory and symbolization'.[104] Either way, if several of my readings do indeed register the wider symbolism of works to the point of allegorical extrapolation, they are still motivated by the sense that an instrumentalizing *obligation* to allegorize—to transcribe symbolic connotations into full-scale, socio-material explanations—can also detract from discerning other planes of signification, where consolation persists as a rich problematic rather than a transient balm.

Consolation's discrepant behaviours in contemporary narrative thus solicit readings that take some account of the equally unusual or unexpected aesthetic experiences they produce. These disruptive, unanticipated reactions may otherwise go unnoticed, if we're too fixated on detecting complicity or pressing textual contradictions into the service of political illustration. Our current climate of methodological flux and vigorous disciplinary self-reassessment has prompted a rethinking of what the stakes of affective analysis might be for literary and cultural studies. Spurred by the acknowledgement that critique can impede 'descriptive richness', as Heather Love observes, varieties of 'reparative criticism' have emerged that share an inclination to relinquish 'hypervigilance for attentiveness'. Rather than aiming for 'powerful reductions' that come with decipherment and indictment, this style of reading 'stays local', in Love's account, 'prefers acts of noticing, being affected, taking joy, and making whole'.[105] *Discrepant Solace* by no means satisfies these criteria, but it does find valuable impetus in them. For arguably, whatever force my readings gain in pursuing counterintuitive or unforeseen manifestations of solace will in part be supplied by consolation's own definitional susceptibility to 'powerful reductions': its propensity to attract historical generalization, despite its inestimable variability over time; its continued predisposition to misrepresentation when viewed as a rather sketchy reason why literature matters.

Yet if one of this book's missions is to manage without the interpretive shorthand to which consolation is prone, another is to avoid the temptation to issue corrective advice for validating solace as an act of intellectual virtue.[106] Furthermore, this study will have deliberately less to say about how we might nurture the benefits of fiction-reading as a collectively therapeutic activity or as an aid to intercultural solidarity. What I try to propose instead is a certain critical disposition: a means of reading in sync with how contemporary writing *thinks* its aesthetic and ethical position as a cultural practice, modelling experiences both familiar and unimaginable, while implicitly commentating on its own relation to the emotive work literature enacts and examines. As Peter Middleton points out, we 'still don't have enough sophisticated methodological vocabulary for identifying (and distinguishing) the intelligence of literary texts and tracing their constructive influence on research, politics and ethics—on the development of human understanding'.[107] In view of this need, I try to recognize—as my initial examples here of memoir and fiction from Deraniyagala and Whitehead have invited us to do—how the complexities and controversies that attend literary solace can epistemically enrich what it means to read such deeply affecting works, where the implications of consolation's forms do not directly hinge on whether or not we come away feeling consoled. The range and inscrutability of solace at formal and thematic levels in literature now challenges preconceived assessments of its artistic assets and experiential intricacies. In practice, this means treating literary works not as mere evidence for the emotions they evoke, but instead as perspicacious equals to the very criticism practiced upon them. As consolation's variousness in contemporary writing expands our affective literacies, it trains us to entertain literature as a site of intellection in its own right.[108]

To be sure, I agree with David Constantine that it remains 'questionable what *consolation* the active beauty' of literature 'might or should bring', because '[t]here is much suffering—man-occasioned—that it would be quite wrong to be reconciled to'.[109] But as we have already seen, the countervailing effect of beautiful articulation is only one aspect of what solace in literature might mean. A pathetic, meticulously described moment that ephemerally offsets the impress of despair; a phrase's unexpected metrical shift, making rhythm surge against diegetic dread; a paratactic sentence whose athleticism seems to defy rather than mirror the chronic longing it enumerates: to be sure, they all contribute vividly and unsettlingly to how writers may allay as much as instantiate the experiential damage they evoke. It's that contribution which has sparked critical controversy. Yet through their command of these ethically agitating forms of redress, contemporary writers are disrupting unidirectional tales of what happens to harrowing realities when language counters in the course of conjuring insufferable loss, the bewilderments of trauma, the overpowering strain of jeopardy. Unsettling consecrations of harm's indescribability, they prompt us to rethink the critical grounds for elevating works that spurn all pretentions to solace.

To close now with a writer who issues that prompt more poignantly than most, consider again Sonali Deraniyagala. At first, she feels bitter towards any sign of rehabilitation, beginning with the flood-torn environment around Yala itself. *Wave* records the day she 'saw the jungle begin to revive' (64), as 'a scattering of young *ranawara* bushes dripped yellow blossoms' (65). A landscape of slow recovery was overtaking her mindscape still in turmoil. Witnessing this, she was drawn to discern—and evoke subtly in kind—the way 'everywhere, on bare ground and between cracks in the floors, tiny pink and white flowers that flourish along the seashore forced their way up' (65). Even as she 'resented this renewal', Deraniyagala nevertheless 'began to experience a new calm' because of what this shoreline had once meant to a family the sea destroyed: 'We loved this wilderness. Now slowly it began pressing into me, enticing me to take notice, stirring me from my stupor' (65). Acts of noticing become consoling, and her behaviour turns from the protections of self-distraction to the purposefulness of observation and intense description. When first confronting the fact that her loved ones 'simply vanished...forever',

Deraniyagala had wondered whether '[i]n order to survive this bizarre and brutal truth' she would 'have to make murky the life I had with them' (114). Living on in her London house seems unthinkable, just as her parents' former house in Colombo is 'no home now, not even one empty of them' (103). As she longs for 'the solace of that space', Deraniyagala cannot help but 'feel dispossessed' (103), realizing that she occupies 'the unthinkable situation that people cannot bear to contemplate', a position that by its very nature 'cannot be imagined' (103).

Gradually, however, Deraniyagala calls to account these tactics for reckoning with this unutterable 'situation' of loss, recognizing that if language is among grief's dispossessions then it isn't unrecoverable. *Wave* thereafter moves from the self-protections of withdrawing into blinkering murk towards the consolation of recollective clarity: 'The more I remember, the more inconsolable I will be, I've told myself. But now increasingly I don't tussle with my memories. I want to remember. I want to know. Perhaps I can better tolerate being inconsolable now' (128). And whereas she saw herself 'loitering on the outskirts of the life we had' (103), *Wave* journeys from that perimeter in, as the pathos of scenes from that former life sustains rather than disarms her: 'More and more now I keep my balance while staring into us. And I welcome this, a small triumph, it lights me up' (206). Of course, the solace of seeing the past in close-up competes with the speculations about the family 'as it would be today' (207). Descriptions of what could have been contain their own hypothetical eulogies for a future that never unfolded, whenever 'details of how we would now be...come striding in, lucid, quite exact' (207). *Wave* reveals how descriptions can be as 'treacherous' as they are restorative, to be sure, inserting 'a new sadness' into the fold of whatever compensations those 'details' impart (207). Yet Deraniyagala also suggests that only by *writing out* this experience of being 'cradled by shock' is she able to negotiate the forking paths of cherished retrospection and nagging projection: 'I have learned that I can only recover myself when I keep them near. If I distance myself from them, and their absence, I am fractured' (207–8).

Instead of being suspicious of transforming and thereby blunting the realities of loss through style, *Wave* endeavours to clasp them, to cradle them in language, affording elegant expression to unrelieved longing. And instead of pre-empting the costs of confronting grief with inevitably inadequate textual portraits, Deraniyagala embraces the consolations of description by resolving to 'want every detail' (184). Her account of a whale-spotting trip off the Mirissa coast that her son Vik would have loved achingly captures this new dispensation for meticulous description, one that takes care to reproduce what he didn't live to witness:

> I want to take in all this blue whale magic, maybe more so because Vik can't. I search the ocean as he would. There is a stir in the water, a foamy mass heralds the head that rises to the surface, its shape an ancient arch. The whale breathes, and a flare of water fizzes in the air. I want to see more now, I want the head to lift higher, that huge pleated jaw, or better still, maybe this whale will breach. But I am left wanting, soon the head is submerged.
>
> They keep their hugeness hidden, these whales, rarely revealing themselves whole to my eager eyes.   (184–5)

Seeing for the son she has lost, Deraniyagala records with crystalline exactness an outing he would have found spellbinding. Her epithetic version of *foam* here recalls the word's first appearance on *Wave*'s opening page, where it anticipated the surging terror that soon followed. Now it no longer serves as the first sign of oncoming disaster: if 'foamy' still reverberates with the horror of that day, its echo here is muffled by the benign 'flare' of the whale's spume. A previously foreboding image is thus reclaimed anew just as Deraniyagala retrieves this moment's 'magic' from her self-reproof, dispelling her own presumption that she couldn't 'endure whales without Vik' (184). And description's reparative work in this sense continues. Resonant sibilance complements acoustically the visual impact of watching 'surface' water disturbed by the rising 'shape' of a whale's awe-inspiring 'hugeness'. Observing the 'same ocean' she once 'was churning in' (185), her relation to the sea is also transformed: 'In this endless expanse of ocean, I feel snug' (186). As her 'earlier discord eases', she no longer feels compelled to 'dread whales without Vik' alongside; 'unclenched and calmed', she is moved to 'savor this relief' (186).

To say in response, then, that these aspects of rhetorical and scenic vividness amount to a distraction from grief, an aestheticizing antidote to the void that subtends this episode, not only feels churlish but distinctly unethical. The luminosity and euphony here supply not some superficial or distorting compensation, one that finds in language an alcove to which the reader vicariously retreats with a writer taking cover from intolerable reality. On the contrary, it is *through* language's commitment to a beautiful yet barely endurable moment—through her hunger for those very details she cannot share with Vik—that Deraniyagala presents us with a form of consolation that encompasses rather than obviates the devastation her style so energetically counterpoints. *Wave* is a testament indeed to how important descriptive moments are for understanding the complex work solace performs. As we'll see throughout this book, such moments at times structurally suspend, withstand even, the prevailing motion of events. This suspension effectively couples narrative adjournment with temporary alleviation, in ways that often magnify consolation's larger social and, in some cases, political entanglements—even when those moments uncoil from intensely individualized circumstances. Although Deraniyagala has 'to compress often and misshape' the 'impossible truth' of her family's loss (186), for this moment at least—*because* of this moment and what it enables her to enfold in style's abundance—she 'can rest with her disbelief about what happened' (186). Not only illustrative but critically instructive, *Wave* sabotages suppositions about what solace expressively means to writing concerned with calamities that seem beyond words.

Building a case for the hermeneutics of consolation, though, still faces a pretty steep path to acceptance. Explicitly negative states of being—shame, melancholy, fury, despair, trauma itself—are consolation's stormy bedfellows; but they are usually cast as its noble antagonists or, interpretively speaking, as solemn counterparts immanently worthy of our critical time and energy. For unlike solace, these damaging, pernicious, often-irreparable feelings are dependably relevant, forever urgent, intrinsically venerable. Consolation, by contrast, is a rather more illicit citizen of literary studies, unlikely to promise critics the same gratification that comes from entering the archives of experiences that possess innate, unquestioned gravity. Yet this same struggle for analytical merit is precisely what makes solace so productively uncomfortable to work on, for it challenges our complacencies about which emotional occasions—and the cultural works they inspire—deserve formal scrutiny and political recalibration. Taking up this opportunity, chapters to come assemble writers who help us to observe how consolation isn't about repairing the object of loss, attenuating grief's duration, or covering up the material causes of psychic devastation. A closer look at consolation as an affordance of style and structure will enable us to rethink solace in active, unruly terms—a more distant cousin of comfort than we might assume. By staging consolation's own acknowledgement of incompletion, these writers uncouple consolation from distraction, appeasement, and soothing repair. A phenomenon that resists the salve of exchange, that's left open, that isn't really concerned with the prospect of substitution: consolation glimmers in the elegant yet unsettling contours of contemporary writing, whose discrepancies we can read more incisively by its light.

1
Fetched from Oblivion

Commemorations can be uneasy occasions for consolation: reappraisals are more likely to elicit sorrow than to offer solace. Voices from commemoration's literary history buck this trend. In June 1940 the journalist and translator Philip Tomlinson showed how commemorative writing, even in dark times, can parley with consolation in his moving 'tribute to a poet for whom loving-kindness was the highest beauty and warfare, a splitting of humanity against itself, utterly ugly'. The subject of his homage was Thomas Hardy, whose birth Tomlinson celebrated in this centenary year by appraising *The Dynasts* (1903–8) as an oracular work that spoke urgently to a moment where 'death is once more astride over pale Europe'. Tomlinson observed 'the eternal irony' of the fact that 'it is to this poet who was called pessimist and other meaningless names we can turn to find fortitude and safety of justice and calmness'. *The Dynasts* lays on few rosy diversions. Forged from inner frictions, this epic-drama possesses 'something of the gaunt beauty of a giant oak, its foliage in the sunlight, its roots deep in the darkness'. Thanks to this striking demeanour, with seemingly 'incommensurable' parts, Tomlinson deemed it a 'book of the day' whose 'eternal meanings' rely on rather than resolve Hardy's 'double vision of a limited and an abstract world'.[1]

On first impressions, this portrait makes *The Dynasts* appear monumentally bleak; looking again, though, the text is also made to seem like a daring consolation at an incipient of juncture global cataclysm. Out of his historical 'panorama of Europe'—now a prescient 'panorama of pain'—Hardy simultaneously 'remembers' certain 'nooks and moments that bloom into the beauty of joy or the beauty of pity'. Such 'lyrical' intervals counterweigh the drama's 'tumultuous happenings', argues Tomlinson, which otherwise do everything to 'emphasize the foulness of war and the pity war instils'. By means of its uncompromising yet lyrically 'full recognition of the coil of things', *The Dynasts* provokes readers in 1940 to confront their own 'poised moment of fate', however 'paradoxical' it may feel 'to turn to the close of this great sad epic for encouragement'.[2] This paradox gives Tomlinson pause. 'Do they create happiness?', he wonders, wrapping up his estimation of Hardy's prophetic and pathetic voices, voices that offer readers ten months into another world war something tougher than wishful escape from present dread. 'If they have not the allurement of a sure promise', concludes Tomlinson, 'which never had a place in Hardy's purpose, they have that better-founded solace that comes from looking squarely at the worst, bracing the heart to endure in order to overcome'.[3]

Writers today continue to take on the ethical and aesthetic demands of countenancing that 'better-founded solace'. Choosing inconsolable situations to register what it means to endure the worst, they mobilize and test what Freud called in 1908 literature's 'techniques of overcoming', whose variety the following chapters will sample.[4] Aesthetic energies and critical controversies arise from those techniques, and these continue to resonate in contemporary writing as a legacy of Tomlinson's own moment—the moment of modernism. Durable consolations are hardly what modernism is best remembered for, still less the reason why its lasting potential for oppositional art is celebrated. Here I play devil's advocate with this assumption to suggest that contemporary fiction's strenuous stylistic and thematic engagement with solace entails a reassessment of how modernist writing faces losses whose impact seems otherwise ineffable, scarcely remediable.

In this conversation between contemporary literature and the affective language of early-twentieth-century fiction, modernism's innovative yet contentious work of consolation becomes the subject of renewed aesthetic and political scrutiny. In critical discourse, that scrutiny has been going on for some time. According to these accounts, the very form of modernist fiction can further its own redemptive propaganda. Motivated by a salvaging, corrective impulse, to recall Leo Bersani's polemic, the most thrillingly inventive novelists cultivate 'the consolations of narrative order', even as they map the personal and world-historical upheavals of modernity.[5] Although experimenters like Virginia Woolf, James Joyce, and Marcel Proust appear to fragment that solacing sense of order via innovations with interiority that simulate disarming or volatile sensations, they never lose confidence (so this account goes) in the reparative efficacy of novelistic design. Indeed, the perfectibility of that design may have offered its own artistic solace in an interwar era when literature's capacity to provide tangible transformations was under unprecedented threat.

This is one story of literary modernism's melancholic allegiance to consolatory form; in the coming pages, I want to tell another. When read by the lights of writers today who are thrashing out their own correspondence with the emotional economy of early twentieth-century fiction, an alternative picture of how modernism deliberated over art's redemptive affordances becomes possible—a picture that brings into better critical definition the multiplex and historically enduring stakes of novelists' alternating faith in and contentions with literature's provision of solace. Such a faith is under duress in Ian McEwan's *Atonement* (2001), my loadstone for this discussion. The pressure comes not only from within the moral drama of this period-novel-cum-historiographic-metafiction but also from McEwan himself. His strained relationship with varieties of modernist style supplies the compositional backdrop to a work that's self-consciously concerned with whether postmillennial fiction can offer an ethically sufficient response to modernism's consolatory potential. 'This highly inventive' novel, notes Dominic Head, 'seems to be an emphatic instance of consolation', for 'it enacts the lifelong consolation of Briony (consolation as theme and form), and offers a form of consolation for the reader, through formal intellectual stimulus', even if that reward is partly 'undermined by the shocking disappointment' of the narrative's final tragic disclosure.[6] Briony Tallis's own 'faith in the consoling power of fiction', in Head's phrase, certainly will be one of my avenues of inquiry here. But I also want to examine consolation in more explicitly literary-historical terms, retracing the lineage of its discrepant manifestations in ways that elaborate a critical and creative backstory for a phenomenon I pursue in contemporary writing across this book. By arguing with rather than passively absorbing the lessons of modernism's negotiation of solace, McEwan shows in turn how vital that negotiation was in its historical moment and how vigorously fiction today is still working through its implications. Arguments with modernist consolations thus provide an occasion for *Atonement* to contemplate the very historicity of fiction's affective potential, including the paradoxes the practice of realizing that potential produces. A novel that dramatizes one writer's tacitly consoling plea for unattainable reparation, *Atonement* produces a narrative about irrevocable time that also reflects on its position *in* time, taking stock of contemporary fiction's assessment of its own ability to redress, ameliorate, even redeem—and to turn that self-assessment into a process that's as formally generative as it is ethically probing.

In this respect, *Atonement* will set important coordinates for chapters to come. McEwan's archaeology of novelistic consolation and its discontents is emblematic of the way contemporary writers throughout this book extend in intensified, often self-scrutinizing fashion, modernism's concurrent assaying of and dispute with art as an antidote to devastation. Through its inquiry into the disengagement of narrative from historical reality, McEwan's novel considers modernism's ticklish association with solace on three levels. First, stylistically, consolation is one of the equivocal fruits of literary impressionism which, in *Atonement*'s verdict, risks aestheticizing the violence of moral errors, diverting our attention with verbal splendour (an impression of impressionism that I'll seek to complicate). Second, on a characterological level, solace—creative, intellectual, personal—designates a potentially self-serving goal of the atoning Briony. While bringing to fruition a 'fifty-nine-year assignment' in contrition by professing her commitment to 'exact circumstances', she reveals just how redemptive her adaptation of demolished lives has aimed to be and how consoled she is by a writing process that should have been more penitential than reconstructive, treasuring as she does 'the correction of detail that cumulatively gives such satisfaction'.[7] It's the affective relay between these formal and diegetic levels which points to the third agent in *Atonement*'s tripartite spar with solace: the reader. We are left to wonder whether it falls to us, at the close, to exercise the appropriate response to the solace McEwan's novel both generates and dismembers. Hovering at the perimeters of consolation, we become spectators to the conflux of compromise and pathos at the centre of Briony's broken experiment in happiness—an experiment that admits how the solace it proffers can only survive while her readers are deceived.

McEwan therefore seems provocatively uninterested in merely dismissing consolation as an antiquated impulse that the literary imagination ought to keep at arm's length. *Atonement* invites us instead to rethink the transhistorical currency of modernism's testing yet moving attention to solace, and to consider how the affective aspirations and consequences of modernist form may be fruitfully addressed to the contemporary. Through its dialogue with Woolf, at once animated and uneasy, *Atonement* suggests that modernism was not necessarily identical to 'an aesthetic of the sublime', as Jean-François Lyotard famously described it, whose 'form', in evoking 'the unrepresentable', presents 'to the reader or viewer matter for solace or pleasure'—a facility that a typical postmodern work reputedly 'denies itself'. By rereading Woolf's work ahead of her somewhat fraught commemoration in *Atonement*, I want to recapture something of her fiction's own resistance to the very 'solace of good forms' with which modernism (in a Lyotardian framework) seems besotted, a resistance that allows Woolf to nurture a formal and thematic relationship with consolation that's unsettled, conflictual, discrepant.[8] In advance of chapters to come, Woolf and McEwan therefore present us with an instructive if perhaps unexpected alliance across literary history, one that points to an imperative we'll see time and again in this book: to refuse the cosmetic solutions and false reconciliations sometimes associated with form as literature's apparatus of integration, precisely in order to allow form to measure the difficulties and contradictions that narratives of solace unfold.

STYLE AS ARGUMENT

The potential for modernism to offer even a smidgen of solace wouldn't sit well with some contemporaneous commentators, of course. In his 1937 verdict on 'affirmative culture', Herbert Marcuse suggests that across 'classical literature since Shakespeare' we're presented with the ideal of an individual who is able to 'overcome' life's 'factual loneliness in the glow of great and beautiful words'. With the deceptive 'unity represented by art and the pure humanity of its persons', such works beguile us with 'the counterimage of what occurs in social reality'.[9] Going further still, he warns that such an 'illusion has a real effect, producing satisfaction' in its audience. Hence 'art pacifies rebellious desire', offering in place of agitation 'the consolation of a beautiful moment in an interminable chain of misfortune'. Thanks to these exquisite moments, 'ephemeral' though they ultimately are, the reader 'tolerates the unfreedom of social existence'.[10] The premise of Marcuse's diagnosis of gratification as pacification has had a lasting impact, influencing the terms today with which modernism is valued for how it fosters disconsolation, how it outlaws repair, how it steadfastly prevents the 'glow' of words from mitigating despair. Neil Lazarus, for instance, endorses a modernist resurgence in later twentieth-century fictions of decolonization and uneven development by asserting that the '*ongoing* critical dimension of modernist literary practice' lies in a form of postcolonial writing 'that resists the accommodationism of what has been canonized as modernism', carrying forward what the most subversive 'modernist work has done from the outset: namely, says "no"; refuses integration, resolution, consolation, comfort', and instead 'protests and criticises'.[11] For Lazarus, modernism's most potent lesson for contemporary writers is the forestalling of consolation. In this vein, Kazuo Ishiguro's novels 'offer us intimate portraits of the wreckage of lives that have been lived wrongly, in the shadow or under the auspices of malign social, cultural, ideological, and familial dispensations', and for the characters involved the 'search in these novels for consolation, justification, reconciliation, is urgent and unceasing'.[12] Yet all the while, argues Lazarus, 'a frail light from utopia shines on, or rather, through, the unseeing eyes and unknowing thoughts of Ishiguro's characters. It is this transcendental implication that engenders "disconsolation" in us as readers.'[13]

Similarly, Tyrus Miller celebrates late modernist writing precisely for its satirically stringent refusal of what he terms high modernism's preoccupation with 'the problem of mastering a chaotic modernity by means of formal techniques', including irony, elaborate multiperspectivism, and the existential glue of 'large-scale symbolic forms'.[14] By 'unsettling the signs of formal craft that testified to the modernist writer's discursive mastery', later figures like Wyndham Lewis, Djuna Barnes, and Samuel Beckett 'sought to deflate' the 'symbolic resources' that Joycean encyclopedism and Woolfian lyricism emblazoned. In place of the consolations of architectonic cohesion or elegant stylization, late modernist fiction gave primacy, according to Miller, to 'those negative forces of the age that could not be coaxed into any admirable design of words'.[15]

Generative though these arguments for modernism's criticality can be—whether in 'late' or postcolonial contexts—they rehearse the assumption that as soon as literature consoles it immediately compromises its own capacity for critique. They also assume that the political options writers face in their rendezvous with solace present black-and-white choices: between indulgence or negation, complicity or rejection; formal compensations versus their unsentimental renunciation, acquiescent resolution versus condonable agitation. In turn, they give the impression that the only alternative to consolation must therefore be disconsolation, an impression that limits our options for considering how literature enables intricate kinds of thinking about troubling affects that extend beyond predictable binaries, soliciting responses from readers that participate in the simultaneous enactment and examination of consolation that writers—whether formally or thematically, purposefully or discreetly—carry out.

Indeed, if we look closer at what is actually happening in modernist fiction's affective environments, it is by no means certain that novelists saw in 'craft' a consoling 'means of managing turbulent forces of the day'. Consider an epitome of 'admirable design': *To the Lighthouse*. Woolf's 1927 novel seems keenly aware of the very 'fragility of modernist attempts to contain contingency and violence aesthetically' that Miller's later cluster of satirists sought to expose.[16] At a diegetic level, *To the Lighthouse* is punctuated throughout by instances of solace. We might recall the 'measured and soothing tattoo' of the waves that for Mrs Ramsay 'seemed consolingly to repeat over and over again, as she sat with the children, the words of some old cradle song, murmured by nature', an ecological solace that, on other days, provokes in her a counterpointing 'impulse of terror', replacing 'such kindly meaning' with 'a ghostly roll of drums' that 'remorselessly beat the measure of life'—an 'ephemeral' life that 'had slipped past in one quick doing after another'.[17] As though to withstand her own intimations of this ephemerality, Mrs Ramsay equates familial creation with her husband to an enduring, melodic variety of 'solace which two different notes, one high, one low, struck together, seem to give each other as they combine' (54). Later, in 'The Lighthouse', where the survivors of dismantling time gather in mournful recollection, Mr Ramsay makes impatient demands upon Lily 'to solace his soul' (207). Knowing 'she could not sustain this enormous weight of sorrow', knowing too his propensity for 'sudden roars of ill-temper, complete annihilation', Lily only has the courage to 'praise his boots' (206, 208, 207). Closer to the climax, the vivacity of haunting supplants dolorous commemoration, as

Lily's longing for Mrs Ramsay manifests ghostly visions of her vanishing with her 'usual quickness across the fields'—this very 'sight, the phrase, had its power to console' (245).

In a novel that is of course about one family's crushing and irreparable fragmentation, Woolf doesn't treat consolation uncritically. Like symbolism itself, with its power to give figurative order to otherwise unmanageable or indescribable experiences, so with solace she leaves it in abeyance, incomplete, even if its desirability remains just as acute as Ramsay's 'insatiable hunger for sympathy' (205). At the level of events, the anguished arc of *To the Lighthouse* makes consolation a recurrent point on Woolf's diegetic compass, all the while unfulfillable, ultimately inconceivable. At the level of style, though, something else is going on. 'Time Passes' at once stages and inspects language's necessarily impossible attempt to redress the absence in this coastal home that couldn't be more self-evident. A discrepancy arises between the section's rhetorical plenitude and the vacancy of its setting, a discrepancy that nonetheless testifies to the fraction of resuscitation *To the Lighthouse* ventures to provide at this mid-point, recognizing in the very act of doing so how gossamer style's salve remains in the face of bald loss. Woolf later counsels that 'beauty offers her lures, her consolations' (182); in 'Time Passes' she appears to pre-empt that temptation by trialling expression's defiance of enervation, its tendency to flourish in the same zone of vacuity it limns:

> What people had shed and left—a pair of shoes, a shooting cap, some faded skirts and coats in wardrobes—those alone kept the human shape and in the emptiness indicated how once they were filled and animated; how once hands were busy with hooks and buttons; how once the looking-glass had held a face; had held a world hollowed out in which a figure turned, a hand flashed, the door opened, in came children rushing and tumbling; and went out again. Now, day after day, light turned, like a flower reflected in water, its clear image on the wall opposite. Only the shadows of the trees, flourishing in the wind, made obeisance on the wall, and for a moment darkened the pool in which light reflected itself; or birds, flying, made a soft spot flutter slowly across the bedroom floor.
>
> So loveliness reigned and stillness, and together made the shape of loveliness itself, a form from which life had parted. (175–76)

At the confluence of presence and absence transpires the paradox of 'a form' that at once testifies to irreparable loss and provides 'the shape' of life it elegizes, all the 'rushing and tumbling' excitement that war has thieved from the house. Though some 'shadows' 'flutter slowly' their compensating animation of 'wall' and 'floor' is short-lived, and Woolf's syntax seems to acknowledge this as it shuttles on, never lingering for long on the images it singles out, clause by cataloguing clause. The very affection aroused here concedes the finitude of its own 'loveliness', a concession intimated grammatically by sentences that cannot rest, that refuse to loll in the 'solitude' the scene 'for a moment' rectifies. If the anthropomorphic picturing of 'form' is consoling, then its articulation in these lines enumerates what 'had parted', calling attention through the irresistible progression of Woolf's phrases to the impermanence of that 'shape' which 'loveliness' and 'stillness' try to sustain. Rhythm soon offers some resistance of its own with those pulsing questions this scene 'scarcely needed' to answer—'Will you fade? Will you perish?' (176)—questions whose anapaestic insistence presses back for an instant against the unravelling momentum of the paragraph as a whole. Rhetorical and metrical components of style thus counterweigh the impression of what can 'remain' against the pace of unravelling description.

And how disruptive description is, how it rocks the scene's structurally self-possessed effort to retain and contain. Even if '[n]othing it seemed could break that image' established by a vacant house 'filled and animated' by its natural environment (176), the language required to track, accrete, and itemize that state of animation yields to the perpetual motion of documenting wind and light—at once embellishing and imperilling 'the air of pure integrity' the home enshrines. Spatially, the moment's focus promises to be 'held', like the 'clasped hands' of 'loveliness' and 'stillness', caught in 'the swaying mantle of silence' under which rooms memorialize what they miss by the extent to which 'a face' or 'a hand' can still be sensed (176–77). Grammatically, though, the rendition of that focus corroborates the unsustainability of such redeeming poise. Woolf ripples the serene surface of the episode's seductive image of endurance, slipping into the purl of her parataxis the tougher solace of expressive reanimation that recognizes what expression cannot enfold and shelter forever—tougher because it vivifies rather than veils that discrepancy between unbreakable 'image' and mutably lovely 'form'.

Such a discrepancy underlies the 'elegiac triumph' of *To the Lighthouse*, as Gillian Beer has observed, since the novel seeks 'to sustain entity' precisely through a 'kind of writing which eschews permanence'.[18] This paradox captures the unsettled, sometimes conflictive dynamic of solace that relinquishes the restorative pledges of form that Woolf advances and that contemporary figures such as McEwan, to whom we'll shortly turn, are extending in ways that illuminate consolation's contestability as an ethical and aesthetic legacy of modernism. To grasp the consequences of this persistence, though, we need to dispense with the critical assumption that solace leaves writers complicit with the negligent pursuit of redemptive aesthetics—where 'good forms' administer counteragents for history's pain. For what we witness in *To the Lighthouse* is neither the outright refutation of solace with a force that 'engenders disconsolation', in Lazarus's phrase, nor a plea to transcend history's harm through the 'admirable design of words', to recall Miller's. Instead, language enacts its own fraught efforts to navigate 'the sands of oblivion' (189), as Woolf puts it towards the end of 'Time Passes', and in so doing navigate itself, its resources of resuscitation, knowing what it has 'fetched up from oblivion' cannot ultimately be 'rescued from the pool of Time' (189).

When Woolf returned for 'A Sketch of the Past' to the autobiographical substrate of *To the Lighthouse*, she also, according to Elizabeth Abel, reconsidered her 'hold over the tightly crafted novelistic form' which the novel exhibits. By embracing 'more flexible' modes of 'life-writing' through the 1930s, Woolf recognized that the 'challenge was to find a shape', writes Abel, 'that could resist both the impersonal unravelling of time and the dubious consolation of aesthetic form'.[19] That recognition, I suggest, was already at work in *To the Lighthouse*, dramatized by a style that seems to argue with its very own capacity to confront the inconsolable. Refusing to aestheticize the grief-work it plots, the novel refuses in turn to substitute melodious description for the raw void its centrepiece home monumentalizes. Rather than wrestling one family's wreckage into the redemptive integrity of narrative structure, Woolf acknowledges yet declines the invitation to 'compose from their fragments a perfect whole' (174). The novel thereby sits 'on the verge of harmonizing' (192), watchful of the footing it finds on the threshold of consolatory cohesion.

WOUNDING IMPRESSIONISM

One of the great innovations of 'Time Passes' is Woolf's displacement of the narration's provenance from any identifiable human centre of consciousness: she disperses perspective and dislocates its implied sources, in order for its resulting vision—depersonalized yet still emotive—to align with 'the insensibility of nature' (187). Likewise, neither the source nor destination of consolation can be attributed to a distinguishable, sensate subject, begging the question of who exactly might be consoled from one season to the next by fleeting instants that 'stir the most sublime reflections and lead to the most comfortable conclusions' (182). All this befits Woolf's opinion in July 1925 of the section as an 'impersonal thing, which I'm dared to do by my friends', punctuated by the deaths of Prue, Andrew, and Mrs Ramsay—notifications of which are, famously, rendered all the more pathetic by stark square parentheses—a decade-long interval that would not only evoke 'the flight of time' but also effect a 'consequent break of unity in my design'.[20] Thinking diagrammatically of the novel's triadic progression in her notes, Woolf visualized 'Time Passes' as a 'corridor' between 'two blocks', a model that deliberately calls into question the roborant of architectonic coherence.[21] By withstanding such compensatory integrity, *To the Lighthouse* invites us to consider what kind of consolation is possible when the wounds of impressionist form are left unsutured. Structurally, Woolf thus documents what fetching from oblivion means in a narrative whose tripartite scheme is centrally fractured and internally unequal; meanwhile rhetorically, her scattered and repeated images stir only then to leave insatiate our hunger to 'read' in the tessellation of 'littered pieces the clear words of truth' (174).

Woolf leaves those pieces where they are. Offering no tonic by accumulating tropes and phrasal variations, she models fractal consolations in *To the Lighthouse* on those 'irregular, intermittent, yet somehow related' sounds encircling the newly cleaned home (192). Even as her imagery inevitably yields resonances and patterns that survive the novel's temporal leaps, images whose permutations the reader's 'ear strains to bring together' (192); even as she seems to prize in natural surroundings the 'half-heard melody' of redemptive continuity (192); and even though *To the Lighthouse* appears especially attuned to that 'ripple of irresistible sensation' which promises the very 'wholeness' Woolf sought to obtain, according to 'A Sketch of the Past', by 'putting' shock 'into words', by piecing 'severed parts together' in order to 'take away the pain'—despite all these potential sources of compensatory amalgamation, Woolf nevertheless confronts rather than completes the imperative to 'make it whole'.[22] In the month *To the Lighthouse* was released, Woolf noted to Roger Fry that she had 'to have a central line down the middle of the book to hold the design together'. But she immediately qualified its purpose, insisting that its effects remain polysemic rather than integrational: 'all sorts of feelings would accrue to this, but I refused to think them out, and trusted people would make it the deposit for their own emotions'. This hermeneutically democratic ethos behind her sense of imagery's impact also underpins Woolf's dispassionate chronicle of solace in *To the Lighthouse*. For there she asks readers to imagine what it means to regard consolation as she does her choreography of symbolism: not as a matter of 'right or wrong' (in her words to Fry),[23] but as the nucleus of a tough, poignant recognition that literature can never be 'fully harmonized' with what it longs to bring back (192).

Bringing people back, though, is for Briony Tallis precisely what fiction writing is all about. We first meet Briony at her most precocious in *Atonement*, where McEwan pictures her spellbound by her own 'love of order' (7). Captivated by 'the pleasures of miniaturisation', Briony will subsequently render this fateful episode in her childhood not in that style of 'impartial psychological realism' she hones and condones late in life but in a pretentious replica of impressionism (41), a pastiche that's all too polished, apparently untouched by the wounding 'break of unity' that Woolf inserted in *To the Lighthouse*'s design. No deferential tribute to period style, this pastiche is instead a deliberate tactic on McEwan's part for snaring what he sees as the indulgences and falsely redeeming aspirations of perceptual density and overt lyricism, unleashing what soon becomes a barbed critique of the critical and artistic values associated with modernism at large. Consequently, Briony has been read as a cipher for McEwan's own well-documented misgivings about modernism's involutions, especially what he sees as its prioritization of sensation over story, elaborate mentation over meaningful action, which amounts to a 'dereliction of duty' (in his view) with respect 'to the backbone of the plot'.[24]

Most pointedly, these sentiments align with the counsel Briony later receives while working after the outbreak of the Second World War as a home front nurse. Here, in Part III of the novel, a fictionalized Cyril Connolly offers feedback on the manuscript she submitted for *Two Figures by a Fountain* to *Horizon*, advising that even her 'most sophisticated readers' will 'retain a childlike desire to be told a story, to be held in suspense, to know what happens' (314). In the end, he 'wondered whether it owed a little too much to the techniques of Mrs Woolf', given Briony's willingness to 'delve into the mysteries of perception' through 'a stylised version of thought processes' that allows, with the help of 'random impressions', 'the vagaries and unpredictability of the private self to be explored' (312, 313). Embedded in this disapproval of mannerism is a concern with the very morality of modernism, something McEwan makes apparent in his notebook dating from 2000. 'What she has written was an evasion', he observes, and the *Horizon* letter's 'indictment of her shortcomings as a writer' confirms that Briony 'had crept behind a bloodless aesthetic, her vision of the modern, to defend or deny her guilt'. Amid 'all its pretensions to a modern method', notes McEwan, the 'novella'—comprising *Atonement*'s ornamental Part I—'perfectly encapsulate[s]' Briony's 'own dishonest avoidance of what really mattered'. A formal obsession there with 'random impressions' betrays (in this reading) her ethically weak venture to atone over the course of the novel by putting on display in its opening stages the defects of her fledging work. Briony's decision to begin her plea for reparation by arraigning her former pleasure-seeking impersonation of Woolf only confirms, damningly for her creator, the fact that '[i]t was not the backbone of a story she needed. It was a backbone.'[25]

In what follows, I want to move somewhat against the grain of McEwan's own sentiments, in order to entertain the extent to which *Atonement* hosts a self-complicating deliberation on the modernist poetics of consolation. What I tried to show in revisiting *To the Lighthouse* is that solace was for Woolf a more contested, reflexively instantiated phenomenon than critical accounts of modernism's will-to-redemption allow. And it's a phenomenon that *Atonement* reprises, through content and form, in ways that don't accord with the rather reductive view the novel initially perpetuates of modernist style as an otiose obsession with 'pure geometry', a style fixated—as Briony is as a wartime nurse, brimming with excitement at completing *Two Figures by a Fountain*—with 'the conscious mind as a river through time' (281). Modernism's supposed impeachment, in that account, serves also to expose how synthetic Briony's reparation ultimately is: even though she has reformed herself as a writer, by the end, having shed her mock-impressionism over the decades in acquiring that 'impartial psychological realism' for which she's renowned (41), Briony seems less willing to reform her commitment to fiction making as compensation for the inconceivable degree of atonement history requires her to undertake. By the close, she may have abandoned modernism (at least on the surface). But Briony never gives up on that 'impossible task' of fetching Cecilia and Robbie back from oblivion (371). In the end, she poses as someone who pretends to have moved on from her youthful misdemeanours as a modernist mimic, while nonetheless still being 'stalked, haunted', in McEwan's own words, 'by the figure of Virginia Woolf'.[26] For at the height of her powers, Briony occupies the soothing autonomy of an orchestrator of hypothetical fates, both confessing and finding artistic nourishment in the idea that she has the 'absolute power of deciding outcomes' (371). As she faces in dementia 'an incoming tide of forgetting, and then oblivion', she regards it as part of her penitence to defend 'the fogs of the imagination' and 'set the limits and the terms' on how her readers experience the ruination she can only mend by make-believe (370, 371).

That, at least, is one reading of *Atonement*: a novel that levels charges at modernism not only for inciting stylistic intemperance but also for aiding and abetting a duplicitous conflation of moral and artistic autonomy. I'm going to follow a somewhat different tack. Setting aside McEwan's rather blunt opinions about 'the dead hand of modernism',[27] I want to ascertain the way *Atonement* prompts us to apprehend anew what Laura Marcus calls 'the "redemptive" nature of modernist time', debating rather than simply indicting the notion that 'a work of art offers compensation for the losses wrought by time and history'. Through *Atonement*'s self-conscious audit of modernist aesthetics, McEwan responds to the legacies of what has critically been seen as a quintessentially modernist promise of temporal redemption 'with the full knowledge of its identity as a consolatory fiction'.[28] A more complicated vision emerges in *Atonement* as a result, one that detects in modernist forms not the distracting transfiguration of history's scars, but a scrutiny of that consolation which such forms allegedly precipitate. It's a vision prototyped in Woolf's fiction, as we have seen; and the stakes of its continuity in contemporary literature will be felt in chapters to come, across the work of writers whose preoccupations and contexts might otherwise seem quite distinct. Laying some critical groundwork for those later discussions, *Atonement* helps us to historicize the modernist genesis of discrepant solace in spite of its author's own antagonism towards literary impressionism—the same impressionism that in a starker, wounded guise, stripped of pastiche, actually enables McEwan to negotiate the traumas of war with such affecting immediacy.

IMMEDIACY AND EXPIATION

For all her devotion to the 'modern method' by 1940, a younger Briony probably couldn't have tolerated the prospect of writing 'the modern mind' as Woolf envisaged it. For that would have required Briony to relinquish her childhood devotion to structure and assume 'the mould of that queer conglomeration of incongruous things', adventurously exploiting (as Woolf urged in a 1927 essay) the novel's formal 'freedom, its fearlessness, its flexibility'. Instead, the playwright Briony 'covets the explosive emotional effect' that Woolf associated with zealous attempts to make prose 'dramatic': such an impulse stems from 'a strict and logical imagination', schooled in the credo that 'everything in a work of art should be mastered and ordered'.[29] Perilously, Briony's 'love of order' as an ethos of creative discipline leads her to sense that the 'truth had become as ghostly as invention' (41), an inkling that joins the many coded charges retrospectively levelled by the adult novelist against her own self-preoccupied precociousness.

Truth does indeed seem spectral when, in a fit of juvenile impulsiveness, she accuses Robbie of raping her cousin Lola. If ideals of order appease Briony as a youngster, the writing process itself is an 'inevitable' occasion for '[s]elf-exposure' (6). She wonders: 'What other authority could she have?' (6), a self-exonerating question that finds a troubling echo in Briony's concluding defence of the decision to do away with her earlier, 'pitiless' drafts of the atoning narrative we have just read—'What are novelists for?' (370)—opting instead for the one that leads us to believe, consolingly, that 'the lovers survive and flourish' (371). Admitting her own life is diminishing in the grip of dementia, she defends her authority to rectify the lovers' devastation and ensure 'their happy ends' (370). Just as she 'cast her narrative spell' over the Tallis family (and police investigators) as a lying child (7), so the elderly Briony attempts to rewrite the relationship she condemned to oblivion in a counterfactual account of Robbie and Cecilia's continuity. Her sometime 'pleasures of miniaturisation'—whereby a whole 'world could be made in five pages' (7)—eventually turn into imperatives of reparation, making the reader wonder, as Briony does at the close, whether she has 'not travelled so very far after all' (370). *Atonement* forks in the home straight: one path points to a cruel undercutting of the survival narrative we have been offered; the other leads to Briony's heartfelt effort to turn fiction into a solatium, an effort whose thought-experiment we might still sympathize with despite our misgivings about having been deceived.

At this dramatic level, then, McEwan plots consolation as a potentially suspect element of readerly gratification and authorial self-justification. At a stylistic level, though, his novel extends the kind of strenuous deliberation on solace—as something alternately enunciated, affirmed, and destabilized by expression—that *To the Lighthouse* conducted through confrontations with lost time. For its second part, *Atonement* modulates quite radically away from the luxuriant idiom of its opening sequence, turning from an elegantly furnished 'big house' romance into a stark and shattering trauma novel. There McEwan captures what James Wood calls 'the bewilderments and the humiliations' of the haphazard Dunkirk retreat, as his descriptions eschew succulent embellishment and instead 'gather their strength not from the accuracy of their notation but from the accumulation of living human detail, so alive that we are persuaded that such a thing might have occurred even if no one actually witnessed it'. Warfare imbues the novel with 'a grave reality', as Wood observes, even as this 'necessarily raises questions about its own literary rights to that reality'.[30] If at one point Robbie himself, drained yet still contemplative, concludes that 'no one would ever know what it was like to be here' (227), the second-time reader will detect Briony's ventriloquism, as she inserts what Peter Boxall calls a 'retrospective recognition' *within* a narrative that seems dedicated to Robbie's immediate reactions, a recognition 'that such experience is beyond reach', beyond too her life-long mission of repair.[31] My concern here, though, is less with the ethical conundrum of how to do imaginative justice to war traumas that haven't been experienced first-hand, than with how *Atonement*, in mobilizing this problem, becomes closer aligned with the very impressionism that Briony appears to repudiate when exhibiting the pictorial opulence of *Two Figures* as an extravagant, perilously distracting appropriation of 'the modern method'. Schematically, to be sure, McEwan seems to stage an ethical interrogation of modernist aesthetics as dangerously compensatory in both intention and effect, raising the question of whether style is but 'a controlling play', in Hermione Lee's phrase, 'a form of escapism, lacking all moral force'.[32] Yet I want to suggest that Briony's apparent renunciation of Woolfian lyricism for Part II, as she bleakly and sparely documents the chaotic withdrawal from Dunkirk, may paradoxically affiliate her (and McEwan) with a modernist practice of dealing with solace as an agitated condition of fiction's possibility—the possibility, that is, of giving words, however insufficient, to traumatic experience and without any wishful pretence to redemption.

Part II is McEwan's 'Time Passes', a sequence that splinters the domestic enclosure of the novel's exposition. Leanly expressed, syntactically declarative, with graphic renditions of visceral destruction: the section switches to Robbie's perspective, and arguably heralds a more vigorous phase in Briony's atonement. One could argue that 'once the ending of the novel is known, the immediacy of the experience is hollowed out'.[33] Nonetheless, her conscious effort to conjure that immediacy with a style estranged from its erstwhile sumptuousness marks an ethical development in Briony's artifice, a development that relinquishes the self-congratulatory frills of ersatz impressionism to attempt something formally and affectively closer to the real thing. In so doing, she pursues an artistic correlative for her ongoing reparation, enlisting a more sharply defined vocabulary of perception that forgoes the gratifications of rich metaphoricity and modifying clauses. Integral to this process is the transfer of focalization to Robbie, as Briony tries to redress Part I's languid interiority by reproducing his mental mix of turmoil and longing throughout scenes of 'silent head-down trudging' (226). Of course, Part II is also a eulogy for Robbie, as we later discover that he never survives the evacuation, succumbing to 'septicaemia at Bray Dunes on 1 June 1940' (370). In an effort to console the dead, Briony thus 'has to find another language', as McEwan describes it, committing herself to 'a starker, simpler, stripped down English prose'. After the 'pastel haze' of Briony's exposition—which, in Geoff Dyer's account, is laced with 'pallid qualifiers and disposable adverbs'[34]—the verbal economy that transports us into the horrors of Dunkirk serves, for McEwan, as a crucial 'part of her expiation'.[35]

Whereas for the first 187 pages, the narrative's lavishly daubed 'slow drift of association' apparently proves Briony's supposition that '[t]here was nothing she could not describe' (150, 165), Part II places the very precepts of description under the spotlight, as Robbie's fatigued perceptions introduce between moments of sorrowful reflection on Cecilia catalogues of commonplace carnage. 'It was a leg in a tree', he observes, soon after the reader has entered this remorseless terrain of retreat (192). Seemingly desensitized, but not quite: Robbie's itemizing descriptions—'a perfect leg, pale, smooth, small enough to be a child's' (192)—evince not so much emotional numbness as a 'refus[al] to be drawn in' (192). He and his accompanying corporals 'had seen enough' (192). What they witness is greeted with almost casual, 'dismissive'—and for that reason self-protective—'disgust' (192). But if Robbie polices his outward emotions in this way to confirm how much he 'intended to survive' (193), inwardly his segues are unruly, cutting in elaborate convolutions between the traumatizing apprehension of 'another vanished life that was once his own' and the forever-imperilled belief that 'there was hope' (202). Briony's incredulously ornamental impressions in *Two Figures* have been superseded here by her simulation of Robbie's oscillation between physical enervation and fragile solace. Style captures in its staccato resolve his gritty determination to endure a desperate situation by repeating words from Cecilia's 'last letter' like wisps of reprieve: '*I'll wait for you. Come Back*. There was a chance, just a chance, of getting back' (202–3). Whereas the pseudo-impressionism that opened the novel became an aesthetic accomplice to the circumstances and (mis)judgements that would lead to Robbie's incarceration, the style of the Dunkirk sequence embodies his reasons 'why he had to survive' (203). Thus if Part II formally seeks to redress the compositional indulgences and ethical injustices of Part I, it does so not by rejecting modernist impulses and defying their influences but by spurning the novel's preceding pastiche of modernism's verbal luxuries, and by refusing to apply style as an anaesthetic for the physical and mental tears of war. *Two Figures* had insulated itself from the historical legacy of modernist fiction's coexistence with military violence, whose felt reality for Robbie, whose 'unexpected detail' (191), attunes Part II to the intersecting and conflicting emotions that were always at the heart of impressionism.

Impressionist fiction, after all, 'was never merely impressionistic', as Jesse Matz reminds us: 'Conventional wisdom might equate it with surfaces as opposed to depths, appearances and not realities, hasty guesses rather than enduring truths, but no Impressionist was content with superficial, merely sensuous, appearances.' Briony certainly was in conceiving *Two Figures*; and Robbie's poignant cultivation of private yet seemingly implausible consolations subsequently answers back to that contentment, requiring her to penetrate surface appearances to evoke his anguished and unceasing efforts to 'lose himself in thoughts' of Cecilia, in order to 'plan his next letter, refining the phrases, trying to find comedy in the dullness' (211). At the very moment its narrative appears in penitence to shake itself free of modernism's influence, *Atonement* comes into proximity with what Woolf was trying to develop: for her, 'impressions rarely kept to the level of immediate apprehension or simply visual stimulation', as Matz points out; instead, 'they partook of a phenomenological awareness in which immediate visual apprehension was one with essential thought'.[36] This synthesis is what McEwan achieves as we track his troops in northern France withdrawing along an unprotected road, determined despite their disarray to reach the coast. Even though the route is initially materialized in recognizably pictorial terms—'Vulnerable to attack and without shade, it uncoiled across the undulating land in shallow S shapes' (226)—this verbal brushwork serves setting more than psychology. Unlike in *Two Figures* where an ornate palate of atmospherics took centre stage—as 'high-altitude clouds in the western sky formed a thin yellow wash which became richer over the hour, and then thickened until a filtered orange glow hung above the giant crests of parkland trees' (78)—in Part II the setting's visual refinement occupies the backdrop to Robbie's mutable contemplations. Whereas ancillary asides populated *Two Figures*, informing us that 'Fauvist dedication to improbable colour might have imagined the landscape this way' (78), here in language shorn of such decorations Robbie surveys a terrain of dread and debility that, descriptively, takes second place to the pulse of worry within, a terrain in which he felt '[n]o responsibility, no memory of the hours before, no idea of what he was about, where he was going, what his plan was' (246). Sentences contract, focalizing Robbie's immediate concern that '[i]t was his mind', from which 'something slipped', an 'everyday principle of continuity, the humdrum element that told him where he was in his own story, faded from his use, abandoning him to a waking dream in which there were thoughts, but no sense of who was having them' (246). Most intense in 'his clear moments' (256), these states of perplexity make Robbie's consoling thought of returning to Cecilia harder to sustain. The uplifting hypothesis that their 'story could resume' is threatened by the sense that 'his own story' is fading, that 'continuity' is ebbing away (227).

As sensory impressions trigger intellect in this way, *Atonement* draws closer still to Woolf. She saw in the impression 'an intuition that is also a removal from immediate experience', in Matz's phrase, 'a measure of imagination, a feeling obscure enough to become subject to thought's designs'. In *To the Lighthouse* we observed how the secretion of solace through evocative description enables an ideational examination of consolation's legitimacy for a family that could never be compensated. The novel's elegant forms of counteractive expression are agitated by plot, where grief-torn individuals weather a consolation famine. Far from rhetorical trimmings, impressions acquire for Woolf 'something opposite to the immediacy for which they are so often held responsible', because they become a vehicle for literary thinking—for tracing the conceptual contours of the emotions they dramatize, for deciphering the valences of solace in the course of showing experiences that are far from consolable.[37]

It's this transition—moment by perceptual moment—from immediate feeling to percipient deliberation, from inkling to recognition, which McEwan makes against backdrop of war. To do so, he invites us to spot in the modulations of Robbie's ruminative language an endangered but resistant impression of consolation's discrepant endurance:

> Tiredness had made him superficially elated and forthcoming. Now he reduced his progress to the rhythm of his boots—he walked across the land until he came to the sea. Everything that impeded him had to be outweighed, even if only by a fraction, by all that drove him on. In one pan of the scales, his wound, thirst, the blister, tiredness, the heat, the aching in his feet and legs, the Stukas, the distance, the Channel; in the other, *I'll wait for you*, and the memory of when she had said it, which he had come to treat like a sacred site. Also the fear of capture. His most sensual memories—their few minutes in the library, the kiss in Whitehall—were bleached colourless through overuse. He knew by heart certain passages from her letters, he had revisited their tussle with the vase by the fountain, he remembered the warmth from her arm at the dinner when the twins went missing. These memories sustained him, but not so easily. Too often they reminded him of where he was when he last summoned them. They lay on the far side of a great divide in time, as significant as BC and AD. Before prison, before the war, before the sight of a corpse became a banality.
>
> But these heresies died when he read her last letter. He touched his breast pocket. It was a kind of genuflection. Still there. (226)

The impression of all that needed to be 'outweighed' yields the intuition of alternative fortunes balanced on 'scales'. Style's alternate tonalities and tempos participate in this mental exercise, as Robbie confronts in order to counter his fears of oblivion: the bluntly functional list ('his wound, thirst, the blister, tiredness, the heat') contrasts with the sentence's fluid second half, which begins with the simple yet lulling iambs of Robbie's talisman ('*I'll wait for you*'). In a phrase whose relative modesty betrays its profundity, the lack of verbal extravagance makes Cecilia's pledge all the more consoling by its equation with 'a sacred site'. Yet the next sentence ('Also the fear of capture') breaks the spell of that treasured comparison, giving way to a series of concessions about memories whose sensuousness is too delicate to withstand 'overuse'. Diction thus recedes as Robbie probes the way recollections 'sustained him', offering little in terms of lyrical rescue from the stark acknowledgement that the more exquisite the memory the more vividly it 'reminded him of where he was'. Then a paragraph break renews feelings of promise, recapitulating the idea of rebalancing scales of contingency. Granted, the syntax remains unchanged—as trimmed and unsentimental as ever, closely synced with Robbie's mental slog from trepidation towards some tentative contact with hope that's '[s]till there'. But it's as though the fundamental presence to which he clings doesn't need amplification; the blunt impression of what he touches is consoling enough. Just as the shadow-play of darting birds and 'flourishing' trees 'made obeisance' on the Ramsays' walls—asserting in their very movement what remained beyond decay, beyond oblivion—so Robbie genuflects at the touch of Cecilia's note. The clipped, tightening sentences that open the second paragraph seem structurally analogous to the contraction of his attention around the letter as a snippet of hope, and the resolute phrasing captures just how adamant he is about taking solace in recognizing that her words alone might, amid this landscape of destruction, drive 'him on'.

This is why consolation for the literary impressionist has little to do with injecting style as a tranquilliser into formidable events. Quite the opposite: style is the place where impressions of solace catalyse a process of thinking through its viability; where intimations of survival aren't necessarily reinforced by felicities of expression; where the 'consolations of a beautiful moment' amid the onslaughts of plot are valuable not because they distract us from painful history but because fiction uses the interruptive moment (a trope so prevalent for modernists like Woolf, and still so generative for many of the contemporary writers we will encounter later in this book) to enmesh consolation as an emotional and ethical problematic for authors, characters, and readers—in *Atonement*'s case, for all three. In McEwan's world, as in Woolf's, consolation looks more like irresolution than reconciliation, and the recognition in turn of consolation's unsustainability is something their fictions transport in compelling forms that refuse to deliver the redemptions of pristine design. Only by this refusal, these novelists suggest, can literature articulate what Tomlinson termed the 'better-founded solace' that comes—as Robbie proves—'from looking squarely at the worst'.

WRITING AGAINST OBLIVION

As it turns to the visceral spectacle of conflict, *Atonement* disturbingly counterpoises Robbie's most 'sensual' if increasingly 'bleached' memories with the recurrent sight of 'more bodies in the road, in the gutters and on the pavement, dozens of them, soldiers and civilians' (227). In this, the novel appears to forgo what Connolly called in *Enemies of Promise* (1938) those 'long sentences with many independent clauses' that typified 'mandarin' stylists 'committed to a tyranny of euphonious nothings', with their 'allusions, metaphors, long images, Latin terminology, subtlety and conceits',[38] precisely as part of Briony's rejection, it would seem, of the fictional Connolly's advice to 'ignore' warfare as 'the enemy of creative activity' (314, 315). *Atonement* transitions away from the counterfeit impressionism Briony mimics in *Two Figures*, providing in its place a more stringent 'illustration', as McEwan has more recently put it, 'of fiction's generous knack of annotating the microscopic lattice-work of consciousness, the small print of subjectivity'.[39] It's a modernist knack that supplies acute pathos in Woolf's case, as we have seen, when she deploys in 'Time Passes' formal resources that trace the 'small print of subjectivity' to mourn its very absence in rooms robbed of a family. A style trained in the depiction of consciousness is occupied there with its remnants, just as Part II of *Atonement* is all the more moving for turning Briony's previously shimmering rendition of 'the crystalline present moment' into a steady lens for trauma. Far from purging impressionism, she ramps up its responsibilities.

In the end, though, it's Briony's own responsibility to historical actuality that falters. 'London, 1999' serves as a confessional epilogue: she discloses her fixation with counterlives that compensate for her realization, clasped in the penitential toil of 'humble nursing' at St Thomas' hospital, that 'she would never undo the damage'—that she remained 'unforgivable' (285). The 77-year-old Briony is in reflective 'mood' (353), discerning the physical and mental sensations of her life drawing to a close, just as the novel itself moves towards its climactic revelation. 'I've always liked to make a tidy finish', she admits, echoing her childhood attraction to order (353). Informed that she has vascular dementia, Briony is told too that still 'there was some comfort to be had', thanks to 'the slowness of the undoing' (354). In McEwan's typescript annotations to the epilogue's first draft, she detects the chilly solace of anticipating dementia's terminal journey; while 'thinking of happy ends', she concedes '[t]here won't be one for me, but the comfort is that I won't know much about it'.[40] As part of her birthday celebrations, Briony's original playscript for 'The Trials of Arabella' is recited, though her response is far from nostalgic: 'I knew the words were mine, but I barely remembered them, and it was hard to concentrate, with so many questions, so much feeling, crowding in' (367). Indeed, her mind has been elsewhere, drawn to what will be her 'last novel, the one that should have been [her] first' (369). In its final version the 'lovers end well', making '[a]ll the preceding drafts' seem 'pitiless' (370). Briony 'can no longer think what purpose would be served' by 'persuad[ing]' readers 'by direct or indirect means, that Robbie Turner died of septicaemia at Bray Dunes on 1 June 1940, or that Cecilia was killed in September of the same year by the bomb that destroyed Balham Underground station' (370). Since she can 'no longer possess the courage of [her] pessimism' (371), Briony measures the worth of writing an account of the brute facts against the minimal 'hope or satisfaction' readers could 'draw from such an account' (371). Only 'in the service of the bleakest realism' could a story of a couple who 'never fulfilled their love' be justified (371).

If *Atonement*'s broader contribution, according to Michael Silverblatt, is to demonstrate how novels 'not only seek revenge for wounding, but seek to redress wounds and heal them',[41] is Briony's commitment to saving her readers from bleak realism part of that healing process or the sign that such compensatory diversions threaten to leave history's wounds more infected than ever? Not everyone would be so satisfied with what's artistically enabled by writing that professes to heal through the experiences it mitigates, however self-consciously it calls into question the ethical legitimacy of fiction-writing as redress. Novelist Anita Brookner considers that McEwan's 'suave attempts to establish morbid feelings as inspiration for a life's work—and for that work to be crowned with success—are unconvincing'. Viewing the very principle of atonement as 'a morbid procedure', Brookner argues that if 'it were more palliative' then 'penance could be embraced with total confidence'.[42]

McEwan's manuscript drafts, available from his archive, cast new light on such misgivings, which may elide the extent to which that suaveness is symptomatic—an intrinsic if revealing feature of the choreographic authority Briony wields across the narrative and whose uncomfortable heroism McEwan asks us to examine at the close. Typescript revisions allow us to appreciate that while McEwan 'never allowed' his heroine too much 'relief from her guilt', there were nevertheless other options for counterfactual compensation open to her.[43] In his first typescript for the coda, McEwan has Briony compose a fifth draft of her 'forensic memoir' (370), one that would have let her publish within the lifetimes of those conspiring culprits (Lola and Paul Marshall) she identifies by concealing their names. 'To be safe', Briony concedes, 'you must be bland and obscure' (370). And 'so it was with version number five, March 1972. What a betrayal, what a foolish dilution that was. Unpublishable, and a waste of time. It was my well meaning husband who talked me into it. He was trying to help me lay a ghost. But I won't lose faith like that again.' It's intriguing that McEwan chose to delete this 'one lapse': it adds an additional layer of complexity to Briony's mission of impossible repair, revealing her susceptibility to the consolation of historical substitution, where living criminals are cloaked in the guise of make-believe characters.[44] But it also suggests that the Briony we see in the published novel is no less susceptible to the idea that it's heroic *not* to 'be bland and obscure'—promoting as she does her brave, single-minded 'duty to disguise nothing' (370). Her defence in that first draft of a 'faith' in lived facts thus appears in McEwan's final variant of *Atonement* to affirm novel-writing as a charismatic process of rectification, showcasing Briony's aura as an 'angel-novelist' who watches over a literary 'act of kindness' that resuscitates two dead lovers with descriptions of imagined 'happiness'.[45] If she won't allow herself to be consoled by the safety net of concocting surrogates for real criminals, she will still permit the solace of exercising imaginative providence over oblivion.

It's this self-exonerating belief in the redemptive force of artistic creativity that McEwan invites us to entertain with unease. Despite a wealth of fictioneering behind her, and with a full knowledge of literature's ethical responsibilities at her disposal, Briony defends the simple consolations of conjuring what might have been. Simple, because the plotting of those alternative fortunes seems quite distinct from the more taxing work of testing language's capacity to counterpoint the psychic lacerations of fear and fatigue, as style so dynamically does in Part II; the same work that Woolf undertook in simultaneously facilitating and examining expression's efforts to fetch time from oblivion, and that McEwan continues when *Atonement* joins the war, notwithstanding his reputation for dismissing experimental modernism as a 'dead hand'.

For Briony, though, the justification for a more uncomplicated variety of solace— the comfort of rewriting fate altogether—is clear, as her closing reflections attest. The very style of her conclusions tells a story too, as the language of her rationale resembles the 'crystalline present moment' that provoked Connolly's criticisms half a century before (312). It's the same style that epitomized, for Iris Murdoch, the solace that modernism's overriding 'sense of form' perpetuated for postwar writers. Writing two decades after McEwan's fictionalized Connolly, Murdoch saw culture's 'desire for consolation' as an enduring condition, an appetite that 'clean, crystalline' writing has too easily satisfied.⁴⁶ Looking back on her own venture, though, Briony is unrepentant:

> I've been standing at the window, feeling waves of tiredness beat the remaining strength from my body. The floor seems to be undulating beneath my feet. I've been watching the first grey light bring into view the park and the bridges over the vanished lake. And the long narrow driveway down which they drove Robbie away, into the whiteness. I like to think that it isn't weakness or evasion, but a final act of kindness, a stand against oblivion and despair, to let my lovers live and to unite them at the end. I gave them happiness, but I was not so self-serving as to let them forgive me. Not quite, not yet. (371–2)

Briony's succession of impressions, including her observation about the unnervingly 'undulating' floor, go some way to confirming the purported fixation of crystalline prose on the 'unpredictability of the private self', in Connolly's words (312). But unlike the 'Fauvist dedication' which *Two Figures* retained, her former artifice of elaborate, 'improbable colour' is superseded here by a more elementary notation of 'grey' and 'whiteness'. Instead of high gloss pictorialism or convoluted imagery, style works harder to *enact* rather than simply adorn emotion, dispensing with the graphic pigments of pseudo-impressionism in favour of more subtle, phonic correlatives for feeling. Sentence by sentence, the diction appeals to an acoustic complementarity between otherwise distinct clauses: connecting verb and object, the /b/ of *beat* is duplicated by the /b/ of the very *body* that's under stress, both percussive labials reinforcing the unrelieved pulsation of weariness.⁴⁷ Bringing each end of the second sentence into alliterative conjunction, the /f/ of *floor* and /f/ of the equally assonantal *feet* again intensifies the unsettling affect that ensnares Briony here, as the sentence—brief, self-contained within its phonic symmetry, and closing on two throbbing iambs—structurally equates with each enervating throb of fatigue's *waves*. Although she was once criticized, then, for devoting all her energies to the plush language of sensation, for 'dedicat[ing] scores of pages', in Connolly's estimation, 'to the quality of light and shade' (313), in this final scene Briony offers another amnesty to impressionism as a mode that can embody without ornament her inconsolable vulnerability. It's as though style, now held taut at the eleventh hour, longs to make up for her elaborate and ultimately self-consoling contrivance of granting fictional happiness to the dead. Merging present fragility with historic remorse, she discerns the 'first grey light' giving way to (if not mnemonically signalling) 'the whiteness' into which Robbie's future that evening was swallowed before the onset of war. Just as Woolf, in Steve Ellis's reading, 'cannot but identify herself with procedures that not only illuminate but "expose" the past', so for Briony too the effort of 'reclaiming stories from oblivion' 'also confesses the guilt of the writerly intruder'.⁴⁸

And intrude she does: throughout the novel, of course, as the omnipresent navigator, routing the narrative towards redress; but most explicitly here, in this last-minute, double-edged self-defence. She makes no apology for bringing Robbie and Cecilia back from oblivion, for granting 'them happiness', even as she also qualifies this whole project of resuscitation as one that cannot end in acquittal. Briony hedges at absolution ('I was not so self-serving as to let them forgive me'), though her readers may suspect that her labour of self-indictment yields its own dissentient consolations. That she won't forgive herself while writing a novel that attests to the strenuousness of that refusal could itself be more consoling than self-abnegating. Such is McEwan's way of ensuring a finale shot through with irresolution, of course. By 'having his narrator', as Kate McLoughlin observes, 'refer to literary conventions—knowing that he or she is being offered "comfort," "the reader" is unsure whether to accept it or not and hence definitive conclusion is avoided— McEwan keeps both outcomes in play'.[49] The solace of counterhistory fades for readers at the very moment when Briony accepts the consolations of authorial self-affirmation. As a result, consolation's equivocality here becomes an internally binding orientation of the novel's equally equivocal ending, where closure no longer feels viable after the epilogue's disclosure.

Authorizing fiction's 'stand against oblivion' sounds consoling, then, because it doubles as a tactic for self-legitimation masquerading as an 'act of kindness', a tactic also for bridging that very 'gulf between literary form and material history' which, as Peter Boxall observes, 'the novel itself works repeatedly to open up'.[50] Yet McEwan doesn't make it straightforward for his readers to condemn Briony outright; indeed, he denies us the satisfaction of feeling that we have arrived at the only possible conclusion, that our ethical prosecution of his heroine is incontrovertible. For a closer look at language reveals that the irresolution of her closing admission of accountability chastens the heroism of Briony's 'stand'. Having executed her counterfactual project, she won't permit herself to find complete appeasement in that endeavour, even if she assumes it might have buoyed readers up to this point. 'Not quite, not yet', she concedes, in a phrase reminiscent of the way Forster brings Aziz and Fielding to the tantalizing brink of intimacy and mutual recognition in *A Passage to India* (1924);[51] reminiscent too of Briony's intimation that the *just* of Robbie's imagined request in Balham—when he insists '"Just do all the things we've asked"'—is 'almost conciliatory', though 'not quite, not yet' (349). It was in a typescript version of *Atonement*'s final paragraph that McEwan added 'not yet' to a phrase that originally ended with 'not quite'. With this extra adverb, the emphasis falls on forgiveness withheld and deferred, denying Briony the solace of climactic peacemaking.[52] Only for now, though. McEwan's late amendment to the script ultimately inserts another layer of ambivalence into the novel's closing lines, as the eventual prospect of 'self-serving' consolation isn't entirely ruled out even if it is presently refused.

For the time being, if Briony sounds unappeased, then so are *Atonement*'s readers by this late stage. Such is the epilogue's disconcerting residue. In the end, we're invited not simply to accuse Briony of deluding herself with the false consolation of reserving fiction's 'power to conjure them' (372)—however gratifying it may be for readers to do so—but rather to reflect on our own susceptibility to partake in the solace she hopes this speculative story of Robbie and Cecilia 'still alive, still in love' will afford (372). Holding a mirror up to readers at the culmination of his narrator's self-inquiry, McEwan provokes us to look back (potentially through our reactions as much as in Briony's actions) at the consolatory conceit of the novel we have just experienced. With that rearward glance, we might ask who, exactly, has she been wanting to console? Now that the integrity of its redemptive storyworld has just been quashed, we are left to gauge how far Briony's counternarrative to oblivion has been jeopardized all along by its departure from 'the bleakest realism'.

CONSOLING BLEAKNESS

For who does she have in mind when pondering what kind of reader 'would want to believe that they never met again'? Is it not risky to assume that readers could never glean 'sense or hope or satisfaction...from such an account' (371)? Not only might *Atonement*'s first-time readers feel compelled to reflect on a book-length compensation that Briony withdraws in the home stretch. They might also wonder what that bleakness might have become had it been allowed to blossom. After all, we have already had a taste of how arresting bleakness can be thanks to the Dunkirk section, where McEwan particularizes sensations of exhaustion and relentless threat that bracingly affirm what impressionism is capable of. Looking back over the novel, readers might wonder too how consoling Briony's substitute tale of fulfilment really is, how presumptuous she sounds by including us among hypothetical readers unable to confront actuality's pain, how generalizing it is to suppose that consolation itself is averse to the work of imparting things as they really are. For on this score, *Atonement*'s readers would come to resemble rather thin-skinned audiences who prefer to remain bewitched rather than bewildered by literature's counterworlds, the mastery of form sating their hunger for redemption. 'Describing things as they are', to recall Julian Barnes, 'rather than as we would like them to be can have a consoling effect': such is the possibility that Briony, as a novelist who worshipped (in her creator's words) a 'bloodless' version of modernism, couldn't really entertain. 'Bleak truths can be purging',[53] attests Barnes; but this is not what consolation is customarily taken to mean.

We can recover some of the implications of that bleaker solace, as this chapter has argued, both by revisiting its genesis in modernist fiction and by tracking its contested legacy in the writing of someone like McEwan whose creative conversation with modernist aesthetics has been far from convivial. Briony's disclosure is not so much a betrayal of her readers and a potential disappointment for those who know McEwan's conceits well (in James Wood's estimation, the 'twist', which makes the book 'a proper postmodern artefact', feels 'unnecessary, unless the slightly self-defeating point is to signal that the author is himself finally incapable of resisting the distortions of tidiness').[54] Rather, as the coda modulates into testimony, it does more to question Briony's insinuation that solace comes from fiction's uplifting substitutions—as though consolation were akin to that tentatively 'conciliatory' feeling she imagines she would have taken away from her visit to Cecilia and Robbie in Balham after the war (348). Indeed, Briony might have been sympathetic to a Marcusean view of what readers find tolerable by dint of literature's ephemerally restorative 'glow'. Across the narrative, her recreation of lives as they could have unfolded trumps ethical obligations to bleak truths she assumes readers would find too disconsolate to bear, complementing the sweeping premise of Iris Murdoch's belief that 'we do often prefer illusions and magic to the hard task of thinking—and that the *half-truth* may be the comforting place where we stop trying'.[55]

Consolation, for modernism, by no means attenuated the tough work of thinking. And the 'consolations of form', as Murdoch herself criticized them, were more often than not shaped in the crucible of fiction's contemplation of lives that exceed the rescue work of soothing illusions, the distractions of deluxe imagery, or the confections of euphonic cadences.[56] *To the Lighthouse* apprehends rather than readily supplies solace; it makes consolation's contestability and desirability thinkable through style. Woolf does this without endorsing her lyrical textuality as an immediately gratifying or intellectually numbing tonic. With no pretensions to heal, style instead animates brute devastation while elegizing the intrinsic insufficiency of those consolations radiant language affords. If anything, pitting elegance against oblivion was a necessarily thwarted mission for Woolf. Reflecting on 8 June 1940, a week after Tomlinson's *TLS* tribute to Hardy's prophetic panoramas of pain, Woolf avers that 'book writing becomes doubtful', now that war 'is at its crisis'. Since 'every night the Germans fly over England', 'the battle' itself 'comes closer to this house'. If 'one solution is apparently suicide', for now she persists: 'But I wish to go on, not to settle down in that dismal puddle.'[57]

Reconsidered with Woolf's perseverance in mind, Briony's closing admission sounds intimately in tune with the icon she once reduced to pastiche. To keep the lovers alive was, Briony insists, to perform a literary equivalent of benevolence—belated, synthetic, and ethically compromised though this performance would always remain. 'It was always an impossible task', she informs us, 'and that was precisely the point', because the 'attempt was all' (371). Briony's assertion echoes the 'vision' Lily Briscoe captures in the painting she suspects will 'be destroyed' but which commemorates with the energy of 'its green and blues, its lines running up and across' an irrefutable 'attempt at something' (*To the Lighthouse*, 281). Ultimately what brings Lily and Briony into a rather unforeseen dialogue, what McEwan in turn seems to share with Woolf—to an extent that cuts against his now-familiar antagonisms towards modernism's legacy—is an effort to 'do justice to' what Susan Sontag called in 1965 'the twin aspects of art'. Which is to say, in their fiction 'the overcoming or supplementing of reality' in language closely accompanies the practice of 'making explicit' 'forms of encountering reality' in all its inconsolability. For both novelists, style remains part of that encounter, not its mitigation. However lyrically style supplements experience, it does nothing to vanquish the actuality of that despair which is fiction's formidable incentive and potentially its representational limit.[58]

DELIBERATING SOLACE

Modernism's influence and continuance has been tracked by recent scholarship in terms of literature's politically urgent reassessments of formal innovation, as late twentieth- and twenty-first-century writers seek to challenge generic and representational conventions in responding to global modernity's systemic inequities, the material alienations or disenfranchisements of racial and sexual identity, and the lived adversities of enduring imperialisms.[59] This chapter has suggested that this legacy also has a crucially affective dimension, one that enables us to see how modernist writers performed experiments for living with consolation in all its difficulty, controversy, and variety. In reconceiving the interaction of feeling and expression, they capture consolation's dialectic of replenishment and confrontation—of 'overcoming' and 'encountering', in Sontag's terms—in the internal operations of style itself. This dialectic plays out in works across this book's coming chapters, where solace provisionally enriches yet also announces its own inadequacy, often its undesirability.

In this contested guise, consolation emerges as a key factor in grasping what C. D. Blanton calls the 'conundrum' of 'modernism's *partial* contemporaneity', including the 'half-life' it leads in works like *Atonement*, where it can 'linger as an aesthetic, available to sense and experience, even as its formative concept and shape of its historical necessity withdraw'.[60] It's the necessity of war trauma, as we have seen, that makes the 'historical wager' of modernist style vital again for a writer who has notably refused to welcome modernism's lessons with open arms, so much more vital than that imitative aesthetic which (in Part I) constituted Briony's 'self-protective fantasy', as McEwan called it in his notebook, thanks to which she 'concocted a method to soften the consequences of her deed'.[61] Despite its apparent antipathy to modernist experimentalism, *Atonement* exemplifies how contemporary literature's testy engagement with solace can adjust the way we historicize the 'sensible forms' consolation has assumed.[62] Undoubtedly, it's hard to overlook McEwan's vilification of modernism as a constellation of questionable priorities that instigate, in his words, '[a] crime committed in the name of literature'.[63] Yet for that reason, *Atonement* appeals to a rather unexpected reading: it turns out that this novel may be better remembered for throwing into relief modernist fiction's own complex (and far from redemptive) treatment of solace, enabling rather than foreclosing an affective analysis of literary impressionism's enduring potential that outstrips its author's misgivings about experimentalism. *Atonement* suggests that attending to consolation's literary history can help us to 'invent the critical language', as Blanton urges, through which modernism's 'disappearing formal coherence might be reconstructed or re-imagined'.[64]

The work consolation performs in contemporary literature thus possesses a series of critical and creative backstories that not only have an originating scene in modernism but also attest to modernism's enduring presence in the very language with which writers today reckon with solace. For her part in that story, Woolf suggested that a 'bad present' was not to be healed simply by subjecting traumatic loss to devastating lyricism; rather, if and 'when it shows the way to transformation' (to adapt Marcuse's claim for theory over literature), *To the Lighthouse* 'offers no consolation that reconciles one to the present'.[65] Developing impressionist forms of expression that distinguish consolation from easy reconciliation, Woolf elegizes the irreparability of the traumatic experiences she describes precisely in order to contemplate the way literary description transforms loss without pretending to screen the scars it leaves. This ambition reaches forward in time to writers who will be our focus in the next chapter, as they carry on the work of unyoking solace from conciliatory purposes. Description will again come to the fore there in shattering narratives whose styles counterpoint catastrophe without mollifying its lived consequences. Woolf herself sought in style not some appeasing withdrawal into a beautifying aesthetic but a means of deliberating and scrutinizing the solace of rendering otherwise indescribable, interminable grief. By virtue of that creative self-scrutiny, she set a generative precedent for late twentieth- and twenty-first-century writers, even those who wouldn't necessarily consider themselves flamboyantly experimental or explicitly engaged—as McEwan has been—in conversation with specific modernist tenets.[66] Distinct though their priorities are, writers in the coming chapters do things with that *friction* between structures of affect and the effects of form that modernist fiction helped to fathom. Knowing this helps us to appreciate the stakes of noticing how consolation is subject to continued ethical and emotional contestation. As in Woolf's moment so for the present: solace persists not as the compromising seed of literature's undoing but as a condition of its critical possibility.

2
Description as Redress

A man and his son are on the move; they have been for months. Now, though, they are fast running out of food. Having observed but so far managed to escape the horrors of cannibalism, they know it's going to be harder to stave off starvation. Across a devastated North American terrain they trudge south towards the promise of warmer weather—also towards the sea. In heading for the coast, the man knows that 'he was placing hopes where he'd no reason to', wishing only the ocean 'would be brighter where for all he knew the world grew darker daily'.[1] Progress to the shore is slow, and they endure '[l]ong days' through '[o]pen country with the ash blowing over the road' (181). But something in the air suddenly changes and the man notices 'open country to the east':

> Then they came upon it from a turn in the road and they stopped and stood with the salt wind blowing in their hair where they'd lowered the hoods of their coats to listen. Out there was the gray beach with the slow combers rolling dull and leaden and the distant sound of it. Like the desolation of some alien sea breaking on the shores of a world unheard of. Out on the tidal flats lay a tanker half careened. Beyond that the ocean vast and cold and shifting heavily like a slowly heaving vat of slag and then the gray squall line of ash. He looked at the boy. He could see the disappointment in his face. I'm sorry it's not blue, he said. That's okay, said the boy.   (181)

What could be more dismaying? The longed-for prospect of the sea as a vestige of ecological endurance, as a zone that's 'brighter' than the land's monochrome charcoal, as proof that those 'aching blue' 'siren worlds' the man has been 'learning how to wake himself from' do still exist (15), proving too that their slog has been worth it—all this is dashed over the course of one onomatopoeic description of despair. The dental diction simulates in its listless rhythm the predictability of what they see, as 'dull and leaden' waves lumber onto a beach that's coupled with the novel's most frequent yet muted epithet: *gray*. Both grammar and lexis reinforce the 'disappointment' the boy can't help himself from showing.

Such is the iconic bleakness of Cormac McCarthy's *The Road*, his 2006 thriller whose horrifying account of a 'world shrinking down about a raw core of parsible entities' leads us about as far from consolation as one could imagine (75). In whatever shape or form, solace is hardly what we expect to find in this realm of catastrophe, not only at the level of harrowing content but in linguistic terms as well. In fact *The Road*, at first glance, 'seems exhausted at the level of style itself', as Andrew Hoberek has observed.[2] Arranged piecemeal, the novel's fractured typography visually compounds this effect of debilitation, with paragraphs set off from one another in spacious isolation. Moving in closer still, one may notice how McCarthy's declarative phrases, shorn of commas and subordination, simulate in their very texture the enervated environment they detail. This equivalence between syntax and scenery, between articulation and exhaustion, is part of what makes *The Road* so memorably distressing, of course; but it doesn't necessarily mean that equation is consistent. To venture indeed that it isn't means considering how McCarthy has other things in mind for the language of description aside from communicating doom.

For that language seems to confront the very 'desolation' it delineates. Description stands up to horrific action. In a striking simile, McCarthy invites us to imagine an 'alien sea' from some undiscovered realm. With this image the novel's perspective departs from the immediate impress of the man's misery, and style joins that departure too: far from defeated, it gathers both metaphoric vitality and metric momentum, building through a crescendo of two successive anapaests ('on the *shores* of a *world*') towards the amphibrach with which McCarthy's portrait of this 'unheard of' domain closes. Likewise, acoustically, the sibilance is not simply deployed in the service of the scene's literal description but instead facilitates its figurative transcription. Sure, this diction provides an apt aural correlative to the melancholy plash of waves. Yet McCarthy's alliterative cascade (*some, sea, shores*) propels us at the same time towards the picture of another world, a world whose 'alien' appearance isn't straightforwardly comforting, to say the least, but whose sonorous depiction runs counter to the abjection that inspires it. Clearly, this simile emphasizes the novel's dismal setting by way of otherworldly comparison; phonetically, though, its surrounding sentence carries an amplified assonance that attends to ecological wounds with acoustic grace.

This attempted suture undoubtedly keeps failure squarely in its sights. But even as McCarthy's descriptions enact the unattainability of the consolation they insinuate, they do so by producing, if only for an instant, expressions that are sufficiently mellifluous to exceed the work of merely reproducing bleakness, flouting any perfect knit between verbal melody and visualized events. Such descriptions acknowledge the unsustainable defiance of their own lyricism, staging through style a level of vigour that remains humanly inconceivable in this fearsome storyworld. Reading *for* such descriptive moments, of course, carries an additional risk, one that always accompanies the selection of instances as demonstratively emblematic. A moment's significance relies upon its exemplarity, when it becomes amenable to close readings that seek to connect such striking instances to a textual whole of which they are but a fractional part. Given this caveat, it would be reckless to make a single sentence like one I have just considered representative of *The Road*'s larger economy of affect. Furthermore, euphony is itself a rather selective unit of analysis, making my already narrow attention to syntax here seem narrower still. But like many of the works we'll soon encounter in this book, McCarthy's novel justifies this sort of attention: to notice how his verbal soundscape resonates athwart the landscape he records is to contemplate microelements of description that criticism on fiction routinely passes over. Description counteracts—only for a moment, but vividly *through* that moment nonetheless—the annihilation it conjures and never pretends to heal, an anomaly that shapes McCarthy's approach to the genre of brutal demise he so arrestingly occupies. Against the weight of biospheric ruin and physiological decline, description phonically and rhythmically asserts itself, redressing the diminishment *The Road* so shockingly catalogues. However futile this appears, description provides a 'stylistic concomitant of the sense of potential' that inheres throughout the novel and in spite of the horrors that ostensibly structure it.[3]

Somewhat overlooked, occasionally even maligned, description is a phenomenon this chapter puts centre stage in order to understand its work as a conduit for consolation. In so doing, I pursue the interpretive stakes of noticing description's defections: here in *The Road* as in other works to come, description shirks its mimetic responsibilities and counteracts events that seem altogether terrible. What McCarthy's wretched tale suggests is that prosodic ingredients of description can reroute the negative affects we expect them to affirm. Refusing entirely to reinforce the turbulence it portrays, description jostles against the discomfiture a text like *The Road* seems bent on imparting. From this competition between content and form several larger, metacritical issues arise that I want to pursue in the following pages. Working at cross-purposes with a work's generic gist in this way, might consolation be a facet of novelistic description that recasts—sometimes intentionally, at other times inadvertently and defiantly—the very diegetic material it serves to record? And if description offsets instead of simply classifying and conveying what it describes, do we need to rethink the very immanence of its mimetic function? Which is to say, description might not be as passive as we conventionally assume, fostering disunities instead between style and scene. Far from being a rudimentary, taxonomical device that frames and names, I argue that description is more vivacious in contemporary writing than traditional theorizations of its properties have supposed. And it's this vivacity that lies at the crux of how literary description consoles: rarely neutral, description in recent fiction draws attention to its own aliveness, its own insurgent tendency to kick against plot. Fathoming the stakes of this dissidence for understanding the poetics of solace means not merely salvaging description as a neglected kingpin of writerly charisma or flair. It also invites us to ponder how description misbehaves, how it hatches rogue aesthetic plans, how indeed it becomes—through the sumptuous pressure it exerts on what it describes—a type of narration in its own right.

This chapter thus considers what fiction's affects might look like once we view them as part of description's agency. It does so by accounting for the complex ethical implications of expression as consolation, of rhetorical felicity as redress, implications that seem nowhere more pressing than in fictions of trauma and catastrophe. In such narratives, the solace of depiction is rarely synonymous with the comforts of reading; inescapably desolate works like *The Road* compel us to consider how style's affirmative effects remain in tension with the emotional convulsions of plot. Later on, this sense in which our responses to expression can sit discrepantly with how affected we are by diegetic upheaval will lead me to navigate between ways of reading *for* description and the varied ambitions of so-called 'descriptive reading'. Gauging the consequences of that difference for rethinking consolation in particular and for augmenting our critical spectrum for narrative affect in general synchronizes my overarching motivations. Oxymoronic though it may sound, description affords a variety of what we might call *critical solace*: if description consoles by 'conjur[ing] a kind of presence', in Peter Boxall's terms, which survives the extremities it evokes, then it nevertheless 'carries a forsaking within' its own performance of redress, critically inspecting the presence that's pictured and for an instant restored. As we witnessed in *To the Lighthouse*, description's twinned affordances in this sense have poignant repercussions—poignant because in the act of describing even a writer as dextrous as Woolf knows that language must forfeit what it longingly animates. In her case, as in the work of contemporary writers considered here, this concession suffuses a moving process by which the irreparability of absence takes form, is felt, becomes known. The pathos of that process depends on description withholding easy compensations, yielding instead what Boxall calls 'limpid, luminous expression and a kind of darkness'.[4] Style's revivifications metabolize the antinomy at the heart of description as a property of literary discourse that can both render and rescript the picture of damage it communicates.

Descriptions considered here generate formal consolations that seem to be aware of their own intimacy with privation.[5] They offer no simple balm through linguistic amelioration. Instead they appraise the solace that style potentially supplies through its vivid depiction of experiences that appear indescribable, even as the full consequences of loss unfold, even when consolation—let alone redemption—at the level of content not only seems unlikely but unimaginable. And unimaginable is certainly what solace remains for McCarthy's wretched man. Despite this, prolonged trepidation in *The Road* periodically triggers unexpectedly lyrical reflections, facilitating if only intermittently the visionary speculations of someone who's in no mood to accept succour. 'Filthy, ragged, hopeless', the man struggles in the end to keep up with his son (230). Increasingly the boy would walk on ahead 'and then stop and look back and he would raise his weeping eyes and see him standing there in the road looking back at him from some unimaginable future, glowing in that waste like a tabernacle' (230). Framed in a spatially alien, presently inconceivable realm, the boy occupies that place of sanctuary he and his father seek from perpetual dispossession, enfolded in a moment yet to come. The closing simile here converts the son into a thing of refuge, emanating against the prevailing despair, as the man envisions the boy's fate 'glowing' beyond his own imminent death. McCarthy's phrasing proceeds by multiple conjunctions between motional and ocular verbs like *stop*, *look*, *raise*, and *see*, thereby insinuating expectation despite the man's dejection. Thanks to this rhetoric of anticipation a promise of survival—again, only for a moment—is recuperated from ubiquitous 'waste'. That McCarthy's man might not register this awful compensation himself doesn't stop description from carrying out some counterbalancing work of its own, discrepant though it remains in this context of impending demise. It's not only *The Road*'s 'pared down, elemental' style, as Ashley Kunsa suggests, that offers 'a triumph over the dead echoes of the abyss',[6] but also the more baroque, Faulknerian 'flourishes' which 'peek out', in

Hoberek's words, 'from its minimalism'.⁷ With these tactics, McCarthy suggests that description is rarely passive. If anything, it triggers dissent between style and story,⁸ unsettling language's purely simulative relation to those actions we expect it not only to convey but also, in mood, to complement—a productive discord that marks the point at which description defects, shirking its mimetic duties so as to reckon with what it shows.

DESCRIPTION AS DEFECTION

As phenomena equally disposed to misperception, both description and consolation happen to have a good deal in common. In literary and cultural studies, description is often 'defined by failure or falling short', argue Sharon Marcus, Heather Love, and Stephen Best. A practice 'insufficiently self-conscious of its own procedures', description never quite fits the bill for what is a 'still dominant view' of its 'deadening' inventories, being 'either too small, focused on minute details' or else 'too large, an exhaustive catalog of inconsequentiality'.⁹ If disrepute hangs over solace—a distractive, substitutive affect, one that supposedly blocks our recognition of systemic inequalities and deters us from suspicious or interrogative readings—then in comparison to description it is clearly not alone. Like the action of describing, literature's ability to console likewise tends to be set in 'contrast', following Marcus, Love, and Best's account, 'to what it is *not*': inadequately grasping loss because of the rhetorical sheen or poise of its literary transmission, inadequately capturing the anguish of others thanks to the surreptitiously assuaging language by which their pain is portrayed.¹⁰

If solace has therefore been seen as common enough but ultimately paltry, then by the same token nothing seems at once so vital and yet taken for granted as description. Mediating and magnifying our view of fictional worlds, its role appears simultaneously indispensable and incidental, a role famously demoted by its terminological separation from *narration*. First propounded by Georg Lukács, this distinction often lies at the root of qualitative assumptions about description's formal influence and affective value. Despite 'all its virtuosity', claims Lukács, 'description is mere filler in the novel'.¹¹ Zola happened to be the primary target here. But Lukács broadens his indictment beyond nineteenth-century naturalism to issue a warning about novelistic production at large, because description had become 'the writer's substitute for the epic significance that has been lost'.¹² (Clearly there was something 'compensatory' about description for Lukács too, though here its substitutions carry a rather despondent ring.) Above all, what worries him is 'the danger of details becoming important in themselves': with the consequent dilution of narration, these 'details cease to be transmitters of concrete aspects of the action and attain significance independent of the action and of the lives of the characters'.¹³ If this sounds rather inflexible in theory, it's even less viable in fictional practice, where we discover the phenomenon of focalization turning characters into active participants of description, perpetually chronicling their own sensory perceptions. Far from 'transform[ing] people into conditions, into components of still lives', as Lukács insists,[14] characters' shifting inclinations result in depictive inflections, their mental states pilot the text between picturing and narrating, and their felt experiences precipitate the reader's empathy or animus. All of which seems a far cry from fictional persons being objectified victims of static portraiture, complying with 'a schematic narrowness in characterization'.[15]

However impractical Lukács's distinction turns out to be, it stands at the head of a steady stream of mild antipathy towards description running across twentieth-century criticism, an antagonism that has persisted even when description's contribution to or detraction from narration isn't really at stake. As Mieke Bal observes, description has become something of 'a bone of contention' in its own right, resulting less in enabling debate or refinement of terms than in what Werner Wolf and Walter Bernhart call a 'conspicuous research lacuna'.[16] One explanation for this, suggests Bal, lies in the 'gap' dividing 'a critique that lauds description' from a body of 'narrative theory that marginalizes it', when analytical priorities split between paying attention to 'the "experience" of reading' and accounting more systematically for fiction's 'logic of structure'.[17] There is no reason, of course, why affective responses to narrative form should be inimical to the pragmatic, taxonomical study of structural patterns, implying as it does a conflict in the reader's experience between emotion and analysis that is just as misleading as the disconnection of 'description' from 'narration'.[18] In a vigorous exposé of these needless binaries, Ruth Ronen points out that the description–narration polarity has 'endured' largely because it has been reinstated by critics themselves, even though there is 'considerable confusion caused by the difficulty in sustaining the opposition in practice'.[19] Indeed, to uphold the dichotomy, one has to take for granted—just as Lukács took for granted the way description reduced characters to the equivalent status of objects in still-life painting—that 'the referentiality of description counteracts' a novel's 'narrative syntax', insofar as description 'follows the logic of the object described rather than the narrative demands to which the object is subjected'.[20] This assumption has spurred 'post-semiotic theorists', as Ronen calls them, to 'claim that description is everything which is negative of narrative (viewing narrative as a structure of signification while considering description as a mode of pure reference)', thereby imposing 'a theoretical opposition incompatible with textual experience'.[21]

It's this experiential element that will continue to concern me here as I examine the consoling affordances of description's unexpected countercurrents of rhetorical and grammatical energy. With this task in mind, let us return one final time to McCarthy's wasteland, where the friction between style and situation is all the more pronounced when the man and his son reach a swamp, whose depiction appeals to both ends of *The Road*'s lexical spectrum from minimalism to elaboration, from spareness to sonority:

> The road crossed a dried slough where pipes of ice stood out of the frozen mud like formations in a cave. The remains of an old fire by the side of the road. Beyond that a long concrete causeway. A dead swamp. Dead trees standing out of the gray water trailing gray and relic hagmoss. The silky spills of ash against the curbing. He stood

leaning on the gritty concrete rail. Perhaps in the world's destruction it would be possible at last to see how it was made. Oceans, mountains. The ponderous counterspectacle of things ceasing to be. The sweeping waste, hydroptic and coldy secular. The silence. (230–31)

On one level, the abruptness of descriptions equals this man's diminishing hope, with the repetitive adjectives (*dead, gray*) also reproducing the prevailing resignation. But through the unadorned notation of features—'dead swamp', 'dead trees', 'spills of ash'—McCarthy prepares the way for sonorous observations about how the 'world's destruction' telescopes its creation. Counterbalancing even as it is focalized by the man's surrender, a regenerative, iambic pulse underpins that elegant speculation about what it might mean 'at *last* to *see* how *it* was *made*'. Even as McCarthy returns in the next sentence to terse, nominal depictions ('Oceans, mountains'), the momentary blankness of these nouns gives way to yet another ornamental prediction, looking ahead to the 'ponderous counterspectacle of things ceasing to be'. Crisply juxtaposing trochee and iamb, the closing three words here invest the cadence with a resounding crescendo that sits incongruously with conjectures about the earth's extinction. Such sounds counterflow the episode's semantics, exemplifying what Michael Chabon called in his review of *The Road* the 'paradox of language undoing the death it deals'.[22] Arguably these phonic and rhythmical energies only punctuate rather than divert in any lasting sense the novel's steady, inexorable movement towards 'silence'. After all, the chances of the world regenerating itself are diminishing, contracting as the length of this paragraph's sentences do—just as the man's time left with his son is short, thanks to the ravages of respiratory illness. Nevertheless, against these foreboding ecological and physical inevitabilities McCarthy's descriptions reassert themselves: shunning a purely imitative relation to this barren scene, they follow a dissident path of their own.

Albeit in the starkest terms, *The Road* throws down a gauntlet for the range of other novels and memoirs at the centre of this project, which recalibrate the barometer of literary solace, a barometer whose measurements are usually sensitive to the consolations of content at the expense of a more differentiated understanding of consolation as an enduring problem of form—a problem which is also a condition of form's ethical as well as aesthetic potential. In McCarthy's speculative thriller, when syntax tugs against sense, when rhythm seems to undercut a scene's ostensible temper, the consolations of description seem suddenly legible—and of course deeply debatable. For ethically loaded questions attend expression's performance of solace, however self-questioning that performance might be: time-honoured questions to do with the writer's responsibility towards the damage she so impressively describes. This is not an especially contemporary dilemma, by any means. To the extent that description might somehow mitigate upsetting or even traumatic scenarios through the way its micro-components—even down to the smallest fragments of metre and grammar, as we have seen in *The Road*—not only modify but seem to mismatch narrative action, it points to an age-old quandary of whether writers should embrace or resist the compensations of aesthetic form.

My goal for this chapter is not necessarily to historicize that dilemma but to entertain the methodological assets of shifting from reception (where we usually go to speak about the consoling effects of literature) to expression (where the critical work of solace may be conceptualized in compositional terms). In the following pages I turn to the late W. G. Sebald, a crucial figure for understanding the difficult viability of consolation in contemporary culture. As selections go, this might seem perverse because Sebald's work has become canonical for trauma studies, a field that privileges experiences which all but evade representational capture. But Sebald himself often pursued a rather different tack: in critical essays and creative works alike, he hypothesized what literature might do with historically or psychologically forbidding material, rather than simply conceding that narrative inevitably fails. To do so, Sebald modelled forms of affective 'restitution', in his term, forms that challenge the premise that literature is forever in a position of deficit when evoking atrocity and its traumatic legacies. And description, as we shall see, lies at the heart of that challenge.

Attending to Sebald in this way also means reconsidering what exactly description constitutes as a unit of analysis. Over the past decade, narrative theorists have produced conceptual and diachronic maps of description in all its shapes and sizes, ranging from the smallest components of syntax to larger organizational aspects of scenic detail, episodic arrangement, or characterological positioning.[23] In the following pages, I lean towards the former unit of analysis: scaling down to a more granular level, we have the chance to observe in close-up how phrasing and diction counter the seemingly inconsolable affects with which description appears inextricably consumed. Conventionally seen as something rudimentary, functional, even dispensable, description's limber moves could actually turn out to be among the most controversial aspects of how contemporary writing formally modulates emotional content. Casting description as an affirmative opponent to emplotment, not just a simulator of its pernicious repercussions, Sebald's work shows just how discrepant consolation becomes when depictions of dreadful loss put literature's capacity for redress to the ultimate ethical test.

DEPICTING AND OVERCOMING

That the literary provision of solace can be coterminous with sorrow sounds like the epitome of a performative contradiction. Yet the paradox is itself critically enabling, opening up ways of apprehending consolation's formal variety without the presuming that we should also as readers feel somehow consoled. Rarely neutral in rendering events that we're likely to find most upsetting, description's affective mediations make possible other critical transactions with what it describes. Certain occasions in Sebald's last work prove that description doesn't inevitably complement diegetic tumult, secreting instead an affective counterplot of its own. In spite of its unpredictable structure, *Austerlitz* (2001) moves strangely unimpeded, assembling past experiences that would otherwise seem condemned to chilling irrevocability. *Austerlitz* is a 'museum of sorts', as Carol Jacobs puts it, one that 'nevertheless exceeds by far our capacity to comprehend'.[24] In its panoramic entirety, the narrative yearns for what Sebald admired in Jean Améry as a 'painful clarity of memory and vision', a clarity that initially might seem to be at odds with the consternation that besets the focal character of Austerlitz along the way.[25] Becoming his creator's enabling surrogate, Austerlitz voyages back to familial torment in ways that synchronize with Sebald's own ethically vigilant 'quest for a form of language in which experiences paralyzing the power of articulation could be expressed'.[26]

In this respect, *Austerlitz* appears to 'obey' what Roger Luckhurst calls 'the injunction to bear witness to the unrepresentable'. This mandate is of course paradigmatic of many contemporary trauma narratives. As they set out to picture experiences so damaged as to seem indescribable, the dominant aesthetic for such works remains 'uncompromisingly avant-garde', notes Luckhurst: 'experimental, fragmented, refusing the consolations of beautiful form, and suspicious of familiar representational and narrative conventions'.[27] One could easily press Sebald into the service of this template. But collectively his writings also comprise a meditation on—hence partly a resistance to—such reassuringly familiar and widely condoned models of trauma literature. In fact, Sebald's work could be seen as a relatively 'late and mannerist addition to the genre', one that 'risks traumatophilia', as Luckhurst puts it, by 'taking a kind of perverse delight in the repetition or abject assumption of a collapsed trauma subjectivity'.[28] However, in the final book of this trauma chronicler states of collapse are rivalled by the compulsiveness of description, and the fluid assemblage of splintered experience—haunting and besieging though it remains—offers a textual opponent to the psychic fragmentation that Sebald is so adept at conjuring.

'From the first', reflects *Austerlitz*'s narrator, 'I was astonished by the way Austerlitz put his ideas together as he talked, forming perfectly balanced sentences out of whatever occurred to him, so to speak, and the way in which, in his mind, the passing on of his knowledge seemed to become a gradual approach to a kind of historical metaphysic, bringing remembered events back to life'.[29] Austerlitz's aptitude for 'perfectly balanced sentences' in making surprising connections and 'bringing remembered events back to life' sounds so commensurate with what Sebald called his 'attempt at restitution'—something imaginative literature can do that factual 'forms of writing' cannot—that it's hard not to see description shading into ventriloquism here.[30] Deraining though the process of partial remembrance and reconstruction often is for Austerlitz, his knack for historical resuscitation corresponds with his creator's project in ways that seem more reciprocal than merely coincidental. And however much his odyssey appears to take over the book's reins, Austerlitz is closely trailed by a distinctly Sebaldian narrator-figure who adopts the ethical injunction 'to maintain neutrality', as Jacobs puts it, suggesting that 'oblique indirection' is as 'necessary' as any 'purposeful refusal of interpretation'.[31] Meticulously unimposing, this narrator cultivates fluency—a more explicit feature of the English translation, perhaps, than of the original German—something he manages to encourage in Austerlitz, too, as his attentive confidante. So while, in content, Austerlitz's trains of association bear the stresses of traumatic reconstruction, in form they also retain a compensating impetus that survives Austerlitz's periodic bewilderments.[32] Determination underlies his self-descriptions in 'bringing remembered events back to life'; but the velocity of these resuscitations coexists with our suspicion that Austerlitz's sentences are 'perfectly balanced' owing to the fact that they are not simply recorded but also recast by his shadowing amanuensis. Consequently, a first-hand yet finessed portrait emerges of an individual who describes journeys and encounters with a decisiveness that overcomes the initial elusiveness of the past he then goes on to reassemble.[33] And as we'll discover, this portrait goes some way to consoling, through its liquid depiction, the force with which 'the thread of chronological time', in Sebald's words, as for all 'victims of persecution', becomes increasingly 'broken'.[34]

Looking to Sebald's work even for inadvertent shreds of solace might seem unpromising, renowned as he is for charting the traumatizing consequences of imperial and military violence. His vertiginous reanimation of personal testimonies as homage to the victims of Nazi genocide carefully guards against the prospect of seeing consolation in webs of reconnection. For some commentators, Sebald cannot quite 'escape the seductions and consolations of systems' by substituting a 'scholar's preoccupations' for the 'historical amnesia' he aims to confront and rectify.[35] But as Timothy Bewes has compellingly shown, Sebald deliberately exposes 'the implied logic or explanatory thread' behind the very 'principle' of patterning, ensuring the intellectual comforts of 'connection' represent less an opportunity for 'resolution' than the further 'posing of a question'.[36] Furthermore, Sebald's own register complements this questioning of consolation, forestalling form's easy recuperations. Restrained, sometimes aloof, the timbre of his writing might appear too inhospitable for solace; this effect is compounded by the way 'moments of emotion tend to be rendered purely visually' in Sebald's prose, insofar as 'emotion itself is never identified or characterized' but instead just described.[37] In sum, because Sebald 'never offers' an 'affirmative vision', as Matthew Hart and Tania Lown-Hecht contend, it's hard to know where in the 'consistently melancholic tenor of his *Weltanschauung*' consolation's countermelody might be heard.[38] In what follows, though, I want to take up the gauntlet by considering how Sebald's style—'characteristically cryptic and unemotional' though it often feels in translation—counterpoints episodes that are far from consoling.[39] As we'll see, it is precisely the unruffled, self-policing sense of emotional distance in Sebald's writing that unlatches another window on his ethical project.[40] Bringing the resources of description to bear upon the frequently unspeakable experiences he traces, Sebald complicates the notion that trauma is intrinsically indescribable, while refusing—by way of his antique vocabulary and equable poise—to countenance the option of style alleviating readers of the burden of confronting the barbarity he plots.[41]

Throughout his career, Sebald engaged the consequences of persecution whose victims can never be compensated. However unimaginable those traumas are, description is what remains, or so it appears from the way his episodic juxtaposition of haunting settings and reconstructed events does nothing to quash their depictive vividness. Reflecting on Jean Améry, Sebald maintains that for 'those whose business is language, it is only in language that the unhappiness of exile can be overcome',[42] a conviction affirmed by his earlier discussion of Austrian literature. There he insists that the process of 'rethinking of one's relation to misfortune' can in fact be 'a form of resistance'. And furthermore, 'on the level of art as a whole', he contends that the emotive and stylistic 'function' of representing this 'relation' is 'something other than simply to be reactive or reactionary'. In a situation where 'melancholy, gazing rigidly, once again realizes that things could have only turned out the way they have, it shows that the origins of desolation and that of insight are governed by the same power. The description of misfortune includes within it the possibility of misfortune's overcoming.'[43] To evoke bleak eventualities—whose terrible logic of inevitability seems only to be confirmed in hindsight—is not, implies Sebald, to accept desolation as a condition of thought and creativity. It's an opportunity instead to access melancholy's epistemology and its expressive potentiality, to reclaim some 'insight' from despair, so that describing adversity furnishes in fact its own 'form of resistance'. This modality of 'overcoming' is not equal to forgetting or wilful denial. Quite the opposite. By making the distresses of misfortune legible, description makes them all the more immediate, tangible, unavoidable. And that, indicates Sebald, is the incentivizing point of writing about what fundamentally cannot be completely redressed. Description dramatizes its own capacity, however insufficient, to bring damaged experience into close-up, in ways that intercept not only misfortune's dissolution through retrospection but also the very foreclosure of its possible consolation.

What does writing look like that achieves this double act, this simultaneous defiance of memory's extinction and consolation's exclusion? At least one model emerges again in Sebald's eloquent commentary on Améry, where he spotlights the ethically contestable consolations of (self-)expression. Admiring his 'scrupulous restraint', Sebald acknowledges that for Améry language becomes the very 'means whereby he counters the disturbance to his existential equilibrium'.[44] This solace of self-articulation, however, 'ultimately proves inadequate as a cure for the precarious condition of a man losing faith in the world again daily when, on getting up, he sees his Auschwitz number tattooed on his forearm'. Distinctions between the solace we might associate with writing's utility as a potentially ameliorative activity and the disconsolation that the writing subject himself endures, contain great pathos for Sebald: 'The words that Améry set down on paper, and which seem to *us* full of the comfort of lucidity, to him merely outlined his own incurable malady.'[45] This is an incisive warning, if ever there was one, against the overhasty quest for consoling affordances in prose concerned with trauma's shattering afflictions.

And yet, despite Sebald's caveats about the curative force of testimony, in the case of his own work the 'comfort of lucidity' isn't so straightforwardly censured. In *Austerlitz*, language's provision for 'existential equilibrium' permeates its central character's unfurling self-descriptions, which counter in their exceptional propulsion the disorientation Austerlitz retraces—the capabilities of depiction offsetting the incapacities recalled. While the book's thematic preoccupations lodge firmly in what Hart and Lown-Hecht call the 'ineffability of individual experience'—focalized by a figure who is 'waiting to remember, waiting to belong, waiting to return to a place that is gone'—*Austerlitz*'s formal preoccupations are with redescribing such experience with a dexterity that reserves a right to console the physical and mental displacements Sebald narrates.[46]

A broken biography of sorts, *Austerlitz* takes place as a series of conversations between its eponymous architectural historian and a distinctly self-effacing narrator, beginning in Antwerp in the 1960s and resuming again decades later after the two men are reunited by chance. We learn that Austerlitz arrived in Britain as a refugee with the Kindertransport from Czechoslovakia, and that only after the death of his Welsh foster parents did he start to learn about his family's fate in Nazi-controlled Europe, including his mother's eventual deportation to the Theresienstadt ghetto. If *Austerlitz* refracts histories of unimaginable atrocity through the familial losses of this perpetually searching individual, it's also the record of Sebald's own creative odyssey that plots his search for a prism capable of that refraction. This 'prose book of an indeterminate kind', as he preferred to call it,[47] is a quest for the 'requisite gravity of language'—in a phrase from his Améry essay—a quest to 'make the literary treatment of genocide more than a dutiful exercise marked by involuntary infelicities'.[48] Carefully bypassing that exercise, Sebald's writing confronts memory's formidable and unforgiving absences, supplying the voice Austerlitz himself struggles to give to the 'bleak prospect' of history's fluidity, with its 'ever-lasting misery and never-ending anguish' (144).

The impetus of redress here reaches beyond the storyworld, integral as it is to the larger ambition of Sebald's oeuvre (leading up to *Austerlitz*) to correct the complacencies and false comforts of cultural amnesia. Austerlitz's pursuit of the lost circumstances of his family's disintegration emblematizes Sebald's effort 'to compensate for an undeniable German deficit of memory and experience', in Andreas Huyssen's words, one that always routes his work obliquely yet inexorably back to the victims of the Holocaust.[49] Pertinent here is the gradual withdrawal of the narrator himself in *Austerlitz*: 'as a German or even as a non-survivor', notes Robert Eaglestone, 'he knows he can never enter into Austerlitz's world, nor properly respond to his request to honour the dead'. In contrast to the motion of Austerlitz's interior pilgrimage, his scribe seems immobilized by the end, repelled by his companion's total submission to the self-reconstructive passage of remembrance, a paralysis which suggests that 'the way in which Austerlitz's character "works through" the trauma is both a critique of the narrator's stasis, and possibly a complex model for overcoming it'.[50]

The book's creator, of course, doesn't exempt himself from implicit critique either. Just as the chilling truth of Austerlitz's origins and infant arrival in Britain had been concealed by his adopting parents, so Sebald reflects in his compelling essay on 'Air War and Literature' that the absence of attention to the allies' strategies for destroying German cities constituted a 'scandalous deficiency' in public discourse on the war: it 'reminded me that I had grown up with the feeling that something was being kept from me: at home, at school, and by the German writers whose books I read hoping to glean more information about the monstrous events in the background of my own life'.[51] Sebald's project thus comes into alignment with *Austerlitz*'s dramatic attention to what Jessica Dubow terms the 'copresence of things that can be neither reconciled nor rendered synthetic', evoking 'historical experiences in which time puts on its truly material – that is, truly conflictual – face'.[52]

This alignment also pervades description. Sebald's 'mellifluous yet painstaking style', as Boyd Tonkin calls it, enumerates Austerlitz's recollections in a backward-facing journey that subsumes much of the book, a journey across which Austerlitz's creator ventriloquizes his fascination (as in the following passage) with the disjuncture between conventionally quantified time and temporality as a vertiginous experience. Austerlitz claims that '[e]ven in a metropolis ruled by time like London' it's 'still possible to be outside time', a way of thinking 'almost as common in backward and forgotten areas of our own country as it used to be in the undiscovered continents overseas' (143). This observation chimes with Sebald's long-standing interest in narrating time in unpredictable, circular, or chiastic fashion, an interest underscored by the belief that time is gauged more effectively by the erratic paths of memory than by external measurement. Orbiting this theme, Austerlitz's meditation grows. Its expansion typifies the kind of rhizomatic extrapolation—moving from a localized, almost offhand aside to large-scale thesis—that typifies Sebald's use of description as a vehicle for philosophical contemplations focalized by a character who is confiding as much as he's theorizing:

> The dead are outside time, the dying and all the sick at home or in hospitals, and they are not the only ones, for a certain degree of personal misfortune is enough to cut us off from the past and the future. In fact, said Austerlitz, I have never owned a clock of any kind, a bedside alarm or a pocket watch, let alone a wristwatch. A clock has always struck me as something ridiculous, a thoroughly mendacious object, perhaps because I have always resisted the power of time out of some internal compulsion which I myself have never understood, keeping myself apart from so-called current events in the hope, as I now think, said Austerlitz, that time will not pass away, has not passed away, that I can turn back and go behind it, and there I shall find everything as it once was, or more precisely I shall find that all moments of time have co-existed simultaneously, in which case none of what history tells us would be true… (143–44)

Sebald's characteristic disruption of temporal linearity is mirrored in Austerlitz's conjectural 'hope' that 'moments' don't 'pass away' but in fact persist in a state of simultaneity, insinuating a proximity between creator and character. With this discursive commonality, Sebald adopts Austerlitz's ruminations as the means 'to make you imagine things', in A. S. Byatt's phrase, which he 'then delicately says are unimaginable'.[53] What cannot be reimagined, what would seem unethical for the writer to render, is what *Austerlitz* formally announces, just as delicately, as its enabling premise. Masquerading behind its own negative capability, the book thereby ventures to turn description—geohistorical, philosophical, personal—into Sebald's most consoling element.

CONFRONTING RESUSCITATION

If *Austerlitz* submits its own historical and biographical enterprise to memory's 'gravitational field of oblivion' (359), this surrender itself becomes the text's regenerative impulse rather than its impediment, as we shadow Austerlitz's 'search of places and people who have some connection with us on the far side of time' (360). Despite Sebald's reputation for generic promiscuity and beguilingly interwoven perspectives, *Austerlitz*'s carefully stage-managed meetings between its narrator and protagonist yield their own mitigating solutions to what seems confounding and unrecoverable. Even when Austerlitz claims to lapse into inarticulacy, Sebald's descriptions of these episodes step in to ensure the narrative rarely loses momentum, making its eddies and digressions integral to its seemingly inexorable unfolding. This compensating rhythm of continuity is squared with his diligent refusal to take aesthetic advantage of memory's volatility. Sebald's descriptions make chronicling 'places which have more of the past about them than the present' thus not only viable but also—as a literary project— somehow condonable (359). Yet the contested prospect of description redressing historical damage goes head to head with Sebald's ethically scrupulous engagement with traumatic experience, thereby leaving us with a qualified sense of literature's potential for 'restitution'.

We might wonder, then, if it's precisely Sebald's point to ask whether Austerlitz's sentences can ever 'bring the past back to life', when the very times they retrace emphasize the 'uncertainty', in Jacobs's phrase, 'that language, art, and even history might ever perfectly recapture the past'.[54] But pressing a little further—pressing, that is, against the truism of trauma's *in*describability, including its familiar resistance to the kind of writer who, in Sebald's words, is too intrusive, too 'eager and persistent, intent on his linguistic framework'—we might also ask whether description is actually a consolation for Austerlitz's 'precarious relation to recountability'.[55] At once eloquent and forthright, Austerlitz's self-descriptions often seem ruptured and incomplete; but they are just as liable to confront the epistemic instabilities and emotional insecurities that accompany his acceptance of the chimera of total recall. In one especially acute account of mental breakdown, Austerlitz describes this experience as a 'constant process of obliteration, a turning away from myself and the world' (174). Just as writing became a panic-provoking activity, so his attempts at reading likewise spelled 'a state of the greatest confusion' (174). In the end the most discrete elements of language, 'even the nouns denoting ordinary objects', enshrouded and obfuscated themselves in his mind as though 'enveloped in impenetrable fog' (175). Consequently the 'very thing which may usually convey a sense of purposeful intelligence – the exposition of an idea by means of a certain stylistic facility – now seemed to me nothing but an entirely arbitrary or deluded enterprise' (175). Yet Sebald does more than simply report this disturbing phase in Austerlitz's life: his rendition of this period of bewilderment and crippling inarticulacy turns into the obverse of the very deficiencies being outlined. Offering a belated kind of rhetorical solace, Sebald reinstates the verbal 'facility' of which Austerlitz had been traumatically robbed.

Descriptions therefore accumulate in *Austerlitz* not simply to collect, catalogue, and manage information for the reader. They do more than that, something more counteractive than the text's preoccupation with journeys into overwhelming, indecipherable pasts would suggest, as Austerlitz's struggle towards self-expression in 'the exposition of an idea' stimulates vivid ruminations. Descriptions of this struggle offset his incoherence in facing the history he has suppressed and whose recognition later threatens to spell a 'silence of unfathomable profundity' (232). Turning description in effect into narration, Sebald counterpoises that silence, ensuring that Austerlitz's fraught sequences of self-exposition don't so much interrupt narrative as initiate it. In this fashion, the book becomes a scarcely interrupted testimony, even as we can also see how aptly the indefinite edges of many episodes capture the way 'certain moments', for Austerlitz, 'had no beginning or end', such that 'his whole life had sometimes seemed to him a blank point without duration' (165). If *Austerlitz*'s movement from one winding excursus to the next resembles such amorphous 'moments', this does nothing to alter the book's strangely resilient articulacy—a level of expressivity that survives the emotional vortex it conveys to redress the 'deluded enterprise' of self-elucidation at its heart.

Oblivion stalks and threatens this resuscitating fluency throughout, however, especially so in the narrator's visit to Breendonk fort near Mechelen in Belgium, commandeered by the occupying Nazis and turned into a notorious prison camp. The fortress is the site where Améry himself was tortured:

> Even now, when I try to remember them, when I look back at the crab-like plan of Breendonk and read the words of the captions – *Former Office, Printing Works, Huts, Jacques Ochs Hall, Solitary Confinement Cell, Mortuary, Relics Store* and *Museum* – the darkness does not lift but becomes yet heavier as I think how little we can hold in mind, how everything is constantly collapsing into oblivion with every extinguished life, how the world is, as it were, draining itself, in that the history of countless places and objects which themselves have no power of memory is never heard, never described or passed on. (30–31)

The run-on sentence (in Anthea Bell's translation) captures in its overflow the illimitable sufferings, with their futile appeal to be 'described or passed on'. Aided by the expanding, gathering force of this parataxis, Sebald's narrator extends the ambit of 'oblivion' beyond his first-hand experience of Fort Breendonk as a monument to atrocity, taking in 'countless places and objects' in a wide embrace that reminds us—at this early moment in *Austerlitz*, as though priming us for the narrative to come—that Sebald's overriding 'concern', as Ruth Franklin notes, is not always with 'the actual events' of the Holocaust 'so much as their aftereffects, which cascade down out of history into the lives of anyone touched even obliquely by war'.[56] Records of this cascade are 'constantly collapsing'; and yet, this menacing void, this seemingly insurmountable obstacle to description, is also Sebald's incentive. Granted, the phrasing here—at once accretive yet volatile, a catalogue that succumbs to its own terrifyingly 'countless' focus—simulates the insurmountable, forever redoubling task of writing micro-histories of those imprisoned, unconsoled, and forgotten, a task that would never be ethically sufficient for what it strives to render. But if there's relatively 'little we can hold in mind', then there's more we can potentially express in the written word—a promise Sebald realizes with considerable virtuosity in *Austerlitz* even as he draws attention to the inadequacies of his chosen form.

The consolations of possible articulation are thus bound up with Sebald's 'paradoxically impossible project', as James Wood calls it, of '[s]aving the dead' through integrated photographs, whose 'pictured people stare at us, as if imploring us to rescue them from the banal amnesia of existence'.[57] Description remains on hand to perform this kind of rescue work. At the same time, Sebald is vividly aware of the moral implications of what literature does to the damaged pasts it revisualizes, so much so that his register in translation maintains a sort of pristine reserve, an unwavering remoteness. Indeed, *Austerlitz*'s narrator assumes a position equivalent to the iron column at Pilsen that Austerlitz passed with the 1939 Kindertransport, which stood by as 'a witness to what I could no longer recollect for myself' (311). By posing as that witness—as the facilitator of Austerlitz's self-documentary, not only a confidante but, in effect, also his muse—the book's narrator faces what is a recognizable conundrum in Sebald's work. It's the conundrum of accepting that one's project of describing the impact of persecution is at once essential and suspect: essential insofar as the re-conveying of what witnesses struggle to impart is ethically necessary, especially when their experiences testify to 'the unavailability of an interpretive structure';[58] and suspect, in that literature—by offering a substitute of its own for that structure—may not only interpolate but potentially embellish distressing events that victims 'could no longer recollect' for themselves.

For critics like Julia Hell, this tension between the ambitions and compromises of description epitomizes the challenge postwar German writers face in producing an 'ethically committed post-Holocaust art', a reconstructive art that needs to visualize what 'cannot be seen, can no longer be seen, could never have been seen, but which still determines both German culture and its subjects'. Like Wood, Hell notices a 'paradox' in Sebald's attempt to write across his oeuvre as though from the position of an 'eyewitness with immediate visual access to things that have long since disappeared'. As Hell admits, this 'craving' to catalogue cultural and psychic forms of annihilation 'that he has never experienced' may also 'be interpreted as the desire of any writer committed to a literature of description'.[59] And while she doesn't address *Austerlitz* directly, it strikes me that this work, arguably more than any in Sebald's career, offers the most ethically pointed reflections on that craving for description. For Sebald adopts a narrator who (like Conrad's Marlow) is by no means excused by the self-effacing conceit of the book's frame narrative; if anything, this observer is drawn *through* close description into voyeuristic proximity to destruction's legacies, in ways that announce the risk trauma literature runs when becoming 'lost in unproblematized identifications'.[60]

As such, Sebald ensures that description carries out a form of self-critical work: both through the ambivalent stance of his narrator, and through *Austerlitz*'s overarching imperative of redress that captures the impulse, in Hell's phrase, to 'speak about what cannot be seen but ought to be seen, what cannot be represented but ought to be represented, what cannot be known but ought to be explored'.[61] For Austerlitz's part, the 'accumulation of knowledge' over time has 'served' as a 'compensatory memory', a fugitive 'substitute' (198). As we might expect, this compensation eventually dissolves; but Sebald records this dissolution in a syntax that sounds rather orderly and calmly enumerative (in Bell's translation), even though its subject is the collapse of Austerlitz's self-protecting ruse of 'forgetting' fresh and 'dangerous' fragments of 'information'. This habitual bracketing of retrospection's revelations,

> this self-censorship of my mind, the constant suppression of the memories surfacing in me, Austerlitz continued, demanded ever greater efforts and finally, and unavoidably, led to the almost total paralysis of my linguistic faculties, the destruction of all my notes and sketches, my endless nocturnal peregrinations through London, and the hallucinations which plagued me with increasing frequency up to the point of my nervous breakdown in the summer of 1992. I cannot say exactly how I spent the rest of that year, said Austerlitz. (198)

Symptoms of Austerlitz's decline are listed with a systematicity that counters their deleterious effects. As a catalogue of behaviours, this account feels tempered amid the description of emotional turmoil, as though the narrator recounting Austerlitz has resisted rhetorical ornament in rendering the hallucinatory time that's being retold. Measured and relatively composed—despite the lengthy, searching penultimate sentence above—Austerlitz's self-description would seem to fulfil the very principle Sebald praises in his study of Hans Erich Nossack's account of Hamburg's destruction. There he commends an 'entirely unpretentious objectivity' that shuns the 'construction of aesthetic or pseudo-aesthetic effects from the ruins of an annihilated world', a 'process' of excessive description 'depriving literature of its right to exist'.[62]

If anything, then, what *Austerlitz*'s descriptions epitomize is the discrepant 'alloy of moods', as A. O. Scott calls it, that Sebald's prose achieves through its 'combination of obsessiveness and calm'.[63] *Austerlitz* exhibits a serene tenacity that diverges from the anxieties and atrocities it depicts, showing how cautious Sebald is about the transfigurative pressure that style can exert on seemingly ineffable material. Such artistic self-control is also apparent in Sebald's watchfulness of what he calls (in 'Air War and Literature') that 'repeated intensification of plot elements'. Quelling 'exaggerated language', he favours a version of the 'documentary approach' that eventually enabled postwar German writing, in his view, to come 'into its own and begin the serious study of material incommensurate with traditional aesthetics'.[64] Such a firm ethos of stylistic moderation, in this view, may be literature's only ethically acceptable premise for redress.

METADESCRIPTION AND THE SPECTACLE OF HISTORY

If *Austerlitz*'s narrator—attentive listener and elegant scribe that he is—appears to compensate Austerlitz for the 'total paralysis' of 'linguistic faculties', then the prose that makes good on the promises of this compensation still remains methodical, unostentatious, despite its occasionally antique register.[65] Ultimately, the book promotes an artistic humility that stems from Sebald's implied provisos regarding the limits of literary solace: limits that mark a definite ethical position on redress;

limits beyond which Sebald would risk aestheticizing the 'sense of rejection and annihilation' that Austerlitz had 'always suppressed' and that now breaches 'the walls of its confinement' (322). Who would question such self-impositions on Sebald's part, such efforts to sustain writing as a relentlessly self-examining activity, one that dovetails with *Austerlitz*'s ethical mission to map a 'place', as Jacobs puts it, 'in which the border between healing and punishment remains uncertain, in which any healing implicitly promised also recapitulates previous suffering'?[66] Who would question the fact that this same scrutiny of description's implicit claims—of its consoling pledge to make memory legible, to make it cohere, if only for a time—is also what leads Austerlitz himself to learn via 'meandering detours' that relaying 'factual history simply won't do, that there is no way to make the telling of the past adequate to the object of its description'?[67] Indeed, it would seem unreasonable for us to spot signs of artistic self-affirmation in Sebald's assiduous inspection of literature's powers of recovery. Yet the relentlessly conscientious moderation of his prose makes another, second-order form of solace available to a writer in his position. Which is this: that even for a world-historical abomination as unrepresentable as the Holocaust, whose postwar legacies make the very principle of consolation seem unconscionable if not obscene; that even when description can never be entirely adequate to the experiences it dramatically recovers; that even here there might be a role for literature to play as an agent of restitution, however incomplete or conflicted its redress remains. Though Sebald seems well aware that 'art alone is no substitute for memory', there is still, as Franklin observes, 'something deeply consoling about his vision of art as capable of offering some sort of recompense'.[68]

In this sense, then, Sebald could be closer than he might prefer to what he termed in 1982 'the traditional idea of a creative writer bringing order to the discrepancies in the wide field of reality by arranging them in his own version'.[69] As *Austerlitz* moves headlong into what Sebald elsewhere called (echoing *The Tempest*) 'the dark backward and abysm of time',[70] its narrative implicitly longs for an aperture that can take in the 'painful clarity of memory and vision' that Austerlitz periodically evinces and that Sebald discerned in Améry.[71] To be sure, description's painful clarities can just as easily confound. Moving testimonies (like that of Věra, Austerlitz's childhood nanny in Prague) reveal that the war spelled a 'time' where 'everything was caught in a vortex whirling downwards at ever-increasing speed' (248), and disarming revelations (especially those of such forgotten moments as the picture of Austerlitz as a child 'cavalier') leave him 'speechless and incomprehending, incapable of any lucid thought' (260). Yet Sebald still makes it possible here for both testimony and revelation to trigger descriptions that redress by virtue of what they restore, reinstating for Austerlitz what has hitherto seemed incomprehensible to his 'field of vision' (261).

Paradoxically, Sebald does this, as we have seen, precisely by *not* allowing description to become an embellishing salve, a cosmetic cure for traumatic content. If *Austerlitz* charts the uncertainties that compel suffering individuals to ask 'what do we know ourselves, how do we remember, and what is it we find in the end' (287), the book seems adamant about specifying this emotional and epistemological consternation rather than entirely rectifying its effects at the level of form. Poised, tenacious, yet often pedestrian: Sebald's prose can indeed be seen 'bringing order', albeit of a provisional, unnerving kind, a prose that seems forever watchful of what he called the 'comfort of language evoking pity'.[72] This idiom enables him to attend dispassionately to the 'abysmal sense of distress' that punctuates Austerlitz's European peregrinations (297)—a sorrow Sebald's style records rather than demonstratively amplifies, announcing *through* expression his own ethically attuned avoidance of grief's literary-aesthetic exploitation.

Such self-moderation can itself become a convention, no doubt. Knowing this, some critics have found the recurrence of convenient devices—such as overblown pathetic fallacy and settings curiously 'empty of life'—across Sebald's oeuvre both unrealistic and 'forced'.[73] But in the case of *Austerlitz* these misgivings might lead us to miss textual elements that strike me as rather more inadvertent and more intriguing to unravel. For one, Sebald's seamlessly realized attempt to give a consoling voice to a figure who often lapses into paralysing silence and uncertainty has the effect of delineating 'unalterable pain', only to curb what his descriptions themselves seem capable of conveying about the very ontology of Austerlitz's condition (362). Which of course may be precisely the point. By the end, remarks James Wood, 'we certainly know a great deal about Jacques Austerlitz...but it can't be said that we really know him', which leads us to suspect that '[a] life has been filled in for us, but not a self'.[74] This sense of reportorial withdrawal—which finds Sebald content to outwardly describe his central subject rather than thoroughly penetrate and simulate Austerlitz's psychic life—may itself be another facet of his ethical stance, another mark of his charismatic sense of culpability in bringing the seismic legacies of the Holocaust into the fold of literary creation. *Austerlitz* epitomizes Sebald's refusal to capitalize on the psychological damage he chronicles. Opting to catalogue rather than adorn Austerlitz's experience of 'memories surfacing then sinking out of sight again', Sebald remains vigilant of the consequences of magnifying 'consecutive images and distressing blank spots where nothing at all is left' (319).

With these successive images, description begets metadescription. In the winding, cerebral pathways of his solitary yet eagerly self-revealing protagonist—here recounting the digressions of a sometime teacher, Hilary—we find asides that indirectly meditate on Sebald's own depictive procedures: 'All of us, even when we think we have noted every tiny detail, resort to set pieces which have already been staged often enough by others. We try to reproduce the reality, but the harder we try, the more we find the pictures that make up the stock-in-trade of the spectacle of history forcing themselves upon us' (101). Sebald discreetly embeds admissions about the possible shortcomings of his method, a method for 'reproduc[ing] the reality' of Austerlitz as confounded witness to a chronic 'spectacle of history' whose atrocities pervade intimate memory. Do these very admissions amount to something like a comforting modesty topos? If Sebald concedes the limitations of literature's capacity to retrieve, reanimate, and restore, he also reinforces by way of this concession the ethical sensitivity of his own historical imagination. Much like *adynaton*—a writer's self-reassuring admission of inexpressibility, a tactic we'll see again in the next chapter—the modesty topos is a potentially consoling device, allowing writers to concede their inadequacies in facing a creative enterprise that they then go on to execute with great intellectual conviction and formal ambition. However, as Sebald shows, this discrepancy between humility and execution need not compromise writers who, in describing 'misfortune', wish to bring about 'the possibility of misfortune's overcoming'.

PARABLES OF SOLACE

Far from synonymous with still life, then, description actively dramatizes the contested premises of fiction's consolatory effects. Anticipating the work description performs for several writers later in this book, Sebald's depictions at once stage and agitate their own recuperative work—announcing yet also examining style's effort to redress the emotional upheavals it conveys. Implying that descriptions have a tendency to appease, Mieke Bal situates them in the service of distraction rather than tonal alternation or counteraction: by 'following the order of perception of the hypothetical object', she suggests, 'description has a soothing, illusionistic effect that is possibly but not inherently realistic'.[75] Yet as we observed at the outset of this chapter in *The Road*, the sonorous cadences and figurative amplifications of even the most disconsolate story prove that description's consolations hardly depend on realistic illusions, nor do they simply produce calming diversions from formidable outcomes. If anything, McCarthy recovers the solace of descriptive superabundance from utter desolation and in the course of impressing upon us— as he does early in the novel—how '[e]verything uncoupled from its shoring' (9–10), when familiar words seem increasingly anachronistic once their material referents have become obsolete. It's as though his style takes a last stand against the scenario it so gravely embellishes, visually propelling us towards—even as it rhetorically defies—the prospect of the 'names of things slowly following those things into oblivion' (75).

There's a metacritical lesson to be drawn from this paradox, as literary depiction in contemporary writing thrives in such realms of obliteration. In one sense, the lesson is that of terminological pluralization: the 'recuperation of description', as Philippe Hamon remarked several decades ago, 'must be accompanied by a certain extension or dissolution of the descriptive'. But that recuperation doesn't stop at categorization; it also involves recognizing how fundamental description is to a work's vigour and volatility. For description, as Hamon observed, can 'be that place in the text where the generative power of language might show itself most clearly and as quite unmanageable'. As a consequence, he adds somewhat wryly, this is partly why 'the descriptive seems to be only partially accepted in the realm of discourse on literature'.[76] Precisely because description is prone to disruptive incongruity as much as it provides the assurance of imitation, it has taken some time for criticism to recognize the import it originally owned and to pay adequate attention to those ethical, affective, and aesthetic implications it always yielded. Conventionally seen as something rudimentary, functional, even inessential, description turns out to be disarming and unruly. Leading a double life, description consoles because it also vivifies scenes whose lexis and tempo modulate the substance of what's evoked, not only conveying but countering seemingly irreparable damage. Striking discords between style and action, description is one of the means by which contemporary writing complicates the perception of solace as one-dimensional, superficial, or suspect.

Far from dilating or shielding our vision of the distresses it pictures, description's contribution to the work of literary consolation warrants a closer look at the stakes of those frictions it sustains—when rhythm reforms what diction captures, when style's euphony reckons with plot's catastrophe. Sebald's eloquent rendering of what seems indescribable also suggests that 'if trauma is a crisis in representation', as Luckhurst notes, 'then this generates narrative *possibility* just as much as *impossibility*, a compulsive outpouring of attempts to formulate narrative knowledge', such that 'trauma's stalling actively provokes the production of narrative'.[77] If descriptions are engines of narrative possibility and thus of literary knowledge, then they also comment, as we have seen, on their own propensity to provoke more than simply evoke.[78] Operating as such, descriptions produce a 'parable', in Sebald's own words, 'of the bridge made by writing between misfortune and consolation'.[79]

*

'There's great comfort' when 'everything collapses around you'.[80] So claims British theatre director, Katie Mitchell, speaking here in Grant Gee's 2012 documentary, *Patience (After Sebald)*. That same year, Mitchell herself took the audacious step of putting Sebald's *The Rings of Saturn* (1995) on stage in Cologne, a city where the absence of pre-war architecture left her feeling 'shocked and unsettled'.[81] Histories of air-raid destruction were among Sebald's leading concerns, of course, making him one of Europe's eminent scribes of urban ruin. For Mitchell, though, it's his method, not just the subject-matter, which allows us to probe the emotive as well as physical implications of demolition. In this Mitchell discovers a more unusual consequence for the reader absorbed in Sebald's attention to what's lost. Against 'all things material', she says, 'that we try to construct, in order to contain the chaos or the fears', Sebald suggests that they 'aren't actually valid, they don't have any meaning'.[82] What she then goes on to imply is that when you're reading Sebald's work there is, paradoxically, a kind of solace in the way he solicits our attention to the shimmering edges of dissolution as he dismantles false protections.

This sense that there's some solace both for the audience and for the writer in witnessing the collapse of superficial consolations chimes with Sebald's overarching project. Conducting a sustained argument with the whole ethical premise of writing as redress, his work scrutinizes its own handling of historical atrocity as material, as we have seen, by testing its resistance to the allure of violence's aesthetic transfiguration. A virtuosic work of psycho-geography, *The Rings of Saturn* continues in this self-inspectional vein. Conscious of its inescapable perspectivism, the book finds Sebald curating an affective archive and historiographic montage about exile, persecution, and imperialism. Readers will recall how he departs on mental pilgrimages, reaching from herring fishing to colonial exploitation, chronicling along the way the banishment of Joseph Conrad's parents from Warsaw in the 1860s and the indictment of Irish Nationalist Roger Casement, who had written damning reports to the Belgian and British governments in the early 1900s about conditions endured by slave labourers in the Congo and Peru.

Famous for being so unclassifiable, *The Rings of Saturn* provides the spur and setting of Gee's cinematographic voyage. Shot in monochrome, with tributes from fellow landscape writers Robert Macfarlane, Chris Petit, and Iain Sinclair, *Patience* offers more a eulogy to Sebald's tone than to the man himself, as the film's itinerant structure and greyscale hue complement the perpetual motion and pervasive melancholy that make *The Rings of Saturn* so iconic. Deserted shorelines, secluded countryside, military relics, and vacant streets aptly capture Sebald's obsession with places where nothing significant yields itself up for description (or so it seems); often everyday places, which then prompt unexpected associations and spirals into the past, as though his repeated encounters with vacancy amount to an essential ritual without which narrative itself would cease to be. That such scenes of topographical blankness and brooding weather recur like a signature style may have been for Sebald a rather convenient pretext for stoking the peculiar atmosphere that has guaranteed his continued renown. Yet these recurrent scenic tropes captured a productive paradox across his career, as time and again from *The Emigrants* (1992) through to *Austerlitz* he launched episodes using recognitions of absence to identify the residual presence of dark history.

Paying homage to these signal motifs, *Patience* is a meticulous sort of visual elegy, the genre around which the next chapter revolves. For Gee aspires not only to salute Sebald's idiosyncratic manner of description, but also to reproduce it in cinematic terms. In this sense, documentary reaches beyond biography: grieving the very mode and sensibility that inspires it, the film mourns Sebald today as an irreplaceable chronicler of man-made catastrophe. *Patience* thus formally consoles for what its portrait elegiacally concedes; simulating Sebald's vision, it also acknowledges that with his untimely death a whole way of seeing in contemporary culture now seems irretrievable. If the documentary therefore offers redress, it does so by acknowledging its own deficit, allowing that acknowledgement to furnish its underlying eulogy. For Gee seems to admit that he can only describe—not entirely reproduce—for viewers a singular method of depiction that feels all the more poignant now that it has passed away.

The poignancy of description meant a great deal to Sebald himself. Affirming and refracting, inflecting and redressing, description is of course liable not only to encapsulate but also to exacerbate the very psychological states or environmental situations it so resourcefully captures. And yet, description equally shows how style has a canny way of persisting amid pathos, as the linguistic production of consolation survives alongside—indeed, in some senses despite—the reader's ethical and emotional discomfiture. Writers of fiction and memoir alike will invite us in the next chapter to consider these intervals between counterweighing lyricism and the demands of coping with bereavement, between elevating depiction and enduring isolation, as they disrupt the internal harmonics of elegy. Expecting from this genre no guarantee of repair, inviting from style no lasting salve, contemporary elegists view consolation through the crosshaired lens of pervasive loss to trouble its viability without refuting its consequentiality. For them, the paradox we have already touched upon looms large, as the words they find for unspoken grief are also the words that readers find all the more compelling when they describe experiences of bereavement so well, words that can turn an elegy's illumination of absence into public recognition and acclaim, words that probe even as they replenish the privations they so plaintively impart.

3

Elegy Unrestored

Divulging grief in detail may not necessarily mitigate your loss. It may even exacerbate bereavement, exposing the cliché that opening up helps you to let go. Elegists have known this for centuries, resisting the assumption that transcribing bereavement into eloquent forms can reconcile let alone restore its churning affects. Even so, of all genres that make some attempt to confront the felt consequences of loss, elegy has done it best: most prominently in poetry, of course, but also in modern and contemporary narrative, where elegy's formal adaptability has itself remained a spur for writers who assert grief-literature's value. By dramatizing retrospection as being as much about self-revaluation as emotional repair, elegy has become in recent years more self-conscious than ever when revisiting past wounds to expose them anew—forever alert to retrospection's healthy supply of sentimental appeasement. Writing by the light of this vigilance, contemporary novelists and memoirists have stressed elegy's generic heresies, refusing to follow the trajectory from searing bereavement to tentative alleviation with which elegies have historically been associated. What might this development in genre tell us about the unpredictable nature of solace itself? Is there a way of seeing elegy's aesthetic taxonomies of grief as fraught acknowledgements of what's left unrestored, pursuing in language not so much a pathway to restoration as a testament to consolation's own fundamental inconclusiveness?

Talk of unguaranteed outcomes hasn't always befitted elegy's generic definitions. Few forms seem more susceptible to being assigned formulaic purposes, thanks in part to elegy's alignment with psychoanalytic schemes for grieving. According to this view, elegy tracks an affective progression from the sudden, psychically numbing assault of loss, through the recuperative phase (however successful) of mourning, towards the promise (however elusive or self-deluding) of endurance and acceptance, if not eventual solace. As Angela Leighton has noted, this layout for emotional advancement encloses 'this most free of literary genres', ensuring that elegy symptomatically becomes 'an act of mourning which may or may not be worked through in the interests of consolation'.[1] Experiences of *working through* are thus tallied with elegy's movement from grief towards turbulent recuperation. In the readings this model inspires the convolutions of mourning are antithetical to solace; from the early twentieth century on, elegists have accordingly sought to deride the prospect of succour.[2] It is not hard to notice how a false dichotomy can creep in between the supposedly reflexive, surprising, on-going aspects of mourning and the sentimental, purportedly self-deceiving closure associated with consolation:

the very notion of what modern elegy does best relies on generalizing assumptions about what solace does worst.

In correcting this picture, it's worth acknowledging that 'the presumed emotions of either writer or reader are not intrinsic features of the genre'.[3] And contemporary elegists in particular attract discussions of elegy's emotional 'conventions' that say much about the critical suppositions this genre attracts. As David Kennedy remarks, both theories of mourning and literary-critical histories of elegy have rehearsed the conjecture 'that loss leads individuals from initial confusion to regained self-possession'. In practice, the genre is far less compliant with these templates for psychological progress, just as it remains constitutively unpredictable—as 'likely to be a distinctive idiom, mode of enquiry or species of self-description as a distinctive form'.[4] Contemporary writers have utilized this inherent restlessness to disrupt expectations of how elegy manages both the diegetic presentation and formal rendition of consolation. By undercutting expected arcs of restoration, the elegists I consider in this chapter alternate between epicentres of loss and intimations of solace while refusing to parody the experience of consolation as an unproblematic or else misleading phenomenon that simply resolves grief's complex persistence.

That elegy can argue in this way with the very premise of repair without spurning consolation as the poorer relative of emotions with allegedly more psychological mileage is a possibility explored by Colm Tóibín. Around the time he released *Nora Webster* (2014)—a work I will be considering later—Tóibín published a short memoir, 'A Grief Observed', borrowing his title from C. S. Lewis's 1961 meditation on the death of his wife Joy Davidman, where Lewis close reads the strain bereavement places on the solace of Christian faith.[5] Tóibín is quite open in this essay about *Nora Webster*'s biographical inspirations; centred on its eponymous widow's sorrow and endurance, the novel is a veiled elegy to Tóibín's mother. The veil is lifted in 'A Grief Observed', where Tóibín does little to obscure the novel's connection to an intimate familial past. Broadening the essay's remit, Tóibín also takes in the wider purpose of contemporary life-writing, announcing his scepticism about the therapeutic implications of writing on loss. As he looks back to the ambitions of landmark memoirs by Francisco Goldman and Joan Didion, Tóibín suggests that their depictions of grief draw attention to how

> novelists have become characters in their own books. By the urgency of the tone, they make clear, however, that, in the aftermath of loss, nothing they can invent compares to it. And that, since they are writers, what happened needs to be written down so that it can be known and shared and understood, so that it can lose its coherence. And so that they, in their powerlessness and helplessness, can at least still do this, can at least write down what it was like.[6]

Note the diverging implications here. Initially Tóibín insists that writing never 'compares' to the experience of loss, nor thereby compensates for bereavement. But he then qualifies this prospect of 'powerlessness' by admitting that writing itself—the very affect of writing's material procedures and proceedings—offers the solace of knowing one 'can at least write down what it was like'. Grief may well leave the writer in a state of apparent 'helplessness'; yet that doesn't always deter one from giving lasting expression to those whom one has lost, as well as to the event and evolution of loss itself. Notice too Tóibín's sense that writing enables the very aftermath of loss to relinquish its 'coherence', a notion that fruitfully counters what has become a convention in critical thought on trauma: namely, that the narration of grief lends it a quantum of shape, of comprehensibility, thereby granting us the illusion that loss is somehow manageable once narrative makes it meaningful. Tóibín tackles this assumption; but in doing so he also implies that grief isn't automatically a deterrent for the writer. That loss can indeed be an artistic impetus prompts further ethical questions, as we'll see, about elegists' creative use of affective experience—not least when proclaiming their own powerlessness.

This conundrum lies at the heart of elegy, especially in contemporary versions of the genre that consciously probe their mission, their own horizons of repair. Sorrow's dextrous evocation prompts us to wonder what happens to the fierceness of grief when it's mediated by formal finesse. As Jahan Ramazani observes, despite 'all their worries about making gains out of losses', elegists' innovations in this sense may 'collectively redeem their mounting losses as aesthetic gains for the genre of elegy'. This 'line of argument', he says, is itself 'recuperative', moving 'the rhetoric of redemption from particular elegies to a historical narrative *about* elegies'.[7] How to square the cultural capital implied by generic or stylistic innovation with humility and ethical self-awareness is one of the distinctive challenges taken up by contemporary writers who have transposed the poetics of elegy to narrative fiction and autobiography. In addition to Tóibín, I examine two fearless, psychologically exposing meditations on loss from Julian Barnes and Helen Macdonald, whose grief-memoirs contribute to that process (in Tóibín's terms) of allowing bereavement to unravel, to 'lose its coherence', while also contending with the prospect of offsetting losses through the linguistic elegance of their articulation. Both Barnes and Macdonald narrate the derailing effects of grief in ways that propel their own writing into what we might call a space of negative potentiality, a space that invites us to consider how inventively literature works in apprehending without entirely mitigating the losses that inspire it.

SALVAGING THE GRIEF-STRUCK

'Nothing humanely great—great, I mean, as affecting a whole mass of lives—had come from reflexion.'[8] So declared Joseph Conrad, in his self-inspecting preface to *A Personal Record*, a 1912 memoir that sizes up connections between subjective contemplation and worldly obligations. Conrad obliquely captures something of the memoirist's concern about who or what elegiac recollection serves, about whether the private consolations the writing process may foster can affect those who read it. With social or philosophical rather than purely subjective horizons in view, elegies can have bi-directional aspirations: dissecting the self precisely as a way of speaking beyond the narrower coordinates of personal recollection and mourning. Across the next two sections, I want to consider memoirs which take an alternative route, as Barnes's *Levels of Life* (2013) and Macdonald's *H is for Hawk* (2014) engage the plight of others in order to excavate their grieving selves: Barnes, aeronautical pioneers; Macdonald, the unsettled novelist and fellow falconer, T. H. White. Both scrutinize the restorative connotations of autobiographical elegy, each pursuing the self-displacing conceit of providing case studies of other figures who strive and fail—inquiries that interrupt their own intimate stories of mourning.

By putting personal loss in conversation with historical figures, these books possess in one sense tightly choreographed structures, despite their periodic alternations in focus and chronological fragmentation. At the same time, their styles are unrulier, working contrapuntally against the mood of measured recollection and historical reconstruction. By tracking these counter-currents, I want to show that even if the 'modern elegist', as Ramazani argues, 'tends not to achieve but to resist consolation' and 'not to heal but to reopen the wounds of loss',[9] then Barnes and Macdonald nonetheless stage and debate the presence of consolation in the very language through which their self-portraits of emotional irreparability are realized.

Unafraid to quarrel with the wisdom of self-analysis through recollection, Barnes's *Levels of Life* is associative rather than straightforwardly confessional or structurally progressive. Part memoir of the loss of his wife Pat Kavanagh, part history of early ballooning, Barnes sets up a dialogue between the perilous romance of human flight and the fact that '[e]very love story is a potential grief story'.[10] *Levels of Life* thus begins in what rhetoricians would call a *paraleptic* mode, insofar as the book seems to pass over its ostensible focus on bereavement through an extended prelude on ballooning, a prelude that then vivifies Barnes's account of losing his wife for which the reader has been waiting in suspenseful anticipation. Elegy thus arrives late in this book, as Barnes first reconjures the events of pioneering ballooning expeditions in stories of risk that preface, before gradually dovetailing with, his own personal meditation on loss.

> You put together two people who have not been put together before; and sometimes the world is changed, sometimes not. They may crash and burn, or burn and crash. But sometimes, something new is made, and then the world is changed. Together, in that first exaltation, that first roaring sense of uplift, they are greater than their two separate selves. Together, they see further, and they see more clearly.... We live on the flat, on the level, and yet—and so—we aspire. Groundlings, we can sometimes reach as far as the gods. Some soar with art, others with religion; most with love. But when we soar, we can also crash. There are few soft landings.... So why do we constantly aspire to love? Because love is the meeting point of truth and magic. Truth, as in photography; magic, as in ballooning.   (31–2, 36, 37)

Barnes abstracts the transformative aspect of love from the particular case by repeating the indefinite adverb 'sometimes', its recurrence pitched between insistence and incantation. *Sometimes* captures both the unpredictability of two people coming together and also the partial manner in which the memoirist extrapolates universal sentiments from individual recollections. Yet as he finds analogues in the documentary of ballooning for romance's combination of recklessness and 'exultation', Barnes also reaches in spare, matter-of-fact, present-tense assertions beyond analogy to the thing that is driving the whole text—love's indissoluble bond to loss.

These symmetries between aeronautical history and romantic impetuousness are what make *Levels of Life* so inventive, even though Barnes's rhetorical agility may seem out of kilter with one of the book's key premises: grief's inexpressibility. Indeed, he offers something of an elegy to the very genre of grief memoir, a genre marked by the pathos of its own concession that the emotional complexities of grieving will forever elude complete elaboration. In Barnes's opinion, we are generally poor at expressing grief, because its quality is highly particular unto itself, irreducible to any strategy of self-articulation that a griever may conceive and hone in advance. Literature also offers less than adequate preparation, however many centuries writers have followed the plight of the unconsoled:

> We are bad at dealing with death, that banal, unique thing; we can no longer make it part of a wider pattern.... So grief in turn becomes unimaginable: not just its length and depth, but its tone and texture, its deceptions and false dawns, its recidivism. Also, its initial shock: you have suddenly come down in the freezing German Ocean, equipped only with an absurd cork overjacket that is supposed to keep you alive.
>
> And you can never prepare for this new reality in which you have been dunked. I know someone who thought, or hoped, she could. Her husband was a long time dying of cancer; being practical, she asked in advance for a reading list, and assembled the classic texts of bereavement. They made no difference when the moment came. (69)

It's hard to disagree with Barnes's frank admission about the power of grief to remain unassimilated, to resist any counterbalancing 'pattern', to fend off blueprints in either written or spoken form. But he may also be having it both ways here: by casting the very motive and subject of his own memoir into an opaque and deceptive space of ineffability, and by adding—in his aside on a practically-minded widow—that literature offers few resources either, when surely to believe this would risk abandoning a project he has already embarked on. Barnes's rhetorical proviso for *Levels of Life* is therefore close to *adynaton*, as he states his topic by underlining what's so constitutively intractable about it. This trope of inexpressibility allows him to preserve grief's resistance, its essence as 'unimaginable'; yet at the same time, his acknowledgement of how unsatisfactory language is in recording loss spurs rather than stalls this compelling chronicle of bereavement.

'One grief throws no light upon another' (70), insists Barnes, echoing E. M. Forster. However, he 'finds consoling' a letter from a friend whose husband died suddenly and unexpectedly, and who reflects that 'nature is so exact, it hurts exactly as much as it is worth, so in a way one relishes the pain'. Cautious about this consolation, Barnes informs us that he 'doubted I would ever come to relish the pain. But then I was only at the start of things' (71). Indeed, he then concedes that '[g]riefs do not explain one another, but they may overlap', leading to 'a complicity among the griefstruck' that makes consoling use of comparing pain (72). Comparisons extend as well to the world at large, as Barnes sets Pat's terminal condition against the scale of irreparable ecological damage:

> They said the world's climate was reaching a point of no return, but it could go to that point and beyond for all it mattered to me. I would drive home from the hospital and at a certain stretch of road, just before a railway bridge, the words would come into my head, and I would repeat them aloud: 'It's just the universe doing its stuff'. That was 'all' that 'it'—this enormous, tremendous 'it'—was. The words didn't hold any consolation; perhaps they were a way of resisting alternative, false consolations. But if the universe was just doing its stuff, it could do its stuff to itself as well, and to hell with it. What did I care about saving the world if the world couldn't, wouldn't, save her?   (74)

The emotive charge of Barnes's anger here is simulated by his shift into a version of free indirect style, whereby the controlled manner of first-person retrospection gives way to irate interior thoughts, whose syntactic momentum captures also that peculiar aggravation which is born out of despair. There's no solace to be found in scale, for Barnes. Or rather, rescaling the irreversibility of Pat's disease in proportion to the grand scheme of things implies that his resigned acceptance of forces exceeding mortal control can offer only dubious consolation. Language once again comes under the spotlight, as Barnes scans the commonplaces—'just the universe doing its stuff'—that soothe us into accepting the environment as beyond our immediate circle of care, rendering our powerlessness strangely reassuring.

This acknowledgment of, and frustration with, how ineffectual we typically are in articulating loss has provided both catalyst and theme for life-writing since modernism, cultivating what John Paul Riquelme has called the equivalent of negative capability in autobiography. Such narratives 'generat[e] a negative capability concerning the self that involves both misrecognition and uncertainty rather than recognition and certainty'.[11] However, Riquelme also flips the term around to produce a concept that seems more germane to a writer like Barnes, who exhibits a variety 'of capable negativity, that is, productive or generative negativity'. Riquelme sees this temperament as particularly 'Beckettian'.[12] But I think it reaches beyond the existential bleakness of late modernism to a contemporary memoir like *Levels of Life*, where Barnes's recourse to adynaton epitomizes his own capable negativity in facing up to seemingly indescribable facets of loss. 'Perhaps grief,' speculates Barnes, 'which destroys all patterns, destroys even more: the belief that any pattern exists. But we cannot, I think, survive without such belief. Writers believe in the patterns their words make, which they hope and trust add up to ideas, to stories, to truths. This is always their salvation, whether griefless or griefstruck' (85–6). Barnes's scepticism about the consolations of restorative patterns doesn't altogether neutralize the 'hope' that mobilizes an artistic investment in the very patterns that 'words make'. This is memoir at its most discursively self-conscious: simultaneously aware of its own salvage work and of the propensity for symbolic patterning to offer the solace of sense-making.

This reflexivity, however, seems productively negative rather than resigned. Scrutinizing his most intimate terms of expression, Barnes refuses to resort this time to adynaton; instead language alone, whether spoken or in fleeting dreams, justifies its own revitalizing role, initiating further acts of memorialization. He notices that the grammar, like everything else, has begun to shift: she exists not really in the present, not wholly in the past, but in some intermediate tense, the past-present. Perhaps this is why I relish hearing even the slightest new thing about her: a previously unreported memory, a piece of advice she gave years ago, a flashback of her in ordinary animation. I take surrogate pleasure in her appearances in other people's dreams—how she behaves and is dressed, what she eats, how close she is now to how she was then; also, whether I am there with her. Such fugitive moments excite me, because they briefly re-anchor her in the present, rescue her from the past-present, and delay a little longer that inevitable slippage into the past historic. (108)

Barnes's grammar of perpetuation is itself a consoling resource, and the very tempo in which it is conveyed here models his 'surrogate pleasure'. The list of fresh reports of Pat in motion renders each clause exceptional, preserved equally without subordination. This enumeration of 'fugitive moments' duplicates in its pulse Barnes's excitement at the restitutive work such moments perform. At the same time, though, his phrasing also reaffirms, in its pacey collation of images, the 'inevitable slippage' of those moments as they pass into a more 'historic' archive of affection. Even as Barnes implies that there's some succour afforded by the 'intermediate tense' of Pat's continuity—snatched from reports of other people's oneiric sightings of her or in recovered fragments of advice—his syntax actually embodies through its urgent rhythms a thrill that's also a recognition of what's already moving towards the past. Previously unseen, unheard, and endearing: these souvenirs offer consolations as transitional as the tense that conveys them. His friends are following a time-honoured method for comforting the bereaved, and his style in turn tacitly acknowledges how willing the bereaved can be to engage in this unspoken custom. Elegy's conventional modulation from mourning to recuperation starts to meet internal resistance as Barnes's descriptions betray the precariousness of the emotional 'rescue' they momentarily convey.

UNDOING ELEGIAC ISOLATION

Style can thus destabilize even as it seems to enable elegy's consolatory affordances. At the same time, style may just as spryly compensate for the admissions of inexpressibility that memoirs invite from their self-examining narrators. Cultivating with loss, expressing seemingly unspeakable grief: such are elegy's 'attempts to conjure with absence', in Julia Jordan's phrase. As a creative venture, this can be 'productive' as well as recuperative, with the work itself 'seeking not just to articulate or perform an act of mourning', as Jordan observes, 'but also to recover the griever to the wider world'.[13] Re-entry into the worlds of social and professional life seemed well-nigh impossible for Helen Macdonald. Following her father's sudden death, Macdonald decided to embark on training a goshawk—one of the most difficult and recalcitrant of all raptors commonly used in British falconry. Over the course of what she calls 'dispatches from the front lines of grief', Macdonald records how her solitary life with her female 'gos', Mabel, 'was fascinating, all-absorbing, wild and often very beautiful', while also revealing the way 'bereavement and self-imposed isolation took me to some very dark places indeed'.[14] Telling the story of that time, *H is for Hawk* helps 'different genres speak to each other'.[15] Just as Barnes traced analogies for love and loss by redocumenting the escapes of early balloonists, so Macdonald integrates her account of grieving with a portrait of T. H. White, the troubled novelist who found imperfect escape from repressed homosexuality not only by writing Arthurian romances for which he's typically remembered but also in his incompetence as a falconer. A 'shadow biography' of White unfolds alongside accounts of the English landscape which are as phenomenological as they are historical, each framed by Macdonald's visceral dramatization of how '[s]udden bereavement does something strange to your powers of recall'.[16]

This amalgamation of genres drew instant admiration. *H is for Hawk* was named 'Costa Book of the Year' in January 2015, becoming also the first memoir to win the Samuel Johnson Prize for non-fiction. As the Prize committee chair Claire Tomalin recalled, her panel reacted to *H is for Hawk* as 'an extraordinary book that displayed an originality and a poetic power', deeming it 'very unusual' but all the more impressive 'linguistically and interesting technically'.[17] Macdonald's scenic and syntactic energy—her cataloguing of Mabel's moods; her account of their communion as 'parts of each other';[18] her candid recollections of deep anxiety about flying the bird free for the first time; her descriptions of place and perception that oscillate between staccato clauses and compulsive, run-on sentences—also caught the attention of reviewers. Janette Currie, for instance, implies that although *H is for Hawk* follows a somewhat familiar arc of autobiographical restoration, as Macdonald 'travels from despair to hope, and denial to acceptance', ultimately 'what rescues the book from cliché is her weird, wonderful style'.[19] The formal logic of piecemeal repair sometimes linked to confessional memoir—that formulaic path from initial confrontation with loss, through mourning and reconciliation, towards the anticipated solace of acceptance—becomes entangled in Macdonald's unpredictable modes of expression, which seek to probe rather than resolve the turbulent ontology of grief.

With its aesthetic inventiveness—its stylistic weirdness—*H is for Hawk* confronts received opinions about '[m]isery memoirs'. Although that label can sound misleading and unfair, Macdonald admits that it often sums up 'what books about grief are' or appear at first blush to be, with their lingering 'connotation of navel-gazing'.[20] Complicating the category, *H is for Hawk* does more than view distress in close-up purely for poignancy's sake; this is not a work of pathos-porn, and it quickly becomes clear that Macdonald intends to lead her readers across a more dispassionate spectrum of distinctly impersonal consolations. Grief occasions a sense of affective distantiation, whereby Macdonald deflects sentimentality on a number of levels: in her withdrawal from social life to absorb herself in 'manning' Mabel; in her submission to 'the grip of very old and emotional ways of moving through a landscape, experiencing forms of attention and deportment beyond conscious control' (5); in her frank warnings about romanticizing the countryside, highlighting 'the danger that comes in mistaking the wildness we give a thing for the wildness that animates it' (275); and finally, in her admission that the text itself is a product of temporal separation, for it took 'seven years to get enough emotional distance for the book to be written at all'.[21] Whereas other 'memoirs about grief have a power because they're written inside that time', notes Macdonald, *H is for Hawk* emerged at some remove.[22] She 'didn't think the book had any therapeutic value' *as* it was being written. 'But when I'd finished', she admits, 'there was a great sense that something was done, and it was a goodbye to my father and to that time. The book traces a time from that shock of the early loss to a point when I realised that the grief had turned into love.'[23]

Completion may not be a cure for heartache. But knowing that writing about her experience of grief and depression 'was done', Macdonald knew too that she was able, echoing Tóibín, 'at least [to] write down what it was like'. It's a process equivalent to the productive 'space' that David Grossman (my focus in the final chapter) has associated with writing beyond the numbness of grief, a creative space where 'death is more than the absolute, unambiguous opposite of life'.[24] Chiming with Barnes's conviction that every story of love is also potentially a story of grief, Macdonald reflects that 'love and loss are so close',[25] while aligning again with Barnes—if we recall his belief that '[o]ne grief throws no light upon another'—in her insistence that '[s]hocking loss isn't to be shared, no matter how hard you try' (13).

Macdonald does make some attempt, though, at sharing bereavement in the course of recalling her initial journey into its depths. At a rhetorical level, the desire to share grief—despite its resistance to mutual support and to the comfort of empathic recognition—slips into her manner of address. Reaching out to the reader, she tells us about a cherished souvenir from an excursion to watch goshawks in their natural habitat:

> Keep reindeer moss in the dark, freeze it, dry it to a crisp, it won't die. It goes dormant and waits for things to improve. Impressive stuff. I weighed the little twiggy sphere in my hand. Hardly there at all. And on a sudden impulse, I stowed this little stolen memento of the time I saw the hawks in my inside jacket pocket and went home. I put it on the shelf near the phone. Three weeks later, it was the reindeer moss I was looking at when my mother called and told me my father was dead. (11)

Macdonald's idiom of instruction ('Keep reindeer moss') summons and appeals to her reader, describing a task. And the colloquial evaluation through which this object is admired ('Impressive stuff') temporarily diverts our attention from personal memory to physical matter, from our anticipation of the psychological drama that's about to unfold to practical advice about identifying and looking after moss. However, the material realm then weaves back into the emotional one, as the 'stolen memento' of moss acts not only as a relic of a fondly remembered hawk-watching trip but also as a remnant of a time unscarred by familial catastrophe. Natural remains from a day oblivious to oncoming grief, the moss possesses an aura of resilience that offers little solace when the unexpected news arrives. Or rather, its capacity for solace, its promise of providing a relic of former normality and benign routine, is held out and promptly curtailed by that news—like a consolatory gesture extended then abruptly withdrawn. As the moss overlaps with the moment of shock, the 'stuff' that epitomizes extreme durability rapidly pales. When the call comes, this 'stolen memento' appears bleakly redundant in juxtaposition with unforeseen woe, a juxtaposition—reinforced by the leap in time between Macdonald's sentences—that of course breaks the spell of this passage's meditation on hardiness. And yet, Macdonald's reprise of that moss, weeks later, in the instant of desolation, manipulates the touching potential of a deceptively ordinary object. Building up to and describing this event of shock, she recognizes without being rhetorically disabled by the numbing inexplicability of loss.

What seems affectively opaque thus becomes vividly apparent, as Macdonald's writing rises to the challenge of rendering what otherwise might seem ineffable. She never assumes the authority to comment on sorrows other than her own, just as the experience of '[s]hocking loss isn't to be shared'. However, her exploration of the deeply troubled T. H. White does offer, at least at the level of structure, a means of orchestrating a parallel to her personal grief, though that secondary narrative never aligns as a consolatory precedent with her own. Thanks to this punctuating second narrative, *H is for Hawk*'s perspective shifts from Macdonald's mourning to a misunderstood figure whose passion for falconry she shares (even as she finds abhorrent White's haphazard training practices and routine cruelty). She presents the tenacious research gathered from White's archive (held at the Harry Ransom Center, Austin) in dramatic rather factually biographical terms. Recreating scenes depicting White's moments of frustration with his disobedient goshawk, Macdonald ventriloquizes his crippling insecurities, and these imaginative reconstructions perform their own consolatory work. Although the individual she revives is someone with whom solidarity seems impossible and undesirable, Macdonald sympathizes with how White 'had to displace his desires onto the landscape, that great, blank green field that cannot love you back, but cannot hurt you either' (39). For Macdonald, likewise, displacing herself into the impersonality of the hawk is ameliorative: 'I was in ruins. Some deep part of me was trying to rebuild itself, and its model was right there on my fist. The hawk was everything I wanted to be: solitary, self-possessed, free from grief, and numb to the hurts of human life. I was turning into a hawk' (85).

The goshawk herself is too capricious to be consistently consoling, of course. Mabel becomes a model of depersonalization; offering volatile companionship, she is not so much a distraction as a paragon for Macdonald of why mourning seems so species-specific. Whatever solace the hawk provides is, we might say, performative rather than merely substitutive: Macdonald reconstructs herself in ways that knowingly *enact* fantasies of ontological transposition. In turn self-analysis—a familiar enough trait in memoir—resembles something more like self-evisceration in this book, as Macdonald finds strange solace in stripping away human sensitivities. By refashioning what she might otherwise be, she alleviates her dependence on recouping the person she once was. In one respect, tending to the hawk offers her the prospect of emotional security through absorbed and concentrated identification, buffering her from the unforeseen vicissitudes of grief. But in another, equally immediate sense, Mabel manifests the possibility of yet another loss. While

Macdonald was 'training the hawk to make it all disappear' (117), she recalls how the 'world with the hawk in it was insulated from harm', such that 'every afternoon I walked out onto the pitch with relief, because when the hawk was on my fist I knew who I was, and I was never angry with her, even if I wanted to sink to my knees and weep every time she tried to fly away' (143). Abandonment becomes a variable that Macdonald has to factor into attachment; it's the rogue element in her companionship with Mabel, a risk she accepts and that also, in fact, makes the training process no less consoling:

> There was nothing that was such a salve to my grieving heart as the hawk returning. But it was hard, now, to distinguish between my heart and the hawk at all. When she sat twenty yards across the pitch part of me sat there too, as if someone had taken my heart and moved it that little distance.... I felt incomplete unless the hawk was sitting on my hand: we were parts of each other. Grief and the hawk conspired to this strangeness. I trusted she would fly to me as simply and completely as I trusted gravity would make things fall. (135)

The 'salve' of Mabel's return is figured here as immanent as 'gravity'. But the solace of communion between hawk and heart depends simultaneously upon Macdonald's cushioning distance from herself. It's an ascetic form of self-evacuation that affords some separation from grief's human fallout, as she 'conspire[s]' to ensure her own inseparability from the hawk. This is the discrepant consolation with which Macdonald becomes acquainted, as she finds refuge after her father's death in the companionship of an expert predator:

> Training a goshawk and not letting it hunt seemed to me like raising a child and not letting it play. But that was not why I needed her. To me she was bright, vital, secure in her place in the world. Every tiny part of her was boiling with life, as if from a distance you could see a plume of steam around her, coiling and ascending and making everything around her slightly blurred, so she stood out in fierce, corporeal detail. The hawk was a fire that burned my hurts away. There could be no regret or mourning in her. No past or future. She lived in the present only, and that was my refuge. My flight from death was on her barred and beating wings. But I had forgotten that the puzzle that was death was caught up in the hawk, and I was caught up in it too. (160)

Confronting 'hurts' with 'fire', Macdonald conjures her absorbed devotion to Mabel's vigour through active verbs (*coiling, ascending*) that culminate in the resolute and terse assurance that she had 'No past or future'—the elimination of retrospection and anticipation that Macdonald finds consolingly all-consuming. Her rhetorical tactic here is to immerse us, through the verve of her sentences' varying lengths and tempos, in her former self's susceptibility to finding (at the time) a sort of grim solace in the hawk's formidable presence and then to highlight (in hindsight) how this solace was itself a compromising 'puzzle' she had felt unable to entertain. Alive with labial diction (*boiling, blurred, burned, barred, beating*), her self-analysis achieves linguistically a self-assured ease that confronts the very psychological maze Macdonald is trying to lead us through.

If anything, Macdonald's readers are 'caught up' too in the recalled commotion from which this memoir, one might assume, is intending to achieve some distance.

Then again, these seemingly split priorities—when artful description and convulsive emotion bifurcate—remain crucial to elegy's simultaneous cultivation of and altercation with solace. In these moments, *H is for Hawk* suggests that 'elegy must offer the consolation of its solid, well-wrought art', as Kennedy puts it, yet must also remain somehow 'insubstantial' or provisionally open, precisely so as to simulate the fraught '*process* of that consolation'.[26]

Extending beyond her private context of grief, Macdonald also takes to task the evolution of a consolatory relationship with nature as distorted national heritage. To do so, she historicizes the longstanding tendency for rural rambling to become a way for people to walk 'backwards in time to an imagined past suffused with magical, native glamour: to Merrie England, or to prehistoric England, pre-industrial visions that offered solace and safety to sorely troubled minds' (103). Macdonald is mindful of her own potential complicity with 'a long vein of chalk-mysticism buried in English nature-culture' (260), raising the question of how one might love the countryside without being implicated in its romanticization. In a more artistically self-conscious move—as a writer whose dealings with rural traditions prompt linguistic innovations—she confronts the issue of how one can refuse the varieties of 'solace and safety' presented by natural environments while still developing a vocabulary for representing such spaces, a vocabulary that not only describes but transfigures the landscape through evanescent, and potentially aestheticizing, impressions. This is the memoir's other conspicuous paradox: *H is for Hawk* works to convey so potently that 'exhilarating, on-tiptoe sense that some deep revelation is at hand' when Macdonald engages with the countryside. Yet it recognizes in turn that this engagement relies on 'a presumption of organic connections to a landscape', a 'sense of belonging' that can 'work to wipe away other cultures, other histories, other ways of loving, working and being in a landscape' (260, 261). Finding consolation in a romantic affinity with the wild tends to rely on a dematerialized view of the social ecology of labour, habitation, and rural belonging. Reviewing *H is for Hawk*, Janette Currie suggests that these moments of self-inspection—whereby the memoir quite vociferously examines the risk of dehistoricizing landscapes when they become the subjects of elegiac lament—suggest that 'Macdonald realizes she has been looking in the wrong places for consolation'.[27] It's not so much the locations themselves which are duplicitously soothing as the pastoral figurations to which rurality remains susceptible:

> Old England is an imaginary place, a landscape built from words, woodcuts, films, paintings, picturesque engravings. It is a place imagined by people, and people do not live very long or look very hard. We are very bad at scale. The things that live in the soil are too small to care about; climate change too large to imagine. We are bad at time, too. We cannot remember what lived here before we did; we cannot love what is not. Nor can we imagine what will be different when we are dead. We live out our three score and ten, and tie our knots and lines only to ourselves. We take solace in pictures, and we wipe the hills of history. (265)

Representation here is itself the adversary, preserving 'Old England' in a distorting archive of romanticized 'pictures' in which there's much 'solace' but little 'history'. Macdonald sees in the problem of environmental scale an unwillingness to 'look very hard', which only perpetuates in the public imagination a presentist vision of rurality, one that typically looks back at regional life through the filter of the 'picturesque'. Knowing the solace this elegiac filter provides, Macdonald de-idealizes the very places she so intimately identifies with.

If this sounds combative, then it suits Macdonald's broader stance on the question of 'where nature writing is heading'. For it's a genre she 'hope[s]' will become 'a little angrier', so that we can 'see more books filled with beauty and fury and desperate hope, not simply distanced beauty and elegiac despair'.[28] Then again, elegy isn't a form Macdonald wishes to escape altogether, even if she refuses the conventions of plaintively rendering sorrow, even though she's watchful of how, '[i]n the imagination, everything can be restored, everything mended, wounds healed, stories ended' (248). Formally, *H is for Hawk* sidesteps these resolutions by taking the varnish off elegiac introspection: instead of lyrically amplifying her perceptions of loss and landscape, Macdonald is adamant that '[t]he only way I could write about grief was to be brutally honest about how it felt', such that a spare and unsparing sincerity becomes the generative premise of her style.[29] The tensions she exposes between rescinding affective repair and cautiously entertaining solace are key to what elegy in our contemporary moment does, as it foregrounds the work of consolation as precarious, processual, unfinished. Those same tensions are also markers of creative opportunity—yet another variety of negative potentiality—that invite us to see how twenty-first-century writers adapt the generic anatomy of elegy in order to inspect more closely the consolations elegies have traditionally sought to vouchsafe.

H is for Hawk thus affords its own literary knowledge about grief by confronting without dismissing the solace that elegiac form has in the past underwritten. Macdonald's jousting with loss as something at once laborious and shapeshifting does nothing, of course, to hide her book's athleticism. In this fashion, her style acts out the 'supreme achievement of memory', as Vladimir Nabokov called it, accomplishing in its rhetorical range the 'masterly use' that recollection can make of 'harmonies' composed from 'the suspended and wandering tonalities of the past'.[30] That the form these harmonies assume in hindsight doesn't seamlessly heal the turbulent content of what's recalled is something that Barnes and Macdonald both make explicit. Their elegies leave solace very much 'suspended' rather than supremely achieved—even as their renditions of that suspension are landmarks in memoir's contemporary development.

FEELING NOTHING POETIC

If one of elegy's most enduring conventions involves the writer's 'reluctant submission', in Kennedy's phrase, 'to language and an accompanying protestation of incapacity',[31] might the formal accomplishments of a work counterweigh the loss it conveys, when eloquence not only assaults the indescribability of sorrow but actively harvests some creative energy and critical esteem from its description? Might grief, in short, do more to further than frustrate its own articulation?

We have begun to see how recent autobiographical narratives grapple with these questions by animating rather than simply denouncing elegy's consolatory impetus, distinguishing it from the gradual upward curve of more uncomplicated recovery narratives. We have also seen how bold Barnes and Macdonald are as stylists: despite the impediments and muting aftereffects of loss, their works never conceal their rhythmic surprises and dictional suppleness.

So how might we approach an elegy that does none of these things, or at least not overtly? With this query in mind, I consider for the remainder of this chapter a novel where very little happens, not only in terms of events but also at the level of expression. Scenes stay local, appearing at first inconsequential. Their spare presentation amounts to an adamant modesty, a determined refusal of ornamentation. This is the world of the writer with whom we began, Colm Tóibín, whose *Nora Webster* strives in its economy to counteract elegy's 'aesthetic gains' (to recall Ramazani's phrase), offering a narrative of loss and resilience that feels all the more suspenseful for being so uneventful.

The values behind this strategic understatement come to light in Tóibín's blend of biography and criticism, *On Elizabeth Bishop*, a 2015 study published in the 'Writers on Writers' series hosted by Princeton University Press. The book has been variously praised by reviewers for being more personalized than its appearance as a critical monograph would suggest: a 'mixed-genre critical study/personal memoir'; one 'writer's exercise in rechristening himself'; 'an incidental treatise on the ways writers affect one another's process'—occupying all of these roles, the volume not only brings into close-up Bishop's life and oeuvre but also delivers a kind of second-order commentary that closely reads Tóibín's own priorities as a novelist.[32] Although his strong sense of affiliation emerging across the book is never defined in terms of influence, Tóibín finds features in Bishop that become precepts for his own language and approach. Prominent among these are affective experiences that seem to elude expression and explanation, inviting us to locate 'emotion', as Tóibín puts it, 'in the commas and the dashes, and in the spaces between the words, and in the reticence, in the silences'.[33] His affiliation with Bishop's practice not only becomes an incisive means of analysing himself, but also offers us the opportunity to observe how elements of that practice translate from poetry to fiction. As we will see, these elements are integral to Tóibín's confrontation with solace in what is arguably his most elegiac work yet, a novel that demonstrates this book's central argument: that the very works that may seem most emphatically ambivalent about consolation invite us to rethink its experiential variety and to appreciate its epistemic value.

Bishop's *Selected Poems* accompanied Tóibín on a trip in the mid-1970s to Barcelona, where he came to discover 'a replacement for home'. Works emerging from this émigré period include the novel *South* (1990) together with nonfiction volumes such as *Homage to Barcelona* (1990) and *The Sign of the Cross: Travels in Catholic Europe* (1994). And migration clearly marks his affinity with Bishop. Drawn to the 'idea' that she 'had travelled, which I was doing now', Tóibín noticed a 'tone that avoided easy or obvious drama'.[34] Plotting his career in retrospect across a transnational arc, his fictions' 'impulse and rhythm have pulled me away from home—Spain, Argentina, the United States, the Holy Land—and then have also nudged me, forced me, pulled me, dragged me, back home to the damp air and the dulled light of the southeast of Ireland, closer and closer to things that happened there, to the place of loss, to the loss itself, to minute details, to the very spaces'.[35] While Bishop's poetry isn't consistently elegiac, of course, loss has become something of a master trope in scholarship on her life and work, a focus that perpetuates what Frances Leviston has called the 'problematic separation of the lyric "I" from lyricism itself in many critical approaches'.[36] Returning to sites and senses of loss has also become a preoccupation for Tóibín, leading his recent fiction into an acutely personal phase, of which *Nora Webster* is the most intimate product so far. Though the material was patently difficult to negotiate, Tóibín nonetheless found when 'back in an Irish landscape' that 'writing about it was easier than writing about Spain, and the sentences came with less strain', even as his focus now revolved around what seemed irrevocable.[37]

Centred on the recently widowed Nora as she adapts to life as a single mother of five, *Nora Webster* is a painstaking account of slow, diurnal rhythms of adjustment, with her young and somewhat withdrawn son, Donal, playing Tóibín's boyhood counterpart. Set in the late 1960s, the novel makes no attempt to hide its proximity to his familial past, emerging as a moving elegy for Tóibín's own widowed mother. In this tribute to an enclosed though resilient Enniscorthy home, Tóibín assures us that 'there is nothing invented about the atmosphere in the house in the small town where myself and my younger brother lived with my mother in the years after my father died'.[38] Given how close this novel is to the biographical bone, it's not surprising for us to learn that writing it posed emotional and compositional challenges for Tóibín. Completing the final scene in particular—where this resolutely realist narrative modulates into an oneiric sequence describing Nora's reencounter with her dead husband, Maurice—proved to be the most testing. In hindsight, Tóibín sounds adamant that ultimately the process wasn't immediately consoling. Viewing it as such would be too convenient, he implies:

> I remember afterwards swimming in the sea, staying in the water for as long as I could. The scene was written. It would be lovely to say that I felt free of it all then, that by writing it down I had somehow erased it, or dealt with it properly for once, broken the silence. But writing requires such an amount of technical care, such cold deliberation, that it is not a form of self-help.[39]

Between 'cold deliberation' (in composition) and the questioning of solace (as theme) Tóibín spots a correlation that he associates too with Bishop's work. The attention he pays to her stanzaic shapes and metrical rhythms, to her everyday objects of attention, and particularly to her economy of means—the meticulous diction and avoidance of embellishment—suffuses his anatomization of grief in *Nora Webster*. Across this formally restrained narrative, Tóibín seems determined to do less, to cut away, to 'seem casual and uncertain' (borrowing his characterization of Bishop's verse) 'as though nothing was happening, nothing poetic, but maybe something all the more real and exact for that'.[40] By close reading Tóibín as he close reads Bishop, the critical stakes become clear of placing *Nora Webster*'s compositional priorities in dialogue with a poet who specializes in nothing visibly ornamental. Throughout his critical comments on her ways of working with language—sometimes *un*working it, by compressing, by streamlining, by stripping away—Tóibín intersperses creative comments on what his fidelities with a writer from the past can reveal about his own priorities in the present.

Tóibín's cultivation of 'cold deliberation' is perhaps what drew him to the 'calm austerity' of Bishop's technique, a trait she shared with Hemingway's 'fierce simplicity'. Pointing to a practice of affective shrouding, Tóibín finds in Bishop a self-disciplined 'use of words in which emotion seems to be hidden, seems to lurk mysteriously in the space between'.[41] Where *Nora Webster* is concerned, this space operates figuratively and literally, as the household at once safe-keeps memories and painfully triggers their recall. Maurice, who dies the same year as Tóibín's father, 'barely appears in the novel, but his loss lies between the words; he is there as a palpable absence'.[42] As Nora becomes alert to mnemonics nested in mundane places, so she discerns how '[e]very room, every sound, every piece of space, was filled not only with what had been lost, but with the years themselves'.[43] This is the understated zone of loss and longing—mundane yet portentous, where vacancy seems freighted with what's unrecoverable—that might well have appealed to Bishop. 'Modesty, care, *space*', she wrote to Robert Lowell in 1958, isolating features she found most impressive in such different modernist poets and painters as Eliot, Moore and Klee. A keyword in her creative praxis, 'modesty' named for Bishop a paradoxical yet valuable 'sort of helplessness but determination at the same time'.[44]

Tóibín's *Nora Webster* exercises a similar commitment to care and restraint in its assiduous record of grief. Refusing stylistic ornamentation just as confidently as he eschews sentimentality, Tóibín narrates the seemingly uneventful, pedestrian progression of his heroine's movement from raw distress to tentative hope. Nora herself keeps close watch over the family's apparent 'helplessness', routinely 'measur[ing] her success with the boys by how much she could control her feelings' (6). Scrupulous about identifying occasions where she could, discreetly, 'let herself feel how much she had lost, how much she would miss' (7), Nora is conscious of her own self-protectiveness, feeling 'nervous' whenever she notices 'someone coming towards her ready to remind her of her loss' (152). Thanks to this guardedness she sometimes 'felt helpless and regretted not having said something kind or special or consoling' to those who attempt to share her family's grief, to mitigate their sorrow (24). And it's through Nora's hostility towards the principle of consolation—whether giving or receiving it—that Tóibín employs the 'watchfulness' he associates in Bishop with 'the solitary figure either speaking or being described'.[45]

Which is not to say that Nora is averse to solace. Indeed she tests the feasibility of escaping small-town life, 'wondering if there was somewhere she could go'. In reveries of consoling speculation, she finds her 'mind moving toward the next thought—that possibility of such a place, such a house', a vision sustained by the deceptively comforting 'idea that what had happened could be erased, that the burden that was on her now could be lifted, that the past could be restored and could make its way effortlessly into a painless present' (31). Recovery of this wishful kind is of course not the outcome Tóibín pursues; instead, he plots the emotional coordinates of Nora's conflicted 'hope' that her 'boys would settle' and even 'become slowly used to the idea that their father was dead but that life would go on' (38). Psychologically exacting, yet domestically focused and dramatically moderate, this novel's suspense rests less on what happens from one scene to the next than on the expectation that 'things would change and maybe some things change for the better' (38).

Tóibín scarcely hints, as the story unfolds, at how or when that expectation might be fulfilled. Events simply don't take dramatic turns. If the narrative's relative serenity seems to jar against the turbulence of grief, it actually befits the way 'an ordinary evening' becomes in time the very thing 'Nora was almost grateful for' (110). Relatively simple and humdrum though they appear, these micro-consolations remain more substantive than the loftier prospect of spiritual acceptance imposed by Catholicism. Nora refuses the solacing logic of prayers, suspicious as she is of their insistence that people who die young (like Maurice) have 'escaped the tremulous hands of age' (51). Religion's bald rhetoric of appeasement through the reassertion of faith 'seemed to be too certain'; in its place, Nora feels instead that 'wherever Maurice was at this moment, he would long for the comfort of this house and for her, as much as she longed for the past year of her life to be wiped away and for him to return to them' (51). Attending the fluctuations of these longings, Tóibín converses with Bishop's renditions of emotion. To deal concisely with the evocation of loss is, we learn, to trust that words 'left out', like 'the holding of breath, could have a fierce, stony power'.[46] *Nora Webster*'s straightforward syntax and undecorated lexis evince Tóibín's attraction to the aesthetic and affective value of compression. 'Words not true enough were cut away', he observes, highlighting Bishop's apparently dispassionate approach to self-editing. And yet, strangely enough, *Nora Webster* seems all the more audacious for attempting similar feats of rhetorical understatement. In a single-minded pursuit of depleted means, Tóibín creates pathos by paring language away, complementing the sense in which Bishop's own 'great modesty', he argues, 'was also, in its way, a restrained but serious ambition'.[47]

Something restrained yet serious characterizes Nora's perception of her situation early on. Tired from the day, and with nothing 'interesting on the television' (28), Nora 'closed her eyes': 'In future, she hoped, fewer people would call. In future, once the boys went to bed, she might have the house to herself more often. She would learn how to spend these hours. In the peace of these winter evenings, she would work out how she was going to live' (28). Succinct, denotative, verb-led— Tóibín's syntax (*she closed, she would*) creates for what is a closing paragraph an internal, modestly climactic pulse, building into something like an incantation. There's a sense of self-affirming resolve achieved through simple reiteration here. Since most of Tóibín's sentences are brief, those with additional clauses tend to stand out both rhythmically and semantically. And it's in these sentences—with the extra clauses—that Tóibín moves from description to prospection, from noting basic actions to mapping Nora's intimations of promise: the likeliness of peace, of savouring the home alone not only as a refuge but as a place to 'learn' again 'how she was going to live'. This knowledge itself is momentarily consoling despite its ordinariness, despite the lack of guarantees here ('she *might* have the house to herself'). Yet it's also a knowledge contained, consolidated, and conveyed by assertive iambs ('how *she*...to *live*'), as though the very momentum of Nora's clipped self-observations performs its own melody of preliminary restoration.

The promise and anticipated consolation of solitude returns in a grammatically similar guise in later episodes, where Nora is pictured swimming: first, after renting a caravan for a fortnight on the coast at Curracloe with her sons; then again on holiday in Spain, this time with her aunt. At one stage the scene echoes almost word for word Tóibín's own account, as we heard earlier, of heading to the sea and 'staying in the water for as long as [he] could' after completing *Nora Webster*'s final chapter:

> She closed her eyes and swam without making much effort, edging out beyond where the waves broke. She noticed the sun's first heat as she lay back and floated. She felt lazy now and tired as well, and yet the energy that had come to her earlier was there too. She would, she thought, stay in the water for as long as she could; she would use up her energy. She knew that a morning like this would not come to her as easily again, the early light so beautiful and calm, the sea so bracing, the promise of the long day ahead and the night that would follow when she would be alone once more, undisturbed, allowed to sleep.   (224)

Once again Tóibín opts for simple subject-verb openings, each sentence creating a pulse across phrases that gently simulate the tranquil motion of the sea as Nora's sanctuary, knowing as she does that this respite ought not to be taken for granted. Tóibín catalogues this peace. Noting each of its facets, the final sentence's cadence rocks back and forth to emulate the mix of repose and energy, relaxation and anticipation, as the effortlessness of Nora's swimming coincides with her expectant sense of oncoming night. The isolation of the anapaestic 'undisturbed' visually and rhythmically confirms its own promissory significance: placed on its own, the adjective pinpoints a precious nocturnal interlude in Nora's grief. By departing rhythmically from the iambic phrases that bookend it, *undisturbed* creates a momentary eddy in the prevailing flow of descriptions of light and water. Metrically cutting away from its surrounding diction, it seems to advertise what it captures best about the ordinary solace Nora savours most.

A good deal of suspense in *Nora Webster* is supplied by what the novel seems to withhold in its diurnal accounts of Nora's bereavement, and Tóibín pinpoints a similar effect in his commentary on Bishop. There he draws attention to the way 'there is always something else there in the space between the words, something that is controlled but not fully, so that the chaos is all the more apparent because it is consigned to the shadows'.[48] Controlled brevity proves unnerving: something potentially disarming is exposed by what is not given away, by what is left only implied, because the language does less, staying composed, unperturbed. Hence the haunting insinuation that the departed still endure; that things left unsaid cue those still living, hoping for expression at last; that the very places bearing the mark of loss play host to lingering presences—these facets of bereavement materialize whenever Nora 'pictured the house' (116). Speculating 'how strangely filled with absence it must be', Nora knows that her sons don't read their home as closely as she does, having yet to cultivate her habit of 'watching every scene, every moment, for signs of what was missing or might have been' (116). Yet they also don't watch themselves, missing 'how uneasy they were'—an unease that might 'not leave them for years'—missing too the habit they had unwittingly formed through a 'suspicion of each other and of everyone around them' (116).

As an acute observer of the relation between what's gone and what could have been, Nora is not only the grief-struck object but also the focalizing subject of the novel's elegy. Consequently, she develops a perspective on the world that alienates her somewhat from the present, knowing 'that she was interested in nothing at all' and that her preoccupation with loss—despite her show of resilience and domestic efficiency—leads her to wonder whether 'she would ever again be able to have a normal conversation and what topics she might be able to discuss with ease and interest' (71). A proficient yet self-protective elegist of her own situation, Nora becomes acutely aware that the notion of '[b]eing released into the world of others seemed impossible' (71).

With the passing of every elegiac reverie, of course, Nora feels the strain of being 'back in the hard world again' (7). Release, however, takes other forms. Music affords its own kind of solace, for instance, as Nora gains confidence among other amateur singers, while also building her own classical music collection. Singing lessons remind her that 'Maurice had no ear for music'. Yet the realization 'that music' itself 'was something they had never shared' is double-edged, consolingly affirming her own sense of agency at the same time as it 'lead[s] her away from Maurice, away from her life with him'. Such is 'the intensity of her time' with music that she feels increasingly 'alone with herself in a place where he would never have followed her, even in death' (204). This unexpected passion for music, though it opens up social opportunities, in fact compensates for her not wanting to be 'released into the world of others'. And it's a pastime she cannot altogether share: what she 'had told no one, because it was too strange, was how much music had come to stand for', since it came to constitute a 'dream-life, a life she might have had if she had been born elsewhere'. Nora abandons herself 'for a time each day' to 'a pure fantasy in which she could have learned the cello as a child and then been photographed' as a performer, 'eager and talented and in full possession of her world, with men beside her who depended on her to come in with her deeper, darker sound'. Temporarily soothing, this parallel universe 'almost made her wince in embarrassment when she thought of her own mornings in Gibney's working with figures and dockets and invoices, and her own morning walk across town, and her own return home each day, and how meagre were the things she looked forward to, and how far these were from a recording studio, a concert platform, a name that was known, how far from the spirited authority of this young woman's playing'. Introspective though this chimera remains, its mental afterglow makes Nora look out into the world and wonder whether 'she was alone in having nothing in between the dullness of her own days and the sheer brilliance of this imaged life' (263).

Such is our proximity to Nora's most secret self-examinations. Free indirect style always entails a certain intimacy between reader and focalizer, of course. But here Tóibín *thematizes* that closeness. We're made privy to a world of harmless make-believe that for Nora can be as embarrassing as it is consoling—and maybe not altogether harmless either, if we think of the chronic and discomforting returns to the 'dullness of her own days' that her excursions into this parallel life repeatedly entail. Tóibín thus prompts us to appreciate how music becomes 'a way to inhabit loss, or to allow loss to have its full weight', without dismissing as superficial the solace of the 'imagined life' it inspires.[49] He also implicates himself to an extent, as though registering the fact that sheer economy of style doesn't necessarily cancel out the stylist's trace. Despite its flawless discretion, its unwavering suspension of rhetorical decoration, *Nora Webster* reveals how indirection alerts us to 'the ways a writing subjectivity conjures other ones', as Lauren Berlant asserts, 'so that, in a performance of fantasmatic intersubjectivity, the writer gains superhuman observational authority, enabling a performance of being that is made possible by the proximity of the object'.[50] It's this sense of authority, including the notion that a writer can never entirely decline it, which Tóibín invites us to contemplate. By close reading his elegy, we realize that the very closeness of grief's psychological rendition—the stunning consistency of the narration's proximity to Nora's interior mourning—counterpoints in its technical adeptness the novel's surface modesty.

Engaging with *Nora Webster*, in this sense, turns into a sort of close-watching, a mode of attention that leaves the reader conscious of her own preconceptions about the experience of grief and consolation. This observational proximity resembles the pure 'noticing' that Tóibín identifies in Bishop's elegy to Robert Lowell, 'North Haven'. Watching prevails in that poem, he argues, overriding 'thinking or remembering or analyzing'.[51] So too in this novel, we're compelled to watch rather than to dissect; to share Nora's 'longing' to be away from the 'noise and confusion' of social gatherings (169); to empathize with how she experiences 'silence and solitude' as a consoling, 'strange relief' (169–70); to sense at the same pace of her dawning realization that 'this was what being alone was like' (170); and, ultimately, to register the language through which all this is conveyed, a language that aspires to be emotionally exact by giving the impression that 'nothing was happening'.[52]

The pay-offs of this kind of phenomenological proximity amount to more than sympathetic involvement. For one thing, close-watching acquaints us with how 'modest knowledge' (in Tóibín's view) names a common ethos in Bishop's work and in regional Irish culture, where a deliberate sense of 'evasion' in 'precise description' exemplifies writers' avoidance of 'ornament' and 'exaltation'.[53] But moreover, when I say that this might not be about sympathy alone, I also mean that it's not just an affective result of beautifully rendered, nimbly articulated free indirect discourse—though of course this does have its own rewards too—because there's a distinctly pedagogical dimension to this proximity, which echoes the emotionally instructive nature of elegy as a genre that models states of distress and redress, without guarantees of repair. Our closeness with Nora gradually teaches us how to read her situation with patience, if also with some degree of impartiality, even scepticism, not least because she can seem 'both brave and difficult', as Tóibín desired, even 'oddly nonchalant in the ordinary course of events'.[54] An occasionally stubborn character, rebellious in grief, Nora is likely to refuse as much as she accepts the very consolations we might wish for her.

THE SOLACE OF SCRUPULOUS MEANNESS

With self-possessed economy Bishop's poetry insinuates unease, in Tóibín's verdict: she 'picks up tiny details' and then 'leaves out any sense of menace, or instead succeeds in filming absence of menace, and thus manages to capture menace all the more truly and effectively'.[55] In *Nora Webster*, this unsettling strategy leaves Nora teetering on the threshold of despair, even while she maintains a domestic sphere of relative protection for the children, screening with workaday tasks her inward consternation. Tóibín allocates his own attention to 'tiny details', as though close reading, through Nora's focalization, the disquieting substrates of ordinary routine— all the more disquieting, indeed, thanks to his unassuming descriptions of the very absence of clear and present danger. Placid accounts of events do little to placate our sense of unspecified menace. It's an effect produced through a carefully managed process of 'statement with no comment', which in Bishop's case, as in Tóibín's, leaves 'description' itself 'so calm and brisk, the rhyme schemes so comforting and soft on the ear, the atmosphere so traditional and local, that something must happen to break all this up', even if ultimately 'it is unclear what this breach of decorum can possibly be'.[56]

That readers have to wait for something to happen in *Nora Webster* is a consequence both of the novel's moderately paced plot and of its punctiliously restrained prose—a register so reticent as to acquire a magnetism all of its own.[57] This approach owes much to the other iconic experimenter and fellow Irish novelist who looms large in *On Elizabeth Bishop*: James Joyce. Perhaps inevitably, Tóibín connects the language of Bishop's poems about Nova Scotia with Joyce's famous promotion, in speaking of *Dubliners* (1914), of 'scrupulous meanness'.[58] Both of these modernists, in Tóibín's view, 'could allow language to compensate and console, then rise above such petty urges and seem to redeem what had been lost, or redress much that they both cared about deeply'.[59] There's an implied hierarchy of value here, whereby *consolation* (construed in this instance as a near relative of *compensation*) is overtaken by two impulses (*redemption* and *redress*) with greater efficacy and integrity.[60] If consolation is at the 'petty' end of Tóibín's scale of aesthetic 'urges', then what does he condone? In this reading of Joyce and Bishop, an alternative take on the modernist ethos of impersonality scores highest. To overcome linguistic compensations, argues Tóibín, Joyce and Bishop 'moved into a space that was impersonal, beyond the personal, and then they allowed this impersonality to transform everything that lay beneath it or beyond its understanding, creating a music filled with risk and repetition, which would mimic the tones of prayer, the mind at its most exalted'.[61]

Here is where things get rather more complicated for Tóibín, following his demotion of solace. His critical metaphors transition from the domain of things that writers care 'about deeply' to a logic of depersonalization whose transcendental formalism, its promotion of 'risk and repetition', simulates without quite aspiring to the act of praying—that profoundly personal and private activity of supplication and self-excavation. Reaching through personal care for a 'space' beyond 'the personal', Tóibín invokes the briefest examples from the texts themselves (the closing 'image of the snow' from Joyce's 'The Dead' and 'the quasireligious images of water in Bishop'), in order to emphasize not only literature's emotional wisdom but also its spiritual leverage.[62] What he tries to offer, in a sense, is a creative theology of image-making, a charismatic compositional practice that aligns with only then to exceed sacred coordinates. Via this account, Tóibín can thus claim that '[w]hen faith disappears, as it did with these two writers, then the language of transcendence can have a special power because it invokes something that was once familiar, once possible, and is now lost'.[63]

Is there a consoling dimension to writing, then, when '[f]aith goes'? Is the very fact that 'language remains' after religion 'disappears' a durable source of solace, despite Tóibín's dismissiveness towards consolation as a 'petty' impulse here? That language delivers aid in the face of spiritual doubt is nothing if not life-affirming for Tóibín, affirming too his sense of the vitality of literary form. If 'faith' should be placed anywhere, for him it ought to be in the quiddity of imaginative language: in the work that words perform to transfigure the pain they detail; in the work they do to create an intensified proximity with 'all the emotions surrounding belonging'; in the work they do to redress the displacements of unknowing, the grinding persistence of grief, the longings loss perpetuates. 'Language is all there is now', he insists: 'And in the ambiguous space created by a precise and exact evocation of the past, a single, concluding image...is allowed to soar above the ordinary universe like a hymn, or an aria, something filled with rising cadence.'[64] Tóibín's similes frame this climactic process of elevation by straddling sacred ritual and musical virtuosity, while the 'hymn' in its modesty is replaced by the more audacious, expressively athletic 'aria'. His point, it seems, is that linguistic dexterity of the sort we encounter in Joyce and Bishop temporarily suspends our perception of ordinary life, even if their images are ultimately drawn *from* realms of everyday action and emotion. This is not an argument for literature as wishful escape. Instead it opens up the possibility that writing and reading alike are synonymous with the translation of 'the world of things' into something momentarily other—'into an uneasy, shimmering, almost philosophical, almost religious space', where the writer makes and the reader faces 'something that has not been formulated or imagined by anyone before'.[65]

'Almost philosophical, almost religious': this is the consoling zone, at the crossroads of sacred and secular discourses, where Tóibín locates literature's potent forms of 'redress', irrespective of his misgivings about consolation as a trivial urge. Even though he dispenses with faith, religion is retained by analogy, an equation qualified here by his carefully placed 'almost'. In place of divine reassurance, writing is an act of salvage and for that reason a source of solace, despite his qualms about praising that payoff. Crucially, it appears that literature carries out this consolatory work not with soothing embellishments but by being deliberately—scrupulously—lean.

And in *Nora Webster* that leanness is what alters the novel's own relationship to the consolatory engineering of elegy. As we have seen, the novel exhibits 'a conscious avoidance of flourishes or bright display' in 'a tone held back, held down', carrying out the conviction Tóibín spots in Joyce and Bishop 'that the words themselves, if rendered precisely and exactly with no flourishes, could carry even more coiled emotion than an ornate phrase or sentences filled with elaborate textures'.[66] For Joyce and Bishop, Tóibín asserts, the imperative was to 'visualize' above all: 'It was essential for them that the remembering be exact and precise, enough for it to draw in and hold all the emotions surrounding belonging, or dreams of belonging, or loss, or dreams of loss, or indeed knowledge of loss.'[67] The emphasis here is on approaching loss indirectly: alert to what emotionally *surrounds* loss, to how one belongs in its devastating wake. *Nora Webster* supplies an arguably oblique account of grief: in place of graphic scenes of raw bereavement centring on Nora's longing for Maurice alone, the novel follows her tentative and materially essential re-entry into some semblance of ordinary life and employment. Recognizing the possibility that longing itself might eventually dissipate, Nora suspects 'that there would come a time when he would not be missed, that they would all manage without him', even as she finds it inconceivable that this recognition would be comforting (263).

Nora is resigned to the acknowledgement 'that there was no other way for them to live', discovering that most of the time she had 'forced herself to believe that he would want them to be happy' (263). Every effort to move on, to think of what lies ahead for the family, leaves Nora haunted by the anticipation of coping well enough alone. This haunting is literalized in a late, dreamlike sequence where she encounters a spectre of Maurice in her upstairs bedroom. As though he were an oracle, she presses him about Donal's uncertain future, but his ability to reply dissolves as the dream-sequence evaporates and the solace of prophecy remains beyond reach. The episode epitomizes that 'tendency', as Kennedy sees it, for late-twentieth-century and contemporary 'elegies to become uncanny spaces where the dead's singularity is perpetually reanimated'.[68] Furthermore, the scene would appear at once to occasion and to fulfil 'the dream of all elegy', in Leighton's phrase, 'that form, in its virtual reality, its empty room, will be able to house the beloved human form again, and so find its longed-for consolation'.[69] Yet Tóibín also resists the inevitability of this formal aspiration, thereby undercutting the sense that Nora simply longs for a solace that the genre she inhabits will eventually afford.

RELINQUISHING ELEGY

This resistance is poignantly mobilized at the novel's close. Here Tóibín's affinity with Bishop—relying on words shorn of amplifiers, 'rendered precisely and exactly with no flourishes'—is especially visible at a point where readers might reasonably expect a memorably festooned climax. As Nora retrieves Maurice's letters from the earliest days of their romance, Tóibín imparts only minimal information—much like the letters themselves, which 'were often short, just suggesting a place in town where they might meet, and a time' (310). Nora knows these letters by heart, so their contents are summarized for us succinctly, relatively factually even, in free indirect style. Yet the very compactness of her synopses is itself pathetic, giving plaintive inflections to the hopeful content of Maurice's courteous notes that document the modest courtship routines he once proposed with endearing formality:

> He often talked about himself as though he were someone else, saying that he had met a man who had told him how fond he was of a certain girl, or how he had a friend who walked home from seeing his girlfriend and all he thought was how much he would like to see her again soon, or how he would like to go to Ballyconnigar with her and walk along the cliffs at Cush and maybe have a swim with her if the weather was good.
>
> She knelt down and slowly fed the letters into the fire. She thought about how much had happened since they were written and how much they belonged to a time that was over now and would not come back. It was the way things were; it was the way things had worked out.   (310)

The paragraph break before the bare, straightforward description of Nora's decision to destroy the letters emphasizes her firm and pragmatic resolve. We then switch from her methodical action beside the fire into an equally methodical, poised reflection about the futility of holding on to mementos from 'a time that was over'. Sentence by declarative sentence, the spare prose could in part reflect Nora's determination to accept that this 'was the way things were'. But with the embers of *Nora Webster*'s main events still glowing, what Tóibín leaves out—what he cuts away in a motion that resembles Nora's cutting loose from attachments to a life that 'would not come back'—is what the reader is enticed to replenish, knowing as we do the weight of feeling that goes unsaid here as memories are 'fed' to 'the fire'. The pathos surrounding 'the way things had worked out' thus seems most acute when Nora departs from elegizing what she cannot repair—what's left unrestored might indeed be what leaves her most consoled.

Decisive like that paragraph break, this departure from elegy marks a retreat from the 'work of losing' inherent to the genre, in Leighton's terms, 'in which language replicates the loss that gives rise to it'.[70] For here, Tóibín's language—increasingly abrupt, determinedly unostentatious—refuses by that second paragraph to simulate the commotion of loss that is elegy's stock-in-trade, discerning instead a raw, stark consolation in Nora's frank admission that this was 'the way things had worked out'. As she readjusts her relationship with grief, so the novel disarticulates itself from the elegiac parameters within which it has hitherto plotted Nora's sorrow. This adieu to elegy is only reinforced by the conviction, the scrupulous control, that Tóibín's language exhibits here, a control that Nora sustains in kind through her gesture of hard-won intentness. A stylistic principle of doing less thus correlates with Nora's implied resolve to do without, the elimination of rhetorical ornament amplifying the poignancy of her acknowledging the irretrievability of her life with Maurice.

Perhaps this is how elegy itself discrepantly offers the consolation of continuity: not simply by dramatizing the sensation of letting go, but by turning finally into something other than it typically is, set loose from its own generic templates. According to this novel's mutable sense of an ending, where Nora frees herself from the very objects that perpetuate mourning, elegy's cessation also spells an unfastening of sentimental attachments to those very forms, like her letters, that are most recognizably comforting.

*

Bishop's quest for 'exalted precision', observes Tóibín, 'made the bringing of things down to themselves into a sort of conspiracy with the reader'.[71] This conspiracy is, I think, a curious part of the pedagogical aspect of the reader's proximity to Nora's progress through bereavement, including the affectingly elegiac route that progress takes (until, as we have just seen, the end). While Tóibín's novel is a far cry from the classic modernist object of classroom instruction—texts that are monumentally difficult because they are exuberantly polyphonic, impenetrably labyrinthine, or replete with rarefied allusions—*Nora Webster* prompts us to learn something about affective aspects of close reading itself. And this is where the novel speaks to a larger context of shifting disciplinary temperaments. When Tóibín illuminates emotive features in Bishop's poetry that he not only admires but endorses as benchmarks for his own fiction, he coincides with conversations in literary studies more broadly, where the question of close reading's sustainability coexists with the turbulence of what Rita Felski has called the 'method wars'.[72]

Against this backdrop, Tóibín's intimate, self-revealing commentary in *On Elizabeth Bishop*—by turns lyrical and biographical, combining prosodic inspection with explicit opinion—captures something of the 'abiding tension', in Rónán McDonald's words, 'at the heart of the discipline'. This tension lies 'between the value of literature—numinous, sensual, and perhaps even transcendent—and the mechanisms of criticism—rational, judicious, and objective'. For McDonald, this is less a cause for concern than simply a reason to be alert to the 'double meaning in "criticism" that replicates the dialectic, straddling as it does observation and evaluation, objective analysis and impressionistic response'.[73] Such a dual-pronged understanding of critical attention shapes the readings I develop across the rest of this book. Thinking back for now on this chapter, the flexibility McDonald has in mind seems crucial to approaching multi-generic memoirs and auto/biographical fictions whose complications of consolation have required us to move from formal conventions to phenomenological reactions, from the characterological/narratorial dramas of recollection or self-examination to relations between metre and mood. Tóibín himself hones the sort of close reading where biography, aesthetic assessment, authorial self-assessment, and technical description intersect. In so doing, he models the way different critical registers of explication can mutually complement each other in attending to portraits of non-restorative bereavement and self-contesting solace that contemporary elegists offer.

With their manifold adaptations of this genre, Barnes, Macdonald, and Tóibín invite equally varied responses to the provision of consolation that has traditionally been attributed to elegy. Just as they reveal that elegy is no longer beholden to that 'laborious and improving effort' of journeying from mourning to recuperation, as Leighton puts it, 'checked along the grid of grief and consolation',[74] so they also imply something about the state of reading itself. Specifically, they point to how needless the split has become between 'two camps' in conversations about the way we read today, with 'one tending toward objective, positivist scholarship, the other toward creative or phenomenological criticism'. These distinctions, as McDonald notes, could well 'mark a more profound division in current literary studies than a putative move from depth to surface'.[75] Doing without that unnecessary split points to a critical attitude that *Levels of Life*, *H is for Hawk*, and *Nora Webster* solicit and repay: not an uncritical or purely appreciative stance, but rather one that allows us to test our own willingness 'to ask', as Tóibín recommends, a given 'scene to offer nothing more than the tone that the words describing it might propose'.[76] This doesn't mean suspending our detection of discrepant or contradictory elements. On the contrary, Barnes, Macdonald, and Tóibín compel us to glimpse in their prosaic accounts of loss not some rhetorical elixir but expressions of grief's emotional fallout that linguistically *enact* consolation's difficulty.

In the process, these writers reflect on language's own affective capabilities and mediations. Entertaining the debatable nature of solace goes hand in glove with their awareness of the fallibility of description, a recognition that Tóibín sees at work in Bishop's 'Poem', which holds the belief that 'to name the loss would be to lose it further, to lose what was remembered and what was experienced, to betray it somehow'.[77] Learning to read the aftermath of grief as something inherently unpredictable, maybe even unreadable, is what these elegies enable as they absorb us in unrestored lives. If they unsettle the legitimacy of consolation, then they also ask us to unlearn what familiar paradigms of mourning have taught us to expect of literature's transmutations of loss. For all their obvious structural and topical differences, the works brought together here open up opportunities to reassess the way the complications of consolation alter elegy's generic constitution.

Retrospection has, perhaps inevitably, loomed large in this chapter; next we'll turn to fictions that revolve around anticipated oblivion. That reorientation will also be accompanied by a different unit of analysis, moving from aspects of genre to microelements of style. Two very different novelists test the work of consolation as an affordance of style. And this test leaves style, to recall Tóibín's terms, in the discrepant position of being 'uneasy' yet 'shimmering', falling short yet somehow flourishing, throughout fictions consumed with the recognition of shame, the endurance of disappointment, the expectation of self-loss. By arguing too with the ease of divine consolations, style occupies an 'almost philosophical, almost religious space' in its own right.

4

The Religion of Style

'Style here is style as consolation, style as redemption, the grace of language.'[1] The 'here' in J. M. Coetzee's crosshairs happens to be Flaubert, who pictured the ideal novel as 'dependent on nothing', its formal physiology virtually self-sufficient. Buttressed by aesthetic integrity, such a work would be 'held together', in Flaubert's words, 'by the internal strength of its style'.[2] Flaubert's idealist vision of style as the essential, binding element of fiction is nothing if not consoling. And for his part, Coetzee approves of Beckett's apparent suspicion of such ideals, even though this vaunted circumspection, this vigilance towards style's mitigating or substitutive effects, may itself constitute a rather comforting, even self-satisfying attitude for a writer to adopt. After all, there's something reassuring about rejecting the allure of verbal finesse, particularly when this rejection also enhances the reputation of novelists prepared to dodge the decoys of adornment. It's in this sense that Beckett would gain prestige as a master chronicler of disconsolation thanks to his 'repudiation', as Coetzee terms it, of the enticing consolations of expressional elegance and transparency.[3] What could be more self-affirming than the writer's dignified veto of style's myriad 'temptations'?

Although Coetzee doesn't entertain this paradox, it shadows his own productive wariness of what he dubbed in 1973 the 'religion of style'.[4] Committed throughout his oeuvre to the utmost economy, Coetzee's lissom language has acquired some notoriety as proof of creative sobriety. Even if this aspect of his prose—and of his settings too—divides opinion, Coetzee's dedicated temperament undeniably garners cultural capital.[5] Over the years his writing has been praised for its alliance of poise and frugality, finding sustenance in what he calls an ethos of 'thrift' that guards against the magnetism of embellishment. 'Spare prose and a spare, thrifty world', admits Coetzee: 'it's an unattractive part of my makeup that has exasperated people who have had to share their lives with me'.[6] As an artistic proviso, thrift befits the way Coetzee would seem, as first sight, to pre-empt solace as an affordance of rhetorical flair. Accordingly, he commends the 1938 *Murphy* for warding off style's 'seductions', staking out instead a 'battleground' with rhythm, cadence, and euphony, from which its narrative emerged triumphantly lean, denuded of polish. Some fifteen years later, *Watt* would fall prey to 'lulling plangencies', according to Coetzee, as though Beckett's resistance to expressional 'grace' had buckled under the weight of 'narcissistic reverie'.[7]

A firm endorsement, then, for Beckett's early prudence. No wonder Coetzee has shown little deference to style's redeeming promises, little intention of becoming a disciple to the credo of aesthetic salvage. As a result, it might be satisfying to demonstrate how this sensibility yields 'thrifty' results across Coetzee's fictional and autobiographical works, something I have attempted elsewhere.[8] In what follows, though, I want to take the more counterintuitive route by bringing together this paragon of austerity with another writer, Marilynne Robinson, for whom expressive 'grace' is integral to the cultural and ethical work she thinks fiction can perform. More than for the sake of contrast, this pairing of an ostensibly secular writer with a passionately Protestant one allows us to probe the points at which consolation's aesthetic, ethical, and theological vectors intersect in novels that inhabit the same genre of anticipatory loss. Shaped around the expectation of oblivion, Coetzee's *Age of Iron* (1992) and Robinson's *Gilead* (2004) invite us to ask, as Paul Ricoeur once did, what role fiction might 'play in the apprenticeship of dying'. Cultivating yet also scrutinizing varieties of what Ricoeur calls 'counterdesolation', these novels show how consolation might be realized in a 'lucid manner—just as lucid as Aristotelian *catharsis*—of mourning for oneself',[9] as their characters work towards provisional, qualified forms of recognition through lyrical previsions of death. By gauging the impact of their loss on loved ones who survive them, they forecast too what writing's vitality will preserve of them. Graceful though their existential apprenticeships are, at the same time *Age of Iron* and *Gilead* volatize their own accounts of reckoning with death through epistolary forms. Intentionally fore-structured yet susceptible to caprice, these novels are records of advance solace; but they also archive feelings that expectancy leaves distinctly unconsoled, as prediction magnifies the perception of self-loss. Two very different writers, then, seem devoted to the same poignant conceit, focusing in on the precariousness of solace for characters who have become apprenticed to their own passing.

We have thus switched directions now. Unlike elegy—a genre that *periodizes* solace, precipitating consolation by measuring the time endured through the interval achieved since the original epicentre of bereavement—fictions of approaching loss don't have the luxury of lengthening retrospect. Time can't really be much of a great healer when life is running out. Coetzee and Robinson dramatize the psychic consequences of this temporal shortage, asking whether the about-turn of anticipation can transform the kind of mourning that we associate with the aftermaths of grief or simply reprogramme mourning to behave the same only now in advance. In fictions that look ahead, to what extent is loss itself even narratable when it's foreseen rather than retrospectively felt, when it's oncoming—and to that extent unknowable—rather than inflicted, encumbering? Kindred questions will resurface in the final two chapters, when I turn to novels from Ishiguro and Grossman that explicitly test whether solace can survive the strain of apprehensiveness. For now, such queries set the scene for bringing Coetzee and Robinson into an otherwise unlikely dialogue: they both generate scenarios of contentious solace for the anguish of impermanency, while drawing attention to style itself as a conduit for and commentator on consolation's contested legitimacy. Arguing with solace even as they simulate the experience of it, their novels indicate that if loss isn't always 'representable according to the narrative explanations that would "make sense of history"', as Judith Butler observes, 'then making sense of ourselves and charting the future are not impossible'.[10]

And this is where my third selection becomes germane, in the shape of a novel that will triangulate *Age of Iron* and *Gilead* by trialling consolation's viability in a context where the 'mark' of historical harm, in Butler's phrase, is all the more 'insuperable, irrevocable': the 1999 *Disgrace*. Epitomizing a moment of endemic disappointment in South African culture, as Andrew van der Vlies remarks, *Disgrace* is a work of negative anticipation, whose 'bad feelings' are in league with a considerable body of literary works 'frustrated with the constraints of colonial and apartheid-era social and political conditions', such that they 'dwell thematically on expectation and enact formally the frustration of readerly expectation'.[11] One thing we might expect in this most violent of post-apartheid novels is the perishability of solace, of course; but at a linguistic level, Coetzee doesn't make that conclusion so easy to draw. For style performs other kinds of affective work aside from directly mirroring or intensifying unfurling deprivation. Unquestionably, *Disgrace* seems, to use Butler's terms, dramatically 'framed and incited by the irreversibility of loss itself'.[12] Yet formally, despite its own diegetic bleakness, this devastating novel invites us to reassess Coetzee's early misgivings about the consolatory contours of language—and thereby to ask, more broadly, what the 'religion of style' might do for works that appear so vigilantly to curb their own scope for redemption.

CONFESSING CONSOLEMENT

'This book represents my farewell to realism and to a duty to the South African scene.' So asserts Coetzee in his *Age of Iron* notebook from October 1988. A month later, despite this resolve, he still seemed haunted by the obligations of political immediacy, admitting that '[t]he pressure for so-called relevance to SA' remains 'too much': 'That is to say, I am capitulating before it.'[13] Born out of this anxiety, *Age of Iron* confronts the social trauma of its historical present through a distinctly private narrative of confession—but confession less as an archaeology of past misdeed than as a process of ethical reckoning initiated in anticipation of oblivion. The novel stands out in the critical literature on Coetzee for representing, at that stage in his career, his most direct engagement with the chronic suffering and social catastrophe of apartheid, while also his most concerted effort to depart from a purely reportorial assessment of state-sanctioned brutality. The novel continues Coetzee's project of bearing witness to the legacies of colonialism from which South African apartheid emerged, while at the same time registering the undesirability—which is to say, the formal and ethical insufficiency—of trying to articulate violence in comprehensive, legibly mimetic terms. Hence the novel's obliquity: apprehending apartheid through Mrs Curren's digressions and self-examinations, the novel's apparent refusal to attempt an all-encompassing documentary viewpoint on the agonies of military and police atrocity secures through elliptical expression and intense perspectivism her implication in a 'landscape of violence' before which she remains 'very directly affected' and 'ashamed'.[14] That state crimes might not only resist verbalization but solicit a narrative form that embodies and reflects on that resistance encourages us to construe *Age of Iron* as a kind of confession within a confession: according to this reading, Mrs Curren—terminally ill with cancer, writing an extended letter to her emigrated daughter punctuated by the local horrors of the state's barbarity and by an unlikely companionship she finds in the homeless Vercueil who accompanies her dying days—is ventriloquized by the '"white liberal" Coetzee', insinuating what Kim Worthington calls 'metaphorical linkages between' Mrs Curren's 'own impending death and that of the white regime'. Given its explicit context, *Age of Iron* could have amounted to a damning case study of oppression and complicity alone. But as it turned out, Coetzee set himself an even greater challenge by tackling head-on the ethical ramifications of writing so gracefully about apartheid's inexpressible abominations, thereby 'elevat[ing] the novel', as Worthington puts it, 'from what could be a self-absorbed, if intensely lyrical, account of personal grief to the higher ground of political truthfulness and integrity'.[15]

Coetzee's reservations about complying with the demands of social realist 'relevance' were already brewing two years before the 1986 *Foe*, when he observed that he has 'always written best out of an adversary position'.[16] Among his creative adversaries, as we have noted, is the notion that writers can, by grace alone, transcribe and somehow redeem the damage they record. How convenient it would be, then, to connect this repudiation of style's consolatory allure to the way Coetzee also refuses to release his characters from their often visceral, shameful entanglement in the 'bare life' of racial division, persistent injustice, and social disenfranchisement.[17] This, in theory, would present a perfect knit of sentiment and drama: bringing the ethics of Coetzee's commitments as a technician to bear on the cultural abominations, historical and contemporaneous, that his fictions obliquely register. But I want to complicate this received portrait of Coetzee as a dispassionate and unflinching artist who strips from his prose the solace his protagonists are denied, because this portrait may distract us from how nimbly his writing often disobeys its own self-discipline. Coetzee's simultaneous cultivation of and antagonism towards stylistic grace forms a dialectic in his writing that becomes as creatively supple as it is ethically provocative. Consolatory components of expression may be as unavoidable as they are apparently incongruous in relation to a work's thematic aspirations. And this sense in which solace can be ineluctable as well as out of place becomes particularly charged for Coetzee's fictions of violence. As we'll discover, his style is nowhere more ethically embroiled in its own affective potency than when it performs the very solace that to all intents and purposes it strives to relinquish. Discrepant though they remain in traumatic narratives, consolation's expressive animations are all the more legible when novels try, on the face of it, to disavow them.

Age of Iron is one such novel. Despite marked shifts in point of view, the manuscript was deeply personal from its conception. Over successive versions, as David Attwell has shown, the novel became an oblique elegy to Coetzee's mother, Vera, whose 'views on South Africa and her place in its history were plainly unacceptable'.[18] Dedicated to Coetzee's son, Nicolas Guy (Talbot) Coetzee, *Age of Iron*'s completion also coincided with a loss surely too great to be assuaged, making its biographical backdrop too salient to be ignored. As his typescript moved towards the final stages, Coetzee received news that Nicolas had been killed in a fall from an eleventh-floor balcony. With awful pathos, on the title page of Coetzee's typescript of Draft 10 of the novel (at that stage called *The Rule of Iron*) there appears an additional handwritten dedication, 'N. G. C. (1966–1989)'.[19] While this terrible loss, as one can only imagine, remains for Coetzee 'a constant, corrosive pain from which there is no deliverance',[20] J. C. Kannemeyer also suggests that Coetzee derived some solace from the fact that 'at the time of his death Nicolas had a postcard from his father in his possession',[21] just as he had been finishing a novel about a woman whose reconciliation with death is enabled by the gift she hopes to give in a confessional letter to her distant daughter. Compounding the trauma, however, Coetzee's former wife Philippa was also terminally ill with cancer. Together, such losses—one unforeseeable, the other distressingly imminent—comprise a formidable 'tragedy' that 'lends poignancy', remarks Andrew van der Vlies, 'to Mrs Curren's anguished negotiation of the meaning of dying at a distance from her daughter', while the novel's dedication can be seen 'memorializing the dead'.[22]

Written in the teeth of bereavement, then, *Age of Iron* is a self-conscious elegy about the challenges of representing personal loss—loss configured in Mrs Curren's case in terms of anticipation as much as longing or regret. Granted, there's still a sense of retrospect, and Coetzee was adamant about finding the right mode for this, as a notebook entry from 1988 reveals:

> Rewrite from the beginning in the first person (woman's point of view), past tense, with that *elegiac tone* that comes from something irreversible having happened between the time of which is being written and the time of writing.[23]

Such is the care with which Coetzee eventually synchronized the novel's perspective and register, creating a narratorial standpoint that could bear the weight of witnessing a history of apartheid leaving irreparable scars on the nation's future—racial injustice an anterior wound of still-unfolding damage. Alongside this retrospection, the novel develops another temporal orientation, a *prospective* one: 'in looking forward to the end', he records in the same notebook, 'one begins to cut one's ties with the land, one begins to die away from it'. In this observation lies the germ of what Coetzee considered to be the novel's 'necessity' of including 'someone who is in fact dying and comes to welcome death', even if that person then reaches 'a point of conversion at which hope is explicitly abandoned'.[24] Embracing oncoming death and losing all grounds for optimism: from of this alloy of competing affects Coetzee fashions an argument with the very consoling impulse that *Age of Iron*'s dramatic arc seems to trace as a proleptic eulogy.

Expecting no reply, the novel's expressive force attests to Mrs Curren's enunciating authority even as her narrative evolves into a kind of ontological self-dismantlement. 'I write', she insists, 'I follow the pen, going where it takes me. What else have I now?' (108). Yet it becomes apparent that her letter is more than a futile substitution, more than a means of expending time till oblivion: 'Death may indeed be the last great foe of writing, but writing is also the foe of death' (115–16). By 'holding death at arm's length' (116), writing consoles not through self-delusion or distraction, but because it invites her to find some reassurance in 'follow[ing] the pen' into the unknown—where the letter alone, its materiality, will remain. There is 'even a sense in which the distance and the necessity of [her] written correspondence', as Derek Attridge puts it, 'make possible for Mrs Curren an exceptional fullness of giving, and hence of love and of living on, in that it enables the gift to be posthumous, without thought of return'.[25] As she insists at one point, '[t]he comfort...should flow forward, not backward' (73). *Age of Iron* pivots on this axis between 'irreversible' loss and the letter's potent afterlife, a prospect that also serves to counteract precisely the question Coetzee posed in his notebook to the novel: 'Have things come to such a state that one may not prepare one's soul for dying?'[26] While finding in writing an equivalent for that preparation, Mrs Curren 'uses her body's breakdown', as Justin Neuman suggests, 'as a heuristic device to help her understand her own ethical place within a disintegrating apartheid system'.[27] Yet she also recovers *from* this breakdown a secular address to the soul that elevates her letter, turning it into something other than an empirical record of the brutal system she witnesses in horror. Voicing Coetzee's 'farewell' to the requirements of moral and social relevancy,[28] *Age of Iron*'s 'uncontestable lyricism', as critics have appreciated, 'cuts against any reductive claims regarding its political realism'.[29] Stylistic felicity becomes in itself a form of resistance, carrying out Coetzee's own insistence that it's 'hard for fiction to be good fiction while it is in the service of something else'.[30]

Which by no means implies that the novel tries to cultivate a Flaubertian dependence upon nothing but its own style at the expense of social turmoil. Rather, Mrs Curren's elegiac address to an 'only child thousands of miles away' is as ethically ensnared as it is rhetorically energized by her witnessing the nation's ravaging 'time out of time' (50):

> In every *you* that I pen love flickers and trembles like Saint Elmo's fire; you are with me not as you are today in America, not as you were when you left, but as you are in some deeper and unchanging form: as the beloved, as that which does not die. It is the soul of you that I address, as it is the soul of me that will be left with you when this letter is over. Like a moth from its case emerging, fanning its wings: that is what, reading, I hope you will glimpse: my soul readying itself for further flight. (129)

The repeated pronoun 'you' builds into a reparative refrain about her daughter's 'unchanging form', a form preserved in the present tense, then perpetuated, with the help of auxiliary verbs, in future predictions. Writing in this vision reaches beyond physical oblivion, towards a daughter who appears (as Mrs Curren will too) not as she was but as she might spiritually remain. This prophetic succour is amplified through analogy, as she pictures the letter's provenance as a moth-like soul, 'glimpse[d]' and retained even when her daughter's reading of it 'is over'. For Mrs Curren sounds adamant, wishfully so, about her daughter's immutability, insisting 'you are' 'not as you were' but 'as that which does not die'. The punctuation, too, heightens the denotative character of what is otherwise a conjectural sequence of claims. Each colon signals the cementing of the image or action that follows on from it in an elaborating clause: the daughter *will* remain 'the beloved'; Mrs Curren's soul *is* something she 'hope[s]' her daughter '*will* glimpse' in the warp and weft of the letter. Colons typically prepare us for further information, of course, opening catalogues with consecutive definitions or qualifications. Here they visibly distinguish and affirm Mrs Curren's restitutive, if perhaps futile, prospect of love's legacy inscribed by the 'ghostly passage' of her own 'pen', projecting an era that could be better equipped in 'trying to keep a soul alive in times not hospitable to the soul' (130).

Given that the present appears so eviscerated of hope, Mrs Curren's letter is a farewell note—a secondary, negative eulogy—to an era 'heaved up out of the earth, misbegotten, monstrous', whose 'age of iron', as she calls it, has remained an unrelieved 'nightmare from beginning to end' (50, 51). Religion can supply few consolations for the country's social calamities, in her view, since the violence reflects only the 'spirit of Geneva triumphant in Africa. Calvin, black-robed, thin-blooded, forever cold, rubbing his hands in the afterworld, smiling his wintry smile. Calvin victorious, reborn in the dogmatists and witch-hunters of both armies' (51). This implied compatibility, even mutual support, between Calvinism and apartheid rule has been debated by scholars concerned with the political appropriation of faith in South Africa. On the one hand, the increasing 'ideological support provided by right-wing Christians from the United States was welcomed by the National Party regime which', as David Chidester observes, 'was attempting to maintain the apartheid system of racist oppression'.[31] During the 1970s, the 'Dutch reformed churches supported segregation', and while 'English-speaking churches', notes Peter Walshe, openly 'condemned apartheid at annual conferences', in actuality they remained 'part of the racially oppressive system'.[32] But after the social uprisings of the mid-1980s onwards, the context from which *Age of Iron* emerges, 'prophetic Christianity became more articulate and more broadly based in its support of the liberation struggle', resulting in 'a sharp escalation in the confrontation between activist Christians and the apartheid state'.[33]

Coetzee is more steadfastly bleak about the toxic affinities between Church and State. Calvin looms in this novel as the grim reaper whose dictates ironically underlie 'both armies', reconciling them only insofar as they share unyielding and dogmatic commitments to violence. Yet this portrait is perhaps intended to be less an accurate diagnosis of Christianity's position on government-sanctioned oppression in this State of Emergency than a symptom of Mrs Curren's own ascendant faith in a 'secular maze', as Dominic Head calls it, into which her language has so purposefully wandered.[34] As a medium for agnostic confession, the letter itself 'has become a maze, and I a dog in the maze', so that although God 'is looking for me... he cannot reach me. God is another dog in another maze' (137–8). Ultimately, it's not the afterlife that appeals but a rather more ascetic notion that the physical world—with her words on the physical page of a letter bound for an uncertain destination—will continue without her. This 'would keep her going, in a manner of speaking, after she was dead', notes Coetzee, in some of his earliest fragments for the novel in preparation: 'The world would go on, as huge and heavy and clumsy and complicated as ever; the world would never, for all practical purposes, cease; and that would be a great consolation to her.'[35]

As it turns out, though, there is a more unlikely, domestically discrepant source of solace to hand. For if theological aid isn't something Mrs Curren foresees or even desires in an age 'not hospitable to the soul', then hospitality is nonetheless what

Mrs Curren in the end receives. The homeless man, Vercueil, on whom she has become increasingly reliant, becomes her final 'carer' and dubious condoler. Events surrounding this unexpected relationship are quite delicately choreographed, albeit disturbingly so. What's unsettling is the way Coetzee's spare, declarative present tense enables prosody to confront plot, as though rhythm itself initiates its own risky form of redress. 'Now I put my life in his hands instead', she confides: 'This is my life, these words, these tracings of the movements of crabbed digits over the page. These words, as you read them, if you read them, enter you and draw breath again. They are, if you like, my way of living on' (131). The robust alternation of iambic and anapaestic phrases here counterweigh her seemingly exhausted self-surrender to Vercueil, their pressing rhythm complementing her investment in words as tools of spiritual continuity. Metre itself shifts athwart the imminence of her ultimate diminishment. Although they're mere 'tracings' and 'crabbed digits', her phrases survive through their very tempo of enunciation: the surefooted vigour of her final belief that 'they *are*, if you *like*, my *way* of *liv*ing *on*' carries out the promised endurance they declare.[36] In circumstances where solace seems unlikely if not desperate, narrative's rhythmical 'movements' offer signs that the graphic action of writing has alone become a consoling venture of self-preservation.

Though seemingly implausible, the sustenance Mrs Curren finds in Vercueil as an unreliable chaperone for her final days affects the very structure of her explanations, which successively counterpoint each other: 'I give my life to Vercueil to carry over. I trust Vercueil because I do not trust Vercueil. I love him because I do not love him. Because he is the weak reed I lean upon him' (131). By moving the conjunction to the head of the clause in that final sentence, Coetzee shifts the register from self-disputing justifications, towards a firmer acceptance of Vercueil's dependability as Mrs Curren's 'weak reed'. Beyond her uncertain stating and negating of 'love' and 'trust', Vercueil is nothing other than what he is—and, in the end, becomes the subject of her conviction: 'When it comes to last things, I no longer doubt him in any way. There has always been in him a certain hovering if undependable solicitude for me, a solicitude he knows no way of expressing. I have fallen and he has caught me' (196).[37] 'Solicitude' comes from the Latin *sollicitudo*, from *sollicitus*, which itself is linked to 'solicit' from the Latin *sollicitare*: to agitate. *Concern* thus coincides with 'hovering' *agitation*, something manifested in Vercueil's own bouts of irritability and self-destructive inebriation. By characterizing Vercueil's 'solicitude' as 'hovering if undependable', Coetzee redoubles Mrs Curren's earlier image of him as a 'weak reed' that she must somehow depend on—present yet mutable. Vulnerable in his own disquiet, the 'solicitude' Vercueil is barely able to communicate cannot be self-administered either. That he is deprived of the very solace he seems unexpectedly though still unreliably to supply is something Mrs Curren recognizes in the mutual company they keep:

> I need his presence, his comfort, his help, but he needs help too.... He does not know how to love. I speak not of the motions of the soul but of something simpler. He does not know how to love as a boy does not know how to love.... The nearer the end comes, the more faithful he is. Yet still I have to guide his hand. (196)

Clutching at the 'comfort' Vercueil habitually conceals, she becomes attuned to a concern 'he knows no way of expressing'.[38] At the same time, she elegizes Vercueil's untimely return to pubescence through a touching, forgiving analogy—mourning his arrested development in ways that momentarily stave off her own physical demise. As the novel's unforeseen agent of belated assuagement, she is compelled 'to guide his hand'. Knowing there is little more than this, that there is little left, she stands as witness, *through* the process of writing, to a bare act of faith that may or may not be reciprocated.

Improbably consoling is Vercueil's final, foreboding embrace; yet it does nothing if not allay utter loneliness. Whatever its haptic inadequacy, the 'mighty force' of this macabre gesture remains (198). Even as it abruptly heralds the novel's termination, the tableau of this enclasped couple resonates on, as elegiac laments are traditionally supposed to do for the living. An image of entwinement set against a 'landscape of violence', it avers futility yet commemorates improbable intimacy, thereby presenting a visual correlative for the discrepant consolations that punctuate this novel's language.

COETZEE'S MOTILE SOULS

Both 'chaste and lyrical without being self-conscious': though Paul Bailey could well have been talking about *Age of Iron*, this was his critical assessment a decade on of *Disgrace*. He deemed it 'quietly stylish',[39] a phrase that nicely captures the *frictional* priorities of Coetzee's prose: verbally bridled yet affectively potent, unembellished yet athletic, it displays a knack for what we might call virtuosic restraint. This makes the agility with which Coetzee dissents from what he saw in the 1970s as the consolatory accessories adjectival enrichment and lyrical ornament sound like a performative contradiction—an exhibition of dexterity that his own sense of economy seems otherwise to dispel. But this paradox has itself remained remarkably generative for this fiction. And also for his audience. Coetzee's style summons us into what can seem like an oddly conflictive aesthetic, where ethical ambitions find expression in a language that often behaves with the utmost reticence, the philosophical gravity of thematic concerns dovetailing with formal self-denial. In fact, one could say that his writing has it both ways: avoiding overexertion without dispensing with vivid symbolism; chiselling itself down to the barest components while still showcasing the rhythmic potential of grammatically simple sentences; finding in the very 'barrenness of narrative', to use Coetzee's own terms, an unlikely sense of melody and 'inspiration'.[40]

However self-monitoring it can feel, then, Coetzee's style by no means forgoes the very finesse which had piqued some suspicion in his early scholarship on Beckett. And by the time he reached *Disgrace*, 'the grace of language' was clearly surviving his idiosyncratic self-control. Rare though they remain in the fabric of this novel's tightly executed use of free indirect discourse—focalized as it is by David Lurie's taut, lacerating self-examinations—intermittent moments of pellucid, even euphonious expressivity play a dramatic role in their own right. As we have seen in *Age of*

Iron, rhetorical elegance often coincides with heightened episodes of self-scrutiny, as though the sustained verve of Coetzee's narration serves as a barometer of ethical conscience—a stylistic correlative for the unabated experience of disgrace. But in his 1999 novel of that name, a certain discrepancy emerges between what style affectively does and the situations it conveys, when Coetzee's orchestration of uncommonly melodic moments entangle shame with the incipient prospect of solace, even as he blocks Lurie's access to moral or spiritual rehabilitation. Moreover, we'll discover that the consolatory 'language of the soul', familiar from *Age of Iron*, resurfaces in *Disgrace*, revealing a correspondence between these novels that speaks to what Jarad Zimbler calls Coetzee's transition from a 'concern with the bareness of life to a concern with how this bareness might be remedied'.[41]

As someone for whom shame has become a whole way of being, Lurie is beset by 'listlessness, indifference', along with the sensation that 'he has been eaten away from inside and only the eroded shell of his heart remains'.[42] Such feelings of evisceration find their earliest incarnations in Coetzee's rough notes for *Boyhood* (1997), where he pictures a figure 'in bed thinking not who he is but what will be left of him when everything else is taken away'.[43] This sense of evacuation will later beset Lurie, too; with his professional life in tatters, stripped of respect, he confronts what remains without expectation of reprieve. Indeed, he views with some scepticism the solacing possibility of ever describing his condition otherwise, wondering whether 'a man in this state' could 'find words' to offset 'the feeling wash[ing] over him', let alone 'find music that will bring back the dead' (156). We have to wait until the final pages of *Disgrace* to discover what Coetzee will do to redress Lurie's ignominy even as the novel clearly denies him any redemption—its plot of ripening shame defying, structurally, any resolving arc of successful penitence. The scenario in question does grant for a time some respite, as Lurie approaches his daughter unawares as she works on her plot:

> Softly he speaks her name. 'Lucy!'
> She does not hear him.
> What will it entail, being a grandfather? As a father he has not been much of a success, despite trying harder than most. As a grandfather he will probably score lower than average too. He lacks the virtues of the old: equanimity, kindliness, patience. But perhaps those virtues will come as other virtues go: the virtue of passion, for instance. He must have a look again at Victor Hugo. Poet of grandfatherhood. There may be things to learn.
> The wind drops. There is a moment of utter stillness which he would wish prolonged for ever: the gentle sun, the stillness of mid-afternoon, bees busy in a field of flowers; and at the centre of the picture a young woman, *das ewig Weibliche*, lightly pregnant, in a straw sunhat. A scene ready-made for a Sargent or a Bonnard. City boys like him; but even city boys can recognize beauty when they see it, can have their breath taken away. (217–18)

This crystalline episode embalms a 'moment of utter stillness', introducing a hiatus that feels all the more fugacious ahead of the imminent close, where Lurie will solemnly give over to lethal injection the 'young dog' 'who likes music' and for whom he has developed special affection (219). At first sight, the scene's language here seems simple enough, almost conspicuously so. Succinct phrases preview the 'functional, even minimalist' realism of Coetzee's later Australian fictions whose idiom, as Elleke Boehmer notes, is even more 'stripped-down', occasionally 'less-than-literary', if not 'perfunctory'.[44] By specifying the moment's discrete components, Coetzee's descriptions do appear quite workaday (what could be more clichéd, arguably, than picturing bees as *busy?*); and while 'stillness' isn't an easy noun to replace, its repetition evinces his typical refusal of elegant variation. At the same time, however, the episode's alliteration (*sun, stillness, field, flowers*) counterbalances this undecorated depiction of scenic elements, as though style acoustically compensates for its own frugal diction—recouping in enunciation what's withheld in vocabulary. In one sense, then, Coetzee's straightforward wording is thoroughly apposite for the 'ready-made' appeal of this scene, which in its combination of figure, landscape, and light sits (for Lurie in any case) somewhere between Sargent's realist portraiture and Bonnard's post-Impressionism,[45] a scene that teeters, admittedly, on the brink of essentialism when Lurie aligns Lucy by allusion with that Goethean trope of the 'eternal feminine'. Despite this proclivity for wistful romanticization, style rescues the moment, and Lurie with it, from irredeemable objectification. Animating sibilance allows his envisioned state of grandfatherly tenderness to gain some level of credence in this present instant, as it connects across phrases 'kindliness' with 'stillness', thereby linking an alternative way of being—a last chance in life to act otherwise—with his surrender to what he now sees. Lexically spare yet also euphonic: what seem like contrary properties of language may also be its dramatic charge, precisely because they also define the extent to which expression flexes here its own capacity for consolation. Style's cushioning acoustics thus have a plot of their own to impart, not a plot of redemption (few readers would expect Coetzee to grant such amnesty to someone who has behaved so unconscionably), but one in which amplified sibilance yields just as it audibly mirrors the possibility of self-effacing 'kindliness', when the awed 'city boy' replaces himself with Lucy 'at the centre of the picture'.

Is this a perversely affirmative reading, all too enthused by spotting a level of sonic springiness normally screened by Coetzee's sparseness, a reading that asks us to acknowledge, against our better judgment, that his seemingly stern frugality can also curate its own remedial effulgence? Probably. And however consolingly eloquent its depiction, the stilling 'moment' inevitably doesn't fulfil Lurie's 'wish' that it be 'prolonged'. As a unit of pause, this painterly scene might appear lightening when set against *Disgrace*'s prevailing backdrop of jeopardy and dereliction. But in the context of what's left to come, this instant—an ordinary encounter that leads to Lucy welcoming her father afresh, as if this represented a 'visitation' for Lurie, 'a new footing, a new start' (218)—anticipates the entirely more sorrowful 'moment when, bewilderingly,' the dog's 'legs buckle' (219). Thanks to their striking proximity in textual space, these affectively contrasting moments perform through their juxtaposition the successive inscription and effacement of solace that the novel enacts throughout.

Throughout this sequence, Coetzee tolerates qualities of expression he once collapsed with suspicion into the work of 'style as redemption', a permissiveness that reveals something about the journey his writing has made from repelling style's consolatory efficacy outright to viewing it as one of fiction's ethical nodes. That journey is also part of his broader 'movement away from the precipice of late modernism', as Zimbler puts it, 'or at least the radical aesthetics' of Beckett, who became as we know a lodestone for Coetzee's early opposition to literary solace. In its closing stages, *Disgrace* movingly brings that movement to fruition. Here narrative discourse appears 'to signal an acceptance, perhaps reluctant, of the process of naming' rather than dispelling the operation of redress on which its irrepressible lyricism is borne.[46] Against the emotive pressure of the novel's ending—as I will unpack now in some detail—Coetzee asserts style's critical potential for contemplating the solace it insinuates.

To do this, Coetzee introduces two vocabularies, spiritual and material, which compete for attention. Refracting these distinct positions, the image of a 'soul' modulates in such a way that unsettles the narration's implied provenance. For as it 'hangs about in the air, twisting and contorting' (219), the soul sets in motion an alternation between theological and pathological lexicons. Familiar from *Age of Iron*, of course, and Mrs Curren's contemplation there of her soul preparing itself for flight ahead of the body's oblivion, the trope returns in *Disgrace* to flag internal discrepancies in the language of its climax. What appears at first to operate as free indirect style contains descriptive inconsistencies that imply another presence, another voice shadowing Lurie's consciousness. And those inconsistencies are nowhere more revealing than in the motivic handling of the spirit. Initially, it is figured in olfactory terms: inside a veterinary 'room' where 'something unmentionable' is performed, Lurie detects 'the smell of expiration, the soft, short smell of the released soul' (219). But as the focus turns to the euthanizing procedure itself, the diction becomes more violently compulsory. No longer seen as involuntarily seeping out into the ether, 'the soul is yanked out of the body' (219), a verb—deriving from late eighteenth-century Scots, meaning a 'sudden sharp blow' (*OED*)—that starkly reinforces the combination of functionality and violation in a procedure that has become routine for Lurie after volunteering at Bev Shaw's animal hospice.

Prototype reactions to that functionalism appear in Coetzee's 1997 notes to the novel, where Lurie 'reflects that animals can teach us how to endure pain and how to die', a training in mortality degraded by the hospice's 'instantaneous deaths', which Lurie finds 'disappointing'.[47] This disappointment doesn't quite survive in the published novel as an overriding mood. Neither heightened into sorrow nor flattened into dejection, Lurie's responses to the transubstantiating moment where buckling dogs emit writhing spirits seem to shift incrementally, conveyed by a narrative voice whose implied position and perspective adjust unpredictably in kind. Perspectival manipulations become more complex still when, amid the soul's agonizing contortions, we're directed to the blank presence of the room where it all happens. Lurie imagines how unfathomable this terminus would appear to the dog; somewhere that 'will be beyond him', this apparently 'ordinary room' denotes less a place than 'a hole where one leaks out of existence' (219). That last verb only adds to the enigmatic layering of alternative figurations of the soul (from releasing to yanking to leaking), a succession of not altogether compatible images for the same soul, which introduces an ambivalent gap between the narration's diction and its (sporadically) focalizing subject. For it's as though Lurie's observations don't quite 'own' the imagery that accompanies them to a degree that would suggest that their vocabulary is consistently inflected by his mentation. Perhaps the resulting sense of detachment is perfectly apt, however: Coetzee's retraction of the sort of emotional intimacy and psychological ventriloquism we associate with free indirect style may itself be read as a formal equivalent to Lurie's own growing sense of emotional self-deletion, of inconsequentiality. In a 1998 draft, for instance, he decides that 'what goes on in his heart will be of the utmost irrelevance' when bearing the corpse of his befriended dog to the incinerator.[48] Yet surely it couldn't be *more* relevant to *Disgrace*'s reader at this point. Moreover, Coetzee's deletion of that draft sentence suggests he wanted to retain the possibility of conveying—from a distance, without the penetration of internal focalization—how relevantly heartfelt, how *in*consolable, the act of giving up this dog will remain for Lurie, even as he distances himself emotionally from that duty by recognizing its inevitability.

Coetzee's motile perspective on the soul thus embodies through its oscillation between impersonal exteriority and genuine pathos the unsustainable 'irrelevance' of Lurie's 'heart' to an undertaking that clearly disturbs him—a ritual whose routine is far from spiritually serene. Although the diction that apostrophizes the dog's soul morphs in ways that disclose a distinct voice in play with the freedom to inhabit Lurie's interiority and to depart from it at will, by the same token Coetzee's language stays just close enough to Lurie's impressions to suggest that this is hardly a dispassionate task either, a task for which he seeks some consolatory rationale in a selfless, unsentimental ethic of justified 'care'. A 1997 note offers an additional means of construing this curious narratorial externalism, where Coetzee sketches Lurie's shift into objectifying self-scrutiny: 'For the first time in his life he stands outside himself watching "himself"', so that consequently, and again '[f]or the first time', 'his thoughts and activities do not interest him. It cannot be a coincidence— it must be that the soul is making its first stirrings as it begins to leave the body.'[49] Paradoxically, then, what Peter D. McDonald calls the 'oddly self-cancelling status' of Coetzee's free indirect style entirely befits *Disgrace*'s portrayal of a protagonist who feels increasingly detached from if not indifferent to himself, and who has little interest by the end in discovering whether he can find solace before his own soul disembarks.[50]

Coetzee's fascination with a soul that's itching to depart evidently endured, even if in the finished novel he transferred those 'stirrings' to the dog Lurie grows to love and whom he's obliged to destroy. As we have seen, *Disgrace* seesaws between the violence of a forcibly released soul and the painfully consoling vindication of euthanizing welfare, the palpable effects of which are not only manifested in the forlorn action of these closing pages but also enacted at the level of narrative discourse. From initially releasing the spirit and affirming Lurie's actions for the dogs as beneficent, Coetzee then undercuts his concluding anthem to unshackled souls by leading us full circle—back to the disconsolate actuality of Lurie's prosaic drill, one that will require him to 'wheel the bag into the flames and see that it is burnt,

burnt up' (220). Rather than categorically resisting the consolatory effects of expressive grace (as his younger writing self might have wanted), Coetzee's insinuation of and serial interference with free indirect discourse therefore provides a stylistic counterpart to the successive emergence and truncation of consolation across this novel of circumscribed reprieve. With these granular effects, *Disgrace* dramatically imparts and formally instantiates the fitful availability of the 'less than little' solace Lurie already assumes he doesn't deserve (220).

Adjacent scenes therefore distil towards the close acts of care and ethical accountability that can't exactly be correlated but do at least bring into alignment the demand for unqualified compassion Lurie confronts. Facing the prospect of reconciling himself to Lucy's decision to bear her rapist's child, he will as an extension of this selflessness 'do all' for his favourite dog 'when his time comes', ministering to his death and disposal (219). In promising simply to 'whisper to him and support him in the moment' (219), Lurie abjures the self-satisfying prospect of his own heroic benevolence, knowing only that this end-of-life attentiveness to the dog 'will be little enough', indeed 'nothing' (220). If feelings of incipient renewal and sudden rapture frame Lurie's 'visitation' with Lucy and temporarily console him, then structurally the novel has other plans: Coetzee counterpoises Lurie's breathtaking recognition of sun-splashed 'beauty' with the subsequently piteous image of him '[b]earing' the dog 'in his arms like a lamb' (220).

By turns engrossingly lyrical and shot-through with sadness, such moments can appear 'lushly autumnal yet edged with irony' (181), to borrow Lurie's description of the kind of harmonies he envisages for his Byron opera. From this it would be tempting to draw a musical analogue for Coetzee's own narration, which does indeed feel fringed by a certain ironic awareness of its own affecting strategies, a rueful awareness of the costs of indulging that 'religion of style'. Lurie himself, of course, turns autumnally self-ironic as *Disgrace* progresses, savagely so when it comes to providing mocking metaphors for his own 'grey mood' (107): 'He has a sense that, inside him, a vital organ has been bruised, abused—perhaps even his heart. For the first time he has a taste of what it will be like to be an old man, tired to the bone, without hopes, without desires, indifferent to the future' (107). The denigrations that accompany such irony are yet another feature of Coetzee's interruptions of free indirect discourse: by insinuating some distance between narration and subject, he decouples style from focalizing sensibility in ways that allow him to parody the neo-Romantic idiom of Lurie's self-presentation. This strategy does nothing to mar the novel's culminating poignancy, as we saw above; but it's deployed for critical as much as moving ends, as Coetzee imitates the discourse of someone who has imbibed the lessons of European Romanticism. Even at the end—and for all his self-irony—Lurie's reactions are couched in a vocabulary of divinity in nature, and we're invited to detect there a wry pastiche of the way he exalts an autonomous, creatively shape-shifting, ascending spirit. If *Disgrace* provokes competing responses as a result, their competition doesn't have to be resolved. Ironic scrutiny and emotional sincerity can often present themselves as two sides of the same stylistic coin. Nonetheless, in Coetzee's potentially consoling, potentially parodic final pages, the reader confronts the option of becoming at least two readers. In the event that we end up feeling both harrowed and wary, compelled and suspicious, *Disgrace* prompts us to track how affective representation manipulates degrees of critical involvement. Unsettling though this remains, Coetzee's multiplying levels of the readerly solicitation are in themselves a foundation for examining what it means for a text to conjure, contest, and not entirely outlaw consolation in moments that seem anathema to its acceptability.

SAD MIRACLES

Interpretive discrepancies are all the more appropriate, in their own way, given that Coetzee's style is not only concerned with representation but also with argument. Style functioning as a kind of argumentation, a medium for reckoning with the very aesthetic compensations it insinuates, is something we have seen throughout this book, first in the modernist lineaments of McEwan and most recently in the scrupulous leanness of Tóibín. In Coetzee's case, style's inquisitional energy generates its very own creed of thrifty beauty. Even in moments of burgeoning irony, where characters' behaviours are dissected as stringently as Coetzee has dissected fiction's pretensions to redemption, style acquires irrepressible articulacy—dare we say, a type of grace. Episodes of 'searing self-interrogation', as Carrol Clarkson has noted, tend to spur rather than stall Coetzee's 'critical and creative acuity' as a writer and thinker.[51] So too those moments in his fiction kindled by shame, by the recognition of irremediable limitation, or by intimations of personal redundancy, tend also to be moments of linguistic brilliance, whose own creative acuity lies in their equivocation over the aesthetic redress such language affords. In this way, Coetzee's style registers without succumbing to the vexed implications of its own consolatory capabilities.

Out of this eagled-eyed yet enriching aesthetic, where self-scrutiny equals replenishment, comes a lesson for the reader. Which is surely no surprise, for Gayatri Spivak is right to say that in Coetzee's work we invariably find ourselves 'learning how to "read" '.[52] And among the lessons is this. No doubt there's some critical satisfaction to be had in entertaining Coetzee as a stern gatekeeper of his own panache, who refuses in advance the artistic temptations he knows all too well, forestalling the phenomenal pleasures of form by substituting austerity for sublimity. In practice, his language doesn't always behave in this manner, as the carefully paced, heightened sequences from *Age of Iron* and *Disgrace* have attested here. Perhaps Coetzee was unable, over time, to measure up to that steely repudiation of 'style as redemption' he once applauded in Beckett. For as we have seen, linguistic grace is everywhere apparent—or at least forever standing by, poised for the appropriate cue—even in narratives backlit by historical trauma or imminent loss whose plots unwind beyond rescue. Where and when these moments of ambivalent grace will turn up is often hard to foresee, and their unpredictability adds to the challenge of dealing with Coetzee's limber yet razor-edged prose as it drills deep into the grammar of moods that look to be self-evident.

Assumptions about consolation's self-evidence in secular and religious discourses are Marilynne Robinson's quarry as well. 'We have forgotten solace', she writes, forgotten, that is, how to distinguish it from the provision of soothing remedies that shield us from sadness. With the help of a seemingly counterintuitive proposition, Robinson wonders whether '[m]aybe the saddest family, properly understood, is a miracle of solace'.[53] She suggests that 'our multitude of professional healers and comforters are really meant to function like the doctor in a boxer's corner', intervening merely 'to slow bleeding and minimize swelling so that we will be able to last another round'. Assuaging rather than confronting the true emotional substance and implications of damage, '[n]either they nor we want to think about the larger meaning of the situation. This is the opposite of solace.'[54]

The novel form has been for Robinson, of course, the choice medium for thinking imaginatively about this larger 'situation' for consolation, even against the backdrop of the 'saddest' of prospects. And in her critical writing, she smuggles in a fictional scenario to reinforce what solace might actually (rather than superficially) mean:

> Imagine that someone failed and disgraced came back to his family, and they grieved with him, and took his sadness upon themselves, and sat down together to ponder the deep mysteries of human life. This is more human and beautiful, I propose, even if it yields no dulling of pain, no patching of injuries. Perhaps it is the calling of some families to console, because intractable grief is visited upon them.[55]

Consolation in spite of, because of, grief's intractability; to console *through* the adoption of sadness, not simply by smoothing it away—these are occasions for discrepant solace that Robinson asks us to hypothesize. Here the familial scenario she proposes is one her readers will recognize. First given as an address to the National Book Foundation and subsequently collected in a 1998 volume of essays, this essay offers a précis for the 'calling' to console that would later become the pivotal circumstances of *Home* (2008), Robinson's second instalment in a series of linked novels beginning with the Pulitzer Prize-winning *Gilead* in 2004. In this case, Jack is the 'failed and disgraced' son who returns to the family property in Gilead where his aging father, Reverend Robert Boughton, grows weaker by the day. Although he was always his father's favourite and remains the child Boughton will still forgive, Jack struggles to bear the weight of disappointment and continues to battle a lifelong habit of self-destruction. His sister Glory, now living at home in her late thirties after a failed relationship, tries to take upon herself the insurmountable labour of allaying his sadness and chronic self-persecution. But Jack opens up only so far. And although he's an atheist, Jack's true source of solace—the person with whom he can genuinely 'ponder the deep mysteries of human life'— turns out to be Boughton's close friend and fellow minister John Ames. In a series of encounters that become as tense as they are touching, Ames tries, with myriad reservations, to unburden Jack of crippling shame without presuming to suture his moral injuries.

The historical moment to which *Gilead* and *Home* belong coincides with the Montgomery bus boycott in 1957. Gilead's racially uniform population remains self-enclosed, ignorant of the tortuous progress of contemporary civil rights. Jack himself ciphers the indefensibility of the town's disengagement in the earlier novel through climactic disclosures to Ames: knowledge of Jack's common-law marriage to the African-American Della, from whom he's forced to remain separated, intensifies Ames's inner conflict over whether he should forgive him. Ames knows that this troubled man's alienation will only be compounded by the racial prejudices of old Boughton, whose provincial bigotry remains endemic in the town at large. As I want to show over the coming pages, that conflict forms an intellectually and affectively turbulent counterpoint to the composed, sorrowful grace of *Gilead*'s language as a self-consoling education for Ames in untying his attachments to life.

Now in his seventies, Ames writes out daily observations and recollections not knowing how they might necessarily end but hoping they will later be given to his boy, Robby, the son he will never see as a man. Time once again is no healer here. But Ames's sense that he's reached a state of joy all too late doesn't make him regret meeting his wife, Lila, in old age; instead, the very fact that he did so has 'enlarged' his 'understanding of hope, just to know that such a transformation can occur'.[56] Marrying unexpectedly, bringing Robby into the world: these events, Ames reflects, have 'greatly sweetened my imagination of death, odd as that may sound' (231). That he recognizes and takes solace in these gifts motivates his preparation for their oncoming loss. In light of this, his feelings for Lila have amounted to 'a foretaste of death, at least of dying', not that this would 'seem strange' to Ames, given that '"Passion" is the word we use, after all' (233).

Gilead thus extends the novelistic subgenre we have been considering here, in which the anticipation of death is integrated with reflections, predictions, hopes, and instructions intended for surviving loved ones. Like Mrs Curren's daughter, Robby is the subject of adoration in a eulogy written by—rather than for—the one who's dying, a eulogy compelled by foreknowledge presently concealed from its own addressee. In years to come, Robby will also be the recipient of a prophetic sort of gift, as Ames distils adult wisdom for a son who has yet to reach adulthood. With its microscopic attention to Ames's interiority as an ordinary preacher with an extraordinarily rich history to impart, *Gilead* 'enacts a Protestant understanding of inner life', as Amy Hungerford calls it, such that both 'thematically and narratively' the novel animates the 'mental discourse of religious persons while also spinning stories that situate those persons within religious life'.[57] Writing this self-documentary—ahead of his own absence and across time to his son's future self—is seen as synonymous with praying, but without guarantees: 'You can feel that you are with someone. I feel I am with you now, whatever that can mean, considering that you're only a little fellow now and when you're a man you might find these letters of no interest' (21–22).

If Ames finds solace in directing stories of himself into the future, then in doing so he has to tolerate poignant, inevitably sombre qualifications. For one thing, he's mindful of the respite they offer as a personal record, watchful of how elegizing his own lack of remaining time can itself be self-appeasing and therefore in tension with his narrative's overarching motive as a gift for his son rather than an immediate salve for himself. Furthermore, faith itself isn't always straightforwardly consoling.

As Laura Tanner points out, though undoubtedly Ames's 'belief in spiritual existence after death mitigates, to some extent, the tragedy of mortality, it also contributes to his tendency to anticipate his embodied absence', thereby intensifying 'the imaginative work' of 'anticipating a world without him in it'.[58] Comfort in *Gilead*—whether through immediate, worldly acts of care or through the prospect of 'looking back from the grave' (141)—is rarely welcomed complacently. The novel follows Robinson's suggestion that '[i]t may be necessary to offer ourselves palliatives, but it is drastically wrong to offer or to accept a palliative as if it were a cure':[59] accordingly, Ames considers solitude the best 'balm for loneliness' and maintains that 'I've spent a good share of my life comforting the afflicted, but I could never endure the thought that anyone should try to comfort me' (21, 45–6). Even the 'genre' that comprises Ames's dual-pronged diary of recollection and oncoming death displaces him from consolation's sights, as the 'journal that would serve as a stay against absence', notes Tanner, 'both represents and enacts the way that old age propels Ames into the margins of the lived world, positioning him as an observer'; perched increasingly on the sidelines, Ames 'watches and records from a position of embodied invisibility a kind of voyeuristic experience of his own anticipated loss'.[60] So, if neither recalling the past nor making ready for the future make up for the unavoidable fact that Ames has become 'so damn old', as Lila fondly puts it, just when he's surrounded by the wife and child he has always hoped for (58), then what modicum of solace in expectation of dying does *Gilead* invite us to entertain?

For her part, Robinson thinks that any consolation is hard won. And her argumentative, often-polemical essays on theological principles and doctrinal histories offer one way of making sense of *Gilead*'s exacting portrait of solace 'shadowed by the consciousness of loss'—a portrait whose presentation sustains its own religion of exquisite style.[61] With clear misgivings towards the remedial patches of 'professional healers', Robinson has taken up the rather formidable task of reviving public interest in Calvinism, a strand of Christianity whose consolations might seem few and far between. Her fiction too defends the pertinence of Calvin's commentaries for contemporary audiences, offering narratives of belief that translate religion into what she calls a 'language of orientation that presents itself as a series of questions'.[62] Austere though it appears by reputation, Calvinism's 'ethic of radical open-handedness' is the lesson Robinson advances, an ethic for which solace entails a commitment to the 'requirement of generosity' towards others.[63] She quotes Calvin himself as advising that insofar as 'every man knoweth the particular needs of his neighbours, so let him endeavour to succour them'.[64] As we have heard, Ames won't countenance the idea that others ought to comfort him, even as his congregation notices his ailing health. In place of such predictable reasons for giving and receiving comfort, Ames seems more concerned with the idea of offering solace— even to neighbours like Jack of whom he is suspicious—in full knowledge of its indeterminate efficacy. Stimulating small acts of ministration beyond the church, these seemingly incidental episodes of contact and succour capture, Robinson argues, the way 'every human encounter' for Calvin is an exceptional 'moment', since 'the other in the encounter is always "sent" or "offered".'[65] To recognize the import of such encounters means cultivating ways of seeing the everyday world that are attuned to wonder. 'Ordinary things have always seemed more numinous to me', notes Robinson, affirming a Calvinist belief that 'you don't simply perceive something that is statically present, but in fact there is a visionary quality to it all'.[66] Perceiving life in these terms involves registering, as Ames himself puts it, 'something in kind but exceptional in degree' (32). At once uplifting and taxing, the rewards of perceptual alertness turn out to be as edifying as the effort is strenuous.

Ames thus serves as Robinson's model observer: alert to the solace of ordinary perception, he reminds us of how 'we forget to find value in the beauty of a thought'.[67] A custodian of quotidian marvels, Ames finds consolation in sheer astonishment at the 'physical particularity' of others (79). Discerning delicate actions, atmospheres, moods, and movements in the fabric of the everyday constitutes, for Robinson, 'not a report on reality' but 'the primary locus of reality itself'.[68] Ames is indeed frequently consoled by feeling his way into the very 'essence of perception', as she calls it,[69] an essence for which *Gilead*'s narration becomes an exquisitely lyrical analogue. 'Existence' alone appears to Ames 'now the most remarkable thing that could ever be imagined', knowing that he's 'about to put on imperishability' (60). Of course, this cheering prospect of becoming 'imperishable' as Ames's son reads his letter in adulthood is conditional on losing the vitalizing, visionary capacity that perception itself enables—a paradox with considerable pathos. Tanner is right to note that '[e]ven as his heightened perception yields some compensation for abbreviated opportunity', the very 'surplus intensity of Ames's experience cannot be banked against the inevitable loss of embodied presence'.[70] However, this downplays the way such intensity is manifested as style, countering *through* the expressive force of description precisely that 'experience of an absence the imagination is powerless to forestall'.[71]

Ames might be existentially defenceless, in other words, but the novel stylistically isn't. To be sure, acquiescence often sabotages his moments of wonder, and Ames concedes that to feel 'more alive than I have ever been' is to realize that he 'cannot imagine not missing bitterly' the 'poor perishable world' he'll soon be leaving (60–1). However, if describing the exceptionality of what he sees escalates Ames's anticipation of losing it, then anticipation's sorrow is itself consoled by his foreknowledge of passing his descriptions on. In this respect, Robinson's style doesn't just heighten perception and the imminent tragedy of relinquishing sensory experience; it also hews from Ames's monologue, chaperoned as it is by grief, an alternative kind of inheritance, one that's less concerned with lessons on life than with preserving in limpid descriptions the solace of ordinary moments. As in the following scene, style safeguards the consolations of everyday details, which seem even more resplendent for appearing at first unremarkable:

> There's a shimmer on a child's hair, in the sunlight. There are rainbow colors in it, tiny, soft beams of just the same colors you can see in the dew sometimes. They're in the petals of flowers, and they're on a child's skin. Your hair is straight and dark, and your skin is very fair. I suppose you're not prettier than most children. You're just a nice-looking boy, a bit slight, well scrubbed and well mannered. All that is fine, but it's your existence I love you for, mainly. Existence seems to me now the most remarkable thing that could ever be imagined. (60)

Light's 'shimmer' finds its acoustic correlative in Ames's abundant alliteration, as the 'sunlight' is answered across the passage by adjectives (*soft, same*) and by the reiterated noun and principal focus of this sequence (*skin*). Delicately linking colours and textures from nature to body, it's a luminous sketch; yet for all the euphony and brimming affection, it's also a consciously simple one. With straightforward, unembellished observations ('They're in the petals of flowers, and they're on a child's skin') Ames records a happenstance glimpse of his boy's splendour, easily missed—and, for him, soon to be lost. Wonder, it would seem, coexists with ascendant mourning though somehow keeps its potentially crippling disposition at bay. Moreover, the consolation on this occasion isn't divine, something that style itself seems to disclose: a discrepancy emerges between the tender precision with which Ames evokes the immediate, physical world and the relative lack of verbal imagination prompted in subsequent lines by heaven's prospect, described there as 'a light better than any dream of mine' (60). Infinitely more uplifting than this speculation is the marvel of what he directly discerns, as the '[r]emarkable', 'well mannered' intricacy of Robby's 'existence' surpasses Ames's conjectures about the afterlife. And for now, the elegance with which that existence is expressed, the very fact that Ames feels that he can *give* it expression, makes the prevision of surrendering this spectacle of life more bearable.

It's not that these earthly pleasures of perception discount the more familiar consolations of celestial 'imperishability' in Robinson's imagination. Rather, depictions of wonderment, and the stylistic energy they supply *Gilead*, serve her mission to correct the largely negative opinion of Calvinism itself in contemporary culture. Despite the renowned severity of his doctrine, Calvin provides a 'model' of perception, argues Robinson, that 'allows for the mysteriousness of life', just as Ames here is consoled by the awe of noticing in the play of sunlight on skin something profoundly enigmatic about his child's ordinary yet radiant presence in the world.[72] Promoting mystery, then, just as Ames promotes the remarkable fact of existence, Robinson invites us to question 'the old faith that everything is in principle knowable or comprehensible by us', a faith in rational, scientific categorization for which 'mystery is banished'.[73] Wonder is a feeling that matures, she suggests, challenging a dominant supposition in secular culture that 'everything is explicable, that whatever has not been explained will be explained'.[74] By turning this feeling into a conviction as much as a consolation, Ames prepares Robby for future belief by suggesting that the effort to describe wonder may itself be one reason for believing at all.

GRACEFUL REMAINS

If his very attempt at evoking astonishment consoles Ames, demonstrating a faculty that he hopes to pass on, then its rewards are double-edged. For he accepts that our 'dream of life will end as dreams do end, abruptly and completely' (118); fascinated with nature, he accepts too that though 'this is all mere apparition compared to what awaits us', the world remains 'only lovelier for that' (65). Concessions here emphasize once more the poignancy of his imminent losses. Among them will be his very own dexterous talent for recognizing how 'the world is available to being seen', in Robinson's words, 'very differently from the way we ordinarily see it'.[75] Passing this aptitude on to Robby will be Ames's only recompense: his extended journal is also a lesson in how to perceive life's immanent mysteries, such that the text we read becomes the discursive consolation for what mortality asks Ames to give up. If eloquence, as Robinson has more recently implied, is synonymous with grace, then Ames's felicity in pondering the inexplicable captures in the novel's form her suggestions that grace might also 'include the fact that we have untried capacities to live richly in a universe of unfathomable interest, and that we can and do, amazingly, enhance its interest with the things we make'—things including the novel.[76]

Ames's account of delicate moments of astonishment dramatize his creator's own inclination 'to feel both intrigued and comforted by the thought of everything we do not know', an account that's gifted to his son in a way that offers its own solace as an enduring testimony.[77] To greet those moments in all their imponderability is to begin an additional apprenticeship in grace, beginning with acknowledging 'what a power you have to experience beyond anything you might ever actually need' (56). In these terms, Ames speaks again to Robinson's own thought about spirituality and subjectivity, representing for *Gilead* 'the solitary, perceiving and interpreting locus of anything that can be called experience'.[78] Bringing experience into close-up, Ames discovers a strange 'assurance' in visionary rumination, a consolation contained in the sensation that arrests him after visiting his grandfather's grave, reminiscent of 'those dreams where you're filled some extravagant feeling you might never have in life' irrespective of 'what it is, even guilt or dread' (55).

That Ames, facing death, discovers some solace in describing this 'extravagant feeling' anew makes him sound like an heir to Joseph Alleine: the seventeenth-century nonconformist pastor who vouched for an equally 'rapturous and ravishing sense of God's presence'. According to one recent scholar of English Calvinism, when Alleine exhibited piety it was 'joyous' rather than morose.[79] Alleine wrote his own premortem handbook, 'The Art of Dying Well', which became the preface to his volume *Remaines* from 1674. Offering a step by step guide to end-of-life self-care, he advises, '[i]n all your undertakings, let conscience have the crafting voice, ask counsel of it diligently, hear its rebukes patiently, thankfully, as a precious balm that will not break your heads'.[80] As someone who listens to inner 'grief, but never without comfort' and confronts his 'loneliness, but never without peace', Ames tunes in to the 'crafting voice' of his conscience, hoping that he will in fact be 'explained a little' by the will-be-posthumous narrative he's producing for Robby while he still can (81). Based on his tenth tip for dying well, Alleine would probably have commended Ames's chosen genre. 'Keep a Day book in your own hearts', suggests Alleine.[81] In modern parlance, a daybook is of course also a ledger for accounts: a means of taking account *of* oneself while accounting *for* oneself and for what will remain. In his own Alleine-style record of diurnal reflection and spiritual self-reckoning, Ames notes the strange solace that accompanies even memories of being 'back in hard times for a minute or two', because 'there's a sweetness in the experience which I don't understand' yet 'that only enhances the value of it' (109).

It's as though Ames finds consolation in knowing that 'there is always an inadequacy in argument about ultimate things' (203), and indeed his effort to map 'frontiers of the unsayable' has 'been among the true pleasures' of his preaching life (218). His failures of articulation emit their own consolatory testament to the way language allows him to confront the limits of knowledge while examining what exactly those limits of apprehension might mean; it is the ongoing, humbling, necessary *work* of apprehension, rather than the hope of bringing it fully to fruition in 'argument', which is consoling for Ames. At the same time, his address to that twinned problem of expression and comprehension, of 'the unsayable', is inevitably elegiac: all along he has 'meant to leave' Robby 'a reasonably candid testament to my better self', but 'it seems to me now that what you must see here is just an old man struggling with the difficulty of understanding what it is he's struggling with' (230). Difficulty lies at the heart of Ames's attitude towards fathoming divinity, and he does nothing to downplay perplexity when mapping for Robby the often-forbidding terrain of belief.

What counters this struggle for articulacy is, discrepantly enough, language itself. Lexically nimble and rhythmically effortless, Robinson's style retains a certain composure despite her narrator's claims about incomprehension. When Ames feels reassured by the bare 'idea of grace' as something that 'takes things down to essentials' (224), he becomes a conduit for Robinson's commitment—her own novelistic homage to Emily Dickinson's poetic economy—to 'stripping down' fiction 'to the essence of perception'.[82] Mark O'Connell echoes praise widely-held among Robinson's reviewers when he notes that the 'simple, unself-conscious beauty of these sentences are inseparable from, and equal to, the beauty they describe', so much so that her 'moral wisdom seems inseparable from her gifts as a prose writer'. Even as she brings these formal virtues to bear on situations scarred by intolerance, shame, or incomprehension, '[t]here is nothing fraudulent about her eloquence', argues O'Connell, 'nothing remotely shifty or meretricious about the beauty of her sentences'. Producing as Robinson does a voice that is 'at once sad and ecstatic',[83] this affective combination is nowhere more pronounced than when Ames acknowledges the fact that memory has no legacy of its own. Treasured past events have an afterlife that survives only as long as our mental archive: 'I wish I could leave you certain of the images in my mind, because they are so beautiful that I hate to think they will be extinguished when I am' (184).

For Ames, however, there's ultimately some solace in seeing memory as all the more wondrous for being so fragile. Recollections console when they confirm rather than smooth over the fact that 'this life has its own mortal loveliness' (184). In these instances, where the elegant description of what's about to be lost is offset against the acknowledgment of oncoming disappearance, Robinson's stylistic transcription of grace becomes all the more legible:

> Our dream of life will end as dreams do end, abruptly and completely, when the sun rises, when the light comes. And we will think, All that fear and all that grief were about nothing. But that cannot be true. I can't believe we will forget our sorrows altogether. That would mean forgetting that we had lived, humanly speaking. Sorrow seems to me to be a great part of the substance of human life. For example, at this very moment I feel a kind of loving grief for you as you read this, because I do not know

you, and because you have grown up fatherless, you poor child, lying on your belly in the sun with Soapy asleep on the small of your back. You are drawing those terrible little pictures that you will bring me to admire, and which I will admire because I have not the heart to say one word that you might remember against me. (118–119)

Initially the plain syntax here somewhat disguises Ames's elaborations in topic and tense, clause by clause. At first, he's in philosophical key, meditating on the importance of sorrow to the cumulative 'substance of human life'. But then he turns to the more immediate 'example' of his son, lying sunlit with the family cat, pinpointing Robby as a paragon of his 'loving grief'—a feeling equivalent indeed to Robinson's 'sad and ecstatic' form. Amid this direct and touching observation, Ames swerves momentarily again, into a more oracular idiom, glancing forward in a snippet of sadness at the adult Robby who 'will have grown up fatherless'. Returning to the present—or rather to events proximate to the present, an affectionately expected moment soon to come—Ames readies his generosity, anticipating his own willingness 'to admire' everything his son does so that he may be remembered generously in kind.

It's not simply that these switches between temporal realms exhibit a stylistic facility that soothes Ames by recasting sorrow in affirmative lights. More than a sweetening glaze, such language—rhythmically and structurally so at ease with itself, despite its thematic weaves between care and apprehension, between paternal love and proleptic pity—suggests that to write with grace means to 'reach', as Robinson suggests, 'toward a greater sufficiency of expression'. Aspiring beyond a mere 'definition or a demonstration of grace or even an objective correlative for it', Ames's prospectus for the end of life's 'dream' consoles not only by its rhetorical dexterity but also by its 'intimation of a great reality of another order'—one that 'pervades human experience', as Robinson argues in an essay devoted to 'Grace', 'even manifests itself in human actions and relations, yet is always purely itself'.[84] Ames seems quite capable, then, of contemplating the mortality of memory without compromising his own venture to give 'some sort of account' of his past. And this ability compensates in its own way for his admission that 'age has a tendency to make one's sense of oneself harder to maintain, less robust in some ways' (239). Writing steps in for Ames at the point of self-doubt. Countering suspicions of infirmity, his enduring perspicacity substitutes the supposed inarticulacies of old age.

LOVING GRIEF

The rhetorical facility of Ames's expository journey between remembrance and wonder, combining testimony and prospection, audibly allays the alarm of unknowing. Confessions of ineloquence in this novel also channel Robinson's larger contemplation of linguistic inadequacy in matters of belief, connecting narrative technique to her Calvinist conviction that the very 'insufficiency of people is the great gift of God's grace'.[85] Ames indeed seems nowhere more articulate than when he is describing 'the full measure of my incomprehension' (23). Though Robinson has him profess that 'I do try to write the way I think' (33), it's exactly in episodes when he reaches the perimeters of thought, when he 'wonder[s] where my attention was' (47), when he portrays himself as 'an anxious, fuddled old man' (60), or when he asserts 'that you never do know the actual nature even of your own experience' (109), that she elevates the dexterity of Ames's reflective moments. Once more, distinctly everyday moments are crucibles for this paradox. Unfathomable yet ordinary experiences breed their own affective literacies, and in so doing answer to what Coetzee cautiously viewed as the promise of 'style as redemption'. It is 'a strange thing', admits Ames, to claim to represent one's 'return to a moment', especially 'in its passing'. And yet, because the 'moment is such a slight thing' its very 'abiding is a most gracious reprieve', even as we also look upon the recalled instant as an occasion to grieve (184–5).

Robinson's stylistic enrichment of such moments makes up for the epistemic shortfalls they occasion. If such consolations arise from the conjunction of lyricism and incomprehension, eloquence and unknowing—that is, from the way she offsets graceful descriptions against her narrator's disquiet—then they occur not only at the level of euphony or rhythm but also in choices of diction. This is most neatly captured, as we have just seen, in Ames's encompassing sense of 'loving grief' for his son. Movingly, such grief is anticipatory: provoked by the vision of Robby or, rather, a future manifestation of him as a man who Ames does 'not know' and who will have 'grown up fatherless'. Loving grief presents a collocation of epithet and noun that might make us pause. That's not because it's oxymoronic, or because grief isn't bound up with love, which of course it is; but because as an emotional state it contains two temporalities at once, as though our present sense of overwhelming devotion can also inhabit the expected devastation we invariably try, precisely *through* love, to resist. Loving grief also finds its structural counterpart in the intimacy Robinson creates between Ames's luminous descriptions of ordinary things and his accompanying recognition that 'there's a lot I could do' but no time left in which to do it (161). Loving grief has a tonal equivalent, too, as the novel unfolds in a tenor of raptured bereavement. For Ames is enthralled, as we have seen, by domestic events that he painstakingly records—with that record itself initiating a kind of prophetic mourning in its own right. Lovingly grieving descriptions accept without succumbing to Ames's foreshortening role in the lives he describes: 'Your shirt is red—it is your favourite shirt—and you fly into the sunlight and pause there brilliantly for a second and then fall back into the shadows again' (127). Temporally speaking, therefore, Ames's perceptions cut in opposite directions at once: they look back to cache precious moments that will only be reappraised when disclosed years after his death; in turn these moments act as mnemonics, prompting him to 'remember those first experiments with fundamental things, gravity and light, and what an absolute pleasure they were' (127). Grieving though he is for the expected loss of all that he so lyrically depicts, this process of coordinating record and retrospection offers Ames the solace of association. If memories burn unquenched for Ames, they light up the present not with the glow of nostalgia but with the prospect that some 'fundamental things' will persist, just as it becomes 'a great consolation' for Mrs Curren (to recall Coetzee's notes for *Age of Iron*) that the world won't cease without her.

Robinson closes *Gilead* with a structural reprise that is also a reflection on what Ames's apprenticeship in loss has achieved. In hindsight, he senses 'a kind of youthfulness' in the original 'expectation of death I began with' (272), musing as he did at the outset that '[i]t seems ridiculous to suppose the dead miss anything' (3). A formal recapitulation of anticipated mortality at the novel's end thus coincides with a feeling of regeneration, of beginning again. Death, like wonder, turns out to be like a kaleidoscope, revealing different facets depending on the mood or motivation with which we begin to contemplate it. With the end in view, Ames retrospectively discerns death's 'novelty' as the source from which his whole record of passionate bereavement flows (272). This instance of reassessment also allows readers to see the trajectory of self-development, of belated *bildung*, that Ames's journey has traced through 'loving grief' for his son and indeed for the roguish yet endearing Jack, who is just as much a catalyst as Robby for the process of 'writing all this out', for Ames concedes that there's no other 'way to let you see the beauty there is in him' (265). For Jack has caused some of Ames's gravest speculations about Lila's domestic future, envious as he is of the mutual understanding that she and Jack intimately share. Ames's encounters with Jack alter the novel's very tempo and tone. As Robert Chodat points out, after the 'processional pace' of its opening half, *Gilead*'s serenity 'gradually disappears, as Jack arrives and slowly initiates a new chain of thoughts, worries, and uncertainties in Ames's narration'.[86] And yet, the cumulative result of 'sifting my thoughts and choosing my words' arguably counterweighs in the end Ames's prophetic concerns about what Jack's agenda might be after his death (22).

For as his testimony culminates, Ames seems consoled not because his agitations are in any way placated (along the lines of the early modern meaning of solace as alleviation), but because he recognizes agitation as a reason to apprehend himself anew:

> My present bewilderments are a new territory that make me doubt I have ever really been lost before.
> Though I must say all this has given me a new glimpse of the ongoingness of the world. We fly forgotten as a dream, certainly, leaving the forgetful world behind us to trample and mar and misplace everything we ever cared for. That is just the way of it, and it is remarkable. (218)

What's paradoxically consoling here is not the conventionally comforting prospect of 'ongoingness' in heaven but the realization that our uncertain legacy in a 'forgetful world' we leave behind is a great leveller: the likelihood of being 'forgotten as a dream' signals a vulnerability no one can escape. Such is the pay-off of Ames's apprenticeship in loss, even if what he learns ultimately makes him 'doubt' that he's 'ever really been lost before'. Equally 'remarkable' as his vision of the world's impersonal continuity is the self-possession with which his 'present bewilderments' are rendered. Robinson's supple phrasing counteracts again the unstable 'new territory' her protagonist's self-examinations move towards. Yes, there's an uncertainty here that interrupts the novel's earlier 'processional' momentum; but the uncertainty is more diegetic than stylistic, as though plot pulls away from expression when Ames's worries become more pronounced. Perhaps that's what it means to understand 'loving grief' as a kind of aesthetic in its own right: in the novel's later stages, increasing consternation trails against without ultimately disabling the lithe rendition of worry. Present and oncoming varieties of grief are lovingly tracked, their effects gracefully particularized. *Gilead*'s primary consolation thus lies not in its action so much as in the performance of rhetorical endurance, when states of perplexity do nothing to undo the pristine articulation of what it feels like to experience them.

We know of course that the account Ames gives of himself is selective, manipulated by his propensity to find solace even at his most solitary, by his tendency 'not to remember grief and loneliness so much as I do peace and comfort' (81). And it's true that despite this selectivity 'later portions of the book offer fewer and fewer of such tranquil recollections', as progressively Ames's 'entries envision a more terrestrial, anxious future'.[87] However, I have argued that the text never quite loses sight of his core injunction—one that Robinson endorses as a neglected facet of Calvinism—that the ordinary world 'deserves all the attention you can give it' (32). Whether discerning his 'present bewilderment' or divulging his fears for the future, Ames enlists the same particularism he brings to consoling descriptions of everyday acts and incidents, with their 'vivid slashes of poetry'.[88] Ames's observations do indeed become increasingly terrestrial, overshadowed by his darker anticipations of what harm Jack might bring into the lives of his widow and son. But the tremor this sends through the novel's calm fusion of observation and reminiscence accelerates rather than derails Ames's preparation for loss—producing apprehensions *of* loss that reenergize *Gilead*'s language even as they diminish its serenity.

FAITH IN RECALCITRANT FORMS

'There are pleasures to be found where you would never look for them' (45), advises Ames, and the details he uncovers often perpetuate rather than placate his habitual self-questioning. But that's the point. Robinson gives primacy to close-watching experience in all its variety—whether treasured or ominous, enriching or foreboding—and she is not content with showing how Ames becomes peacefully reconciled to the imminence of bodily 'perishability'. Consolation is both enabled by and questioned throughout Ames's process of self-description, especially when his narrative founders in episodes of unknowing: where inarticulacy intrudes, where he bleakly notices how '[c]ataract...this world is' (219), where Robinson fosters rather than resolves everyday mystery. That such episodes are rendered so elegantly proves her interest in not only instantiating but also formally amplifying those very experiences for which 'language is not an appropriate tool'.[89] Active 'demonstrations of the failures of language' are for Robinson, as for her narrator, 'paradoxically, demonstrations of the extraordinary power of language to evoke a reality beyond its grasp, to evoke a sense of what cannot be said'.[90] Perhaps this is one explanation for why her characters can be consoled even when they reach the very limits of phenomenological literacy; when they 'discover', as Ames does, 'a kind of equivalency of considerations that is interesting in itself but resolves nothing'

(159); and when everyday perceptions—as commonplace as 'the feeling of a weight of light' (59), or as unsettling as the question of whether 'provision will be made' for a boy like Robby stepping into the social 'wilderness' of the future (135)— exceed the perimeters of intelligibility.

In its exactitude, as I have tried to show, Robinson's language redresses these perceptual and spiritual consternations. She drafts a non-pejorative space in style where solace is allowed to flex in acts of description that tenderly memorialize a world that's about to be lost. These rather unstable, worldly consolations seem more distinguished, more multi-layered, and more enduring than the sort of comfort associated with divine assurances of everlasting continuity. This might sound counterintuitive, given that we know Robinson's belief is such a steering presence in her fiction, to an extent that characters like the compassionate, self-reflexive Ames seem to be channelling the conceptual and historical questions of faith she unravels in her essays. However, what her writing formally suggests—despite itself, in a way—is that fiction's consolations aren't to be found in uplifting lessons about spiritual promise, but in the recalcitrant movements of form. Grace not as act but as language in *Gilead* draws readers into an affecting intimacy with the losses Robinson describes and for which there is no repair aside from the intricacy and pitch of their evocation. Aching, elegiac, ardent: descriptions of Ames's embrace of the inscrutable, 'cataract' world of everyday life call attention, I have argued, to Robinson's sensuous, gently reparative manipulation of diction and syntactic rhythm, as much as they intensify our pathetic response to what's dramatically occurring in the text. There's no reason why these alternative reactions can't go hand in hand. Nevertheless, it's telling that *Gilead*'s most concentrated episodes of grace take as their generative premise Ames's utter humility, a humility whose antipode is the verbal lustre of Robinson's language, the poise of which (to borrow her own lovely phrase) 'can *seem* like virtuosity regaling itself with its own brilliance'.[91]

Form as an artistic correlative for the possibility of thinking grace; descriptive brilliance as a conduit of spiritual intellection—such ideals are liable to rouse suspicion in a writer like Coetzee, wary of a faith in style becoming equivalent to theological succour. At least, that's the standpoint that interviews with him lead us to infer: 'As for grace, no, regrettably, no: I am not a Christian, or not yet'.[92] Typically so for anyone who has worked on him, Coetzee refuses to be drawn here on the question of what has traditionally been seen as the supreme consolation— that soothing reliance on the expectation of a divine presence, coupled with the promise of an afterlife. But it's intriguing to see how a theological lexicon inflected his early sense of the novel's proximity to atonement and reparation, as his vision of Mrs Curren's impulse began to crystallize in November 1988: 'The task is to find an action for her to redeem her life, despite the fact that the only life she has to give up is virtually worthless.'[93] A day later he ventures that the 'book will only work if I work on things like <u>angelhood</u>', conceding 'perhaps not even then'.[94] Unsurprisingly, therefore, the vocabulary of the spirit pervades Mrs Curren's own commentary on what she has been composing: 'This was never meant to be the story of what happened to my body. It was meant to be the story of what happened to my soul'. And in the version here, from Coetzee's manuscript in late February 1989, she then goes even further: 'It was meant to teach me how to die.'[95]

Teaching the process of dying, including 'how to endure pain' to recall Coetzee's notes for *Disgrace*, has brought this chapter's markedly different writers into the fold of the same genre. Strictly religious models of consolation can't quite do justice to its affective variety in such novels of imminent loss, especially when solace performs its most unexpected work through defiant expressions rather than in the conventional guise of divine consolation. And yet, glancing back there at Coetzee's equivocal response over the matter of 'grace', I'm tempted not to take him entirely at his word. For he seems to disclose, or at least wants to imply, something about himself through the very attribute he 'regrettably' negates—leaving us with a revealing shard of indecision or, better, an augury of what has still yet to be resolved.[96] In a similar way, *Disgrace*'s commentary on the soul is notably more animated than it might otherwise have been. In a 1996 draft, Coetzee corrected a less openminded version of David Lurie, who comforted himself for his handling of animal remains by insisting that 'dogs do not even have souls that live on after that death'. Coetzee deleted this belief in his revisions. And the deletion suggests that a greater challenge would be put before Lurie's conscience if he were made to entertain the idea that those creatures he helped to euthanize had souls after all, a possibility that makes it harder, as we have observed, for Lurie in the published text to console himself by assuming dogs without souls wouldn't 'care if their carcases were dishonoured'.[97]

With its calculated undecidability, Coetzee's response to the sacred thus ratchets up the ethical predicaments facing his characters and also justifies his fiction's alignment in this chapter with a writer as theologically devoted as Marilynne Robinson. To satisfy the perennial dilemma of selection in this fashion, though, makes me aware that I'm not altogether able to disentangle myself from the critical attractions of approaching secular and religious modes via deliberately counterintuitive juxtapositions, attractions I can't indulge without demur. Still, I wouldn't concede that a conversation between Robinson's and Coetzee's work is therefore inadmissible. Robinson seems to humanize Calvinism to such a degree that invites worldly readings of *Gilead*, much like the one I'm conscious of having offered here. Coetzee's picture of Calvinism's transnational legacy becoming 'grafted onto the nationalist paradigm' of South African apartheid is undoubtedly mordant;[98] yet this doesn't altogether foreclose the possibility of widening *Age of Iron*'s emotional frame to include aspects of spiritual fortitude which one may instinctively distrust in Coetzee's secular universe.

'We embrace to be embraced', after all, insists Mrs Curren at the novel's outset (15). Her meditation there on 'the true meaning of the embrace' anticipates in a perverse though structurally prescient way the climactic return of this motif when Vercueil takes her 'in his arms' at the end (198). She had 'longed' for her daughter 'to be here, to hold me, comfort me!' (15), not so much to assuage the fear of dying, as to help her anticipate what it might entail, irrespective of the consolation that something may lie beyond it. Though wishful, her prospect of this embrace is comforting because the embrace, like her letter, has a proleptic dimension. For Mrs Curren, '[w]e embrace our children to be folded in the arms of the future, to pass ourselves on beyond death, to be transported' (15). Through its reiterations, *embrace* shifts as a verb from an offered gesture to a reciprocal gift; her enumerations of its 'true meaning' grammatically help to propel her notion of being enveloped in the future—a notion that consoles her, despite being directed at a daughter she has effectively lost.[99] Opposite ends of this novel thus hail each other across narrative space, suggesting that Mrs Curren's increasingly necessary association with Vercueil turns out to have been an apprenticeship in losing the solace she imagined seeking in her still-absent child. If this union in *Age of Iron* seems ambivalent at best, it's distinctly unusual for also capturing at least one credo from Calvin himself: that, for neighbours in need, we should 'neither exempt ourselves from their want, nor seclude them from our abundance, but gently make them partakers with us, as folke that are linked together in an inseparable bond'.[100] This isn't to imply that Coetzee's improbable couple here cipher his fiction's religious unconscious. That much would suggest I'm reading rather too much against the grain, perhaps. And yet, when approached in light of Robinson's narrative of spiritual preparation and self-dissemination, Coetzee's premortem novel seems no less secular but certainly more spiritually attuned—to say nothing of how his style magisterially upholds a faith in frugal grace. Such a comparison is one that his fiction does everything to earn but that Coetzee himself probably wouldn't encourage—'or not yet'.

Just as Ames claims some comfort in *Gilead* from his grieving love for a family he will soon leave behind, so in *Age of Iron*, Coetzee dramatizes the 'paradox of finding succour', in Dominic Head's phrase, 'in that which is damaging to the self'.[101] Such is the novel's 'dominant mood', by which Coetzee seeks to advance an alternative kind of discursive 'authority based on self-effacement', even though a good deal of Mrs Curren's narration 'has to do with the *process* of relinquishing personal authority which is matched by an inverse accumulation of narrative authority'.[102] Self-demotions assume dissentingly graceful forms, just as the effects of Coetzee's style can be reconstructive in spite of his idiomatic impulse to strip novelistic discourse back to its barest components. Over the course of this chapter, I have also been concerned to reveal yet another discrepancy, relating as much to what Jarad Zimbler calls Coetzee's 'language of the soul' as to matters of compositional authority.[103] For although Coetzee would seem to be the least likely ally of Calvinism (including the more sympathetic version of its legacy that Robinson endorses), Mrs Curren has nevertheless been described as an 'agnostic confessant',[104] and it is ultimately through 'a secular vision of Calvinist grace', as Michael Neil points out, 'that Coetzee imagines' her 'release from ... the endless labyrinth of confession without absolution'.[105] Such is the surprising, if perverse upshot of placing these writers together, as their fictions gesture in directions that run counter to their respective convictions. Where Robinson increasingly substitutes conventional piety for the impression that grace may be detected in prosaic spheres of everyday wonder, whose beauty serves to 'push at the borders of intelligibility and create new eloquence as it does so', Coetzee reinstates a numinous vocabulary of the soul that destabilizes the rigid binary between ethereality and materialism, indicating a postsecular ethos that takes exception to the outright redundancy of spirituality.[106] This is not to imply there's a bizarrely improbable yet sufficiently concrete affinity between these writers that surpasses their theological disparities. Rather, it is to appreciate the dialectical sense in which phenomenal traces of grace and the gracefulness of style are stress-tested by the very circumspection they attract in fictions charting the anticipation of self-loss.

Backdrops of racial injustice and uprising in these works, however, struggle for precisely that kind of expression: late twentieth-century century uprisings against apartheid's systemic brutalities, for Coetzee; mid-century resistance to pervasive discrimination against African Americans, for Robinson. Though these upheavals don't exactly amount to silences for *Age of Iron* and *Gilead*, as historical flashpoints they are afforded less diegetic prominence than their narrators' immediate reflections and self-examinations. Pointed questions abound. For we might wonder whether a faith in graceful self-scrutiny can become a diversion from collective injustice, reaffirming the ethical primacy of conscientious yet individualized contemplation at the expense of social commentary.[107] With their style 'regaling itself with its own brilliance', do these novels compensate for the very perspectivism that can produce social blind spots? Do they vindicate through virtuosity narration's suspect swerves away from a more panoramic view of the conditions and legacies of racial injustice, as though such a view of actuality were somehow unutterable or rhetorically unmanageable? Perhaps: if one reads them, that is, in search of reports on the historic political storms they flank. Maybe the effect in question is less unambiguous, though. For when Mrs Curren declares, in a snippet of dialogue Coetzee drafted in April 1989, that she wishes 'to release' her daughter 'from this charm of words', she also implicitly confesses that she has not yet observed enough: 'I am going to let go of you into the future, into the land I will not see.'[108] In one sense, rhetorical charm—her private religion of style—has become a mitigating occupation, veiling a land riven with segregation. But in another sense, that's precisely the novel's critical catalyst rather than confirmation of its complicity. Release from compensatory words into a more direct vision of the country's racial 'future' is what the text arguably affords readers in the afterglow of its disturbing events, obliging us to see the realities of social injuries that have only peripherally entered its diegetic purview. Similarly, in *Gilead*'s case, if there's something strangely discrepant about Robinson's decision 'to tell the story of race and racism in America in a small all-white town in Iowa with white Anglo-Saxon characters', then that is her means of arguing—*through* the novel's enclosed cast, community, and form—that 'the experience of life, for black Americans', as she asserts, remained at that historical moment 'very strongly formed by people who don't think about them at all'.[109]

Works that asseverate what they miss, *Age of Iron* and *Gilead* invite us to notice how the 'charm of words' may, counterintuitively, serve as an interpretive provocation: when language artfully shields it doesn't genuinely console. These novels seem alert to this distinction, compelling us to notice what we 'will not see' if we immediately take the grace of expression to mean a distraction from the pain of disenfranchisement. Their potential (self)implication, then, in the perpetuation of history's relative illegibility is something these novels confess, testifying as they do, through the testimonies which they are, to the forever fraught 'temptations' of showcasing the consolingly transformative work of language in evoking eras of profound division. Robinson has insisted that 'you have to be engaged with the world to write fiction',[110] and these novels respectively endorse that conviction by dramatizing the very costs of withdrawal.

LESSONS IN DISSONANCE

If solace has a sense of direction, then what we learn from Coetzee and Robinson is that it follows several routes at once. For elegists, consolation's compass points them to anterior routes; following paths that bisect recollection and reflection, they generate occasions for memorialization that are also excuses for self-analysis. Commemorating its own subject, contemporary elegy tends also to scrutinize its maker, as we saw in the previous chapter. In this most reflexive of genres, a good deal of the work consolation does for writers—and by implication for empathic readers, too, who are stirred by elegists' arguments with solace—remains retroactive. According to this logic, literature intervenes in the fallout of dejection to script alternative templates for comprehending and coping with loss. Indeed, it's 'precisely because of the elusive character of real life', suggests Paul Ricoeur, 'that we need the help of fiction to organize life retrospectively, after the fact'.[111] But Coetzee and Robinson reveal something of consolation's other bearings in fictions whose temporal orientations help us to unyoke solace from derogatory assumptions about its belated assistance, assumptions that make solace seem redundant not merely because its affective aid is delayed but because it seems superficial when it arrives in grief's wake. They test forms of anticipatory reconciliation with loss that work under the sign of their own emotive limitations, acknowledging the liability of consolation's incompleteness without renouncing it altogether. Likewise, their 'apprenticeships' in mortality recognize their own formal insufficiency without foreclosing the productive role that solace still performs, not least in narratives where oblivion itself is forever close at hand.

If these fictions stage what might tentatively be called lessons—ways of making mortality thinkable and affectively legible as opposed to obscure, fearful, unmanageable—then they speak to the pedagogical context of Elisabeth Kübler-Ross's pioneering research on aging and death from the 1960s and 1970s. A psychiatrist and hospice reformer, Kübler-Ross campaigned to confront the lack of adequate training for medics and palliative care-workers in attending to terminally ill patients well before their final days. (Four decades after her original cause for complaint, the surgeon Atul Gawande sums it up well in the opening sentence to *Being Mortal*, his 2014 meditation on the administration of end-of-life care: 'I learned a lot of things in medical school, but mortality wasn't one of them.')[112] By examining attitudes to loss across cultures and faiths, Kübler-Ross observed that while '[i]t is unlikely that any group has ever welcomed death's intrusion on life, there are others who have successfully integrated the expectation of death into their understanding of life'.[113] Instead of viewing death as 'a dreaded stranger,' she suggests, we ought to 'reintroduce it into our lives' as the 'expected companion to our life', allowing us thereby to 'live our lives with meaning—with full appreciation of our finiteness'.[114] If the brute fact of that finitude doesn't exactly sound consoling then learning how to engage with its prospect can, she argues, be enriching, life-affirming. 'Clearly, not everyone who is dying ever reaches a level of acceptance', grants Kübler-Ross, 'but if you can do so *before* you are faced with your own or a loved one's death, then you will be able to live and die more meaningfully.'[115]

In his 1977 epic, *The Hour of Our Death*, the French medievalist and historian of childhood Philippe Ariès pursued a similar line, reflecting that '[i]t is not…at the moment of death or in the presence of death that one must think about death', but 'throughout one's life'. Then problem, as Ariès saw it, continues to be the 'heavy silence' that 'has fallen over the subject of death', leaving us disengaged socially and imaginatively from any 'close relationship between living well and dying well'.[116] The role contemporary fiction might have in reinforcing that relationship is one Coetzee and Robinson also probe. If writing about death ahead of its physical actuality or psychological repercussions 'invites man's reason', in Ariès's words, 'not to become attached to life', then Coetzee and Robinson prompt us to consider what consolatory behaviour this peculiar genre of anticipation displays.[117] Kübler-Ross was perhaps right to suggest that 'it's not really dying that's so hard' but living itself—'living until you die'.[118] How much affective work might literature today have left to do in consoling for this recognition of our own finitude? Might its job therefore be to make more 'transparent' to us, as it was for the young David Foster Wallace, the fact 'that, if we forget how to die, we're going to forget how to live'?[119]

That worry is certainly apparent for a surgeon like Gawande. How to live life more meaningfully in fuller recognition of its finitude is the question that concerns *Being Mortal*, a personal memoir that integrates clinical reflections on the ethics of interventionist treatment and palliative care for the terminally ill. 'For human beings', asserts Gawande, 'life is meaningful because it is a story'. With this premise, he argues 'that our most cruel failure in how we treat the sick and the aged is the failure to recognize that they have priorities beyond merely being safe and living longer; that the chance to shape one's story is essential to sustaining meaning in life; that we have the opportunity to refashion our institutions, our culture, and our conversations in ways that transform the possibilities for the last chapters of everyone's lives'.[120] Shaping stories that grapple with the seemingly bleak consolation of seeking meaning in life's final episodes is the tough work Robinson and Coetzee undertake. Uninterested in escapism, they raise the stakes of recognizing how literature, as Ricoeur once put it, can allow us to 'have the experience, however, incomplete, of what is meant by ending a course of action'—involving us in 'a slice of life' before life's own denouement. Doing so, literature arguably helps us to discern the affective 'outline of these provisional ends' ahead of any lived sense of such endings—thereby allowing us also to notice what, beyond our own preconceptions, those myriad 'priorities' of the dying might actually be.[121]

No uplifting bromide is administered here. As we will continue to see, contemporary writers tend to be circuitous with their salves. Specializing in the insatiate, there's nothing they like more than kindling the 'troubling hunger', in Claire Messud's phrase, with which readers are drawn to literary 'accounts of grief', perhaps in 'the hope that the shared revelation of pain may assuage—or perhaps stave off?—our private sufferings'.[122] Alert to this voracity, Ricoeur cautions that at best fiction asks us to be 'prepared to take as provisional and open to revision' what it tells about the experience of loss. Nonetheless, these provisional lessons lead him to wonder: 'do not the narratives provided by literature serve to soften the sting of anguish in the face of the unknown, of nothingness, by giving it in imagination the shape of this or that death, exemplary in one way or another?'[123] If so, would it not be churlish to say that this shape, when given compelling form, proves that all consolation amounts to in literature is the seduction of aesthetic design? Refusing to sentimentalize or universalize the anticipation of mortal ends, Coetzee and Robinson disrupt too an anodyne 'revelation' of what reconciliations with death consist of.

Despite clear divergences over the question of belief, these novelists are therefore attentive to 'a certain kind of ontological discomfort', in Robinson's phrase, 'that seasons thought', while our attention to the equally discomforting sense in which their fictions disarticulate themselves from history, by rendering their central figures less-than-articulate witnesses of their own implication in social environments beyond the contemplation of their own mortality.[124] Discomfort, of course, is the very incentive for their novels' provision of counter-desolation, an incentive too for sustaining what Ricoeur called a 'fruitful exchange' 'between literature and being-toward-death'.[125] One important spur for Ricoeur's defence of this exchange in relation to literary consolation was of course that renowned chronicler of anticipated loss, Frank Kermode. In *The Sense of an Ending*, Kermode argued that while the literary 'imagination...is a form-giving power, an esemplastic power', a 'maker of orders and concords', the most valuable fiction does not in fact 'falsify' the unpredictable realities of experience 'with patterns too neat, too inclusive'. Instead, the writing itself registers the sense in which 'there must be dissonance'.[126] It's in precisely this element of discordance that form's potential for redress is realized: the chapters so far and those still to come concur with Kermode 'that without paradox and contradiction our parables will be too simple for a complex poverty, too consolatory to console'.[127] For their part, Robinson and Coetzee suggest that if books 'continue to interest us', as Kermode speculated, when they 'move through time to an end, an end we must sense even if we cannot know it', then those same narratives avoid the easy solace that would 'sever us from our losses' and venture by choice towards 'discoveries of dissonance'.[128]

A child of that dissonance, whose turbulent past animates the analepses of Robinson's 2014 novel of her name, Lila wonders whether '[f]ear and comfort could be the same thing'. Becoming Ames's young wife, Lila acquaints him with what it means to glean solace from hardship, having pursued long enough an apprenticeship in '[f]inding comfort where there was no comfort'.[129] As we have seen, characters confront in different situations their own versions of her paradox, an affective paradox that imbues rather than undermines the felicity with which novelists discern subjective reckonings with sorrow. This is not to suggest that ultimately fiction's consolations betray an exercise in aesthetic distinction, one fuelled by the promise that, with the aid of language alone, psychic distress or social duress can somehow be mended. Rather, it is to notice how inventively novels behave when they simultaneously amplify and cross-examine style's role as an antagonist of loss, an antagonist whose imperfections enjoin writers to appraise their own work's sponsorship of solace.

Foreclosure isn't always literature's preferred habitat, when it patrols the precincts of consolation. Endings can be left unwritten, even reversed, disclosing in that reversal the hunger to outmanoeuvre the immutability of error or the blight of unalterable misfortune. As definitive as loss has appeared in this chapter, next we'll see how memoirists have trialled the solace of reassigning fate altogether. Imagining what might have been, they glance at the chance for dejection never to take hold, performing inconceivable resuscitations that only magical thinking can bring off. By courting these counterlives, Doris Lessing and Joan Didion reorient the temporal gist of consolation once again: from anticipating woe to redacting the script of sorrow; from teaching us how to die to picturing the dead's return.

5
Life-Righting and Magical Thinking

Pondering how life might otherwise have turned out can be tempting. If we have such thoughts, it can be equally tempting to consider that if we think hard enough about the way these parallel, relinquished, or potential lives could apply to ourselves or others, then the thinking itself will bring some trace of them into being. To wonder whether this could be so is not necessarily to nurture delusions of omnipotence. But it can still lure us into weighing up our imagined influence over unrealized lives, prompting us to consider whose wishes we fulfill and whose frustrations we solve by venturing to rewrite ill-fated futures in compensation for thwarted pasts. Depending on the occasion, this venture alone can be as consoling as what it hypothesizes; an anticipation of how a life might be re-led can soothe as much as it dismays. Such twinned feelings occupy Robinson's Glory at the end of *Home* (2008). 'Maybe this Robert will come back someday', she hopes, against all odds.[1] Her father's namesake, Robert is the son of Glory's brother, Jack, and his African-American partner, Della. Theirs would be a marriage that Gilead's uniformly white Christian community would never welcome, let alone accept. After an unforeseen visit from Della, however, Glory imagines a scenario of conciliation with Jack's grown son that defies the town's intolerances. A consoling idyll, it's a transparently wishful one too. Glory clearly knows this, yet pursues her line of thinking to its comforting climax regardless. Jack has just left Gilead, this time maybe for good—unable to bear the expectation of an imminent family gathering ahead of their elderly father's death. As Glory begins to accept that Jack won't be returning in old Boughton's lifetime, her vision of accommodating his son in the family home not only sustains her as she mourns Jack's disappearance and their ailing father together; it also becomes her means of conjuring a double homecoming. Glory's vision, that is, generates a kind of magical thinking with a twofold objective: it aspires to alter the course of a seemingly unavoidable future of disconnection for her siblings; and it satisfies too her yearning to repair Jack's intractability and subsequent estrangement, the repercussions of which have weighed on the family for decades. Although Glory acknowledges 'she could never change anything' (337), her self-granted wish that young Robert will return of his own volition is precisely her way of opposing that impotence. By affording '[w]orn, modest, countrified Gilead' a racial openness it has done nothing to warrant (338), she will have telepathically 'answered a longing' of her brother's, going so far as to picture how Jack himself 'could even imagine that their spirits had passed through that strange old house' (337). This alone, the consoling 'thought of it', 'might bring him back' (337).

Poignantly, Jack will also come back in the son his family is unlikely ever to meet. Except for Glory, that is: in her corrective, reconciliatory vision, she alone is the privileged witness to Jack's return in his son's guise.

> What of Jack will there be in him? And I will be almost old. I will see him standing in the road by the oak tree, and I will know him by his tall man's slouch, the hands on the hips.... He will be curious about the place, though his curiosity will not override his good manners. He will talk to me a little while, too shy to tell me why he has come, and then he will thank me and leave, walking backward a few steps, thinking, Yes, the barn is still there, yes, the lilacs, even the pot of petunias. This was my father's house. And I will think, He is young. He cannot know that my whole life has come down to this moment.
>
> That he has answered his father's prayers. (338–39)

Up to this point, events in the novel have been narrated in the third person, filtered by Glory's perspective. With the shift here into her direct first-person future tense (framed only briefly by 'She thought') there's also a shift in tenor, as longing conjectures give way to assertive predictions (*I will, he will*). Through this sense of assertion the scene not only consoles by satisfying Glory's every expectation of a beneficent future with her at its liberal core, but also enacts the ideal that she wishes she could share with her absent but still-troubled brother. Doing so might divert the course of Jack's potentially irrevocable path of self-destruction. Across an episode where fantasy is consciously fostered, fully accepted for what it is, Glory enacts a private atonement on behalf of the Boughtons, as Robert's fantasized visit instantiates the kind of mutual recognition and racial accommodation that presently seems unthinkable in Gilead. Scripting the future as a movingly self-fulfilling prophecy of reunion, Glory distills her own sense of purpose 'down to this moment', a moment that affirms her faith in divine grace but also performs a wish-fulfilling experiment in righting the course of wounded lives.

Nothing if not a belief-affirming climax—'The Lord is wonderful' (339), runs the novel's final line—this closing scene seems to be conspicuously offset, both rhetorically and thematically, against *Home*'s preceding chronicle of Jack's chronic dissolution. A sublime, uplifting sequence, it is nevertheless rooted in prosaic rumination. Indeed, the scene seems to endorse Robinson's own position in her essays, which we considered in the previous chapter, where she poses as an ambassador for everyday wonderment. Glory vouches for the numinous within the ordinary, alert to the way momentary encounters or perceptions, which at first appear merely 'statically present', go on to obtain a 'visionary quality'.[2] Yet despite the consoling aura of *Home*'s finale, broadcasting Glory's confidence in how her charity will be received, Robinson holds resolution in abeyance. When read this way, the novel's last paragraph feels like a self-enclosed bubble, a reparative coda through which Glory assumes the illusory authority of a seer who is licensed to forecast how future events will redress present dejection and past damage. These envisaged circumstances promise to console too for Jack's more recent and decisive departure. But if so, they risk amounting to the mere 'dulling of pain' and 'patching of injuries' that Robinson herself distinguishes quite pointedly from what she calls a 'miracle of solace' that's far from superficial.³ Lyrically redemptive though its ending is, *Home* draws to a conciliatory close only to leave unanswered questions about the sort of consolation one gains in reimagining the lives of others.

Rewriting as strategic reparation; speculative counterplots that try to ameliorate the consequences of loss; assuming an existential vantage point that's sufficiently omnipotent to rectify the course of derailed lives—as manners of behaving that also influence modes of narrating, this cluster of consoling activities set my coordinates for what lies ahead. Distinct in emotional context and aspiration though they are, these strata coalesce under one category in particular: magical thinking. As *Home* suggests, it can belie spontaneous wishes for what might have been; but at the same time, magical thinking may also describe a more considered, self-consoling investment in outcomes that could yet unfold otherwise, in yearning alternatives that might still be fulfilled. Magical thinking therefore combines two temporal directions. While it's normally associated with 'the belief', as Pamela Thurschwell observes, 'that thoughts and desires can directly transfer themselves to, and transform, the material world, other people, the future', I will also be examining depictions of such 'magical transmissions' as they orient towards the past.⁴ By approaching it not simply as an emotive or psychic facet of dramatic events but as shaping style and genre, I read magical thinking in works of life-writing that function as opportunities for life-righting.

Building on the account of form's contrapuntal relation to content this book has been advancing so far, I consider here how scenes and strategies of magical thinking further our understanding of solace by disarticulating it from straightforward, fantasy-fuelled comfort; and in turn, by approaching style as that place where the alternating promotion and interrogation of life-righting unfolds. As we'll continue to see, consolation and its conflicts play out in narrative situations of irreparable loss, enduring regret, and other inhospitable pretexts for aesthetic redress. One burden of this chapter is to take a closer look at what contemporary writers do in these instances, as they register literature's potential to console precisely by calling wishful compensations to account. And it's just as well that 'life-writing' as a critical category has become capacious enough to encompass not only memoirs of personal distress, but also period-specific chronicles of domestic life and counter-historical romances. For we begin with a generically hybrid book that combines them all.

LIFE-RIGHTING WITH A STOIC

'I used to go particularly to novels to find out how I ought to live my life. But, to my loss, I see now I didn't find out.'⁵ Such was Doris Lessing's stance in the 1970s on literature as a source of edification, one that could also make up for the familial instruction that hadn't for her, it seems, been part of growing up. While Lessing's admission is very much in line with her anti-instrumentalist view of fiction's value—'literature shouldn't be treated as a kind of blueprint for a better way of correct thinking'⁶—it's rather less in tune with the hybrid form of her last book.

In *Alfred and Emily* (2008) she offsets fiction and memoir to explore what lives her parents might otherwise have lived without the perennial struggles that in reality they endured. Representing Lessing's final 'bold experiment', in Blake Morrison's estimation, *Alfred and Emily* might be considered as 'not life writing so much as the righting of lives'.[7] Lessing rehearsed the narrative's factual section in a 1984 *Granta* memoir, 'Impertinent Daughters', where she reflects that 'it has taken me a lifetime to understand my parents, with astonishments all the way'. To document those surprises, Lessing embarked on a 'mysterious process', in her words, one that was all the more 'frightening because there is nothing whatsoever you can do about it' when moving 'from fierce adolescence' towards 'a place where you can stand where they did, in imagination'.[8] In her youth, the literary imagination became a place of refuge. 'It was my mother who introduced me to the world of literature', she recalls—a world, ironically, 'into which I was about to escape from her'.[9] Lessing embarked on 'very strange novels, almost as a deliberate counterbalance' to the 'dreadful provincial little hole' that was Salisbury (now Harare).[10] In an earlier essay from 1957, Lessing insisted that even when she turned to more canonical figures of classic realism as a young reader, she 'was not in search of the pleasures of familiarity' but rather 'looking for the warmth, the compassion, the humanity, the love of people which illuminates the literature of the nineteenth-century'.[11] Providing the sort of 'warmth' forever missing from her relationship with Emily— 'I can't remember a time when I wasn't fighting with my poor mother'—literature was Lessing's consoling 'safety line, something to hold on to'.[12]

Years later, though, it was the task of '[w]riting about [her] mother' that Lessing would find most 'difficult'.[13] Their combative relationship affects the very fibre of *Alfred and Emily*, the novella half of which grants Lessing's parents two alternative futures—without each other, but also without the shattering legacy of the First World War. Despite this being a somewhat 'charitable fantasy', as Frank Kermode noted, Lessing still 'could not bestow on her mother a satisfactory marriage'.[14] Becoming 'Mrs Martin-White, the doctor's wife', Emily discovers that she's 'desperately unhappy',[15] unable to 'account for her heavy heart, her anxiety, her feelings of wild panic that took her over for no reason, without warning' (49–50). After her husband dies suddenly at fifty, Emily is 'torn loose, floating' (64); through this fallout, Lessing hatches the circumstances where the 'formidable machine of that energy' in Emily could finally be switched on (55). For in this fantasy scenario, Emily's life into middle age and beyond turns out to be reasonably fulfilling, as she establishes a 'Martin-White Foundation' investing in schools. A mock-postscript later informs us that 'Alfred Taylor was a very old man' we he passed away and that Emily McVeagh died of a heart attack at 73 after reprimanding a group of boys 'tormenting a dog'. So revered was she that '[h]undreds of people came to her funeral' (138).

How different colonial life actually was for Lessing and her parents on their maize farm in Southern Rhodesia (now Zimbabwe). Operating at a loss, Alfred wishfully turned his attention to 'divining as a new science', for which he 'believed he was creating a new method for finding any mineral, gold only one of them'. In Lessing's portrait, this vocational dream left him 'alone in the world, so he saw it, with no one sympathetic to talk to' and hoping that '[o]ne day his family would take him seriously'.[16] Emily, meanwhile, 'no longer talked of going back Home' as the Second World War raged on.[17] According to Lessing, her mother 'felt their lives were ending before they had really begun, for the time on the farm did not really count', and in any case Emily 'had always been waiting for life to begin when she could move off it'.[18] The interminable waiting also inevitably affected Doris. 'I personally had some pretty amazing beliefs', she admits, 'generated in me by that long, long nightmare, watching the slow grinding down of my parents'.[19] Radical beliefs caused further friction, prompting Lessing '[i]n retrospect', to 'pity' her mother, 'stuck with this incredibly difficult child who never thought or did anything "conventional"'.[20] Politically incendiary and married at 19, Doris must have seemed all the more recalcitrant to Emily, who 'did not mind the conventional in the way my father did', who 'was still, in every fibre of her, a Londoner', and who had resigned herself to a farming life—the 'isolation' of which Alfred 'revelled in', even though it 'was destroying her'.[21]

An audacious, impertinent child; a life of cultural disengagement and geographical seclusion; a marriage verging on misalliance: the biographical backdrop of *Alfred and Emily* seems primed for a comforting surrogate-story. But that's not the consolation Lessing pursues. Not exactly. Part I ('Alfred and Emily: A Novella') isn't quite the fulsome compensation we might expect it to be, ahead of the record of disappointment and displacement that ensues in the factual Part II ('Alfred and Emily; Two Lives'). To be sure, the novella *seems* to perform the work both of reconciliation and consolation: Lessing reconciles herself through fiction with the mother who forever angered her, by writing a sympathetic portrait of a feisty woman who lives a perfectly enriching life without children or a long-term husband; and she consoles her father as well, since Alfred lives to a ripe old age liberated from the traumas of war and diabetic complications. However, I suggest that there's more to this than meets the eye. Recuperative though the novella doubtlessly appears, its serene events are matched by a placid style and pedestrian pace that undermine the degree of redress in Lessing's vision of her parents' alternative lives. That the novella is so subdued thus calls into question, as we shall later see, the very consolation that might appear to be its principal interest and goal.

Alfred and Emily hasn't really been read against the grain in quite this way. Even so, the book's bifurcated structure and contrasting styles attracted some equally polarized reviews upon release. For Heller McAlpin, the novella half is 'richer than the meandering, fragmentary commentary on her parents' ill-fated, stifling attempts at Edwardian colonial life that follows'.[22] By contrast Caroline Moore felt that 'as a work of fiction in its own right, the novella is oddly ungripping', noting that Lessing's 'prose is kept deliberately flat, mock-factual'.[23] Rather than weighing in on either side, other commentators have more fruitfully pointed to the dynamic 'interplay between both parts of the book', wondering as Susan Watkins does 'whether Lessing would consider the speculative half of the text or the memoir as the liberating element'.[24] In a similarly even-handed view, Blake Morrison characterizes Lessing's impulse to tell the 'same story in two different ways' as 'a double throw of the dice', whereby that portrait of her parents in the 'novella allows them to be truer to themselves than they were in life'.[25]

A truer picture isn't necessarily a more consoling one, of course, and the one *Alfred and Emily* paints is no exception. The counterfactual novella offers only modest compensations in recreating what might have been, an affective shortcoming compounded at a formal level by its manner of expression. Lessing's curiously restrained, functional prose seems intentionally to counteract the gesture of resuscitation performed by her plotting of replacement fortunes. If there's such a thing as solace in rewriting, in Part I it is qualified by the uneventful tenor of her surrogate life-stories—as though Lessing renounces, *through* the novella's narration, the very consolation her counter-historical biography seems to intend. In an effort to explain the text's two discrepant halves, some critics have implied that *Alfred and Emily* is best appreciated as the sum of its parts. Unshrinking and resolutely candid, the memoir of Part II exemplifies what John Plotz calls Lessing's 'unsentimental stoicism: remaining open to the feelings of others while simultaneously restraining one's emotions'.[26] But despite its restraint, it's also vigorous; the withholding, in other words, might be essential to the memoir's affective pressure. Voicing Lessing's vexation over the bleakness her parents faced, the memoir makes up through its honesty for what Caryn James deems the novella's 'flat-footed' register. Following the example set by Julian Barnes in Chapter 3—testing as he did certain patterns of language to make sense of calamity—we could therefore read *Alfred and Emily* as Lessing's tool for giving 'artistic shape to her own indignation'.[27]

Instead of entirely suturing the book's two parts, in what follows I want to preserve something of that breach between them. Doing so enables us to consider how (in Part I) Lessing's reserved, consciously underwhelming animation of 'lives as might have been if there had been no World War One' hedges rather than embraces the solace her fiction provides when placed, as it is, in anticipation of that grimmer autobiography to come (vii). Thematically speaking, the novella does go some way to satisfying Emily's documented wish in real life: '"If only we could live our good years all over again," my mother would say, fiercely gathering those years into her arms and holding them safe' (24). Formally speaking, though, novella forestalls through its inactive, reined-in prose the very redress it insinuates. Resembling what Plotz terms Lessing's '*insensible* aesthetics'—whereby she invites readers to 'take a long chilly walk away from their feelings'[28]—*Alfred and Emily*'s novella suggests that Lessing defers the easy consolation of closure, a sense of closure that she might well have claimed for herself by writing this book in order 'to get out from under that monstrous legacy' of a 'war that would end all war', 'trying to get free' (viii).

In the novella's initially sunny world of 'peace and plenty' (3), a village cricket match is Lessing's excuse for bringing Alfred into proximity with the Emily he's intrigued by but never romantically pursues. It's 1902 and Emily is upset over her father's 'pompous' reaction to her decision to work as a nurse in London's Royal Free Hospital (8):

> Alfred watched the cricket, but not so that he didn't hear the girl whose head was on Mrs Lane's shoulder say, 'I know it is the right thing for me. I know it is'. Alfred seemed to need to escape, but changed his mind and from the tea urn fetched more cups of tea, which he handed to the three women, with a bowl of sugar. As he gave her

> cup to Daisy, he asked, very low, 'Who is she?' and Daisy said, 'She's Emily', as if nothing more need be said. 'She's my friend', she added.
>
> Oh, so that's Emily, Alfred thought, for of course he knew all about Emily, had heard so much. As often, faced with the reality of a real person—in this case a sobbing and dishevelled young woman—he was thinking that it was not easy to see, looking at her, why she meant so much to Daisy. (9–10)

The commentating clause, 'as if nothing more need be said', encapsulates the studied banality of the novella's style. It's as though Lessing is cautious about over-rectifying her parents' dismal (real) lives and replicates that vigilance in a language estranged from its own élan. Determinedly descriptive, rarely oblique, Lessing's third-person narration only occasionally modulates into free indirect discourse ('for of course he knew all about Emily, had heard so much'), such that she rarely grants clausal tempo and inflection the liberty of variation. Alfred's and Emily's respective viewpoints are conveyed with the minimum of information and with the least amount of ornamentation. This is not the kind of economy that facilitates connotation (the ethos of *less is more* one finds in J. M. Coetzee, Kazuo Ishiguro, and Toni Morrison, for instance).[29] Rather, it's a mode that polices its own rhetorical amplitudes and sonorities, reproducing *as* style the tempered solace this novella emits.

Consider the following chapter climax, which is decidedly anticlimactic not just in respect of any romantic developments for Alfred, but also in relation to depictive pulse and crescendo:

> 'We cannot stay long', said Emily and Daisy. They were both on night duty. Not probationers now, Mrs Lane had to remind herself. They were in their second year, were actually nursing patients. How time did fly, they all agreed.
>
> Alfred, tea-time announced for the players, came over. He greeted Daisy, whom he had always known, but not Emily. He did not recognize her. He remembered Emily as a robust, tall girl—surely athletic: he had witnessed her leap over the fence.
>
> He said to Mrs Lane, 'One reason I'm glad not to be going off to Luton or somewhere: I like dropping in for a bit of your fruit cake'. And his smile was certainly enough to win the heart of anybody at all who was not his mother.
>
> 'You know', he said, 'I couldn't be in the bank. You know me.'
>
> 'Yes, Alfred, and I'm so glad you won't be going away.'
>
> Daisy did not hear this, or pretended not to: she thought Alfred did not know she would be even more glad. (17)

The short paragraphs are largely composed of denotative descriptions of state ('They were both on night duty', 'Not probationers now', 'They were in their second year') or verb-led indications of attitude and action ('He greeted', 'He did not recognise', 'He remembered'). Itemizations of situation overtake insinuations of inner feeling. Lessing refuses a more speculative and symbolically suggestive idiom, even while working within what are the speculative coordinates of fictionalized biography. With this anti-style, she recognizes embellishment's propensity for aesthetic redress and opts for parsimony in response. Verbal intensity and syntactic variety are seen as compensatory qualities in their own right, qualities from which Lessing seems intent on differentiating the novella's prose.

Which could be exactly her point. In writing of a blissfully war-free world in which she was never born, Lessing declines style in a way that seems bound up with her self-extinction. This apparently depersonalizing move is also integral to her exercise in magical thinking, including the projection of that exercise onto her audience, when we're encouraged to participate in re-envisioning historical and social constraints. With her 'unquenchable confidence in any character's (and any reader's) capacity to *imagine*, dispassionately, the existence of worlds in which those constraints look entirely different', Lessing specializes in apprehending 'other worlds with cool comprehension'.[30] From one standpoint, then, the novella's flatness could imply that Lessing's imagination is simply less engaged by the novelistic version than by the biographical one. As a result—again, to play devil's advocate—there's an absence, if not an exhaustion, of writerly personality. And with that goes all sense of flair. But in another reading, such a withheld register evinces a sort of inverted audacity, the product of Lessing's weirdly vivid sense of self-composure. With its unsentimental surveillance and suppression of surplus lyricism, this formal composure serves as a striking analogue of her own biographical self-erasure.

Yet ripples start to emerge across this impersonal aesthetic, once we consider what Lessing presumes or claims to know about the characters whose consoling counterlives she shapes. At a dance hosted by Mrs Lane for Daisy and Emily, we're told that Emily knew 'she looked gawky and uncomfortable' (19), and we're told also that 'Mrs Lane was dissolved in love for her little flower [Daisy] and sick with shame because she had done so badly for Emily' (20). But in a summary of the night's split fortunes, Lessing reports the outcomes for those young women in ways that seem both functional and yet all at once more suppositional: 'Emily did not do so well. Alfred did dance with her but she was awkward and stiff, probably because she hated how she looked. A triumph, then, for Daisy, and something to forget as soon as possible, for Emily' (20). The insertion of 'probably' here either suggests that we have suddenly switched to Mrs Lane's perspective, who's suspecting, as we already know, that she's 'done badly for Emily' by not helping her to make her look more dashing. Or alternatively, we have switched to the perspective of an external yet epistemologically restricted commentator, who shies away from gaining psychological access to inner compulsions that free indirect style affords, and who is content instead to give us explanations for characters' outward impressions that are *probably* the case. This idiom of supposition is curious indeed, when we think of this novella's basic premise: a methodical recreation of a counterfactual past that takes as its catalyst what is actually known of the life that Alfred and Emily as a couple endure. The fleeting speculation implied in *probably* therefore belies an odd dissociation of authority on Lessing's part towards her own compensatory vision of an alternative past, a vision over which she has complete choreographic command.

Lessing's verbal skid there into feigned unawareness captures in miniature an aspect of what is a thoroughgoing oscillation in this novella. Marrying two competing impulses, Lessing's desire to self-authorize a corrective biography coincides with a certain watchfulness that undercuts the magical thinking intrinsic to her 'righting of lives'. As I have suggested, her refusal to embellish the counterhistory she conveys in the novella section of *Alfred and Emily* suits Lessing's own self-eradication: an attempt to formulate a dispassionate literary aesthetic that bears no footprint. The resulting absence of personal inflection supplies a perfect device for envisioning the world without her. But at the same time, Lessing's insinuations of narratorial uncertainty do everything to reintroduce her as a foiling presence, a querying opponent to the performance of historical restitution she orchestrates. By hesitating over the idea of fully realizing the psychologies of her fictional characters, Lessing equivocates too over the prospect of fully consoling the lives she rewrites.

RECKONING WITH RECUPERATION

If Lessing's narratorial persona in *Alfred and Emily*'s novella is by turns assertive and pedestrian, intrusive and impersonal, frankly descriptive and beguilingly equivocal, then at other times she has no qualms about reminding readers of the fictional frame she's willing to fracture. Lessing introduces her mother's imagined fiancé, Dr Martin-White, as a somewhat diffident figure, whose habitual reserve made him 'very different from the people Alfred was surrounded by most days, all farmers, labourers, country people. He was tallish, perhaps too thin, with a hesitant manner, as if he felt he presumed, with a thoughtful, sensitive face'. Before this sequence of counterfactual characterization progresses, the paragraph then breaks:

> This happened in 1916.
> In life, my father's appendix burst just before the battle of the Somme, saving him from being killed with the rest of his company. He was sent back to the trenches where shrapnel in is right leg saved him from the battle of Passchendaele. 'A pretty lucky thing', he might say. But, later, 'That is, if you set so much store on being alive'. (31)

Lessing steps forward to detail actual events that might seem fortunate in terms of diverting her father's fate. Until, that is, we hear from the real-life Alfred firsthand. For him, fortune is relative for the survivor, especially if he has been condemned (as Alfred really was) to endure post-traumatic stress and the long-term complications of uncontrolled diabetes. The solace of knowing how horrific things might have otherwise been is subdued here, if not cancelled out, by Alfred's chronic mental and physical sufferings.

What effect, then, does this sort of interruption have? For one, bare facts infiltrate the novella just at the point of romantic fulfilment for the fictional Alfred, allocated his imaginary fiancé, Betsy. Lessing's record of her father's *actual* stance on 'being alive' is thus also a way of disrupting the novella's seamlessly consoling development towards marital contentment. Back in the storyworld, ensuing pages tell us that '[n]ow things moved fast' for Alfred, as he finds himself unable to avoid the fact 'that the looking over of Betsy could not be postponed' (32). Intervening raw facts '[i]n life' are bookended with the fantasy of Alfred's awkward engagement then speedy coercion into wedlock. By doing this Lessing creates through interruption something equivalent to the self-correcting, sceptical vision of lives lived out in plenitude that moderates the novella's action as a whole. As she breaks the diegetic frame here, Lessing also suspends our immersion. Tampering with our involvement in events, she also tempers the solace they yield through less than idyllic accounts of her parents' separate marriages.

Things change considerably in Part II. Here in the domain of biographical actuality, Lessing's prose starts to take off. Memoir, it turns out, elicits more lexical energy and phrasal brio than her previous excursion in compensatory rewriting. Consequently, the blankness the novella's voice is replaced by Lessing's own probing and confessional manner of address, as she calls into question memoir's generic means of production—'One may write about a life in five volumes, or in a sentence' (152)—in ways that enliven the narration, elevating it well beyond the novella's deadpan record of concocted events. Lessing tacks swiftly between emotive circumstance and authorial self-scrutiny, characterizing crucial junctures in her parents' struggle to establish life in Southern Rhodesia that twist into examinations of her own method: 'When she was ill', she tells us of Emily, 'shortly after reaching the farm, she was intolerably sentimental, and this leads me straight into the hardest part of what I am trying to understand' (156). This labour of recollection and understanding assumes syntactic form as she unleashes phrases extending to length of a paragraph, moving in a suspenseful, paratactic arc towards the troublesome target she draws into uneasy focus: the question, that is, of who Emily really was, both despite and in light of all that she experienced.

> Nothing that she ever told, or was said about her, or one could deduce of her in that amazing girlhood, so busy, so full of achievement, or of her nursing years, about which we had the best of witnesses, my father himself, or the years in Persia, so enjoyable and so social, nothing, anywhere, in all this matches up with what my mother became. (156)

Emily's multisided identity—once fulfilled, later dismantled—becomes the memoir's motive interest and distinguishing impetus. Echoing her opening sentence above, Lessing notes that '[n]othing fits, as if she were not one woman but several' (156). In formal contrast, then, to the novella's measured, chronological plotting of brief encounters, sunny cricket pitches, romantic disappointments, and marriages founded on mild resignations, the memoir becomes Lessing's occasion for interrogating the very recuperations and clarifications borne by retrospection. 'I have got ahead of myself', she admits, 'or beside myself. It is because of the impossibility of making sense of Time in its boundaries. Known boundaries and that is the point' (159). Paragraph sizes and rhythms fluctuate; scenes from Emily's perspective are realized with greater vivacity than any episode relayed from either her standpoint or Alfred's perspective in the novella. Lessing's writing gains propulsion, driven by her manner of '[t]hinking about those years', in which—*because* of which—'it is easy to feel them now like parallel streams of experience: the books, the talk of her, the reminiscences, then, the illnesses, physical and mental. Stronger than all of these, the bush, being in it' (172). Incisive diction here, complemented by her decisive use of the list, forestalls the nascent sentimentality of Lessing's retrospective undertaking.

She keeps dispassionate watch over the affective enticements of envisaging what might have been. And yet, this dispassion is nothing less than an affirmative element of her writing. Formal self-command enables more than it conflicts with Lessing's consoling conviction that 'the grimmest fictional world', in Plotz's phrase, 'is made into something different by the realization that its grimness too had to be imagined, written down, read, and recreated'.[31] Blunt though her style in the memoir often seems—as though warding off the sentimentality she witnessed in her mother—Lessing's candid, conspicuous economy emphasizes what is not only traumatic but also transformative about *Alfred and Emily*'s tussle with brutally unchangeable times and her parents' irreversible decisions.

Could it be, then, that for all its harrowing detail it's in the memoir, not in the novella, that style instantiates its most vivid forms of redress? Autobiography turns out to be more linguistically agile than the fictionalization of biography, surpassing the novella's patent goal to compensate blighted fortunes. In this manner, Lessing exploits discrepancies between our aesthetic expectations of these two genres: it's not the war-free novella devoted to the uplifting prospect of lives lived long and free of trauma that affords the most potent salve, but instead the ferocity and agility of a memoir devoted to the pathos of decline. Spry in comparison to a 'flat-footed' novella where Lessing writes herself out of existence altogether, the memoir facilitates a more substantive process of arguing with the past. By contrast, the novella's attempt to carry out repairs on parental history seems consoling in generic kind but not in emotional degree.

To test this assessment, I want to turn finally to a scene in Part II that epitomizes how Lessing departs from the quelled, often listless mood of her counterfactual novella. The episode concerns 'a memory that is one of the most important I have', according to Lessing, one that she owes to Biddy O'Halloran, the family's au pair. Biddy had entered the room where the young Doris was sleeping and placed a lit candle beside her bed, the flame only 'half an inch from the mosquito net' (161). When Emily 'enters just behind Biddy' the action goes into slow motion. Noting in horror the risk Biddy has obliviously taken with the candle, Emily imagines a terrible sequence of outcomes, narrowly avoided, ending in a 'tempestuously burning hut [that] would have set off the whole group of thatched huts across the homestead' (161). Lessing too is contaminated by this nightmare scenario, as she senses that what her mother 'is imagining is reaching me', for even as a young child she was 'already aware of and wary of fire' (162). '"But nothing happened,"' Biddy 'says pertly' (162), a nonchalant self-defense which is of course Lessing's cue to tell us that in her 'mother's imagination everything was happening':

> She sat staring at Biddy and it is this that will never leave my mind. She is uncomprehending, bewildered. Her lips are white. Between the clever, foresightful people of this world and the ones without imagination there is a gulf into which we will all fall one day. My mother can't believe that Biddy—or anyone—could do what she did. (162)

The acceleration into an urgent present tense happens almost imperceptibly, via Lessing's segue into first-person reflection in the latter half of her opening sentence, seizing there upon an image of Emily's stillness 'that will never leave my mind'. Two descriptive and succinct sentences follow, grammatically straightforward but no less effective for giving a simple portrait of shock. Taut, subject-led clauses are familiar to us by this point after reading the novella, where domestic depictions of what characters do tend to mute any vivid suggestion of what they feel (beyond, that is, what their outward behaviours functionally reveal about what they feel). But here description offers a more emotive lens: magnifying Emily's terror, before bringing it into close-up. Extrapolating from her mother's reaction, Lessing thereafter moves into a gnomic register. Backing away from the action temporarily, she articulates that 'gulf' between foresight and neglect by drawing our attention there to a spectrum of accountability running from intelligence to negligence on which she posits Emily and Biddy at opposite extremes—without allowing her readers to congratulate themselves on being anything else than somewhere in-between. By virtue, then, of its subtle yet simple shifts in tense and tone, the episode is not only dramatically vivid but also ethically instructive. In a scene of what we might call negative magical thinking, Lessing tests out the way imagination isn't only cerebral but instrumental, a vehicle for potentially life-changing foresight.

Such instances are worth pausing over, not simply to point out how rhetorically vital or thematically engaging Lessing's memoir appears when measured against the synthetically reparative novella that precedes it, but also to show how interplays between *Alfred and Emily*'s two halves raise questions about the responsibility of rewriting pivotal events. Lessing brings the very recuperative pretensions of life-writing under the spotlight, via the conjunction of these two parts and the comparisons they invite. Doing so, the book proceeds by way of creative self-assessment: proof of what she called in 1981 her continued 'close work of the imagination on my experience of the past'.[32] In this kind of close (self-)reading of Lessing's past, hindsight itself becomes a contested subject, however inevitable hindsight seems for spells of recollection and revaluation:

> What was to blame?
> How attractive are the tidy conclusions of hindsight! How satisfying the *of course* of the back-looking perspective. *Of course* if you do this, then that will happen...
> Now it is so easy to see that nothing could go right.
> It was entirely their fault, but how could they have seen it? First, you have to be able to see yourselves in relation to circumstances, see the family and that house, wrapped in myth and the perspectives of 'If only...' or 'If we had known...'   (173)

Virtually derisive towards hindsight's neat 'conclusions', Lessing spurns what's 'attractive' about retrospection, scrutinizing the clichés that usually accompany one's 'back-looking perspective'. Phrases routed through regret, *If only* and *If we had known* cipher not only self-persecution's futilities but also—perhaps inadvertently for Lessing—guilt's strange comforts. For is it not consoling, after all, to condemn the uselessness of indicting oneself over 'circumstances' that couldn't have been avoided? Might there be some curious solace in admitting the futility of wondering whether one could have foreseen lamentable outcomes whose prevention can only be recognized well after the blow has been dealt?

Lessing's suspicion of hindsight casts the whole impetus of *Alfred and Emily*'s novella in a different light, if we regard it as the compensatory story that it's set up to be in advance of Part II's painful facts. Hindsight's advantages aren't really borne out by the alternative fortunes the novella proposes—reimagined fortunes that are far from 'satisfying'. Lessing is clearly watchful of finding solace in a conveniently different 'relation to circumstances', especially if that becomes a comforting distraction from understanding in retrospect how 'nothing could go right'. Still, the very critique of hindsight provides its own discrepant consolation: the consolation of claiming some intellectual satisfaction from the fact that if we cannot adequately redress historical damage, we can reassure ourselves that we're able to resist retrospection's fantasies of how life could have turned out.

SURVIVAL TACTICS

As Lessing's novella unfolds against an idyllic peacetime backdrop 'wrapped in myth', it thus announces a compromise that's also a creative impetus. Recognizing 'the *of course*' that is retrospection's advantage, *Alfred and Emily* also observes the 'tidy' gesture of hindsight's explanations. 'Life is not, after all, exquisite butterflies with the afternoon sunlight on their wings', she notes, after giving us a nonetheless crystalline depiction of 'the most exquisite sight' in Rhodesia of 'hundreds of butterflies' 'fluttering their pretty wings' (224). This kind of double-edged reflexivity informs the book as a whole. Recalled instances of wonderment or nostalgic endearment are summoned before Lessing's unromantic jury. If she has 'moments of sentimentalizing the bush' (225), they are typically undercut, pitted against her knowledge that without fertilisers, machinery, and vets the farms that thrive on an agriculturally challenging landscape are 'nothing'—they fall into 'neglect', with 'the lands going back to the bush' (227). Unlike some other narratives encountered in previous chapters whose formal expression counterpoints their evocatively tumultuous plots, *Alfred and Emily* offers a rather different example: that of a text's form undoing the compensations its own narrative reaches towards in both action and design. The novella's structural conceit as a counterbalancing prelude to the dark times of Lessing's memoir finally calls that consolatory manoeuvre into question—not only in light of Part II, but also as a result of what Part I itself formally *doesn't* do.

When taken together, then, it's not only that Lessing's novella and memoir amount to something more emotionally and technically substantial than they would do in isolation. More significant is how Lessing's fictional part of this life-writing experiment invites a critical perspective on the consolations of counterfactuality implied by her juxtaposition of alternative and actual lives. Indeed, what her novella offers is a self-eulogy of sorts: it implicitly mourns the way Lessing never joins that hypothetical generation, alleviated from the First World War, whom she charts, while deferring her most enlivened and bristling prose, as we have seen, to the factual section of *Alfred and Emily* where disenchantment takes centre stage. The book's aesthetic dynamism thrives in proportion to its most moving episodes of decline. As a result, when the book bids farewell to the novella's fantasy, the prospects suddenly improve for consolatory form in spite of the text's increasingly depressive content. Lessing's writing thereby gains immediacy and tonal variation as it gains ground in the harsher, visceral realm of historical experience.

'If you're writing a record', advises Lessing, 'a personal history, you're really writing from a different part of yourself, very much more detached'.[33] Whereas for Lessing, detachment was a choice, a posture that matched her tenaciously impersonal prose, for Joan Didion it becomes a more unpredictable phenomenon—a stance she can't altogether control, still less exploit so as to lever grief into lucidity. Notably, the experiment in self-effacement that *Alfred and Emily* pursues is directly at odds with a portrait of Lessing's prose offered in 1971 by Didion herself. 'For more than twenty years now', exclaims Didion, Lessing 'has been registering, in a torrent of fiction that increasingly seems conceived in a stubborn rage against the very idea of fiction, every tremor along her emotional fault system, every slippage in her self-education'. A vivid picture emerges of the writer in stubborn conflict with her own medium. In Didion's opinion, Lessing 'views her real gift for fiction much as she views her own biology, as another trick to entrap her'; as a result, she doesn't even 'want to "write well"', cultivating instead a 'leaden disregard for even the simplest rhythms of language' along with an 'arrogantly bad ear for dialogue'.[34] In part, Didion rehearses what is a familiar set of complaints against the novel of ideas, a genre that's prone to a 'common criticism', as Michael LeMahieu points out, 'that because its primary concern emanates from the conceptual realm', it 'necessarily subordinates plot and character: action is sacrificed to discussion between persons who function as personifications of concepts or mouthpieces for ideas'.[35] When it therefore 'succeeds', such a novel will do so 'inasmuch as it is not quite a novel'.[36] We're given a flavour of these misgivings in Didion's claim that 'Lessing writes in the service of immediate cosmic reform': this predilection leads Lessing to present not so much 'the play of ideas in the lives of certain characters' as situations where 'characters exist only as markers in the presentation of an idea'.[37]

Didion's qualms moved beyond genre too. A more personal, biographical conclusion about Lessing lay in store. Lessing's Rhodesian childhood, argued Didion, left her 'imprinted ineradicably by precisely the kind of rigid agrarian world that most easily makes storytellers of its exiled children', having grown up 'knowing not only what hard frontiers do to women'—one of *Alfred and Emily*'s indictments—'but what women then do to the men who keep them there'.[38] Didion seemed impressed by the gravity and political urgency of what Lessing has to convey; but she was eventually frustrated with the idiom that conveys it, an idiom marked by uncertainties that compromise Lessing's creative confidence in her own convictions. Spotting in 'the granitic ambitiousness of *The Golden Notebook*', for instance, a thinly-veiled memoir of its creator's 'sheer will', Didion discerns 'the fracturing of a sensibility beginning for the first time to doubt its perceptions'. This in turn unsettles narrative form, producing a 'teller' who, in Didion's account, 'berates herself for clinging to the "certainty" of her memories in the face of the general uncertainty', betraying Lessing as a writer 'driven by doubts not only about what to tell but about the validity of telling it at all'.[39]

Doubt doesn't really sound apt for characterizing the assertive self-reflexivity of works written decades later, like *Alfred and Emily*. The relevance of Didion's remarks may have waned. What does remain pertinent, however, is the extent to which her own terms of critique from the early 1970s—as they question that preference for clinging to memory's compensatory yet deceiving certainties—would apply to the habits Didion scrutinized several decades later. Across two late memoirs that are themselves 'driven by doubts', Didion's testimonies to loss involve a 'fracturing' not only in 'sensibility' but also in style, simulating grief's disintegrations and curious delusions. Most curious of all—most self-alienating, for Didion, because so out-of-character—is that consolatory phenomenon of magical thinking. Noticing this behaviour for herself, Didion comes to 'realise how open we are to the persistent message that we can avert death'.[40] When stimulated by the most sudden losses, however, magical thinking turns out to be more perilous and disarming than comforting or self-affirming. Speculations about how unavoidable loss could have been averted—along with the self-questioning such speculations then provoke—are subjects of *The Year of Magical Thinking* (2005), where Didion counts herself among those '[s]urvivors' who 'look back and see omens, messages they missed' (153).

Winner of the 2005 National Book Award for Nonfiction, *The Year of Magical Thinking* is now hailed as something of a classic in the modern grief literature. It chronicles the year following the death in 2003 of Didion's husband, the novelist, screenwriter, and critic John Gregory Dunne. As that year unfolded, Didion's grief was compounded by the repeated hospitalization of their daughter Quintana from pneumonia, septic shock, and eventually bleeding on the brain. Quintana died, aged just thirty-nine, of acute pancreatitis in August 2005. At the time Didion was still writing *The Year*, but she left the manuscript unaltered and instead made her daughter's death the subject of a sequel memoir, *Blue Nights* (2011). One might think that the appalling concatenation of these losses would make writing about them impossible, let alone consoling. Yet Didion was quite clear about her chosen means for negotiating grief, quite willing to place 'the validity of telling' (to echo her views on Lessing) under examination: 'I had to write my way out of it. Because I couldn't figure out what was going on. By the time I started [*The Year*]—John died December 30, I didn't start writing until October—I was out of the phase where I didn't know I was crazy. I was still crazy, but I knew it. So, it was a step back.' Stepping back sounds again synonymous with the detachment Lessing defends as model for prose; for *The Year*, though, Didion opted to assert rather than subvert style as a vehicle for unrestrained mourning. She insisted that the memoir ought 'to be really raw' and 'not as concealed as my style usually is'.[41]

This rawness affects both the language and structure of Didion's record of contemplating alternative outcomes, a record that tracks over months how she noticed signs and theorized circumstances that, for her, could somehow have circumvented John's unavoidable death. She wrote 'it with reporter's eyes', said Hilton Als, towards the end of an interview that spanned Didion's career.[42] Als draws attention to how the dispassionate optics of her path-breaking journalism from the late 1960s and 1970s endured in her postmillennial memoirs. More implicitly, Als highlights the sense in which Didion refuses in *The Year* to take solace in style; instead, she confronts the bleakness of bereavement with the utmost coolness, with tenacious restraint, her crystalline language counterpointing the extravagance of magical thinking as a symptom of sorrow. Among the 'raw' features of that language we find phrasal repetition serving as a means of resisting mental improvement;

jagged patterns in paragraph organization emulating such affects as hesitation, realization, and alarm, when Didion's sense of her own fragile, obsessive attention grows; and finally, rhetorical questions enabling her to circle over the past and subject memory to reassessment. Each of these strategies offers a variety of emotional reprise that holds the consolations of closure in suspension. And yet this retrospective act of writing about unmanageable grief yields a narrative of gradual self-reformation, whose structural solace, so to speak, counters the disorienting year it plots. Architecturally speaking, *The Year of Magical Thinking* prevails, its prose forever in check, as we'll discover later in this chapter, despite the perplexities it recounts. However closely she delineates magical thinking's erratic form with its varieties of craziness—and however inconceivable a survival-narrative seems from within the maelstrom of grief to which she retraces her mental steps—Didion's own chiselled form wins out.

For her part, Lessing never really doubted her ability to give retrospection some sort of textual shape, purpose, and clarity, even as she admitted how difficult it was for her to confront the heavy legacy of her parents' unhappiness, framed by two catastrophic wars. Didion, by contrast, tackles straight away the adequacy of autobiographical language in registering the impact of loss, surveying with disappointment the paucity (as she sees it) of available literature on bereavement. 'Given that grief remained the most general of afflictions' across history, she argues, 'its literature seemed remarkably spare' (43). This supposition doesn't quite hold up under scrutiny; but Didion does at least acknowledge the emblematic status of C. S. Lewis's *A Grief Observed* (1961), and she also takes in such earlier touchstones as Matthew Arnold's 'The Foresaken Merman' (1849) and Auden's 'Funeral Blues' (1936/38). Unimpressed by these works' 'abstracted representations of the pains and furies of grieving', Didion also indicts 'a body of sub-literature' with therapeutic claims, those 'how-to guides for dealing with the condition, some "practical," some "inspirational," most of either useless' (44). This whistle-stop tour through an underwhelming archive enacts a brisk ground-clearing exercise, thereby assigning *The Year* a corrective function even though the long and flourishing heritage of writing on loss hardly needs redeeming.[43] Didion's conviction that there's a dearth of grief-writing situates her own plaintive memoir as a compensation for the psychological blindspots and formal infelicities of existing self-help and professional 'guides' to loss. Where the teachings of Freud and Melanie Klein were concerned, Didion felt merely that 'I learned...many things I already knew', even though such knowledge in itself 'seemed to promise comfort, validation, an outside opinion that I was not imagining what appeared to be happening' (45).

Magical thinking, however bizarre, thus became Didion's motor of generic nonconformism: her means for not confirming what she already suspected about mourning's mental mischief; for resisting the predictability with which people offer compassionate charity as a first step towards believing that you will soon manage on your own; and finally, for eluding the undeniably complex yet somehow schematic prognoses of psychoanalysis. These tactics complement her insistence that '[g]rief, when it comes, is nothing we expect it to be' (24). As Sandra M. Gilbert notes, 'the phrase "magical thinking" summarizes the initial (and overwhelming) madness of grief, especially what is called "unanticipated grief"—a mental state marked by a shocked refusal to accept the absolute disappearance of the beloved and a simultaneous, perhaps paradoxical quest to uncover explanations for an absence in whose reality the bereaved does not fully believe'. Forever expanding its affective radius into everyday life, magical thinking 'comes to permeate even more aspects of the mourning process as the griever struggles to acknowledge and accommodate the multiple, often devastating ways in which the death of an intimate partner reshapes the quotidian experience of survival'.[44] By avoiding generic models in the interests of conveying this sense of grief's unpredictability, *The Year of Magical Thinking*'s intervention is double-edged: it inserts itself into what Didion regards as the insufficient body of grief literature; and it simultaneously announces its distance from the emotional pragmatism of hands-on carework, looking instead to the aid of experimental imaginings. Yet arguably the book gains distinction by differentiating itself from a rather selective history of literary and psychological discourses. For Didion summarizes yet ultimately surpasses grief-therapy's eclectic trends. Offering in their place her own elegant addition to the contemporary archive of mourning, she affirms *The Year*'s singularity in both mode and aspiration.

At the same time, however, Didion never hesitates to interrogate her own medium. She broaches head-on the issue of whether memoir, as a genre, will ever be capable of conveying the irrationalities of magical thought as an unpredictable, involuntary symptom of grief. In a cautionary prelude, Didion debates the rationale for *The Year*'s engagement with mourning's derailments. Can loss be documented if it's so recent as to resist assimilation, all the more evasive thanks to its proximity? Didion's answer sizes up the means on offer, the first to do with style itself. Despite this being a memoir concerned with convoluted counterplots to death—magical thinking's substitutive fantasies of out-smarting oblivion—Didion keeps a careful watch on linguistic transparency, exercising authority over the material, erratic though that material originally was. Hence she could, in principle, 'show' her reader 'simultaneously all the frames of memory that come to me now, let you pick the takes, the marginally different expressions, the variant readings of the same lines' (6). And yet, '[t]his is a case in which I need more than words to find the meaning. This is a case in which I need whatever it is I think or believe to be penetrable, if only for myself' (6). Needing something more than words, even if that means whatever *is* grasped is articulable only to herself—such is the premise of a memoir that stages the very encounter with magical thinking it recalls, while also maintaining a running commentary on its own reproduction of the past.

One rhetorical tendency of this self-commentary is to collate questions that are at the same time self-revelations. Honing 'a mode of urgent testimony', as Gilbert describes it, which is also alert to the 'bitter repetitiveness of grief', Didion poses hypothetical queries that probe the magical thoughts she otherwise perpetuates.[45] As questions go, they seem unanswerable, or answerable only within the realm of further yearning conjecture: 'I was trying to work out what time it had been when he died and whether it was that time yet in Los Angeles. (Was there time to go back? Could we have a different ending on Pacific time?)' (29). Time's brutal irreversibility becomes a motif in *The Year*, with verbal or phrasal repetitions simulating longing's reiterations as well as Didion's recurrent expectation of John's impossible return.

Yet magical thinking is not entirely self-deceiving, not entirely conditioned by wilful fantasy. If anything, it carries and requires a kind of self-analysis: a willingness to register what's possible beyond the bounds of responsible and logical thought; but also a willingness to recognize the perilous satisfactions of doing so. A process of reflexive hypothesizing, magical thinking makes us wary of the surrogate fortunes it concocts even as we indulge them, allowing us thereby to see how substitution and solace are by no means the same. Didion mobilizes this wariness, knowing she was 'still crazy' while also taking 'a step back'. Magical thinking isn't consistently consoling in *The Year*; that much is for certain. Yet it rarely seems anything less than inevitable, just as the prospect of dispensing with John's shoes seems unthinkable. At first, Didion assumes she can 'handle what remained of the shoes, a start'. But then

> I stopped at the door to the room.
> I could not give away the rest of his shoes.
> I stood there for a moment, then realized why: he would need shoes if he was to return.
> The recognition of this thought by no means eradicated the thought.
> I have still not tried to determine (say, by giving away the shoes) if the thought has lost its power. (35)

Brief, staccato, even insistent—the single-sentence observations in this sequence rhythmically capture Didion's abrupt, segmented apprehension of fantastical thinking for what it is. Yet her shift into the present tense (in that final sentence) only ratchets up the memory's ambivalent afterglow: a good deal of time may have passed since this episode of delusion; but that does little to alter its allure. Hindsight's sober rationalism doesn't really take hold where we might expect it to do, in the clear light of Didion's self-analysing present. With that, the consoling thought of John's homecoming prompted by keeping his shoes freezes into an enduring possibility, reinforced visibly on the page here by the scene's syntax, which remains coolly succinct, segmented, unfazed. A talismanic 'recognition', her 'thought' confirms without undermining the solace of implausibility she conserves, a consolation the continued existence of those shoes prolongs. However measured and even-tempered her style seems, it does little to dispel magical thinking's lasting attractions.

There's an intriguing friction, therefore, between style and recollection in this memoir, whereby the raw precision of Didion's prose provides no mitigation, let alone remedy, for the disarming irrationality of the behaviour she plots. 'I did not believe in the resurrection of the body', attests Didion, 'but I still believed that given the right circumstances he would come back' (150). Point-blank self-portraits like this further *The Year*'s work of self-examination. In fact, Didion readily affirms the very appeal of the magical thinking she also distances herself from, a double-act that finds her eyeing the deceptiveness of moments she so movingly documents—moments, like the one above, freighted with the consolations of conjecture. Given her rhetorical penchant for questions, Didion pits absolving facts against incriminating uncertainties, as the reality of what's happened collides with suspicions about her own accountability towards the notion of writing as resuscitation. Implicitly ruminating on its own resurrections, *The Year* thus 'opens up questions about the divide' we face between death's brute actuality and our indelible impressions of the departed: 'If the dead were truly to come back, what would they come back knowing? Could we face them? We who allowed them to die? The clear light of day tells me that I did not allow John to die, that I did not have that power, but do I believe that? Does he?' (153).

By ending whole sequences of text with such questions, Didion seems to want to resist the successive, small-scale closures implied by episode breaks, or at least to suggest that such miniature endings are by no means synonymous with affective resolutions. Instead, whatever finality these sectional intervals insinuate soon dissipates. Typography advertises Didion's preference for deferring resolution, even if that means resorting to repetition across the book. One of her choice tactics for refusing simple appeasement is to re-circle over the same verbal fragments (including *Life changes in the instant, You sit down to dinner and life as you know it ends, The question of self-pity*). As these capsule statements reopen unfinished arguments, so too the motivic recurrence of certain phrases draws our attention back to stray lines couched in bafflement, defying not only explanation (despite their simplicity) but also the solace of familiarity, of renewal, that comes with a reprise. Such sentence fragments pulse like refrains, instantiating Didion's 'sense'—now as a writer yet 'even as a child'—that meanings are 'resident in the rhythms of words and sentences and paragraphs' (5), though meaning here remains opaque, obscured by death's inexplicable suddenness. Accentuated with each recurrence, isolated captions thus remind us of what Didion can't quite decipher about the portentous aura of actions and dialogue leading up to John's final seconds:

> *You sit down to dinner.*
>
> 'You can use it if you want to', John said when I gave him the note he had dictated a week or two before.
>
> *And then—gone.* (24)

As Christopher Nealon has observed, 'since Faulkner, at least, modulations into italicized prose have come to signal reverie, lyricism, a matrix in which anguish can be given shape, but not too rigid a shape'.[46] In Didion's case, such italicized segments—which encompass retrospective, 'omniscient' reflection as well as reported speech—accumulate in ways that don't necessarily unpack their implications. Accreted rather than analysed, their lingering blankness is part of the point. Repetition captures for Didion grief's nagging, echoic reminders not only of loss itself but also of signals she might have missed in advance of death's irreversible instant. Recurrent fragments don't necessarily contain in their own right any narrative purpose or impetus; they resonate as accumulated relics. Statements of fact or, as above, seemingly offhand remarks from John, are left unembellished—untouched by retrospection's factual advantage. This places the reader in a position of perspectival restriction akin to that of the griever: through unadorned, reiterated, unprocessed phrases, Didion seems to emphasize the disconsolate coexistence of bereavement and bewilderment.

Not knowing what to expect or proportionately feel is a common enough experience of mourning. Particular unto itself, each episode of grief allows no dress rehearsal. That bereavement 'is nothing we expect it to be' represents a mental deficit which magical thinking works to rectify, producing compensatory illusions of how and when our losses could have been intimated in advance:

> Grief turns out to be a place none of us know until we reach it. We anticipate (we know) that someone close to us could die, but we do not look beyond the few days or weeks that immediately follow such an imagined death. We misconstrue the nature of even those few days or weeks. We might expect if the death is sudden to feel shock. We do not expect this shock to be obliterative, dislocating to both body and mind. We might expect that we will be prostrate, inconsolable, crazy with loss. We do not expect to be literally crazy, cool customers who believe that their husband is about to return and need his shoes. In the version of grief we imagine, the model will be 'healing'. A certain forward momentum will prevail. The worst days will be the earliest days. We imagine that the moment to most severely test us will be the funeral, after which this hypothetical healing will take place. (189–90)

The whole passage is oriented around the collective pronoun to assert—in pointed, declarative syntax—what *we* might tend to *anticipate, misconstrue, expect,* and *imagine* in reacting to death as something both inevitable yet obscure. In speaking about what *we* do, of course, Didion is no further from herself: this excursion into a universal condition enumerates reactions which are also peculiarly hers, as readers will have already discovered by this point in *The Year*. Couched therefore in a serial diagnosis of our common notion of grief's unfathomability is a testament to responses that are singularly Didion's own. Confessions about what she couldn't foresee about herself entwine with, if not ultimately overtake, general statements about all the '[w]e have no way of knowing' in the process of bereavement and supposed 'healing' (190). Didion resists this 'model' of developmental recovery, despite the memoir's basic conceit of following a year in the life of her evolving grief.

The deviation between feeling and form is itself consequential for the larger picture Didion aims to paint of mourning's unforeseeable recapitulations. For a book premised on the unstoppable succession of months, *The Year* paradoxically plots a discontinuous progression of affective reactions. Didion records the distance she doesn't necessarily want to travel away from the period immediately before and after John's death, a period that she compulsively revisits. Though structurally determined by that temporal unit of a year, on a rather different, expressional level the memoir counters the assumption that 'forward movement will prevail' (190), especially when Didion introduces repeated phrases, as we have seen, that highlight the circularity of reflection over the solace of continuity and resolution. Time is no great remedy here because the temporal experience of grief itself remains more recursive than progressive. As such, *The Year*'s episodic linearity is held in tension with the verbal iterations that punctuate each chapter: a discrepancy thereby shapes the book's very form, a discrepancy between progress and repetition, between overcoming loss and orbiting its origin. And these frictions help us to appreciate how Didion intervenes in customary understandings of what, in reality, recovery from bereavement might mean. If the weeks and months after loss beget any recuperation at all, she implies, this rehabilitation has to contend with the circular manner in which grief returns mourners to its source.

Disrupted assumptions about the way bereavement unfolds also underscore *The Year*'s account of funerals. Organized around the implicit social obligation 'to get through it', the ceremony's progressive ethos is contradicted by the way 'the funeral itself will be anodyne', remarks Didion, 'a kind of narcotic regression in which we are wrapped in the care of others and the gravity and meaning of the occasion' (190). In her view, the crucial and vivid 'difference between grief as we imagine it and grief as it is' lies in our having to live on in 'the unending absence that follows, the void, the very opposite of meaning' (190). This incomprehensible vacuum includes 'the relentless succession of moments during which we will confront the experience of meaninglessness itself' (190). *The Year* is at once a record of that confrontation and an inevitable compensation (not only in its evocative honesty but also in its material status as a critically lauded, award-winning memoir) of the strange vacuity grief represents, all-consuming though its effects might be. Intimations of *succession*, as I have argued, are counterbalanced by Didion's structural and lexical use of repetition, a feature that gives the effect of a purposeful reprise. By returning to—and reprising—valued moments she lends them some quantum of meaning despite the very absence they instantiate. Evidently such 'fragments mattered' to Didion, quoting as she does Eliot's *The Waste Land*: 'These fragments I have shored against my ruins' (192). But fragments are also viewed for what they are, rather than as raw material for filling grief's enduring 'void'. By the same token, Didion isn't content even to take solace in the view of death's unknowability; in fact, we suspect that she would regard with some suspicion Esther Schor's reassurance, in her cultural history of bereavement, that mourning is 'a recognition that the loneliness of death is something we are blessed with not being able to know in this life'.[47]

If anything—if at all—solace in *The Year* resides with speculation: the speculation about whether one can know in advance the telltale signs of death's trespass on life. Didion's thought-experiments in prediction seem like the only available consolation for the impossibility of foreseeing when and why 'Life changes in an instant' (1). Depictions here of implausible pre-emption and equally implausible wishes of return demonstrate how the very 'description of misfortune' (to recall Sebald's phrase) may be enframed yet also strangely propelled by loss, as Didion hypothesizes the consoling 'possibility of misfortune's overcoming' through the fiction of resurrection.[48] As we'll see, though, the book's language seems to enact, as a very condition of that possibility, Didion's recognition that loss remains the thing she struggles most to describe.

Life-Righting and Magical Thinking 169

RECOLLECTION AS REPOSSESSION

Those who are 'grieving have urgent reasons, even an urgent need, to feel sorry for themselves' (194), insists Didion, admitting that in grief we 'are repeatedly left with no further focus than ourselves, a source from which self-pity naturally flows' (196). Didion never assumes that her readers would be compassionate towards this self-pity; if anything, she invites us to question the assumption that such projected compassion is intrinsically virtuous and sufficiently sensitive. Instead, Didion tussles with 'the satisfactions of grief', as Deborah Nelson describes them in her account of the unsentimental aesthetic of writers, artists, and activists like Susan Sontag, Diane Arbus, and Mary McCarthy. These chroniclers of false solace, in Nelson's reading, 'imagined the consolations for pain in intimacy, empathy, and solidarity as *anesthetic*'; in opposition to such palliatives, they shared an insistence on cultivating a 'painful mode' for their postwar audience, 'one that deprives the reader of consolation, certainty, predictability, gratitude, company'. In Didion's journalism, that mode underlies the values she attaches to a 'directness of statement' capable of conveying the 'detail and specificity of experience'. As Nelson points out, Didion eventually sought to 'reevaluate this hardness' in her style. And *The Year of Magical Thinking* would later offer an opportunity to assess the point at which rhetorical austerity pivots into complicity with a kind of 'emotional self-indulgence disguised as stoicism'. Consequently, by the end of the memoir, 'Didion makes her peace', observes Nelson, 'suggesting that the ideal of avoiding self-pity is impossible' and may itself be tacitly consoling, insofar as valiant 'stoicism is a self-delusion that comforts us'.[49] Didion thus comes face to face with a paradox: how to write a heartfelt testament to the brutal effect of losing her husband (also eventually Quintana) without reproducing the potentially distorting succour of self-pity, which in her estimation 'remains both the most common and the most universally reviled of our character defects' (194)—a flaw that cannot be entirely evaded.

The Year's style has a role of its own to play in this conundrum. No doubt the hardness of Didion's prose is one factor behind the memoir's resistance to renditions of emotionally overt, lyricized poignancy. But there's one significant exception, in a scene with which I'll soon finish, where Didion no longer seems intent on warding off solace with an unsentimental rhetoric of restraint, and where she vividly documents an intimate memory without condemning that intimacy as a dubiously compensatory distraction from anguish. There, as we'll see, style participates in a more permissive conversation with consolation throughout a closing episode that still wrenches the reader clear of any mitigating resolution.

The scene in question is all the more noticeable because *The Year* for the most part remains so stylistically guarded, matching in language Didion's unflinching, adamant pursuit of grief's susceptibility to misunderstanding and cultural generalization. It's not that the book is affectively quelled, or so replete with intellectual reflections or detours as to preclude a more immediate, visceral sense of what life can be like (to recall Julian Barnes's term) for the 'grief-struck'. Rather, Didion's way of confronting raw emotion through intellection—her assiduous revaluation of grief's rituals and pathologies, her probing of discrepant partnerships between the work of acceptance and the illusions of undying—can lead us to sidestep rather more uncomfortable questions for the reader. For does her constant debate with the mental unpredictability and social customs of bereavement forestall in *The Year* the possibility of *simulating* grief's commotion in linguistic terms? Does the meticulous exposé of culture's inadequate resources for confronting loss leave Didion's own plot of mourning so measured, so carefully couched in a 'penetrable' style devoid of 'polish', as to bleach its verbal texture of the disorientation she periodically describes (6, 5)? Grievers find themselves prone to the prevailing social view, according to Didion, that '[v]isible mourning reminds us of death', such that bereavement is 'construed as unnatural, a failure to manage the situation' (193). Yet her own withheld prose reproduces a version of the self-management she queries. Perhaps she was trying to avoid the sort of 'clotted and sentimental' style that 'didn't work' for her 'on any level' when she first read D. H. Lawrence as a literature major at Berkeley.[50] Perhaps in turn this was why she had chosen to tackle grief, as Hilton Als would later suggest, 'with reporter's eyes'. Whatever the shaping motive, *The Year* holds expressivity in check. Grammatically taut, figuratively trim, Didion's prose verges on the very 'corrective thinking' she indicts, the kind that bridles extravagant displays of grief by persuading those in distress to concede that their 'own loss is nothing compared to the loss experienced... by he or she who died' (193). Despite her attunement to magical thinking's volatile states of being, Didion's prevailing aesthetic seems inadvertently analogous to that traditional obligation to handle mourning through self-command which *The Year* interrogates.[51] It's as though the book's expressive options have been mediated, contaminated even, by the same mentally unhealthy yet socially sanctioned rites of recovery Didion critiques.

Even to make these observations, however, feels uncomfortable. That's not because it's inherently unethical to read grief memoirs against their own grain, but rather because, in attempting such a reading, one evaluates renditions of affective turmoil for which there are ultimately no artistic goalposts. And for this reason, what does seem unethical is the corollary suggestion that some styles of grief-writing can somehow be more appropriate than others. All the same—and despite my unease with this line of inquiry—surely no memoir is beyond evaluation, however candid its content may be, however emotively its drama of vulnerability solicits the reader's sympathy, however insistently it thereby ushers that reader into a corner of respectful appreciation. In Didion's case, our prompt *for* evaluation comes in the end from what *The Year* decides to do rather than from what it lacks. In a tender closing scene recalling her time with John on the Palos Verdes Peninsula, Didion's evocative lyricism seems almost out of character: as the sea swells, so does her style, and this amplification invites us to reflect back on the more contained, denotative idiom of her foregoing chapters.

> I think about swimming with him into the cave at Portuguese Bend, about the swell of clear water, the way it changed, the swiftness and power it gained as it narrowed through the rocks at the base of the point. The tide had to be just right. We had to be

in the water at the very moment the tide was right. We could only have done this a half dozen times at most during the two years we lived there but it is what I remember. Each time we did it I was afraid of missing the swell, hanging back, timing it wrong. John never was. You had to feel the swell change. You had to go with the change. He told me that. No eye is on the sparrow but he did tell me that.   (229)

This closing passage seems designed to evade neat extrapolation, intercepting memory's transcription into the sort of commentary that might take advantage of a scene whose poignancy appears both distant and durably vivid. Didion refuses to reframe the sheer simplicity of 'what I remember' in view of all the terrible losses ahead. And she refuses to cherish the episode for its obliviousness of future sorrow or to mine its symbolism for auguries of anguish. Instead she lets allied impressions (of 'missing the swell', of 'feel[ing] the swell') accumulate and stand on their own unanalysed terms. Ending unresolved—or, rather, resolved only insofar as Didion's recollection of John's emphatic advice that she 'had to go with the change' of the tide *sounds* conclusive—this scene behaves differently from the narrative that precedes it, where Didion is determined to unpick our assumptions about grief by scanning the effects of magical thinking with a frankness that's sometimes anything but irresolute. In this final image, the book therefore shifts key. In contrast to its earlier use of punctuating dates and stark diagnoses, *The Year* modulates into a sensually visual mode, one that resembles the way literary impressionism makes impressions themselves 'dramatically significant (rather than randomly meaningless)', in Jesse Matz's words, but meaningful here, it seems, only unto themselves. Only, that is, for Didion herself, not for us; and certainly not for the reader who would be tempted to extract from this ending a clear insight into the relation between memory and mourning.[52]

At the last minute, then, the reporter's eyes have been superseded by painterly ones. Didion has spoken about how much she 'missed' the West Coast after moving back to New York in 1988, in particular the coastal view of 'horizons', which she found 'very soothing'. In a sense, nothing could be more ordinary than picturing or finding routine solace in 'the sky doing all its brilliant stuff' over a crepuscular horizon; but that's the point.[53] At the heart of impressionism, as Matz reminds us, 'are moments in which an ordinary perception spurs revelations because of its relative nullity'. And in the concluding passage of *The Year*, Didion preserves that perceptual nullity for its own sake, emphasizing above all—which is to say, above any definitive sense of conclusion—the private significance of a venture for her and John that was possible only 'half dozen times at most during' their stay in the region. Hence in its lush closing lines, *The Year* turns militantly in on itself, away from the sober scrutiny of grief's delusions or social customs towards the simplicity, the ordinariness, of John's instructions. Didion reproduces his imperative ('[y]ou had to go with the change') in a form that invokes recorded speech and recasts it in the past tense. Talismanic, this fleeting caption of what John 'told' her now resurfaces and inflects her own retrospection. Because she omits punctuation that would signal them as dialogue, the words themselves sound for an instant closer to *her* discourse than his. The phrase 'to go with the change' thereby seems all the more poignant because it swaps ownership, if only for a beat—epitomizing how recollection can repossess the very diction it elegizes. Claiming words that were not her own as though they are now hers to reabsorb, Didion suggests that their provenance has been passed on, allowing language to requite even as it registers what has physically gone.

Maybe this is ultimately another instance of magical thinking, but one that's reserved for expression rather than recounted action: words once heard as advice from someone else now merge with a vocabulary much closer to one's own, their survival in cherished thought consoling for their lamented source in conversation. Maybe this is also why Didion chooses to conclude her narrative with phrases that possess no conclusive gloss, free of adorning commentary and overt profundity— there's no lesson in good grieving to be gleaned from this glimpse. If early twentieth-century impressionist fiction evolved out of the belief 'that perceptual immediacy has an innocence required for sophistication, that aesthetic susceptibility is a form of justice to what is real', then Didion carries forward this conviction without exactly fulfilling impressionism's epistemological promise: the promise that would 'stake' significant 'meaning on the barest glimpse', where 'something substantial emerges' from 'rudimentary awareness'.[54] For if *The Year*'s close offers a measure of solace, it stems from a somewhat different promise: to preserve a moving impression simply for what it is, not for the sagacity it may yield. Following the memoir's previous journeys into how 'we mourn our losses' (199), this suddenly lyrical incident consoles the text it finishes by letting go of self-scrutiny, by attaching no unnecessary gravity to intuition, by being nothing more substantial than the abiding impression it leaves.

STORIES TO LIVE BY

Readers will already have noticed that endings seem important to this book, even though I'm cautious about recycling a familiar way of associating consolation with the resolutions and satisfactions that finales sometimes bring. On this matter, as for so many others, *The Year of Magical Thinking* prompts us to think about the ethics of drawing conclusive lessons about mourning from episodes that bring books to a close, even as Didion's writing performs sudden, climactic modulations, as we have just seen, to counter the affective obliterations it elsewhere anatomizes. 'It occurs to me', she reflects, 'that we allow ourselves to imagine only such messages as we need to survive' (215). If counterfactual speculations can be consoling, as Lessing's novella half of *Alfred and Emily* implied, then they need also to be selective. Didion appears to accept this proviso, which is a version of her assertion in the title essay to *The White Album*: 'We tell ourselves stories in order to live.'[55]

Therein lies Didion's double-bind in reconjuring John: since she is a writer, '[i]magining what someone would say or do comes to me as naturally as breathing' (197); yet she recognizes that for her 'to imagine what he could say only in my edit would seem obscene, a violation' (197). Taking advantage of creative license, she confronts the consequences of literary reconstruction becoming a self-soothing activity—an analgesic resource to live by. This confrontation extends to the level of structure, too. When *The Year* draws to an end it becomes troubled by the implications of closure. Summing-up a record of bereavement is not nearly as consoling as structural completion implies. And by unpicking closure, Didion counters the idea that mourning facilitates or even requires progressive self-healing of the sort that eventually stems grief's persistence:

> I realize as I write that I do not want to finish this account.
>   Nor did I want to finish the year.
>   The craziness is receding but no clarity is taking its place.
>   I look for resolution and find none.   (226–7)

Over the course of the writing process itself, Didion comes to 'know why we try to keep the dead alive: we try to keep them alive in order to keep them with us' (227). Moreover, despite her reluctance to finish the memoir, its completion will itself be a tangible acknowledgment 'that if we are to live ourselves there comes a point at which we must relinquish the dead, let them go, keep them dead' (227), even though this feels like 'betrayal' (228). Without implying superficial reconciliations with loss, Didion brings her debate with the tendencies and temptations of magical thinking to an irresolute conclusion. *The Year* does so by highlighting the consoling illusions of keeping the dead alive, not as evidence of damaging denials that lurk in the grieving process, but as a way of bearing witness to the griever's imaginative adaptability and to the expressive demands that grief entails—which, for that reason, are worth recording.

Writing in full consciousness of the consolations of believing in death's undoing, Didion recognizes that recollection can perpetuate a substitutive fantasy of collapsing time, offering the therapeutic impression that '*Time passes*', as she would later put it in *Blue Nights*, albeit not '*not for me*'.[56] As a work of reflexive self-portraiture, *The Year* alerts us to those thresholds that distinguish unconsoled mourning from the survival tactics that grief itself affords the bereaved imagination. It also prompts us to notice how misleading it is to regard such tactics simply as deflections of loss's irreparability. Thus Didion forestalls the two-dimensional understanding of solace as a self-destructive denial of mourning's durability over time, or as a solution for sidestepping grief's formidable cycles of recession and intensification. If anything, thinking consolation with Didion's help is more disarming than appeasing, a testament to her kinship with Lessing's celebration of literature as 'unpredictable', 'maverick', and 'uncomfortable'.[57]

At the same time, both of these writers suggest that narrative—even as it captures affective ruptures—remains a 'safety line', to recall Lessing's analogy, 'something to hold on to'. Both highlight too the ethical ramifications of scripting lives—whether actual or alternative, be they damaged or redeemed—with great verbal panache. For Didion, expression is kept on a tight leash, suggesting that innovation in self-revealing memoir is never far from the all-consuming diversions of magical thinking. Style remains under close watch, as though embellishment in manner can belie extravagance of mind. Yet for Lessing, her prose appears most energetic, as we observed, when it turns from substitute circumstances to the world of auto/biographical fact. What these writers undoubtedly share, though, is a desire to reflect in compositionally self-conscious terms on what memoir recuperates from its chronicles of the unsalvageable. More implicitly, they reflect too on what it means to generate formally striking sequences from the emotional privacies of mourning and self-reproach, from visions of averted misfortune, from knowingly deceptive fantasies of perseverance.

'You can not libel the dead', reflects Veronica in Anne Enright's *The Gathering* (2007), 'you can only console them'.[58] Didion would no doubt agree; as might Lessing, who battled her own resentment towards Emily by ejecting herself from a fantasy that replaces parenthood with two destinies flourishing apart—the gendered work of consolation (including its withholding) in a chronicle of such familial anger and disappointment could not be more apparent. Yet both writers also implicate themselves, testing the pretensions of writing to attenuate bereavement and redress familial tragedy. Taken together, Didion and Lessing further our understanding of solace precisely through their refusal to iron out the discrepancy that makes consolation at once sought after and invariably unfit for the purposes of grappling with loss. Rather than rehashing for-and-against arguments about literature's facilitation of solace, they produce new and vigorous versions of those arguments as a problem of style—one that style itself in their rhetorically self-troubling texts doesn't necessarily solve.

Magical thinking, channelled towards the rewriting of alternative fortunes, does raise ethical questions about who is being consoled and what exactly is being restored—especially when we know what the outcomes actually are. As Fredric Jameson has observed, 'counterfactuality and alternate worlds play out their solutions by way of a shuffling of a limited number of tokens given in advance: we must know what did happen in order to enjoy the consolation of modifying it'.[59] Such are the solutions in which Didion and Lessing entangle us, processing the painful knowledge of what has already happened by subjecting irrevocable losses to alternative sequels. Consoling the dead is one of their unattainable yet inescapable targets.

From these retrospective memoirs I turn for the final two chapters to fictions of fearful anticipation. Plotting the apprehension of oncoming sorrow, Kazuo Ishiguro and David Grossman reveal dread to be consolation's most formidable opponent. Their novels tussle with the question of whether solace is even thinkable when there's no way of dodging the torment one foresees. Like proleptic elegies, they seek against the odds, ahead of time itself, to contemplate the stakes of forestalling the inexorability of desolation; but they also withstand consolation's prospect in the first place, holding out against the imminence of its emotional indispensability. With auguries of unbidden solace, they lend us the binocular vision required to see how future compensations can be both coveted and undesired.

6

Apprehensive Alleviation

There's no consolation without the foretaste of its unpredictable cessation. And yet nothing could be less consoling, surely, than dread. Few other feelings would seem to militate more stringently against solace. With apprehension as its accomplice, dread gnaws away at appeasement, coaxing us into conjecture while eroding our willingness to imagine respite from the looming shadow of future harm. Though we tend to equate foresight with being reassuringly forearmed, apprehensiveness suggests the converse may be true: trepidation forecloses our best efforts to allay anxieties, however unfounded, over oncoming calamity. Dread thereby seems to reverse the temporal arrow of Emily Dickinson's memorable assertion that 'After great pain, a formal feeling comes', by convincing us of the need to steel ourselves in advance of some impending damage, even if its arrival is unspecifiable.[1] Before the pain, speculation gives prophetic shape to states of concern that we cannot verify as likelihoods for certain—convincing us that worry feels warranted in a time of unrelieved expectancy, regardless of whether it turns out to be unjustified in actuality. The 'Chill' and subsequent 'Stupor' that mark, for Dickinson, grief's passage from shock to mourning coalesce in dread's case, halting us in anticipatory suspension.[2] Prompting grim forethought, jeopardy blunts the potent solace of magical thinking by shutting us off from the mental refuge of reimagining the course of what seems unavoidable.

This sense of foreboding is of course dread's signature mood, its very own 'formal feeling'. Since they can feel so persuasively proleptic, intimations of apparently ineluctable harm repel consolation, coercing us instead to make rough estimates of pain that somehow already feels tangible. Triggering irresistible worry, dread sidelines solace not simply by causing alarm too acute to be assuaged, but also by seducing us into believing that future adversity is already too palpable to be averted. In fact, dread is all about specifics, even though we might not foretell exactly whether our portents are reasonable or proportionate. Which is why dread is so tough to redress; why it resists being quelled with rational explanation or offset by the comforting reassurance of probabilities; why its oracular narratives of injury, loss, or demise can seem so immune from mitigating counterplots. If paranoia is a fear of *un*specified threat, then dread gives presentiment clearer directions, making fear's justification in turn easier to grasp. Attuned to this distinction, writers in these final two chapters criss-cross the connotations of *apprehension* itself: when their characters' informed anticipation of what lies ahead does little to quell the consternation this foreknowledge produces; and when alleviation may be the very cause of apprehensiveness, because the prospect of having to be consoled is precisely what these individuals seek to avoid.

Dramatically ominous though all this may sound, contemporary writers have also housed the fraught coexistence of solace and apprehension in quieter, apparently unremarkable neighbourhoods of contemplation. Graham Swift is a seasoned explorer of these everyday precincts, where consolations for domestic tragedy divulge their own fragility. A widower in his fifties, Swift's Eric knows the end of his relationship with the beautiful 26-year-old Tanya is 'coming one day'—'Of course it is'.[3] For now, though, he seems oddly consoled by that prediction, as it does nothing to detract from the fact that he has had this time, however limited, a period remains for now a rare tonic: 'You've drunk the glass, I tell myself, till it's filled next time, but there's still this last drop. Don't waste it' (76). There's even a curious solace for Eric in anticipating the very circumstances of Tanya's departure, after which he envisages himself living alone again yet finding some respite from solitude in the mind's eye, some modicum of succour in projection: 'Just to imagine her being in the world is something, and may be all I'll have one day, any day now' (76). Be consoled by what you have, by what you've shared, and want no more—with this injunction in mind, Eric isn't altogether resigned. But he does keep a lookout for the false consolations of hubristic expectation; only arrogance would permit him to take solace in the idea of the relationship lasting. 'Half a loaf', he reflects, a homely phrase that lends this story its prosaic title, one as unexceptional as any other in Swift's rather exceptional 2015 collection. Eric nonetheless wonders 'isn't this life, the whole of it? Shouldn't I be thanking, praising heaven?' (76).

Perhaps Eric should, given that his father was a 'churchman'. In the Second World War he served as 'an RAF padre', routinely providing solace rather than receiving it. For traumatized pilots, Eric's father 'had to be their comfort' (77). Eric himself has a less indoctrinated sense of the great beyond, reclaiming the afterlife from theological piety as a space for dialogue with his wife when he visits her grave. Three years have passed since Anthea's death, and Eric reflects on how in its wake he 'willed' his own demise, coming at the peak of grief 'close to making it happen' (78). His mourning led to Tanya; or rather, to the 'mental breakdown' in the middle of his osteopathic practice that drew her—a patient at the time—into his life: 'Perhaps for some women, charm, if I have any, is well mixed with a little vulnerability. But this was hardly vulnerability, or a little of it. Was it naked bribery? A performance I'd somehow mustered. I don't care' (80). He consoles himself further by speculating that 'if Anthea is watching' him, 'as God is supposed to watch', then 'she might not wish to punish' 'or even reproach'. It ought not to seem implausible that she would offer encouragement instead, ushering him into a new phase of life beyond loss: 'About time, Eric, about time something like this happened' (79). Even as he takes Tanya on their first date he 'still had the thought: Anthea is willing me on, this is all under her aegis' (80).

To that extent, Eric doesn't want to be consoled if it leads to the complete alleviation of grieving, since Tanya is part of a process that 'has continued for nearly two months' (81), one that amounts to a journey with loss not simply bereavement's libidinal remedy. As time periods go, this is 'already beyond any due allowance – whatever that might be' (81). Consequently, Eric doesn't let himself indulge the fantasy of perpetuity in which this dalliance would flourish into lasting love. Neither does he 'dare believe that she comes because of something [he] give[s] her' (81). Instead, Eric's offbeat consolation stems precisely from his acceptance that Tanya 'has the power to destroy [him] at any moment' (81), an acceptance that carries with it the additionally consoling recognition that at least he knows this about her, even as he concedes that 'people are a mystery, period' (82). Deliberating on the precariousness of their relationship; picturing himself as the object of Tanya's 'thrill' in 'having another human soul dangling from her fingertips' (81); confronting rather than denying the reality of her having an existing, 'regular boyfriend' her own age (81) – all these admissions carry discrepant consolations because they also keep alive for Eric the feeling that Anthea has 'come back' in the guise of an advocate who hopes (as he himself always hopes) that Tanya 'comes back' (82), a fellow supporter of a grief-born intimacy that might otherwise seem foredoomed.

What leaves Eric decidedly unconsoled, therefore, is the prediction that when Tanya leaves, so will the revenant Anthea who has recently felt to him so 'present' (82). To withstand this desolate prospect, he clings to the notion that from his wife's perspective the charge of betrayal will be absolved: displacing insinuations of infidelity, the couple reconjoin in conspiracy. Disloyalty becomes the paradoxically consoling pretext for celebrating the partnership he once had and whose vitality the grave site so inadequately monumentalizes. In spite of that solace, he 'know[s] it will end, of course it will end':

> The day will come. And when it comes I know one other terrible thing for certain. This sense that Anthea is with me and is glad for me, even egging me on, this sense that I'm wrapped in her generosity and that she no longer has to mourn for me, locked out here in the cold zone of life—that too will be gone. I won't feel her presence, won't hear her voice in my ear. I'll just be another lost, dutiful man going once a week to mutter words to a stone and getting no words back. (83–4)

In Swift's scenario, stoical forethought seems all the more touching because it ultimately doesn't allow Eric to predict exactly when that 'terrible thing' he anticipates will occur. To be sure, he feels he can 'know' 'for certain' the consequences of the loss he envisions; but such pre-emptive habits ultimately offer none of the reassurances we typically associate with foresight. In any case, Eric doesn't want to be alleviated of Anthea's present haunting, for that would spell his return to being the 'dutiful' widower appealing for a more conventional rite of condolence. His intimacy with Tanya has become, through magical thinking, an intimacy with the dead, making plausible an alternative way of working through loss, one that contemplates the destructiveness of wanting back 'what cannot be restored'—in David Grossman's words—without simply disregarding these longings or sating them with surrogate company and sexual fulfilment.[4]

Swift is too shrewd a writer to allow sympathy to build towards his narrators without complication. 'Half a Loaf' is no exception, moving though the story remains. For Eric's 'dialogue' with Anthea is a knowing contrivance: a tacitly if harmlessly self-reassuring monologue, which he conducts on his own beneficent terms. That he presumes the affair will console his dead wife because 'she no longer has to mourn' the husband she's left behind could been seen as a self-serving compensation for his having to endure 'the cold zone of life'. But at the same time, Swift invites us to pause before we condemn this effort to unpick the knot of grief and guilt. If those consoling rendezvous with Tanya seem to us blatantly self-seeking, then this indictment competes with Swift's presentation of Eric as someone who remains unwilling to accept the comforting prospect that time with a new partner will inevitably beget repair, who recognizes that moments spent with Tanya are nothing less than a measure of consolation's volatility. Solace in Swift's tale augurs its own indeterminate yet inevitable termination. The story's punctum—the pathetic tear it makes in its brief chronicle of uplift—thus brings into poignant focus consolation's habit of facilitating our apprehension of its own brevity.

But when might the source of sorrow be the expectation of consolation itself? How could the very prospect of solace effectively morph into a jeopardizing moment from which one wants to flee or, in wishful desperation, to forestall? And in such situations, whether immediate or remote, what other resources of emotional rescue are at our disposal when consolation wears out its welcome? Across the following pages and then in the final chapter, I take up these questions with the help of novels that combine retrospection with expectant threat and anticipated mourning. These works dramatize the ways in which apprehending loss coincides with recollections that promise to shield characters from what they dread. Intensive, lyrically intimate descriptions of the past serve not only as a rhetorical counterpoint but also as an emotional deterrent to future scenarios that give the impression of being both unmasterable yet all too predictable, scenarios that bear the equally threatening likelihood of necessitated solace. These affective provocations direct our attention to quite different formal strategies and historically contingent circumstances in the work of Kazuo Ishiguro and David Grossman. When read in succession, though, their novels will offer opportunities to reprise the critical optics that throughout this book have refracted the ethics and poetics of solace: modernism's troubled efforts to fetch forms of presence back from the brink of oblivion; description's capacity for redress in the most dramatically unlikely contexts; writers' scrutiny of elegy's dynamic work of recuperation through retrospection; flights of magical thinking that navigate tempests of grief; and those expectant novels of inexorable loss considered in Chapter 4, whose narrative arcs of anticipation will return for a stirring encore in novels to come, where consolation is just as likely to trigger trepidation as to meet the expectation of alleviation.

CARING ABOUT APPREHENSION

To address what solace might mean for those who feel apprehensive about needing or receiving it, we need to step for a moment beyond the perimeters of literary and cultural studies. Perspectives from scholars of palliative nursing, in particular, help us to recognize, first, how consolation's expectation can turn into something we want to evade rather than embrace and, second, to account for what might be left for the consoler in this situation, where comfort is not only feared but refused because of what it heralds. Research on the ethics of care has shown that 'constant vigilance becomes a way of life' for patients enduring 'the anticipation of dreaded or painful experiences'. As Janice Morse, Joan Bottorff, and Sally Hutchinson explain, because it's so 'hard to find a language to define comfort states', it can also be hard to calculate what consolation signifies for people who are 'hypersensitive to ominous signs of impending pain or discomfort'.[5] In a hospice context, this challenge becomes especially acute unless, as Birgit H. Rasmussen, Lilian Jansson, and Astrid Norberg suggest, patient and carer find 'it possible to talk about dying and death openly, and learn from one another'. They point out that '[o]ne may even be comforted by the death of a fellow patient', and that medical practitioners need to find ways of articulating experiences in which 'dying does not have to be horrible, but instead can be peaceful and dignified, a dying one can hope to have for oneself'.[6] Shifting expectations from dread to some level of ease is partly what the 'meaning of consolation' might be in this sort of care environment. Solace, these researchers found, entails for patients something like 'a shift of center from me as a suffering person to something in between, to experiences of belonging, and feeling at-home with others and the world'. To be consoled, accordingly, is not merely to be comforted; it is rather to recognize, through communing with others, one's own sense of 'becoming in suffering'.[7]

While a great deal of work on the ethics of consolation in patient care is empirically based—substantiated by concrete data from case studies—as the terminology of 'becoming' and 'belonging' here implies researchers have incorporated phenomenological models of emotional self-identification as well. Using this rather more conceptual framework, they have been able to study consolation as it occurs through conversational exchange, empathy, and mutual understanding. What we learn from these findings is that solace lives a mutable, discursive, intersubjective life. Description between patient and carer becomes vital in communing about oncoming eventualities that might otherwise provoke dread. Idealist though they might seem, such arguments are invested in the practical work of altering institutional perceptions of care, so that the practice of administering care itself might be about consoling dialogue, unconfined to pain relief alone. The implication is that nursing practices ought to reflect explicitly on the balance they're able to strike between medicalized treatment and more interactive, verbal forms of comfort, in light of research that suggests that '[w]hen the suffering person becomes open and expresses suffering and the person mediating consolation becomes open they share suffering', entering a relation of 'communion' whose 'prerequisite' is 'a shared affective state, rather than a shared cognitive interpretation of the situation'.[8]

This secularized notion of communion with actual or anticipated distress might sound wishful, even utopian. But the model serves to remind us of the interactive nature of solace itself in situations of care, where consolation's efficacy often cannot be conceived and calibrated in advance of the interpersonal encounter that occasions and requires it. Solace can't really be prescribed, just as the success of communion can rarely be guaranteed. And the unpredictability of interactions in care reminds us that 'the most difficult aspect of hospice nursing' is often the carer's own capacity, 'when *un*able to console', for 'still remaining present in the midst of profound powerlessness and helplessness'.[9] Trepidation's turbulence complicates any notion of solace as immediately therapeutic; and fear's particularity often quashes the hope that delivering consolation might be somehow portable—easily transferred between patients with comparable emotional states and medical conditions. If sufficiently attentive and sympathetic, a nurse may well be equipped to offer consolation as a form of what Janice Morse calls 'compathy', giving comfort by empathizing with a situation of existing or imminent distress. But however empathetic the consoler, however keen their 'ability to identify with the patient's *physiologic* state', there is always the possibility that presumptions about what it is people desire when in distress will misread the actuality of needs, volatile as we know they are.[10] For anyone who has been involved in care, whether professionally or for family, it's not difficult to see how problematic it can be to decide in advance—affectively or medically—what form solace might take, just as there's always the chance that 'nurse and patient perspectives in relation to what is therapeutic and what is comforting might differ'.[11]

In both method and objective, we have entered quite distinct terrain here. It's a far cry from the tone and ambition of critical thought in emotion studies and affect theory, where the emphasis has been on celebrating the diversity, mischievousness, and promiscuity of feelings as they interlock and destabilize each other as well as our preconceptions of them. At times the findings of nursing ethics might seem (for readers in the humanities) too empirical for comfort, too systematically geared towards proving hypotheses about emotions that literary and cultural critics have been trained to regard as evasive. Nonetheless, there are insights to be gleaned from such research. For one thing—at the risk of being blunt—it takes solace seriously. Held up for ethical discussion, consolation in this body of work is refreshingly uninflected by suspicion or habitual qualification. As a result, consolation is uncoupled from superficial diversion and distinguished from the kind of temporary calmative that quells and even aestheticizes pain without solving its causes or consequences. Palliative care researchers ask instructively tough questions about the *practice* of solace in circumstances where we cannot 'assume that if pain is reduced', then 'the patient must be comfortable'. Understanding how the lessening of pain or trepidation might not, indeed, be 'all there is to attaining comfort' strikes me as peculiarly suited to the affective thinking that contemporary novelists cultivate.[12] Soon it will be time for us to take a closer look at how that thinking unfolds for Kazuo Ishiguro. Examining the ethics of care and imminent loss in *Never Let Me Go* (2005), Ishiguro dramatizes, first, the ways in which consolation may endure against backdrops of dread even when it becomes undesired and, second, what it means to console when bodily comfort alone is no longer the horizon of relief.

Ishiguro takes the whole vocation of caring a step further. A novel he conceived, as his archive now reveals, 'with only little hints of doom', *Never Let Me Go* leads unostentatiously into disturbing territory where the ethical scrutiny of nursing no longer relates solely to the provision of comfort but also to the monstrous reasons why patients need caring for in the first place.[13] Like Graham Swift, Ishiguro is a connoisseur of the everyday. This informs his narrators' periodically humdrum yet often-suspenseful ruminations, whose unsettlingly measured tone only exacerbates the effect Salman Rushdie first spotted in *The Remains of the Day* (1989), where '[j]ust below the understatement of the novel's surface is a turbulence as immense as it is slow'.[14] For *Never Let Me Go*, Ishiguro combined that stylistic understatement with artful manipulations of genre that facilitate an ethical meditation on biomedical experimentation. The novel gestures to—though without altogether satisfying—the conventions of dystopian writing, replacing an apocalyptic future with a forbidding past.[15] In the early writing stages, Ishiguro seemed intent on 'not emphasizing the period too much', so as to avoid the 'temptation to connect period with the story'.[16] And indeed the counterfactual portrait of late-twentieth-century England he ended up providing is largely a backdrop for the novel's principal focus: a hypothetical society where the most fundamental subject of institutional care (personhood) has been reduced to purely instrumental use, all but erased from public conscience. In this realm, harvested organs from cloned humans delay the onset of most common fatal diseases, exponentially increasing life expectancy for the general (non-cloned) population. Palliative nursing research emphasizes the importance of patients' 'experience of an empathic relationship with their nurses', an experience best 'captured in the category of "affirmation as a person"'. Hence the problem for Ishiguro's clone characters is that they struggle against the impossibility of ever being acknowledged as having a sense of individuality at all—of ever being 'affirmed' as persons with whom nurses can empathize.[17] That society has legislated this heinous voiding of care is clearly the novel's central ethical abomination and its core thematic preoccupation. Yet the perversion of care itself—including the costs borne by clones who take both pride and comfort in caring for fellow clones who are making donations that will imminently kill them—is also crucial to the pathos the novel generates in troubling the plausibility of solace as such. Denied the very principle of compassionate carer–patient interaction that recent work in nursing ethics adopts as its basic premise, Ishiguro's clones are denied too what Astrid Norberg, Monica Bergsten, and Berit Lundman call the promise of 'consolation as a spontaneous unselfish manifestation of life in an exclusive atmosphere of giving and receiving in mutual trust'.[18]

Unless, that is, they get a carer like our heroine, Kathy H. Having decided to commit her remaining years to nursing clones—including her difficult, jealous friend, Ruth, and the love of her life, Tommy—Kathy accompanies them on successive donations, affording them post-operative solace until the day comes when they 'complete'. She's adamant about the necessity of maintaining care standards as well, regardless of the pointlessness that haunts the whole enterprise and that Tommy insinuates in a brief quarrel late in the novel, where he asks '"is it really that important? Okay, it's really nice to have a good carer. But in the end, is it really so important? The donors will all donate, just the same, and then they'll complete."' Countering the bleak, intrinsic dread of Tommy's observation, Kathy insists: '"Of course it's important. A good carer makes a big difference to what a donor's life's actually like."'[19] Never losing sight of that possibility, Kathy has excelled at what she does. Having 'developed a kind of instinct around donors', she intuitively seems to 'know when to hang around and comfort them, when to leave them to themselves; when to listen to everything they have to say, and when just to shrug and tell them to snap out of it' (3). Knowing how to enable her patients to describe their feelings to themselves—while knowing too when to take up that description herself—partly constitutes the comfort she provides.

Yet Kathy has her own reasons for description on a more existential, self-excavating level too. For the novel itself might be viewed as one extended redescription, as Kathy leads us back to childhood and the friendships forged there with Ruth and Tommy whom she subsequently loses to a life-determining regime she has no capacity to change. What's more, the very genre of Kathy's retrospective story of 'unwanted freedom and remembered anticipation' gathers together poignant instances like collected shards of solace.[20] Resembling a personal memoir both in register and in the confinement of its setting and thematic purview, the narrative compositionally performs—perhaps desperately so, from the reader's perspective—an extended consolation through reminiscing self-description. Kathy's painstaking process of memorialization outweighs, by virtue of its sheer exhaustiveness, the more immediate, dreadfully finite prospect of her time as a carer drawing to a close.[21] As notes from Ishiguro's archive indicate, he pitched the novel's retrospective mode in a rather different register to that of *The Remains of the Day*, where 'memory was something to be searched through very warily for those crucial wrong turns, for those sources of regret and remorse'. By contrast, 'Kathy's memories are more benevolent', observes Ishiguro: as 'her time runs out', they are 'principally a source of consolation'.[22]

Meticulous retrospection, then, serves to moderate fateful apprehension as Kathy's 'world', in Ishiguro's own phrase, 'empties one by one of the things she holds dear'.[23] Memories will endure 'safely in my head', she predicts, comprising 'something no one can take away' as she faces the prospect of that imminent—and, for the reader, ominously—'quieter life' she expects to lead after a decade of nursing a community of donors she'll now join (262). Servicing her sometimes tense relationship with Ruth and her belatedly fulfilled love for Tommy, Kathy's retrospective descriptions console in a structural sense too: they defer the point at which she will need to reorient the stance of this whole testimony to youth, facing it towards a macabrely predetermined end. And what's all the more unnerving about her recollections is the 'assumption', as Mark Currie observes, 'that the reader shares in the knowledge of future events, or belongs to the community of recollectors concerned, so that prolepsis is an unwitting effect produced between the assumed and the real reader'.[24] What we *don't* share, of course, is the same response to the foreknowledge of what's ahead, a fissure that alters the nature of dread because 'a gap begins to open between her own remembered false anticipations'—as relationships with her closest friends make unexpected turns—'and our own increasingly accurate ones'.[25] For Kathy, the effect of recollecting moments freighted with portents is never proportionate to the unalterable destiny that awaits her. Thanks to this discrepancy, 'the very idea of dread', as Currie points out, 'develops an irony produced in the chasm between Kathy's remembered anticipations, and the anticipations made by a reader of the more extreme horrors that lie in wait'.[26] As a result, that reader is also likely to be cautious if not sceptical towards any solace Kathy finds in recovering her 'half-forgotten past'. However sympathetically involved, we feel inclined, urged even, somehow to keep our distance. Even as we pity her condemnation to an awful future that's already hailing her, we're never drawn 'so close as to prevent judgment of her', in light of what we can predict about future horrors she doesn't actively seek to alleviate, let alone resist.[27]

Kathy's labour of recollection may indeed seem all the more pitiable—and, for some readers, no doubt infuriating—as a thought-consuming diversion from unavoidable grief, most personally her expectation of losing Tommy. Retrospective detours structurally delay Kathy's narration of the losses she knows will come and that only figure in the final stages of the novel. In Bruce Robbins's astute account, her 'thoughts are preoccupied not with her imminent end, but with her professional success', and by 'dispatching that success down the track towards a nightmarish terminus, Ishiguro would seem to be querying both the institution of the welfare state and the ideology of upward mobility'.[28] Kathy's measured pre-emption of premature death thus seems all the more unsettling for being side-lined for so long by her unfurling recollections—including recollections that evince what Currie calls the 'absence of knowledge of the future in hopeful anticipation'.[29] With the delay that sidelining entails, Ishiguro insinuates that Kathy's digressions of memory permit the compensations of nostalgia, keeping sentimentalism's drip-feed of succour flowing. They also become an excuse to deflect—and thereby make only more apparent for the reader—what Ishiguro in his archived notes calls the 'discrepancy between our expectations of life and the reality of our life-span and mortality', a discrepancy that for him reveals 'something both sad and noble about our determination to ignore this and carry on making plans', in an effort 'to make the best of our lives'.[30]

Through her role as a highly adept carer, then, Kathy triggers a question at the heart of *Never Let Me Go*. Namely, in Ishiguro's own words, 'What really matters if you know that this is going to happen to you?' It's a question that offers up several options, among them elegiac recall and consolidation ('What are the things you hold on to?') but also the urge to redress ('what are the things you want to set right before you go?').[31] The answers Kathy builds towards seem from the outset like the stuff of utter compliance. Only 31, she has 'been a carer now for over eleven years'; and yet, she still seems grateful for being allowed 'to go on for another eight months' (3). What's obscene for readers seems acceptable, even pleasing, for her, while caring routines—that 'quintessential activity' of the welfare state, as Robbins reminds us—present their own equivocal consolations by affording 'a grateful semblance of meaning and legitimacy to the stopgap efforts of every day'.[32] Such is the now-infamous relation between the novel's carceral regime and its characters' acquiescence, as the clones accept their expectation of losses we find unequivocally abhorrent.

Yet from his own reflections on the novel, it's clear that Ishiguro wanted more universal dilemmas to be in play. Beyond the basic conceit of this bio-technological dystopia, he sought to pose wider issues about the actions and thoughts we assume would occupy us when expecting an end we can do nothing to preempt.[33] While 'we will all fade away and die', Ishiguro sees that the novel counters its own unambiguous gloom by implying that 'people can find the energy to create little pockets of happiness and decency while we're here'.[34] One might say that this invitation feels like a flimsy compensation in comparison to the bleaker force with which Ishiguro also 'obliges us', as Robbins notes, 'to wonder whether the freedom on which his uncloned readers pride themselves is anything more than a similarly managed ignorance of what in all probability awaits them'.[35] Yet some interviewers have shared Ishiguro's seemingly counterintuitive sentiment by recognizing, as Karen Grigsby Bates does, that if you 'were someone who knew that the clock was ticking a little more quickly than for the rest of everyone else, this would be a comforting book', carrying the 'message to do things that you want to do while you have a chance to do them'.[36] Ishiguro certainly is 'urging us to perceive the horror that floats just beyond the horizon of our daily routine', while raising the 'question of what makes action against it almost unthinkable'.[37] Equally, though, he makes integral to our experience of reading *Never Let Me Go* that friction between macabre events and the options for weirdly affirmative extrapolation they yield: 'By having this rather negative, bleak scenario, I thought it might highlight what is actually quite positive and valuable about being alive.'[38] Grasping the value of life isn't intrinsically consoling, of course, not least if that life is facing imminent threat. But for Ishiguro the presaging nature of dread raises the stakes for solace. 'What do you regret,' he wonders: 'What are the consolations?'[39]

THE SYNTAX OF AMELIORATION

In Kathy's case, that final question becomes especially loaded. For what does it mean to find solace in caring for persons whose fortunes (physiological and existential) are determined in advance? How do consolation's requirements—including the reasons for granting it—change for subjects who aren't immanently motivated by a normative will to survive and who deem themselves designed for a premature end? Is there any place for solace in a realm where prolonged dread hasn't really entered the emotional vocabulary of daily experience, where anticipation doesn't give way to foreboding speculation, where friends are compelled to leave a 'cosy state of suspension in which [they] could ponder [their] lives without the usual boundaries' and thereafter seem to resist crippling apprehensiveness (130)? How can Kathy attempt to provide forms of what clinical nursing scholars have called 'sustaining consolation' for patients whose lives have been certified as unsustainable?[40] What happens in this scenario to the 'mutual influence' of solace, as Åsa Roxberg, Katie Eriksson, Arne Rehnsfeldt, and Bengt Fridlund describe it, a phenomenon that occurs when a sufferer's consolation redirects some assurance back to the carer, or when the nurse takes comfort in hearing a patient recount valued experiences?[41]

In Ishiguro's world of foreclosed destiny, care is distorted and undermined in at least two respects. First, it's inevitably complicit with the system that condemns clones to prescribed use and that allows them to expect nothing more. Kathy's admiration of care extends back to what she now recognizes as a 'privileged' childhood at Hailsham, that parody of an exclusive, privately run boarding school set in the English countryside. As one of Hailsham's former 'guardians' later explains, pupils there received exceptional care in comparison to welfare standards for juvenile clones housed elsewhere in subsequent decades. With its resources and relative seclusion, Hailsham was 'able to give you something,' claims Miss Emily, 'something which even now no one will ever take from you, and we were able to do that principally by *sheltering* you' (245). The very institution, then, which to us seems ethically unconscionable is held up as a paragon of care whose venerable legacy Kathy and Tommy should feel consoled to be part of. Also uncomfortable for the reader is the notion any such compensatory association with Hailsham's reputation rests precisely on its students having been deceived: their untainted memories of a seemingly idyllic childhood depend on condoning the systemic benefits of not 'knowing what lay in store' (245). Placing the reader's pity in something of a quandary, Ishiguro tests the limits of fellow affection. For if we sympathize with Kathy's taking comfort in memories of Hailsham—even after learning that, as Miss Emily admits, 'in many ways we *fooled* you' (245)—then we're likely to feel as though we're in danger of implicitly sanctioning a self-promoting programme of deception. Encouraged to hold dear their memories of that place and time, Kathy and Tommy furthermore aren't permitted to be conclusively devastated by the false rumour of 'deferral' (the alleged promise of obtaining an exemption from donation if they can prove their love for each other). Instead, they are invited to find some residual comfort in knowing their 'happiness at Hailsham would have been shattered' had they been able to foresee their true purpose in life (245), had they known their futures will inevitably 'run the course that's been set for it' (243).

Which paves the way to the second problem surrounding the exercise of care: now, as an adult, Kathy ploughs her energies back into the same system by committing to the tough work of nursing donors with unquestioning earnestness. With illuminating readings of this aspect of the novel, Anne Whitehead wonders whether the 'form of labour' that constitutes Kathy's care work is itself a pacifying consolation, diverting her from the notion of rebelling against the values she perpetuates. In this account, care consoles the clone in her small, blinkered circle of duty, thereby 'preventing resistance and unrest, securing passive compliance through endless, exhausting activity and minor compensation'.[42] This observation is taken a stage further to include the very emotional quality of responses Ishiguro solicits: the reader's attachment to Kathy despite her helpless submission to the policies that encage her; our emotional connection to the plight drawn out by retrospections that seem unable to admit unavoidable doom. Absorbing despite its frequent clichés, suspenseful even though her path towards surgically enforced death is preordained, Kathy's 'confessional narrative', argues Whitehead, in fact 'positions her reader as fellow victim and passive observer (preoccupied with the same minor compensations and injustices as herself)'. Consequently, 'by the end of the novel we too have become "carers" through our involvement in and affective engagement with her story'.[43] Picturing a thoroughly implicated reader, Whitehead suggests that *Never Let Me Go* allegorizes the way 'both literature and care work' can 'uphold social inequalities, by producing consoling (but false) fictions of legitimacy and meaning'. These fictions operate as a 'diversion from activist agendas', typically 'by enabling us to feel good about our actions without interrogating too closely the power structures and relations that underpin them'.[44]

Later I hope to offer a rather different account of where the reader might emotionally end up by the novel's close. Avoiding the proclivity to yoke consolation with collusion, I'll suggest that Ishiguro invites us to contemplate the predicaments of our own complicity, and thereby to contemplate the very goals of interpretation itself. He does so by inviting us to look again at how the self-gratifying demystification of compensatory fictions testifies to the comforts of prosecutorial reading, to the pleasures of exposing textual affects that would otherwise, allegedly, beguile us. Insofar as the production of 'consoling fictions' across the novel might simultaneously be a mark of the clones' imaginative autonomy—after all, 'the students' true creativity', as Whitehead remarks, 'lies in the narratives of possibility' which 'they relate to themselves and each other'—Ishiguro calls to account the critical temptation to dismiss such narratives of solace, speculative and arguably ineffectual though they remain.[45] In other words, the novel's ethical provocation is not only diegetic, concerned with the milieu of moral atrocity and violent inequity that it hypothesizes; it's also directed outward, aimed at the preconceived suspicions of a reader bent on associating solace with sentimentalism or self-delusion, eager to uncover in turn the complicity of those audiences who refuse automatically to condemn as a pernicious fallacy what vulnerable figures use to console. Ishiguro prompts us to wonder whether in fact there could be something tacitly satisfying about the default critique of consolation for its supposed reinforcement of political passivity. And his prompt disposes me to look again at what solace, beyond superficial compensation, might mean in the finale of a novel that so potently mixes abiding dread with momentary comfort—a scene of transitory remission where consolation's complexities are brought to light again through the micro-operations of style.

Stylistic features of a granular kind indeed have a crucial bearing on how we ethically construe the consolation of care in this novel. Sometimes clichéd and pitched in the tenor of 'commonsensical resignation', as John Mullan characterizes them, Kathy's retrospections are 'untormented by her knowledge of what will happen to her'.[46] As a result, the novel's narration remains unruffled, strangely equable—discrepantly so, given the ethical outrage Ishiguro pieces together for us. Rebecca Walkowitz suggests that while *Never Let Me Go* clearly 'is disturbing because of its premise', the novel 'is all the more disturbing because our knowledge of Kathy's role'—including our prevision of 'her existence as a future organ donor and as an accomplice to the organ donation system'—is in fact 'obscured by the aleatory style and vague diction of her narration'. Given that this narrative trait, 'which encompasses the entire novel', appears 'to be one of the unoriginal expressions that Ishiguro wants us to value', Walkowitz observes that there is in what Kathy says 'a kind of doubling between the novel's story and the novel's discourse', so much so that 'Kathy H.'s unoriginality seems to be Ishiguro's too'.[47] Precisely because the novel's style is so steady, unagitated, even purposely banal, readers might therefore feel that the onus is on them to identify phrases, or even particles of phrases, which counteract the habits of what is otherwise a monophonic voice, one that 'feels deprived of resources'.[48]

More troublingly still, this sense of linguistic deprivation tallies with Kathy's impression of her own palliative role. Granted, Ishiguro pictures the solace of carework not as intrinsically self-deceiving but as a practice whose intentions, in this novel's alternative universe, are institutionally distorted with appalling consequences. But even with this in mind, and even as she squeezes what little munificence she can from this seemingly futile situation of care, it's hard to sympathize entirely with Kathy's enthusiasm for this work. That caring has signified for her a source of esteem, of pleasure even, appears both disconcerting for what it reveals about her personal expectations and disturbing for what it ethically says about a system that nurtures dubious self-worth. Not only does the solace she finds in the way 'it's brought the best out of me' sound distinctly compromised (189); the very fact that she has 'learnt to live with it'—with 'the long hours, the travelling, the broken sleep' and 'the solitude' in dealing with the shock of donors who 'complete', thanks to 'complications', 'out of the blue' (189)—does more to unsettle than endear her readers, whom she regards (one suspects) as fellow clones. In a further turn of the screw of self-deprivation, Kathy seems highly adept at pre-empting her own distress rather than recognizing its side-effects for what they are or, indeed, for what they augur about systemically guaranteed horrors to come. Knowing that 'when things go badly' she can get 'upset', she consoles herself with the acceptance that 'at least I can feel I've done all I could and keep things in perspective' (190).

Ishiguro's ameliorative syntax becomes central to the novel's deliberation of what would appear to be untenable, self-deceiving avenues for consolation. Consider that last, subordinate clause there ('at least I can feel I've done all I could'): it epitomizes the sort of line with which Kathy often defends and justifies her caring role. Through the construction of such clauses, later qualifications mitigate the conceded detriments noted in sentences' leading phrases. Early on, for instance, Kathy admits that while 'the work gets a lot harder when you don't have that deeper link with the donor, and though I'll miss being a carer, it feels just about right to be finishing at last come the end of the year' (4). It's as if the loss of the 'vocation' that she has 'got a lot out of' (34) can be offset here against vague estimations of when it might be 'just about right' to stop. By this syntactic tilt of emphasis from existential resignation to temporary alleviation, Kathy consoles herself with the thought that her own sense of 'finishing' aptly coincides with instructions over which she has in reality no control. Moreover, carework carries its own comforting rewards despite the isolation: 'Even the solitude', she insists, 'I've actually grown to quite like' (190). This solacing loneliness is again explained syntactically, not through subordination or qualification this time but through paratactic itemization in a strangely twee self-portrait that sits discrepantly with the drudgery of a care-routine from which she draws it: 'I do like the feeling of getting into my little car, knowing for the next couple of hours I'll have only the roads, the big grey sky and my daydreams for company' (190).

Many forms of company are there to be lost, of course, as the reader discovers with horror. But Kathy's reflections on them aspire to a serenity that seems immune from apprehensiveness, embracing inevitability in a language that leaves the very thought of loss unblemished by dread. Indeed, rather than portents of more sorrow to come, losses even assume the status of consoling snapshots of cherished moments in time. Recalling her final visits to Ruth's recovery centre, Kathy once again generates in the latter half of the sentence a consoling satisfaction, with her conjunction (*but*) instigating the compensatory contrast: 'When I think about Ruth now, of course, I feel sad she's gone; but I also feel really grateful for that period we had at the end' (215). Even those final weeks with her beloved Tommy record a period characterized not so much by the suspense of presentiment as by the suspense of all motion towards the end they both know is in sight. Perhaps they 'were making a special effort to be nice to each other', we're told, 'but the time seemed to slip by in an almost carefree way'. As though sensing the reader's incredulity, Kathy adds: 'You may think there would have been an air of unreality about us being like that, but it didn't seem strange at the time' (259). And yet, even if we take her at her word (unlikely though that sounds) by believing this portrait of unreal time in anticipation of Tommy's death, there's still an 'air of unreality' about the very syntax of her self-consoling recollections. Ishiguro's qualifying subordinate clauses and pedestrian parataxis not only amount to what Robbins calls 'evidence of minor compensations, improvements, or advantages within what might otherwise be seen as an irredeemable disaster';[49] they also launch pre-emptive strikes, subjecting inextinguishable dread to countervailing details of experiences Kathy feels she should be grateful for. Although she 'won't be a carer any more come the end of the year', she forecasts a 'welcome...chance to rest' and thereby 'to stop and think and remember'—appearing even to find some relief in 'preparing for the change of pace' (34).

That these conciliating clauses buffer the novel's larger pressures of imminence makes them more than negligible compensations. A rhetorical habit of Kathy's they may well be, a verbal tic that compounds the vanity of her trying to read inevitable losses by affirmative lights: such clauses nonetheless remain her only interlude, her only recess from the dreadful biomedical design that has been imposed on all that she can expect from life. The consistency with which Ishiguro introduces these consoling clauses suggests that they forestall with great efficiency the apprehensiveness that readers acutely sense but that Kathy circumnavigates. Yet their frequency in her narration also implies that the dread they leave unarticulated is made present by its absence. In their very accumulation, such syntactic structures therefore provoke acute pathos: it's hard not to feel compassion for Kathy's unspoken expectancy, fixated as she is on the past. Linguistic compensations that substitute dread are fragile and ultimately futile. We can see that. But what's more moving, more appalling, is the way these same clauses also enable Kathy's oblique confession. Clauses in which she reveals as much as consoles herself, their very mannerisms enunciate how far she has become accustomed to the jeopardy she apprehends.

PHRASING COUNTERLIVES

In an interview from the mid 1990s, Ishiguro suggested that 'consolation' applies to 'something you can't fix or heal; all you can do is caress it'.[50] For her part, Kathy leaves that caress till the close, regarding the temptation to glimpse a counterlife for Tommy and herself as an 'indulgent thing' (263). Successive, often laborious phases of retrospection have till now waylaid the point at which the grief she has been trained to pre-empt calls out for expression. But in the novel's final lines she eventually yields:

> That was the only time, as I stood there, looking at that strange rubbish, feeling the wind coming across those empty fields, that I started to imagine just a little fantasy thing, because this was Norfolk after all, and it was only a couple of weeks since I'd lost him. I was thinking about the rubbish, the flapping plastic in the branches, the shoreline of odd stuff caught along the fencing, and I half-closed my eyes and imagined this was the spot where everything I'd ever lost since my childhood had washed up, and I was now standing here in front of it, and if I waited long enough, a tiny figure would appear on the horizon across the field, and gradually get larger until I'd see it was Tommy, and he'd wave, maybe even call. The fantasy never got beyond that—I didn't let it—and though the tears rolled down my face, I wasn't sobbing or out of control. I just waited a bit, then turned back to the car, to drive off to wherever it was I was supposed to be. (263)

'It's a kind of consolation that the world isn't quite the way you wanted it', reflected Ishiguro in 1990, so that as a writer 'you can somehow reorder it or try to come to terms with it by actually creating your own world and your own version of it'. Such is the consolation of imaginative possibility in confronting a 'wound' that 'hasn't healed', in Ishiguro's words, knowing that 'it's probably too late ever to resolve it'. In this vision of what it means to 'write out of something that is unresolved',[51] he echoes Sebald's implication (from Chapter 2) that, for creative writers, there's some solace in lending 'order' to the 'discrepancies' of reality by 'arranging them' in one's 'own version'. We might also spot vestiges of these shared sentiments in that closing paragraph above. It's not that Kathy can or should simply 'come to terms' with her world of premature loss. What's moving instead is the self-consciousness with which she tests her own capacity to be consoled by envisioning alternative outcomes in a private thought-experiment, one that's framed by the portentous expectation of having 'to drive off to wherever it was [she] was supposed to be'. The reader is steered into a partial lee, tucked away from the storm of inevitability—knowing as we do that what awaits Kathy has of course only been deferred temporarily. And the elegance with which description itself escorts us into this fallible refuge from what Nancy Armstrong calls 'the empty heart of biopower' exemplifies one of those instances where Ishiguro 'provides a source of positive push-back that works its way through the very network that channels clone bodies into donation centers'.[52] Style itself thus takes on its own counterlife. The looser syntax and sibilant-rich lexis reflects Kathy's temporary and tentative submission to this 'little fantasy thing', breaking with what has become a sort of conventional, laboured depiction of recalled events, depictions that throughout the novel have ensured small-scale reconciliations overtake Kathy's expectations of how lives might otherwise be. Here, by comparison, language relaxes. Up to this point, moments of descriptive lushness have been pretty rare; now style modulates into swelling parataxis, as Ishiguro liberates Kathy's diction from the composed, largely declarative mood of her foregoing recollections. Though she sets foot rather gingerly into this realm of gratifying speculation, accumulating conjunctions enable the paragraph to pick up lyrical momentum, just as we see the figure of Tommy in her mind's eye 'gradually getting larger'. If this precarious, perhaps recklessly soothing fantasy seems out of character for Kathy—someone who's habituated to accept the fate she foresees—then that fantasy is all the more eerily affecting for the reader due to the stylistic and behavioural departure it represents.

Inanimate, congregating rubbish might seem odd as a correlate for lives whose meaning this novel wants to reclaim. Yet the 'shore-line' of gathering detritus befits in its everydayness the appalling vision of cloning as a normal component of a proficient regime, one that increases life-expectancy at the expense of a second-tier population whose suffering seems masked from public view. 'I wanted the characters in *Never Let Me Go*', recalls Ishiguro, 'to react to this horrible programme they seem to be subject to in much the way in which we accept the human condition, accept aging, and falling to bits, and dying.'[53] However, his extended metaphor of the caught debris here flexes beyond this parabolic function, pointing to what this scene rhythmically and melodiously performs, not only what it allegorically signals. For these final lines create a sense of discursive uplift, whose pathos revolves around the prediction of consolation's own brevity—stylistically capturing too 'the poignance', as Ishiguro puts it in notes from the mid-1990s, 'of growing older and necessarily leaving behind things one once loved'.[54] If solace, as I suggested at the start, rarely materializes without a foretaste of its indeterminable cessation, the language here embodies this prediction, this temporal alertness to consolation's foreshortening. Suddenly heightened, style's reverberations momentarily ambush us before Kathy dutifully turns to go, snagging her in place if only for 'a bit'—like the litter indeed, but unlike the melancholic neglect that litter seems to symbolize. Description intervenes for an instant to impede the onset of her abandonment once again to predetermination.

In the manuscript, this ending has another counterlife of its own. After that final sentence, as Kathy leaves her field-side reverie, Ishiguro adds 'But as I was driving off, it occurred to me...'.[55] A tantalizing, aborted qualification: the excision echoes the phenomenon of consolation's enunciation and deletion at the end of *Disgrace*. As we saw in Chapter 4, Coetzee both trials and erases the emergence of solace, as he suspends and intrudes in the novel's free indirect style to undercut if not ironize Lurie's consolatory intimations of ascetic redemption. As in that novel's climax, so here Ishiguro invites us to become two readers: one moved to sympathy by Kathy's fantasy; and one who's entirely more suspicious and who finds it appalling to witness how her lyrical vision only typifies her acquiescence to the system. Ishiguro's deletion thus couldn't be more appropriate, performing in that simultaneous conjuring and cancellation of hope the dual responses his published version would eventually solicit—testing the reader's willingness to hold this scene's forking feelings of uplift and acceptance together. Ishiguro's crossing out seems equally apt for Kathy, since it visually captures the alternatives (the hope that creativity can prove individuality and thereby a reprieve; thoughts of how things might otherwise be for her and Tommy) that she's quite capable of glimpsing but which the reader knows she's disposed to retract. In this sense, the deletion is a handwritten analogue for the prospect of alleviation from obliteration that's too dreadfully consoling to unleash in Kathy's imagination. Just as she reins in her fantasy as 'indulgent', so Ishiguro curbed in his draft the counter-fortunes that seem to be implied in that syntactically embryonic arc of a thought that suddenly, epiphanically 'occurred', whose upward slant towards a potentially buoying thing that springs to mind is cut short. It would seem that Ishiguro himself was apprehensive too about alleviating Kathy with a dawning realization. His revision captures what many works in this book have done, when they inscribe only to override consolation in the moment of its initial materialization, emending its viability just as it becomes emotionally legible.

*

Never Let Me Go provokes us in the end to oscillate between what we might call circumspect and consolatory readings. Yet that oscillation is by no means the novel's takeaway message. For although his readers may be 'caught' at the close 'between staying and leaving, holding on and letting go', facing what Whitehead calls an 'unresolved dilemma of care or empathy',[56] Ishiguro also provokes us to consider the critical comforts such binaries offer—and to consider how they may indeed resolve aspects of emotional involvement which aren't satisfactorily unravelled by readymade glossaries of aporia. One of those aspects relates to the way Ishiguro models not only the reader's potential desire for some shred of solace—despite Kathy's sobriety as she entertains then dispels escapism—but also alerts us to how enmeshed that desire might be in the very predicaments of interpretation itself. *Never Let Me Go* embroils us in a way that questions the tendency to regard detachment and compassion, scepticism and love, or critique and care as somehow irreconcilable—along with the tendency as well to find interpretive security in preserving antinomies as explanatory mechanisms. To the extent that the novel reveals something about what it feels to be an implicated reader who might be willing to probe rather than simply overcome her own complicities, it helps us to grasp unpredictable responses to conflicting affects without immediate recourse to the comfort zone of unsentimental distance.

The drama we have observed in *Never Let Me Go* surrounding the apprehension of what cannot be diverted speaks to a novel at the centre of my final chapter, one that puts us in touch with the anticipation of 'intolerable pain', in David Grossman's words, while also narrating a 'way to heal it'.[57] Insofar as Kathy cautiously performs a kind of magical thinking in that final scene to restore what's irrevocable without fully indulging it 'beyond that', without denying the elegiac fantasy that it is,

Ishiguro fulfils his counterintuitive sense that writing consoles precisely by focusing on the 'wound' that 'hasn't healed'.[58] By this Ishiguro suggests that there are important distinctions between consoling and curing, because solace is not necessarily synonymous with the promise of rehabilitation. Consolations that acknowledge their own inefficacy as sure-fire salves occupy Grossman, too, as he advances a vision of literature as that 'place in the world where both the thing and the loss of it can co-exist'.[59]

7

Walking with the Unconsoled

What can we expect imaginative writing to do in the midst of unalleviated grief or incessant trepidation? If one of literature's fortes remains its expression of irreducibly singular minds, its nuanced probing of individual states of being, what role then might it play in unbinding the griever from self-isolation? By now these are familiar questions for the occasions and articulations of solace this book has encompassed. And their answers encounter moving limits in the work a writer to whom this final chapter turns. In the early 2000s, David Grossman sensed a reorientation in his work towards the current occupation and historical conflicts of the Middle East, more explicit perhaps than any work since *The Smile of the Lamb* (1983). This compulsion was immediate, urgent: his eldest son, Yonatan, was already serving in the military; his second son, Uri, also was preparing to enlist. During this time, Grossman recalls, 'I could no longer remain where I was.'[1] And so after years of writing fiction that deliberately avoided 'disaster zones' and 'the reality of the latest news bulletin',[2] in 2003 he embarked on a novel that dealt directly with 'how the cruelty of the external situation invades the delicate, intimate fabric of one family, ultimately tearing it to shreds'.[3]

The result was *To the End of the Land*, whose English translation appeared in 2010, when it was praised for taking on 'great questions of love, intimacy, war, memory and fear of personal and national annihilation', in an epic mission 'to scrape raw the human heart'.[4] It follows an Israeli mother, Ora, as she hikes through Galilee in defiant refusal to wait at home for the worst news ahead of the release of her younger son, Ofer, from military service. In fact, Ofer had already finished his requisite term in the army, but decided to volunteer again following an 'emergency call-up' for a renewed offensive against the Palestinians in the ongoing Second Intifada.[5] Gripped by dread, Ora squares up to her imagination's unremitting 'capacity for disaster' (72). Surprising even herself, she pursues an avenue of magical thinking to pre-empt the news she fears, news that would be brought by official 'notifiers'. Yet magical thinking isn't inherently consoling, as Didion and Ishiguro in their markedly different narratives have already demonstrated. And in the case of Grossman's Ora, magical thinking prompts predictions of the worst imaginable outcome in the most quotidian circumstances, spurring her to plot the variables of catastrophe's unanticipated yet everyday onset. As she prepares supper the evening after leaving Ofer with his regiment, she wonders 'What if they come in the middle of the potato?' Paralysed by this scenario's sudden likelihood, it 'gradually dawns on her that every movement she makes may be the last before the knock on the door'. To alleviate the terror of this conjecture, she 'reminds herself again that Ofer is unquestionably still at the Gilboa, and there's no reason to panic yet, but the thoughts crawl up and wrap themselves around her hands as they clutch the peeler, and for an instant the knock on the door becomes so inevitable, such an intolerable provocation of the capacity for disaster embodied in every human condition, that her mind confuses cause with effect and the dull, slow movements of her hands around the potato seem like the essential prelude to the knock' (72).

Apparently benign activities around the home thus become oppressive. Distorted and transcribed by magical thinking, simple acts spark ominous overtures to outcomes that now, all at once, seem 'so inevitable'. Laced with these triggers, mundane domestic tasks are soon insuperable, even unthinkable. I suggested in the last chapter that dread loves detail; its cultivation of threat relies on making outcomes that aren't inevitable seem so specific as to be ineluctable. So it is for Ora: dread sketches threats to Ofer with sufficient definition for her to feel apprehensive about their likelihood. In her agitation—caught in that 'essential prelude to the knock'—she latches on to a plausible chain of wretched events whose circumstances remain sufficiently vague for her not to know exactly when the worst-case scenario will unfold.

Against the paralysis of grim anticipation, Ora decides to move. In order to avoid the military notifiers—those who 'come even at five in the morning' and 'get you sleepy, dazed, defenseless, too weak to throw them down the steps before they can deliver their punchline' (75)—Ora leaves her Jerusalem house altogether, sensing that 'every moment she spends at home is dangerous' for them both (79). Refusing to explain to Ofer this inner imperative, in many ways so unlike her, she knows 'there's no point hoping he will' appreciate why she still wants to set off on a walk into the high ground of the Galilee, an excursion much like the one they had planned to undertake together before he volunteered (79). Nor does she attempt to justify its purpose as a protest at the risk to which Israel's militarism has once more exposed her family. She does speculate, though, on what Ofer must think of this impetuousness, on how he'll be unsettled by her decisiveness, 'guess[ing] that what scares him is not her vow but the fact that she—*she*—is suddenly starting to flip out with all kinds of magical thinking' (83). Given his bemusement, the hike she once hoped to share with him now becomes a personal enterprise, legible at first only to Ora—one that she hopes will obtain a 'deferment, for her and, more important, Ofer' (94–5).

That Ora's trip doesn't have his blessing is precisely the point. She has to defy Ofer in order to defy the state, knowing 'from her experience' with his brother, Adam, how military service contaminates both their world-view and their most private attitudes. Even when they're 'out of the army', she recalls, 'they don't really come back', at least '[n]ot like they were before'; so much so that in Adam's case 'the boy he used to be had been lost to her forever the moment he was nationalized—lost to himself, too' (68). Ora knows that her reasoning won't go far with Ofer, and that he would dismiss her fears that 'from one moment to the next everything became decided, inevitable' (68). If being at home risks provoking disaster, then not being at home will baffle him. But Ora doesn't expect him to appreciate her determination, for she acts athwart Ofer's present outlook. The apparent irrationality of her magical thinking moreover contradicts the 'measured restraint' she felt obliged to assume as 'she escorted him to the battalion "meetery"', abandoning the pretense of that 'proud grin of helplessness' she'd worn at the drop-off ceremony to match 'the other parents who were making all the same moves' (80).

Repelled by this performance of pride, Ora envisages her walk as a way of suspending the military pact Ofer devotedly serves, calling off that 'arbitrary deal that dictates that she, Ora, agrees to the notification of her son's death, thereby helping them bring the complicated and burdensome process of his death to its orderly, normative conclusion' (95). Leading her out of contact—and in Ofer's eyes, for all she knows, out of her mind—this journey into the countryside will press back against the tide of inevitability, even though she worries time and again about its efficacy as 'a meager and pathetic sort of protest' (94). For the hike takes her across the mental topography of her worst speculations and self-doubts, even though Ora feels convinced that '[s]he's leaving him for his own good' (82). In 'her continuous resolve', however, Ora's consolation is her 'desperate and determined' belief that 'people and events' will 'proceed exactly as she wishe[s]', allowing 'no leeway for bargains or compromises'—the consolation that any oncoming harm will submit in 'blind obedience to the new rules that her mind is constantly legislating' (130). Among these rules, 'quite possibly the most important one, is that she has to keep moving, has to be constantly in motion' (130).

Peripatetic, without a firm route-plan, this self-consuming walk is in essence—that is, in genre—intensely lyrical: a reflective, individualized effort to impede war's pitiless forestructuring of events. However much she adheres, though, to 'the regulations of this emergency state that has befallen her' (130), Ora still intimates dread's conversion into actuality, taunted as she is both by previsions of harm and by misgivings over her venture in 'continuing her journey instead of going home right away to receive the bad news' (202). Still, this venture becomes her way of both registering and coping with 'something ominous in the vitality' of Ofer's presence whenever it 'suddenly emerge[s] inside her' (150). To counterbalance the menace, she hopes that walking will free him from the destiny-deciding cogs of Israel's military machine, that against the likelihood of grief's terrifying delivery '[t]he parcel will be returned to the sender, the wheel will stop for an instant, and it may even have to reverse a little, a centimeter or two, no more' (95). This precarious promise, this act of pre-emption, 'is the thing that grows brighter by the minute, with needle-sharp flashes of furious cheer' (94).

Over the outcome she dreads, Ora has little agency, of course. Yet her foretaste of the worst eventuality provokes a paradoxically consoling idea that she might at least oppose the 'entire system' in principle, even if she can't overthrow it in actuality. That '[t]his is possible'—even though it's seeded in her single-minded abandonment to magical thinking that seems so out of character—offers Ora the solace of self-affirmation: 'it is within her power, and in fact it is the only thing possible for her, the only thing within her power' (95). To safekeep Ofer, she knows she must act in spite of him, against his own wishes. And in turn her sense of withdrawal, of ascetic self-isolation, that comes with Galilee's rocky terrain, serves as her antidote to his boldly patriotic sense of allegiance in solidarity with the nationalist cause. Henceforth, the plan takes shape, galvanizing her hike as an occasion for pre-empting the hypothetical yet horrendously credible prospect of her needing to be consoled for Ofer's death. The entire enterprise 'gains clarity inside her' when she resolves that the 'whole time he's there, she cannot be found. That's the thing. That's the law. All or nothing, like a kid's oath, a crazy gamble on life itself' (82).

Ora decides, though, not to go it alone. She needs an audience with whom to share her 'furious cheer'. Recently separated from her husband, Ilan (who is currently abroad on a trip with Adam), she calls on the love of her life, Avram, Ilan's adored friend and father of Ofer himself. Years after she and Ilan raised him as their own, Ofer's paternity remains undisclosed to both her sons. For Ora's part, this concealment evidently yields some solace: it counts as an achievement, a consoling endorsement of her ability, shared with Ilan, to rewrite a life story for Ofer, a story spun out of 'secretive silence' and inscribed in 'inverted letters' that 'no one else in the world—not even Avram—could read' (271). Although it has since dissolved, this erotic triangle reached back to adolescence. Over the years Ilan and Avram were 'both necessary to her. They were essential, like two angels who ultimately fulfil the same mission: Avram, whose presence was inescapable down to the very last thread, and Ilan, who was entirely absent' (332). The horrific turning point for them all arrived with the Arab-Israeli war of 1973, where Avram was captured at the Suez Canal and tortured in an Egyptian prison. Traumatized by witnessing both sides' atrocities, he withdraws from what he sees as an irredeemably inhumane world. Thereafter Avram plays no part in Ofer's upbringing, a decision that he will come to regard as 'undoubtedly' the 'mistake of his lifetime' (151). Over two decades on, Ora's Galilee walk presents Avram with a chance to correct that mistake, just as she needs him there as a vessel into which she pours descriptions of Ofer 'in minute detail, especially his body', knowing that in order to protect him she 'must give a name to every eyelash and fingernail...to every kind of laughter and anger and wonderment' (465).

Indeed, the very act of description 'is it', affirms our narrator: 'This is why she brought Avram with her. To give a name to all these things, and to tell him the story of Ofer's life, the story of his body and the story of his soul and the story of the things that happened to him' (465). Describing Ofer so intensively, with such virtuosity, is her consolation: when Ora depicts piece-by-piece 'just a few little things' about Ofer's childhood, she finds solace in the fact that *through* those descriptions 'at least [Avram] would know this person he had brought into the world' (144). Description 'weaves the feeling of Ofer inside her like a game of connect the dots, and she finds that things are all right' (198). There's no 'game' more serious than this, undoubtedly. But the solace it yields survives the severity of her undertaking, even though she doesn't allow herself to accept description as a refuge, even though the premise of her hike is to obstruct the terrible outcome from which she'll emerge wanting nothing but to be consoled, and even though her descriptions themselves are shot through at times with the disconsolate feeling of being 'tormented by a very familiar fear, the fear of what she might perceive and what her imagination might show her when she thought of him' (150).

Re-evoking her son, then, becomes for Ora as necessary as walking to preserve him. Description and perambulation enmesh in this mission of magical thought, whereby the 'point is to be in motion, the point is to talk about Ofer' (279). Yet the strange consolation of her sense of necessity here is a far cry from comfort; it stems instead from the form it assumes, a form investing passionately in detail so as to defy the generalizing hubris of nationalism's war machine. At stake in this chapter will be the contribution such detail makes to alternative ways of thinking about the politics of solace in a novel that is not always consoling to read. More than for any other text in this book, I have often found the prospect of doing justice to Grossman's work insuperable. And, of course, any time spent theorizing the resulting confluence of emotional and intellectual challenges is time taken away from developing degrees of close reading that *To the End of the Land* demands and repays. Without further metacritical ado, then, my hope is to sustain over the coming pages an attention to affective details in a novel where tragedy and solace interflow across lyrical descriptions, which mourn through their consoling plenitude the poverty of a social reality numbed by chronic hostility.

RECUPERATING THE TRAGEDY OF THE ONE

As Ora's recollections celebrate the domestic intimacies of life with Ofer, they attest to her strenuous effort to protect him with details alone, loving details whose nemesis is the austere functionality of conflict data that only redoubles human losses by compressing them into impersonal statistics. For Grossman himself, this functionalism is especially vexing because, over time, it allows military rhetoric to infiltrate and deform cultural self-identity. When language itself turns staid and unreflective, it becomes woven into culture's '"normative" social fiber'. Against that 'fear', 'the writing of literature', Grossman suggests, 'is partly an act of protest and defiance, and even *rebellion*'.[6] This also stages an aesthetic resistance to an increasingly homogenized political imagination, countering Israel's incapacity to articulate futures beyond enduring animosity, victimhood, or revenge. In an ideological climate where language contracts into predictability, Grossman suggests that it's up to literature to model alternative outlooks and behaviours, to imagine how one might 'break free from the all-too-familiar Israeli tendency to approach reality with the mindset of a sworn survivor, who is practically programmed—*condemned*—to define the situations he encounters primarily in terms of threat, danger, and entrapment'.[7] Dread, then, has come to shape Israel's social imaginary. Yet this is fiction's spur, implies Grossman, its urgent motive for exploring ways of being that counteract the 'paralyzing existential paradox' of a people 'that throughout its entire history *has survived in order to live*, and now finds itself, at least in Israel, *living in order to survive* and not much more'.[8] To oppose this paralysis is not to ignore a population's very real 'longing to find refuge and meaning', as he puts it, in the crucible of conflict. Indeed, literature has long been a connoisseur of that longing. But its task now, proposes Grossman, is to evoke 'the feeling that there is a way to fight the cruel arbitrariness that decrees our fate',[9] to defy what Ora herself 'senses' as the 'randomness in everything' that leads her to ask 'what good can she do for [Ofer] now, on this silly, pathetic journey', with its 'baseless bargain with fate' (298).

How, then, might a novel pre-empt this culturally endemic and persistent expectation of violence? To what extent can it console the 'paranoid identity' that has become, Grossman argues, the status quo in Israel, a paranoia that 'only generates more wars'?[10] What sort of affective defence or recompense can fiction offer without diminishing the fact that 'when one lives in a disaster zone', as he admits, 'one is constantly on guard, and one's entire being anticipates imminent pain, imminent humiliation'.[11] And if dramatizing this deep-seated sense of anticipation generates vivid pathos, how might fiction describe so as to redress this foreboding sensation without inadvertently reinforcing an inherently tragic view of Jewish existence, a view Grossman associates with 'the failing left in us by history, the terrible tendency to view life as latent death'?[12]

Working towards his own answers to these questions in public lectures, journalism, and critical essays, Grossman has emphasized fiction's opposition to the discourse of antagonism and retribution, fuelled by the twinned banality and bellicosity of reactionary nationalism. The bombastic 'language of war is narrow and functional', he insists: 'Writing is the opposite.'[13] Reporting in early 2000 on the Israeli army's occupation of southern Lebanon, he urged withdrawal by asserting that '[e]very soldier killed now is an unnecessary victim of military arrogance'.[14] Ora knows this, of course, sensing how that arrogance has always threatened to change her sons irreparably, even when they're no longer serving. Meanwhile, arrogance also threatens the very 'process of accommodation' for Israelis and Palestinians alike, reinforcing what Grossman calls the 'armor that all of us in this region have become accustomed to living in'.[15] Given that the 'language used by the citizens of a conflict to describe their situation becomes flatter and flatter as the conflict goes on',[16] one of literature's tasks, he implies, is to expose the 'clichés and slogans' for what they are, with the view to mending the 'insult of describing ourselves in coarse language' teeming with 'generalizations and stereotypes'. Along these lines, Grossman suggests that ultimately 'literature can be kind to us: it can slightly allay our sense of insult at the dehumanization that results from living in large, anonymous global societies'.[17]

Such is fiction's social and existential efficacy in Grossman's model: when it reveals a people 'so submerged in our warped perception that we barely grasp the true price we are paying for living alongside our own lives'; when it records how 'the grip of stereotypes and prejudices' stifles other ways of imagining political collectivities released from the sanctimonies of jingoistic protectionism; when it pictures a population 'so afraid of death' that people are forced by dread to 'condense the range' of their own 'emotional, psychic activity'.[18] Yet literature's value, implies Grossman, comes not only from exposing how things are, but also from its pre-emptions—through its resistance to the foreclosure of identity within defensive, fear-fixated coordinates. By this he suggests that writing can 'redeem each character... from alienation and impersonality', that it can anticipate and 'reclaim some of the things that this "situation" tries relentlessly to expropriate', including 'the precision of words and descriptions'.[19] More than a mere compensation or shelter from nationalistic bluster, fiction's precision foils the generalities of ideological unanimity and the manipulations of state newspeak. Description's detail retrieves 'for us the tragedy of the one', as Grossman calls it, 'from the statistics of the millions'.[20]

This is the recuperative mission pursued in *To the End of the Land*. Through Ora's exhaustive retrospections on Ofer, the novel enumerates the personal and familial make-up of a single person, so easily destroyed.[21] Grossman attests that 'no one wants to describe his nightmare with too-high resolution'; yet he 'insisted in this book to describe with nuances everything'—from the flora and topography of Galilee to the everyday commotions and delights of parenthood—in order to 'regain the language the situation has confiscated from me'.[22] Thus Ora sets out to recount 'the smallest details about Ofer', those 'little effects, the many acts and deeds and efforts that we do in order to accumulate one human being in this world'. Her feeling is that 'by telling these facts she in a way builds a wall around him', one that will 'envelop' Ofer and 'protect him'.[23] This formidable task of description by no means guarantees her solace, however much it rescues intimate vocabularies of family life from nationalism's dull uniformity and ideological piety. For detail itself trades in a moving discrepancy: to exhibit, as this novel so eloquently does, 'language's natural richness and its ability to touch on the finest nuances of existence can be truly hurtful', warns Grossman, 'in a state of conflict', precisely because such richly expressive nuances 'constantly remind us of the exuberant reality that we have lost, of its complexities and subtleties'.[24] If anything, Ora has to tolerate this discrepancy, knowing that while descriptions may protect Ofer (in her imagination at least) their evocative 'richness' can be simultaneously elegiac— anticipating the unrecoverable loss of what they passionately describe. If she gains some reprieve from dread in devoting these lovingly animated sequences to her son, then the aid they offer also coincides with apprehension, haunted as her lyrical notations are by their proximity to the threnody she hopes they will never become.

PARTICULARISM'S REDRESS

If descriptions of Ofer are Ora's defence, then, they also remind her (and us) of what Grossman calls fate's 'cruellest arbitrariness', by giving definition to that capricious destiny which Ora dreads and so strenuously aims to defer.[25] This concession—that description periodically conjures in prospect the very cruelty it strives to redress—coincides with the consolation Ora obtains by reclaiming her son in words from the military's undifferentiated chauvinism. Her objective in particularizing the everyday developments of Ofer's upbringing is twofold: shielding him from omnipresent peril; and gradually introducing his life thus far to the father he has never met, the father whose self-exclusion from their lives she laments. Regret about Avram's absence can only be compensated by her redescribing the most singular moments he missed, as the 'lasso of distant memory floats over and tightens softly around her throat', compelling her to delineate 'Ofer's swollen little fist right after he was born' (98):

> From the moment he was born she drew strength from him. And now she saw his tiny fist—*fistaloo*, Avram would have said had he been with her in the delivery room; even now she finds it hard to accept that he wasn't there with her and Ofer; how could he not have been there with them?—with the deep crease around the wrist, and the bold red of the tiny hand itself, which until moments ago had been an internal organ and still looked like it. The hand slowly opened and revealed to Ora for the first time its conch-like, enigmatic palm—What have you brought me, my child, from the deep, dark universe? —with the thicket of lines drawn all over it, covered with a white, fatty layer of webbing, with its translucent pomegranate-seed fingernails, and its fingers that closed up again and gripped her finger tightly. (98–9)

The description's poignancy stems less from its raw immediacy—its simulation of the visceral, overwhelming sensations Ora might have been feeling in those first ecstatic minutes after giving birth—than from its composed, sonorous comparisons, striking up for this freshly-minted hand analogues in 'organ', 'conch', and 'pomegranate'. Paratactic yet poised (in Jessica Cohen's translation), the syntax unfurls with a measured tempo that befits the affection Ora projects from a distance, an affection that's no less acute for all the years that have passed. Her particularizing and colorific account of one 'tiny hand' reproduces in its steady momentum—in its unhurried, studied accretion of 'lines', 'webbing', and 'fingernails'—the pace with which that 'enigmatic palm' itself had 'slowly opened', its features 'revealed' in a way that only perpetuated its mystery, consolidating the hand's aura of indescribability. With its composure, the whole sequence momentarily suspends the narrative: it intrudes between ongoing events to allow the 'moment he was born' to exist for its own exquisite sake. That this luminous memory is in turn shadowed by the eulogy that it could still become intensifies the pathos of what could otherwise have been just a tender recollection.

At the same time, though, description defies this portentousness through its interruption—its stubborn impulse to adjourn the onrush of Ora's dread. There are both structural and rhetorical levels of redress at work in these moments. Structurally, descriptions of this kind intervene to postpone plot, in a sense, cutting across the urgent motion of the perambulatory main story; and rhetorically, accounts such as that of the hand's physical specificity defy the arrogance of militaristic uniformity and its homogenization of human vulnerability. From personal, treasured flashback, then, comes description's tangibly political implication. Thanks to its interruptive placement in the narrative—imposing an interval in the awful inevitability of the fate Ora feels Ofer is hurtling towards at times—and with the particularism of its diction, description instantiates the talismanic assertion that Ora asks Avram (her temporary amanuensis) to write in her notebook: "'*One person, who is so easy to destroy*'" (454).

As it happens, 'descriptions were always [Avram's] thing' (178). But over the course of their walk Ora takes up the baton, knowing that the traumatic legacy of torture has left Avram barely able to describe himself and only gradually able to receive a verbal portrait of his son. Against these odds, she hopes that by virtue of her recollections at the very 'least he'd know who Ofer was in general outlines, in chapter headings' (144). With painstaking precision, events of childhood are replayed, Ora's scrupulous reconstructions tentatively compensating for the fatherhood Avram relinquished—tentatively yet impossibly. For however detailed they are, Ora's descriptions are premised on their own deficits, their own partial adequacy for a man who knows he cannot rectify those lost years. Nevertheless, conjuring up Ofer both through dialogue and through written reflection (she records notes in a journal as the walk progresses) provides the consolation of imagined care. Writing about Ofer, talking about him to Avram, hearing Avram in turn say his son's name—all this is, for Ora, confirmation that '[h]e's preserved' and 'protected' (234). At first she worries that 'the minutiae, the thousands of moments and acts from which you raise a child, gather him into a person', might not 'really interest him' (182). But she persists, convinced that '[t]his is exactly the sort of thing she should tell him: sweet slices of life, trivial Ofer episodes, nothing complicated or heavy', instructing herself to 'just calmly describe the mornings of that year' which saw the 'meticulous daily construction of a brave fighter, erected on the fragile scaffolding of little Ofer' (182).

Plagued though she is by the implausibility of attempting to 'describe and revive a whole person' (183), Ora's discourse 'goes on, consoling' Avram (217). When she tells him how the growing Ofer 'sprang up all at once', he in turn feels both impaled and solaced, 'refusing to part with a strange new pain, like a cruel pinch of the heart that ends with a light caress' (217). A similarly discrepant blend of tender contentment and sharp poignancy touches Ora, too, while she recounts from more recent times a birthday meal for Adam. Suddenly the image of '[t]hat weekend, those final moments of the careful, fragile happiness' (447), bestows a painful caress, when 'she realizes what she's been doing here all these days: reciting a eulogy for the family that once was, that will never be again' (447). All the same, it's the description *of* her family, however elegiac it abruptly seems, that promises to save Avram from his own impassive self-destruction, to encourage those fleeting moments Ora notices when he 'allowed himself to try out a different possibility, a redemptive one' (168).

Description, of course, is a potentially fallible vehicle for grasping what you attempt to particularize. To depict a person is not necessarily to know them, as we saw in the case of Sebald's Jacques Austerlitz in Chapter 2, whose enigma only deepens as his self-descriptions expand. Ora herself spots this fissure between evocation and apprehension, diagnosing the 'fear that is pressuring her brain, the discomfort that has been eating away at her for some time'—the concern that '[s]he doesn't really know her son' (182). Nor can she tell whether Avram will continue to 'have the patience' for her encyclopaedic aspiration to 'tell an entire life' (182). Such is the pressure Grossman exerts on the compensations of description even as the novel clearly evidences the passion with which he set out 'to describe everything with the most nuanced language I could'.[26]

Depiction's simultaneous endorsement and examination (exhaustion, even) is something we have encountered at this book's outset. Whereas in *The Road*, however, Cormac McCarthy lyrically evokes a world where there is apparently no use for such descriptive energy—a blasted biosphere where every depiction plaintively records its own redundancy, its own melancholic testament to the ecology that's no longer there to be described—Grossman's Ora feels compelled to describe Ofer to someone, in Avram, who assumes he has no use for such descriptions, when in fact they may be the only thing left to console him. Gradually he realizes this for himself. Welcomed in for a communal meal at one remote village, they make a pit stop; and Avram, having momentarily been handed a baby to hold amid the bustle of gathered hosts, gives Ora 'a very slight nod of recognition, of acknowledgment' (175). This signal of consent arrives just in time, 'in contradiction to the despair that had consumed her': for his nod is her cue to 'start from a distance', as Avram requests (175), and impart 'what for years had embittered and sweetened her life at the same time' (300).

That Ora describes Ofer to protect him—to pre-empt the notifiers, to stave off the time when she herself will need to be comforted—doesn't diminish the solace she finds meanwhile by recounting his childhood for Avram. 'Conjuring up in words', notes Alan Mintz, 'the twenty good years of the family cell that has now broken down provides a consolation beyond lament or embitterment'.[27] Although Ora's recital is intended to shield her from envisioning the time ahead when people will condole with the family if Ofer falls, paradoxically it also consoles her when she notices how Avram is gradually enthralled by her delicate recollections of lost years—details from which he had initially recoiled. If only cautiously, precariously, her monologue consoles insofar as it suggests that 'in some dim way Ofer is even growing a little stronger while she talks, while Avram listens' (198). For some, this mutually consoling activity—imaging that she's preserving Ofer, sensing in turn that she might be healing Avram—provides something of a formal solution in sync with the narrative progression implied by the walk. In Iris Milner's subtle reading, Grossman 'enables cure of and liberation from the constitutive trauma, as the mountain hike ultimately succeeds in converting the fixated, compulsive repetition into a linear progression towards a rehabilitating solution, just as the gradual clarification of ambiguous details and the filling of information gaps organize the fragmented story into a coherent narrative'.[28] By the same stroke, however, this forward momentum, this will-to-repair, makes for a temporally discrepant conceit for plotting the distresses of Avram's recalled trauma and Ora's anticipated loss. However rehabilitative the narrative present seems, it sits in tension with harrowing retrospection and perpetually disquieting conjecture. Over his anguishing pasts and her dreadful version of the future the novel circles, compromising the remedial thrust of sequential form. This tension between the novel's diegetic digressions in time and the salving linearity of the hike is one that Grossman seems to want to sustain rather than resolve, a tension that finds an analogue at the level of register, as we'll later see, in the novel's final scene.

Still, the animating force of description, along with the perpetual motion and mental perseverance required by her taxing journey, offer Ora combined resources for countering the side effects of apprehension: what Grossman identifies in *Death as a Way of Life* as the way Israelis' 'expectation of the next collision' readily proves 'how dread and despair transform the fingers of an outstretched hand into a fist'.[29] To break out of this enclosure, *To the End of the Land* shuns sensationalism in favour of specificity, as we have seen, mapping the condition of a nation without pretending only to allegorize it, focalizing pandemic dread through the private magnitude of one woman's dissent. This novel's militant particularism shapes not only the consolation Ora finds in setting meticulous depictions against her trepidation,[30] but also the effort Grossman makes to evoke 'contemporary political reality in a language that is not the public, general, nationalized idiom'.[31] Particularizing accounts of a family that could so easily be torn apart interweave with lush depictions of a landscape that already bears traces of the tearing threat.

Against this backdrop of domestic and spatial detail, Grossman confronts the kind of military aggression that continually chokes the cultural imagination, consigning it to what Jacqueline Rose has called Israel's politically 'numbing sense of sacrificial destiny' that 'shuts out the world'.[32] *To the End of the Land*'s particularism thus becomes an aesthetic counterpart for Grossman's opposition to the generalities of chauvinistic nationalism. Through meticulous expression, it defies what he called a year before starting the novel that rhetoric of '[s]anctimonious self-righteousness', with its bland yet infectious 'wave of crude and sentimental patriotism'.[33] Furthermore, the novel's counter-insistence on conveying the wonderment of 'minute detail', its attentiveness to 'every passing expression' (465), also signals Grossman's resistance to the pretensions of nationalist epic—however much this novel has been applauded in those terms, an antiwar masterpiece celebrated for its scale.

REFUSING THE LUXURY OF DESPAIR

A journey striving to pre-empt the sense of foreclosure that originally motivated it, Ora's walk is also, of course, about *not* looking ahead. She steels herself against her own forebodings and parries the anticipation of circumstances in which she will need, without doubt, to be consoled. If, in contrast to helpless waiting, Ora hikes in defiance of military 'notifiers', then she also tries to escape the psychic barbs of foreshadowing; in fact, her notion of perpetual motion as formidable care depends precisely on *not* speculating about what lies ahead for her son. Hence, she avoids opportunities for divining Ofer's whereabouts and wellbeing: predictions, whether good or bad, are banished as she polices her own desire to know, rescinding for the most part that consoling fantasy-scenario of his safe return. Prospective calamity is what her portrait of Ofer—any conversation, any thought about him—is designed to counteract, in ways that refuse the grim temptations of turning feelings of dread into definitive foreknowledge. Ora tries to ferret out prospection, spotting and ducking away in advance from visions of a time when, caught in grief's vice, she will need to be comforted for the truly unconsolable loss of her son. Magical thinking remains her mechanism for surviving the as-yet-unknown outcome of Ofer's latest patrol, even though she doesn't permit herself to construe solace in this strategy. Consolation is the eventuality she effectively wants to evade.

Eventually Ora begins to wonder whether she ought to stop entertaining the whole venture as well. In the novel's climactic sequence, the hope of perambulation as protection begins to fade, and Grossman momentarily assumes Avram's point of view in a way that positions readers at a certain remove from Ora at the very point her belief in magical thinking falters. Ora has made a rash decision to pick up recorded messages, including those left on Avram's apartment phone. All is well, for now: Ofer called to say he's '"okay, the bad guys not so okay"' (561); yet she also conceals, at first, the fact that she dialled into Avram's answerphone as well, retrieving there a message from his girlfriend, Neta, who suspected she might be pregnant but has called to confirm a 'false alarm' (572). By initially hiding this from Avram, by feeling unable 'to say how good it would be for him to have a child and what a wonderful father he would be' (572), Ora falls into a sort of manic silence, hostilely sprinting ahead and thereafter cold-shouldering him when they meet two hiking boys, whom she welcomes with exaggerated camaraderie. Thrown off balance by her inflated affection and hyperactive chatter with these strangers, Avram in his bewilderment 'dwindles as he watches her, all bustling chumminess, as clumsy as an elbow in a rib, her conduct, foreign and grating, until it occurs to him that she is doing this to spite him' (567). They resume the walk, but he struggles to keep pace with Ora's ferocious urgency. Bemused then panicked by her continuing silence, he senses 'that they were running to reach Ofer in time, the way you dash to rescue someone from the ruins of a building: every second counts' (569). Grossman does periodically shade into Ora's perspective, but even then he doesn't quite disclose the source of her growing 'disquiet' (569), or her sudden coldness towards Avram. Strangely enough, the effect of this distance (for Avram, as for us) occurs structurally in the novel's culminating phase, where one might expect to feel the greatest sympathetic intimacy with a couple whose efforts at counteracting dread unravel towards the close.

For the time being, Grossman thus denies us—through the alienated perspective Avram assumes, through our resulting alignment with his abrupt isolation from an intractable, unreadable Ora—resolving explanations of what she so keenly withholds. Momentarily, too, the responsibility for magical thinking, for sustaining the protective work such thinking carries out, has been handed over to Avram, as he observes that '[i]t's not good that she's quiet', realizing indeed that '[n]ow is when we have to talk about [Ofer], when she has to talk about him' (569). When Ora finally does speak, the momentary relief of relaying the message from Neta gives way to further consternation: she snaps at Avram irritably, 'snorting into her hands' (573), hounded by prophetic visions of 'people standing on either side of the street that leads to her house', some of whom—having 'already gone into the yard'— ominously 'wait for her silently, eyes lowered' (573). Creeping doubt once again overshadows the whole enterprise of magical thinking, compelling her to demand from Avram further descriptions of '"what he is for you"' (574), while wondering '[m]aybe we got it all wrong, from the beginning' (575). All they can do is vow to each other to '"remember Ofer, his life, his *whole* life"', which she has exhaustively particularized for uncertain ends (576).

Compounding this inconsolable sense of uncertainty, the novel's perspective seems to back away, shedding the compensatory abundance of immersive, intricate interiority. Once more we're somewhat shut out, as Aram is. And because we too no longer have sustained access to Ora's thoughts, the narration solicits an affectively unusual form of engagement that no longer depends on our direct sympathetic responsiveness to her alternation between hope and dread. By the end a more reserved, if not attenuated style steers us away from the effortless absorption of uninhibited pity. Just as 'all she gives him is the shell of her face' (576), so the reader is offered a carapace of the novel's hitherto luscious expressivity, its former sumptuousness giving way to an impersonal, controlled register. Clipped dialogue prevails, shorn of interweaving descriptions, as Ora questions again the whole project of pre-emption—'Maybe we were wrong' (575)—a project that has finally come to rest in a state of austere irresolution. Whatever pathos survives in this closing episode does so without relying on our affecting proximity to Ora's inner perceptions: of herself, of what awaits her and Avram on their return, of Ofer's fate, of the whole venture of magical thinking which she now so disconsolately calls into question. The competing textures of these final lines match the tension Grossman posits between the rejuvenating force of her familial descriptions and the stark reality of their situation, between the verbal world she has created to shelter Ofer's '*whole* life' and the military action that could still extinguish him. In what becomes an internally discordant tableau of trepidation, evocative sounds and scents are juxtaposed with the glacial posture of Avram and Ora, conjoined as they are in a freeze-frame of unknowing and beset by unalleviated dread:

> They sit for a long time, hidden away in the small crater. Holding each other like refugees from a storm. The sounds slowly return. The hum of a bee, the thin chirp of a bird, the voices of workers building a house somewhere in the valley.
> Then Ora detaches her body from his and lies down on her side on the rock ledge. She pulls her knees into her stomach and rests her cheek on her open palm. Her eyes are open yet she sees nothing. Avram sits beside her, his fingers hovering over her body, barely touching. A light breeze fills the air with the scents of *za'atar* and poterium and a sweet whiff of honeysuckle. Beneath her body are the cool stone and the whole mountain, enormous and solid and infinite. She thinks: How thin is the crust of Earth. (576)

Abrupt, denotative sentences initially reinforce a paradoxical sense of detachment from these mute and motionless figures with whom we have spent so much intimate time across the novel, in harrowing and life-affirming episodes alike. By telescoping back, by suspending his previously immersive focalization of inner reflection, Grossman reciprocates in language a degree of affective disengagement that seems curious at this climactic moment. Eschewing free indirect style, he asks us instead to engage the scene's impact in a visual rather than vicarious respect. In place of fervent empathy as a gateway to heart-rending involvement, it seems as though we're invited to observe—if not to extrapolate and socially allegorize—the outward structure of human vulnerability, so as to notice in the tableau these 'refugees' form the 'legacy of pain and conflict' for both Palestinian and Israeli cultures, one that's 'written', in Colm Tóibín's phrase, 'into the gnarled and beautiful landscape through which Ora and Avram walk'—written here onto their bodies stilled and silenced on the 'cool stone'.[34]

Nowhere more than here does consolation seem inconceivable. But the formal construction of this tableau makes it nonetheless thinkable. An enduring function of tableaux, as David J. Denby describes it in the context of sentimental texts, is to 'hold up for contemplation an intensified and heightened vision', and thereby 'to suspend temporal progression so that the set of forces with which the narrative has brought together in a particular moment may be allowed to discharge their full affective power'.[35] Grossman's closing picture of gnawing irresolution certainly combines intensification and suspension in this manner. But it does so to channel the political connotations of affective inflections that counter the scene's otherwise shattering inconclusiveness. Grossman achieves this by situating the reader as an implied observer—an abruptly distanced one, as we have noted—while reconstructing the goal of sentimental tableaux to issue an 'affirmation and celebration of the possibility of a common, communicable human experience'.[36] This is not a wide-eyed appeal for mutual recognition or benevolence between nations in ceaseless conflict, but a solemn warning against what Grossman sees as the most ubiquitous form of fellow-feeling in the Middle East: despair.

As such, the tableau is suspenseful not just because of what it leaves untold about Ofer's fate but because of what it implies about dejection's ubiquity in the region. Doubling as an intercultural diagnostic, the tableau petitions readers to watch from their relative remove how two isolated characters, in whose histories of trauma and love they have hitherto been so absorbed, now metonymically come to exhibit a 'state of mind with no horizon', in Grossman's 2014 account, one that's trapped, 'dully comatose', in 'a self-induced numbness'. In this condition, despair prevails for Israelis like a normative symptom 'of living in a self-satisfied democracy, with pretensions to liberalism and humanism, that occupies and humiliates and crushes another people for decades on end'. It's the 'paralysis' of 'this pessimistic worldview', as Grossman would later describe it, that besets Avram and Ora, a paralysis that's reproduced formally as the tableau halts the novel and yearns in that moment of standstill to communicate the 'fateful' side effects of despair that Israelis and Palestinians have been compelled to share.[37]

This yearning, however forlorn, yields the scene's discrepant solace. By devoting more descriptive space to external, environmental observations than to the simulation of internal sensations, Grossman collocates the creamy lexicon of 'sweet' flora with the bleak image of detached bodies held in suspense on a 'rock ledge'. It's not that ecology here simply compensates for dread; if surroundings envelop Ora and Avram, embalm them even, they still edge towards the verge of enervation. Rather, when 'sounds' mingle with then overtake the 'storm', there are glimmers of quotidian calm, glimmers that Ora and Avram aren't in a position to detect for themselves but in which readers might discern the seismic 'hope' Grossman defines as 'the healing power of the everyday'. To be sure, the tableau serves to bring into stark definition the emotional extremity his characters have now reached, appearing starker still when set against an indifferent environment where builders and bees carry on regardless. At the same time, those noises from ordinary life whisper as they eventually return some hint of 'existential security'. And that, for Grossman, is the consolatory if forever vulnerable upshot of common hope—the hope that families from two peoples might one day feel secure enough to build home lives and 'raise children without abject fear, without the humiliation of occupation or the dread of terrorism'.[38]

Throughout *To the End of the Land*, the reader has come to associate pre-emption with Ora's effort to withstand what she dreads. The novel's final lines, however, lever the stress off forestalment with a clarion call to 'resist the gravitational pull of despair'—a resistance that Ora and Avram, for their part, seem scarcely capable of in the end.[39] What makes this concluding episode all the more haunting is indeed the way their crippling dread contrasts the persistence and thus also the promise of everyday life, whose fragile, consolatory intimation of existence beyond fear remains obscure to the couple who actually need it, as they seem on the brink of becoming emblematic of the hopelessness Grossman sees as endemic to the Middle East. Such is the hermeneutic twist—as politically urgent as it is poignant—that the novel provides, as it sacrifices the inconsolable individuals with whom we have become affectively involved, precisely in order for us to recognize despair as the common condition that condemns as a 'deluded dreamer' 'anyone who still hopes'.[40] If throughout *To the End of the Land* Ora is able 'to find refuge and meaning', in Grossman's terms, in the lush language of description, then in this closing instance he tempers that language to articulate a different kind of solace, one that finds in a discrepantly detached register the means of giving 'words to the mute', to those denounced as dreamers. If this also instantiates a warning, it ultimately does so 'to bring about *tikkun*—"repair"'—by warding off the 'luxury of despair'.[41]

REALITY'S ECHO: THE UNANTICIPATED ELEGY

To the End of the Land supplies devastating momentum to Grossman's reflections as an observer of cultural desperation: 'Sometimes, if we reformulate a situation that already seems beyond hope and set in stone', he insists, 'we are able to recall that there is in fact no divine decree that dooms us to be the helpless victims of apathy and paralysis'.[42] By the close, readers are invited to become distanced enough to see how Avram and Ora skirt the perimeters of this paralysis, and this distance in itself conveys something of the political impetus of Grossman's increasingly thrifty language, of his sudden tableau, of his stark colligation of opulent scenery and unmitigated dread. With these manipulations of affective register, the novel lends vivid form to Grossman's sense that '[i]n this struggle, the battle lines today are drawn not between Israelis and Palestinians, but rather between those who are unwilling to come to terms with despair and those who wish to turn it into a way of life'.[43]

The stakes of description's seemingly improbable solace could not have been higher for Grossman: 'Writing a precise sentence, imagining, fusing life into characters and situations, I felt I was building my home again. It was a way of fighting against the gravity of grief.'[44] Most of *To the End of the Land* was finished in draft when in August 2006 Grossman joined fellow writers Amos Oz and A. B. Yehoshua to urge their government to accept a ceasefire with Hezbollah. A halt to the Israeli offensive arrived too late for Grossman's twenty-year-old son, Uri, who was killed in the closing moments of the Second Lebanon War by a rocket strike on his tank. Just as Ora in her 'continuous resolve' believes that she 'has to keep moving, has to be constantly in motion', in order to safeguard Ofer (130), so Grossman sensed 'at the time' of completing the novel that he had 'the feeling—or rather, a wish— that the book I was writing would protect' Uri.[45] He recalls holding on to 'this magical thinking', while recognizing it for what it was: 'I do not believe that words can really protect a life', he admits, 'when you're in the heart of war'. And yet the conceit endured, for he saw that it was his 'duty to accompany [Uri] through writing'. After the tragedy Grossman returned to the manuscript, convinced that by going back to the task of finishing the novel he was recreating a 'home in this chaos'. On the frontline of torment, writing afforded 'the slight satisfaction of doing the right thing', of 'choosing life again'.[46] If much of the plot was already in place, '[w]hat changed, above all'—he notes in a devastating postscript—'was the echo of the reality in which the final draft was written'.[47]

It seems inconceivable now to read *To the End of the Land* without hearing this echo for ourselves, without the book's emotional voltage being continually raised by the searing pathos of that postscript. Though the 'borders' between life and fiction, as Grossman insists, 'have been violated by reality not by me', the shocking accuracy with which imagined events predicted his family's trauma has made the novel horrifically iconic.[48] As Jacqueline Rose remarks, the fact that it 'will never be read now without that knowledge, without that unspeakable pain', risks 'conferring on the book a mythical status'. Entertaining its impact solely in these terms, she warns, we 'do the novel, and Grossman, no favours if we turn it into a sacred object, beyond critical scrutiny and outside the reach of the history to which it so complexly and sometimes disturbingly relates'.[49] On this score, I too feel vigilant, mindful of these critical perils, given that my readings in this chapter have by and large run with rather than against the novel's grain. What's more, by summarizing a biographical backdrop that seems impossible not to incorporate, I risk sanctifying the novel further still by regarding it as a supreme case—a paragon of how literary consolation might be subjected to the ultimate personal and political tests. And yet, however ethical one deems one's readerly inclinations to be, it's difficult—indeed, it may itself be unethical—*not* to consider the fact that for Grossman's family this novel, he recalls, proved 'both painful and comforting', that '[i]t wasn't easy for them to read', and that only by reading it a 'second time' did they understand how 'it could be a source of comfort to us all'.[50] By the same stroke, it's not necessarily dubious to suggest that a book devoted to forestalling consolation could turn out to be a discrepant source of it, when the story of one character's apprehensiveness about solace became the starting-point for her creator to find some way of coping.

'I would not have chosen this catastrophe', reflects Grossman. 'But since it happened, I want to explore it. I feel I was thrown into no-man's-land and the only way to allow my life to coexist with death is to write about it.'[51] The eulogy it never wished to become, *To the End of the Land* was his unexpected apprenticeship in loss. Read by the glaring light of his grief, the novel occupies that elegiac idiom that Ora does everything to withstand in telling her retrospective story of a son she hopes is still living, just as Grossman imagined the writing process as Uri's protection. In the years since this unanticipated elegy, he could understandably have submitted to the 'paralyzing effect' he associated in the 2007 'Arthur Miller Freedom to Write Lecture' with the all-consuming 'power of memory'.[52] But in that lecture Grossman also set out a number of reasons why making fiction, the very 'act of writing' itself, continued to enable him not to succumb or be 'fossilized' by this life-altering event.[53] Confronting 'what cannot be restored', as he put it, 'what has no comfort', he found a kind of asylum in composition, where 'the correct and accurate use of words acts like a medicine.'[54] Grossman likens inventing lives through language to the work of 'digging people out of the ice in which reality has encased them'. Speaking a year after Uri's death, he turned the analogy around, admitting that 'the person I am digging out at the moment is myself'.[55]

It would be tempting, then, for us to admire Grossman's subsequent book, *Falling Out of Time* (trans. 2014), as the brave product of all these excavations. But this latest work wants also to transcend the singularity of his ordeal, to be a collective rather than solely personal elegy. Tacking between testaments of bereavement, the text encompasses a disparate ensemble: a mender of fishing nets, a midwife, a centaur, all of whom have been 'blighted,' as the woman net-mender describes it, 'by the frost / of randomness,' by what Grossman terms, as we have heard, 'the cruelest arbitrariness' of fortune.[56] These characters bear witness to their absent children, producing a resonating polyphony of mourning punctuated only by a 'Town Chronicler,' whose voiceover—initially somewhat removed, much like a Greek chorus—is increasingly implicated in the lives of distress he records. Before we meet this varied cast, however, the action of this play-cum-narrative-poem begins with one man's determined resolve:

>—I have to go.
>—Where?
>—To him.
>—Where?
>—To him, there.
>—To the place where it happened?
>—No, no. There.
>—What do you mean, there?
>—I don't know.
>—You're scaring me.
>—Just to see him once more.
>—But what could you see now? What is left to see?
>—I might be able to see him there. Maybe even talk to him?
>—Talk?!   (3–4)

This opening episode gives a slice of the spare, fractious mode of address influencing the register and typography of what ensues, as the unnamed man struggles to enunciate to his wife a sudden compulsion to begin slowly orbiting at first their house, then the entire district. The 'walking man,' as we come to know him, is eventually joined by a throng of neighbours who recognize that 'a small luminance of sorts encircles the town' (39). Scarred parents, their voices congregate to produce alternating elegies as they eventually begin to move in step with the man's circuit, initiating a journey of memorialization that encompasses the entire town. In testimonies to the pain of outliving their children, they lament 'things that grow / old, that renew, / that change,' because those who are missed have 'fallen / out of time' (62).

If memories carry an incapacitating weight—just as they have silenced the mute couple whom we encounter at the opening—then they also 'gradually fade', thus compounding and repeating the original loss. Noticing the extent to which his son's 'vocabulary', for instance, 'diminishes as / the years go by', the perambulating man wonders, 'are you purposely / robbing me / of solace?' (86). This question condenses a more fundamental and perhaps controversial hypothesis about what literature can offer those who are drawn to art with 'a longing,' as Grossman put it, 'to find refuge and meaning.'[57] To the walkers of *Falling Out of Time*, who in grief have 'learned / to live / the inverse / of life' (14), the solace provided by a collective means of voicing the dead's separation from the trauma of their deaths is not without its compromises. As the centaur reflects at the close, 'still it breaks my heart, / my son, / to think / that I have— / that one could— / that I have found / the words.' But despite these misgivings, even he accepts that 'at least / language / remains, at least / it is still / somewhat free, / unravelled' (192–3). Likewise, in his criticism Grossman suggests that while articulacy itself makes the living feel ashamed, encumbered with presumption that one can describe what is irrevocable, at the same time writing has 'the power to give words to the mute', to bring into being some form of 'repair'. On this point, he would appear to share something with J. M. Coetzee, who insisted in an interview about *Age of Iron* that '[w]hat matters is that the contest is staged, that the dead have their say'.[58]

The repair words bring, of course, may only confirm rather than overcome disconnection among the bereaved. For the problem, as Grossman dramatizes it, is that often 'mourning condemns / the living / to the grimmest solitude' (24). If *To the End of the Land* asks us to think about what's left of consolation when forecasting an occasion where solace would be at once required and undesired, *Falling Out of Time* moves in a rather different temporal realm. Travelling into grief's isolating aftermath rather than towards its forbidding prospect, Grossman acquaints us with another kind of apprehension: that the impact of loneliness is often underestimated when one is consumed with foiling loss. Without diminishing this isolation, *Falling Out of Time* hypothesizes the affective viability of more communal varieties of 'counterdesolation', to recall Paul Ricoeur's term, in ways that aren't just thematic but also timbral, insofar as the book also ponders whether its gathered voices afford cumulative consolations even as they lyrically elegize those who are missed. At the same time, this polyvocal texture seems conscious of the risk it runs in amplifying—and thereby even aestheticizing—the loss its tenor tries to ease. This much seems clear as Grossman shuns structural coherence and verbal clarity, reminding us of Colm Tóibín's insistence (in Chapter 3) that what's productive in writing about grief is that it enables the experience of loss to *lose* its coherence, to become 'unravelled'. Hence, Grossman opts for terse and unembellished sequences of stichomythia, where characters pronounce alternating lines of narrative splintered into verse. They express a common will 'to separate / memory from the pain,' to circle together the perimeters of solace, to walk the 'threshold' of consolation without losing sight of that 'void' of bereavement beyond its reach, without indulging delusions of recovery (175). As they approach that 'one last line shared both by here / and there, the line to which...the living may draw near' (133), without imagining it as anything less than absolute, Grossman both resists the desolation of solitary grief and insists that even the most enigmatically elegant writing ought never to assuage what cannot be replaced.

SCALES OF CRITICAL SOLACE

Description humanizes, allegory universalizes: no doubt this distinction has left some residue on the past two chapters. As contrasts go, it doesn't entirely hold up, of course, even if my readings of description have implied that particularism takes precedence over extrapolation in works here that argue with consolation in narrating dread. For even though description's late surge in *Never Let Me Go* petitions readers for a fleeting moment to entertain counterintuitive responses to the novel's devastating ending, then that by no means fades the text's afterglow as a social parable of welfare gone wicked. Likewise, Grossman's suspenseful, indeterminate close may imply that making fiction speak allegorically to the state of a nation is all too satisfying, because it confirms what the critic already wants to see the contemporary novel enact as a channel for timely political diagnosis. Recently Grossman himself reflected that being an Israeli writer typically 'dooms' the writing to be read allegorically.[59] By the same token, though, *To the End of the Land* doesn't wholly discourage us from translating the particularism of private suffering into the collective pandemic of despair that Grossman regards as the greatest threat to hope in the Middle East. If anything, when we place his lyrical style in dialogue with his cultural commentary, it allows us to appreciate the sheer pathos of Grossman's effort to redress conditions of disconsolate pessimism by modelling alternatives for lives 'lived amid a deafening media clamour, much of which', he attests, 'is deliberately intended to distract the senses'.[60] It's that modelling process which turns microscopic depiction—with its specific treatment of individual consciousness compensating for otherwise ideologically saturated worldviews—into a pressing allegory of social experience.

So, resolving the seemingly forking paths of description and allegory is not really the interpretive point when reading for the politics of solace. If the study of apparently neglected or 'minor feelings' (of which consolation is surely one) seems to call for 'scaled down' forms of attention, in Mark Seltzer's phrase—namely, a certain kind of recovery work that lends specificity to typically fuzzy or traduced affects—then the work of solace in contemporary writing also asks us to scale up. Rather than a blunt choice between the satisfactions of macro-cultural diagnosis and the modesty of appreciating the 'political minimalism' of 'small moments of unaccountability', novels like *Never Let Me Go* and *To the End of the Land* solicit ways of mediating between such scales of response in order to gauge what solace means, in all its troubled viability, within both private and social coordinates of vulnerability.[61]

'Like it or not, today's literary-historical scholar can no longer risk being *just* a close reader', claims one commentator on the plight of critical practice.[62] Apprehending consolation from the infrastructures of genre right down to the scintillas of grammar shows why that risk is sometimes still worth taking. What appear at first blush like incidental modulations of register, rhythm, or perspective significantly direct the emotive currents of pivotal moments (including those in which intimacies or fellow-feelings, as *To the End of the Land* proves, dissipate and withdraw), moments that across this book have reflected the way writers entertain and contest consolation in equal measure—resisting the pretence of mending the damage they evoke, cutting off the supply to readerly appeasement. To discern this simultaneous production and scrutiny of solace has meant travelling between wholesale arrangements of plot and the most granular levels of syntactic inflection. Tracking the unpredictable behavior of consolation's forms as they traverse these analytic scales isn't just a functional exercise but an emotionally loaded undertaking of its own, offering one motivation for what we might call affective criticism. How this approach converses with methodological developments in literary and cultural studies, and to what extent discrepant solace marks in turn a creative zeitgeist for contemporary writing, are questions I take up next in the Epilogue. There I reflect on what literary consolation's historical moment can tell us about the current movements of critical desire.

Epilogue
Bribes of Aesthetic Pleasure?

Banishing 'the Muses of poetry', Boethius's Lady Philosophy 'frowned' on their 'seducing' attempt at 'furnishing words to articulate' 'grief'.[1] She seemed wary of poetry's deceptive balm, not simply because it fosters superficial distractions from despair but also because it presumes to have the capacity to alleviate anguish through artful expression; instead we need to grip that anguish, advises the *Consolation*, in a vice of Platonic reasoning. Only then are we able to metabolize our grief, fortified by a vocabulary of reconciliation that has no truck with poetic relief. Syncing cerebral dialogue with spiritual devotion, Boethius distinguishes the solace of philosophical intellection from the compensations of poetic elegance, anticipating what Freud would describe in 1908 as literature's 'formal—that is, aesthetic—yield of pleasure'. Because it so effectively 'bribes us' with this pleasure, the work sublimates its maker's daydreams yet 'softens' our resulting 'feeling of repulsion', thereby allowing the writer an outlet for fantasy while granting us readers a 'liberation of tensions in our minds'.[2] *Discrepant Solace* has by no means defended outright the consolations of reading, including Freud's implication here that the pleasure of engaging with aesthetically impressive texts can unshackle us from inhibitions and encourage us 'to enjoy our own day-dreams without self-reproach or shame'.[3] And yet, as much as I want to distance this book from this notion of consolation as an inducement, as the gateway to freedom from manacles of mortification, the point Freud makes about literature's aesthetic 'yield' remains pertinent. It is precisely that notion of form as an enduring 'technique of overcoming'—reprocessing distressing material 'by altering and disguising it' in bewitching language—which lies at the crux of why it can seem difficult at times to speak affirmatively about literary solace.[4]

If accepting bribes of formal pleasure isn't something that critics are normally content to do, then the bribes themselves might be worth attending to, because they contain a certain strain of solicitation that helps to explain why consolation is relatively quarantined from discussions of literature's ethical potency—let alone its political efficacy. By consolation here I don't mean the kind of reading experience that encourages acquiescence to conditions we should otherwise resist, but rather the unusual marriage of expressive potentiality and dramatic apprehension, of stylistic amplitude and diegetic turmoil, which preceding chapters have tracked. Freud hints at this when highlighting what writers 'make possible', and thus potentially compensate, through 'purely formal' means.[5]

Therein lies a longstanding—and understandable—bone of contention that has been shared by writers and theorists alike, one that reprises Adorno's worry when he distilled an ethical conundrum for the postwar literary imaginary. Trauma's description, he advised, can leave it 'transfigured', ameliorated by artistic form, with 'something of its horror' inevitably 'removed'.[6] The legacy of this stance can be felt in Lennard J. Davis's caution, at the height of the postmodern era, that novels 'have created or helped develop a mass neurosis'; enraptured, 'sitting passive', we readers are fiction's 'victims'. Thanks to the seductiveness of its 'hidden agenda', we are unlikely to see that the novel merely 'serves a defensive function in helping us carry on and live in the world', allowing us imaginatively to 'make contact with reality and buffer that reality'.[7] In this universe, where fiction is a wellspring of delusion, the job of responsible criticism is presumably to recognize how literature serves to 'help' a given culture 'to get by, to cope, to operate'. In his call for 'resisting' such consolations, Davis advises that we should 'detach ourselves' from the 'rhetoric that protects literary forms'; by doing so, he alleges, we will be able to stand back and register the consequences of readers 'visualizing, analyzing, experiencing a fantasy not their own'.[8] Albeit inadvertently, Davis rounds up his polemic by sounding rather idealist about 'the collective enterprise of the novel': although the widespread effects of literary reading upon people's attitudes surely remain empirically uncertain, he suggests that fiction, 'with its in-built ideological defenses, can and does alter our behavior *en masse*'.[9]

If only that were the case. The prospect of fiction remaining an attitude-influencing force in culture now seems unlikely at a time when personal attention has become, willingly or otherwise, acclimatized to technological distraction and saturation. As I have argued elsewhere, if social media continues apace the work of spatiotemporal compression that postmodern globalization helped to engineer, then this presents literature with an intriguing new task of evoking what Heather Houser names the *infowhelm*. And yet, far from being paralyzed by this representational challenge, writers now seem primed to tackle it, without simply administering anti-glut therapy as a consoling antidote to virtual realms of habitual yet intensifying bombardment.[10] In any case, as we have witnessed throughout this book, the ethical and emotional vectors of life-writing and fiction follow unpredictable trajectories, resisting the assumption that consolation is synonymous with literature as a mass-cultural coping device or as an anachronistic remedy for digitally overwhelmed senses. Through the kinds of reading experiences they provoke, these works defy in turn the distorting portrait of perilously swayed audiences who—when subjected to the supposedly 'passive and crippling effects' of aesthetic pleasure—are easily bribed by seductive prose into feeling soothed by what they read.[11]

But why *now*? Such is the blunt, politically freighted question scholars of contemporary writing are often obliged to answer on behalf of the tendencies they track. However customary that obligation seems, no doubt my reader probably feels that by this late stage she has waited long enough for some answers. For what does the work of consolation in literature now reveal about the historical currents that might engender it? Mindful of the ways in which periodization can be possessive and universalizing, I have had no desire to ringfence discrepant solace as an exclusively contemporary 'turn' whose repercussions are rife in world literature. Instead, my selections and comparisons have attempted to show how consolation's implications in one writer's work can illuminate its conflicts, risks, or fulfilments in that of another whose culturally and artistically contingent aims might otherwise seem very different. To say that all this is happening now is not to say that it is happening everywhere. And to say that it is happening in contemporary literature with peculiar intensity and variety is not to say that it hasn't happened in other literary-historical eras (a motivation for Chapter 1, which retraced an important genealogy for the eloquently agitating consummation of solace in modernist aesthetics). Nonetheless, with these spatial and temporal caveats now aired, it's worth reflecting here on literary consolation's contemporary mainsprings, particularly if this also allows us to gauge how far twenty-first-century developments in writing emotion coexist with recent developments in critical practice.

What do we make, then, of the historical coincidence of geopolitical instability with narratives that draw stylistic and emotive energy from consolation's discrepancies? Have we entered a peculiarly fertile age for writing that models the difficulties and possibilities of solace without simply offering aesthetic compensations for political maladies, as emboldened xenophobia and rampant jingoism continue to make fiscal and ideological protectionism the order of the day? It would certainly be appealing to invoke such questions as the basis for accounting for literature's resistant or edifying work in a world of division: commending contemporary writing for its progressive antidotes to the gloom of escalating chauvinism and mutual disconnection between nations, while endorsing criticism's causal and instrumentalizing accounts of how writers have been confronting prevailing disenfranchisement, economic individualism, and social disaffection. *Why now?*, though, may answered just as fruitfully from the other direction. Rather than presupposing that contemporary historical conditions reveal something about the capacities (and complicities) of twenty-first-century writing because literature symptomatically reflects such conditions, we might ask instead what developments in narrative form tell us about the politics of subjectivity as it anchors and mediates literary representation. The astonishing rise of the literary memoir since the 1990s would seem pivotal to this line of thought, especially if we think of the genre as peculiarly suited—if not self-consciously attuned—to neoliberalism's tentacular reach into all corners of private life. Moreover, many of the novels we have encountered strikingly resemble memoirs in their perspectival notation of intimate experiences, buffeted and broken over time: *Atonement*'s life story of unfulfilled reparation; *Austerlitz*'s accumulation of auto/biographical fragments, curated by a confidante; those first-person recitals of self-examination, catalysing the process of reckoning with imminent self-loss, which shape *Age of Iron*, *Gilead*, and *Never Let Me Go*, novels that ask what consolation there might be in 'the idea', as Ishiguro formulated it in his rough notes, 'that to die is our ultimate mission in life';[12] and finally, even *To the End of the Land* may be read as Ora's memoir of gemstone recollections, moments of familial fullness whose description becomes her imaginative equipment for withstanding the vulnerability they encapsulate—a vulnerability that's often the motor for memoirs, from Sonali Deraniyagala to Joan Didion, about seemingly inconceivable solace.

Against the backdrop of neoliberal individualism, however, this generic affinity may imply something rather more problematic about literary-aesthetic responses to contemporary political times. Given how entangled memoir remains in private worlds of feeling and action, it has become ideologically compromised for some critics, who regard it as 'uniquely outfitted to articulate the ways in which neoliberal reforms have isolated and limited, while championing and privileging, the individual'.[13] In this vein, Daniel Worden persuasively shows that throughout the 1990s and early 2000s 'the erosion of common meaning and the proliferation of the personal authorized by neoliberal reform' set the cultural and economic scene for formally ambitious memoirs (his example also being Didion's *The Year of Magical Thinking*) in which the 'tension between style and fragmentation, coherent narrative voice and that voice's dissolution as it articulates disparate and irresolute events, produces a literary form that captures key facets of neoliberalism'—including, above all, the promotion of 'entrepreneurial individualism'.[14]

The alignment of evolutions in literary form with regimes of neoliberalization satisfies a certain critical hunger for diagnostic equations, analogizing textual interiority with the credos of personal self-governance and enterprising self-advancement. But suppose we observe instead that only by giving voice to this coexistence of coherence and disconnection do novelists and memoirists convey the affectively 'rich interiority' and 'poetry' that, in Wendy Brown's account, remain antithetical to 'the grammar and terms' of neoliberal 'rationality'.[15] Far from reconsolidating 'the personal's negligible status under a regime for which personal initiative is purportedly all', the works we have considered recuperate 'common meanings' for seemingly commonplace feelings—those like solace—precisely by rescuing their peculiar ontology from the generalized 'hyperindividualism fuelled by neoliberal culture'.[16] And these texts do so through their devoted particularism: proving that the depiction of emotionally singular, individuated situations need not be commensurate with the ideological promotion of protective self-reform.

Although it can be genuinely alluring, then, to spot in the tendencies of contemporary writing tell-tale symptoms that supply up-to-the-minute cultural-political dissections, memoirs and novels can equally become the grit in this hermeneutic machine. In no small part this is because their 'force', in Derek Attridge's terms, isn't always 'predictable or harnessable for an instrumental purpose'. By animating solace and its discontents, the works I have brought together demonstrate 'that there is something of exceptional value in the experience undergone by the writer and the reader with regard to the text'—an experience, in my reading, that is enriched by analysing consolation precisely in narratives that make us distinctly uncomfortable. In such cases, the very contentiousness of solace arouses what Attridge calls the reader's 'sense of an entrance onto new ground and a relishing of language's powers to make this happen'.[17]

My early efforts to understand what language does to make consolation happen—especially in texts that trouble its attainability—in some ways miscalculated what my corpus had to offer. Knowing that the project I was embarking on would be making deliberately counterintuitive choices in plotting emotionally shattering parameters for solace, I thought I could nevertheless shed light on two kinds of books: those that aren't ostensibly *about* consolation and those that are. Two species, behaving differently. But I also hoped to prove that solace, as an affordance of narrative form, can be discerned and defined in nondiegetic features: in countervailing facets of grammar or metre; in frictions between the affective register of what happens and the register of its description; in those instances where books occupy genres imbued with sorrow yet also confront the very conventions by which loss is conveyed in penetrating, stylistically energizing terms. I thought my argument might therefore revolve around the implications of form behaving at odds with action. By zeroing-in on the conflicting resonances of what a work rhetorically or structurally does and how its plot emotionally unfolds I intended, first, to disrupt the homologies that position form as a reflective embodiment of the affects it conveys and, second, to propose in the place of such equivalences that form's dissentious relation to content prompts us to redefine what consolation in literature might mean. It turns out that I underestimated the very writers I hoped would disrupt mimetic accounts of how literary language and emotionality interact. Rather than inviting us to locate solace in that disjuncture between syntax and content—as though style reliably compensates for, precisely by colliding with, the trauma or trepidation it details— these writers suggest that it's not enough simply to celebrate texts' resistance to the isomorphism of expression and experience. Rather, they require us to entertain how language itself plays host to a forum where consolation's contentiousness is aired and examined. In the more unpredictable story I found myself telling, style is rarely substitutive or merely aestheticizing, still less redemptive purely thanks to its graceful opposition to the harm it conveys; it is instead the mechanism by which memoir and fiction offer up to scrutiny—and yes, to ethical misgivings and political reservations—the solace that arises when linguistic plenitude meets pitiful deprivation, disappointment, bereavement, shame, or dread.

As a result, it would seem schematic to conclude that the kinds of expression on display in this study—style as consolation and style as argumentation—are distinct, though the claim wouldn't be entirely unwarranted. For in some works, language graphically counters plot (*Austerlitz*, *Never Let Me Go*, *The Road*), when description seems to triumph over anguished recollection, present calamity, or the apparent foreclosure of lives in jeopardy. Holding out the tentative—if presently perverse— promise of futurity, style itself models intimations of 'living on after great pain' (to recall Christina Crosby's Dickinsonian subtitle), magnifying and rendering comprehensible the damage it so agilely records, without blocking out or dematerializing the kind of experiential duress that solace is traditionally meant to assuage (*H is for Hawk*, *Gilead*, *To the End of the Land*). By the same token, style on other occasions offers no such buoyancy or recompense, reinforcing instead those ethically loaded arguments with solace around which fictional or autobiographical events revolve (*Alfred and Emily*, *Disgrace*, *Levels of Life*). But while these scenes and figurations of discrepant consolation are markedly different, in each case lacerating situations generate forms of expression that actively inspect the prospect of solace to which persons in distress, regret, or grief cleave (or from which, as we have seen, they may also recoil), without discrediting or dismissing it.

As these books seize hold of consolation's ideological and cognitive slipperiness, they achieve several things. They add epistemic flesh to the skeleton of an affective phenomenon that's not infrequently invoked quite unthinkingly. They complicate the supposition that the consolatory impress of aesthetic form is at best beguiling for its reader, at worst a mere diversion. And they ask us to give some thought to how solace is neither analogous to pleasing outcomes nor necessarily synonymous with neat resolutions, but can happen in the course of searing authorial self-examination and at uncertain plot junctures: as a moral pivot on which atonement is exposed as it tilts towards self-appeasement; as a stimulus for elegists to argue with their own medium, seeking no easy repair in forlorn reconstruction; as a reason for writers to eye up the mitigations of rhetorical grace, to audit the restorative undercurrents of eloquence. These strategies make consolation newly legible, thinkable, critically recuperable. They suggest in turn that contemporary literature can offer a historical and conceptual portal for accessing the complex imbrications of aesthetics, ethics, and politics that characterize consolation's often-ambivalent representation.

This intersectional approach enables us to deal theoretically, contextually, and phenomenologically with literary solace in mutually informing modes of reading its artistic, emotional, and ideological consequences. For some writers, as we have seen, the stakes of wrestling with solace are conspicuously acute, making biographically-informed responses virtually inescapable: from Sonali Deraniyagala's unflinching excavation of anguish through to David Grossman's confrontation with fiction's sudden symmetry with his own family's catastrophe. Between these bookending figures, our treatment of solace has encompassed the intentional and the inadvertent. Novelists turning to memoir, Barnes, Didion, and Lessing purposefully contend with the impression of writing as 'working through', refusing to countenance any relief or reconciliation. Unorthodox adoptions of genre models, in the case of McCarthy and Ishiguro, offer unexpected occasions for rhetorical replenishment in the scenes that seem irrefutably inimical to solace. Across this spectrum, consolation's vigorous contestation features as prominently as its winning instantiation. Reading more for the disruption than for the triumph of solace, I have discussed works that by no means leave us feeling consoled, precisely in order to account for how literature compositionally engages with consolation's ethical, affective, and epistemological substance. And what these works suggest is that one of the things that defines our contemporary literary moment is the sheer commitment writers show to the constructive capabilities of their own practice. Trying to stay alert to the ever-evolving shape of this moment, this book has argued that if writers today perform consolation's quandaries, they do so not in the negative sense of prosecuting literature's contact with solace as inherently compromised but instead to trial new conditions of linguistic and emotional articulacy.

To say that these impulses might usefully adjust the tenor of criticism itself wouldn't sit easily, of course, with commentators for whom positive stories of what literature is capable of are liable to drift into sentimentality or enfeebling tolerance. 'The impulse to be affirmative', warns Carolyn Lesjak, 'to talk about what texts do rather than what they don't do, occludes the negation upon which such affirmation is based'.[18] To indulge such 'attempts to be affirmative', according to this account, is to 'fall prey to nostalgia and accommodation'.[19] Regarding aesthetic attention to a text's ingenuous surfaces as ill-equipped to plumb its perturbing depths, Lesjak insists that 'unlike a dialectical reading' affirmative responses—and, by implication, readings of what writers themselves affirmatively achieve—provide 'no way of actually registering or thinking the occlusion that structures the surfaces being privileged'.[20] One aim of this book has been to apply some pressure to criticism's familiar reservations about affirmation; in the process, I have tried to stay alert to how tempting it can be to see the 'act of negation', in Lauren Berlant's words, as intrinsically meritorious, consecrating the rightful home of literary and cultural studies in a 'self-confirming scene of disappointment'.[21] When contemporary writers enact their own formally productive debates with solace, they invite us to pause before perpetuating the inclination to see consolation as an indicator of aesthetic deficit (for the work of literature) or intellectual complacency (for the work of criticism).

An affirmative critique of solace—as part of a willingness 'to talk about what texts do' rather than how they misfire—need not mean withdrawing, then, to a 'space of minimal critical agency', as Sharon Marcus and Stephen Best put it in their prolegomenon to surface reading.[22] Rather, I have wanted to suggest ways of taking solace seriously by subjecting it to accommodating readings of its creative, experiential, and philosophical ramifications, without insinuating that even to entertain consolation invariably means lapsing into uncritical equanimity, an insinuation that would come close to rehearsing the cliché that spending time with the pleasures of form (including the 'relishing of language's powers', to recall Attridge's phrase) precipitates apolitical objectives for literary studies. If anything, solace summons interpretive 'work that attends', as Best and Marcus propose, 'as much to the complexities of the critic's position as to those of the artwork'.[23] Indeed, the practice of looking for consolation's discrepant forms in ways that affirm literature's own acuity helps one to resist the self-satisfaction of assuming that representational insufficiency is the only worthy horizon of sufficiently exacting analysis. For what do we miss by equating affirmation per se (either in critical discourse or in creative practice) with supine acceptance, especially when contemporary writers endorse as much as they examine the transformational capacity of language to engage with apparently ineffable regions of experience?

Just how much we can miss is made clear by the poet, philosopher, and feminist critic, Denise Riley. The loss of her adult son, Jacob, inspired two striking books of bereavement, the latest a collection of poems, *Say Something Back* (2016). There Riley has no hesitation in scorning the superficial succour of elegant, metonymic substitutions. In her celebrated 'A Part Song', that critique includes the appeasing apostrophes of elegiac lyrics: 'I can't get sold on reincarnating you / As those bloody "gentle showers of rain" / Or in "fields of ripening grain" – oooh / Anodyne – nor yet on shadowing you / In the hope of eventually pinpointing / You bemused among the *flocking souls / Clustered like bats, as all thronged gibbering / Dusk-veiled*.'[24] Riley defies the idea that 'formal devices', as Jenefer Robinson argues, should act as 'coping mechanisms'. Formal techniques, for Robinson, 'help to redirect attention and to change our conceptions of or beliefs about the content so that it becomes less painful', such that 'we find the content to be less in conflict with our own goals and interests, so that we are less saddened or disturbed by otherwise troubling content'.

By supplying this mitigation, she continues, literature's formal 'devices help us to focus attention on positive aspects of the content, to divert our attention from painful aspects, and to modify our wants and goals'.[25] This model of aesthetic compensation seems redolent of Samuel Johnson's definition of *solace* as 'alleviation'—a remedy that allows us to get on with enjoying the 'recreation' of more positive 'goals and interests'. A defence of diversion, this leads to the kind of misleading equation of solace with substitution that Riley closely inspects. 'Does sifting through damage ease, or enshrine it', she asks, wondering how in these poems she might 'grasp / a past, but not skid on embittered accounting'?[26] *Say Something Back* takes us into the very heart of those 'painful aspects' Robinson sees literature placating, as Riley robustly affirms that language need not shield the reader from grief's lashes or file down its barbed edges into lachrymose imagery; on the contrary, loss provokes grief's voracity, its longing for verbal reanimation. 'The souls of the dead', she attests, 'are the spirit of language: / you hear them alight inside that spoken thought'.[27] This possibility—this conviction that language can be the medium through which the lost subject can be revived without easing or 'enshin[ing]' death's 'damage'—is the essence of what solace means in works that confront head-on the vestigial comforts of 'anodyne' lyricism, arguing with the rhetorical prophylactics of panache.

Rediscovering loss as the germ of linguistic promise is a venture Riley has pursued before, though on this occasion in narrative. *Time Lived, Without Its Flow* (2012) is a virtuosic meditation on the repercussions of her son's death, focusing specifically on the sensation of living in the wake of such a tragedy without familiar durational coordinates, immersed in an 'extraordinary feeling of a-temporality' perpetuated by grief.[28] Unfolding in successive intervals of time, the book plots Riley's recognition that the increasing distance from his death guarantees no imminent clarity, let alone reconciliation. And like many of the writers in this study who have chosen themselves as subjects, Riley is keenly aware of genre. Adamantly she tries 'not to lapse into melodrama or self-regarding memoir' (8); and near the start, she introduces a ground bass of self-consciousness towards her own technical decisions that resounds throughout the ensuing sections of self-scrutiny. Riley anticipates misgivings about the representability of her own time-twisting sense of loss, wondering 'how could such a striking condition ever be voiced?' (8). Whether one can evoke this condition 'is also a question about what is describable, and what are the linguistic limits of what can be conveyed' (8). But Riley admits that she is 'not keen on conceding to any such limits' (8). Acknowledging this conundrum, building it indeed into its very texture, *Time Lived* sustains an extended dialogue with these paradoxical 'possibilities for describing' (8). These seem all the more discrepant in two respects: because they emerge from an experience that's '[h]ard to put into words' even as it remains 'absolutely lucid as you inhabit it daily' (10); and also because Riley's confrontation with grief's inexpressibility anticipates additional loss, for 'to concede at the outset that it's "indescribable" would only isolate you further, when coming so close to your child's death is already quite solitary enough' (11).

Orbiting ineffability, Riley recalls how the 'prospect of recounting it in a written form stayed...both repugnant and implausible for well over two and half years after the death' (10). *Time Lived* memorializes this subsequently fraught attempt at writing; in so doing, it affirms the 'triumph of metaphor' as she navigates the 'crisscrossing and slippage of emotion, which you can only recount through descriptions which serve the dead and the living indiscriminately' (37). From eyeing up description's improbability to subsequently vouching for its necessity, Riley dramatizes the 'struggle to convey this sharply distinctive life inside a new temporal dimension' of bereavement, and her book thereby enacts what it means, for a writer, to 'want to save [grief] from being treated as unapproachable, and exceptional' (52). With its search for the right depictive mode, *Time Lived* showcases astonishing particularism, such that the poignancy of 'allowing myriad specificities of loss their distinctive impacts on lived time' provokes the reader's admiration as well as compassion (52). Responding in these terms need not spell obsequious or reverential acclamation; instead, she encourages us to think *with* her as she conducts philosophical and personal analyses of the turmoil her book strives (and often strains) to describe. We thereby enter a conversation with a text that grapples with feelings that at first exceed words, a conversation that affords a level of intellectual and emotional intimacy that Riley urges her readers to sustain rather than to mistrust.

'No subject', declares Riley, 'can easily be conceived as extinguished. Language doesn't want to allow that thought; its trajectory is always to lean forward into life, to push it along, to propel the dead onward among the living' (56). *Time Lived* previews the solace of finding in properties of description the 'souls of the dead' (as they are defined in *Say Something Back*) when she observes that 'the continuing possibilities for discussing the no longer existing person induce a curious linguistic quasi-resurrection. Perhaps language, at least, possesses a belief in spirit' (55). Like several of the works we have considered—from Sebald's traumatic vortex of partially recovered memory, to Didion's unsentimental enchantment with magical thinking, to Grossman's advocacy of fiction's exactitude when evoking lives made fragile by routine desensitization and endemic despair—*Time Lived* provides a commentary on how loss, whether actual or potential, presents us 'with serious problems of what's describable' (57), an admission that becomes for Riley the very reason to seek linguistically dexterous ways of answering back to the unutterable. If this is a consolation, it belongs to the work: it's not for us to decide whether Riley finds solace in solutions to her own acceptance that '[a]ny attempt at descriptive writing soon reaches an impasse' (56). And it's not for the individual critic to assume other readers will find consoling the achievements of a book that boldly aims, 'however much against the odds, to convey' how the 'so-called "work of grief"' turns out to be 'a shatteringly exhausting apprehension of the needed work of *living*' (12, 14). In short, the issue at hand, the quality to look out for, isn't simply to do with whether this book is *about* the meaning of solace in the epicentre of desolation, or with how it imparts some residue of the turbulent attainment of consolation that it autobiographically records. What's important is how it instantiates the very aesthetic-affective contestation that brings it into being, when style embraces the kind of experience of suspension that 'systematically undercuts its own articulation' (58).

Just as Didion was wary in *The Year of Magical Thinking* of the stale protocols of grief-writing, so Riley argues that 'through the usual memorial outlets, most published expressions of sentiment tend to be highly convention-bound' (58). 'Nevertheless', she remarks, the 'search for any evidence of fellow feeling is restless, almost comically so' (60–1): hence the typical desire 'to comb through any writing that might carry the reassurance that this cessation of your time is both well known and fully recorded' (61). Watchful of this, Riley adjusts the implied sympathies of her stance on solace. From being a hymn to the inconceivability of living beyond ever-evolving pain, *Time Lived* moves on to speculate about what it might mean to defend imaginations of solace, earmarking the need to review the assumption that consolation betokens mawkish self-appeasement. For literature today, this need constitutes an unfinished venture:

> At times of great tension, we may well find ourselves hunting for some published resonances in literature of what we've come to feel. I realise that this might quickly be condemned as a sentimental search for 'identification', and for the coziness of finding one's own situation mirrored in print. Still, I think we can save it from that withering assessment. Instead we might reconsider the possibility of a literature of consolation, what that could be or what it might do. (61)

Time Lived takes its own purposeful step towards seeing what this alternative genre might look like, as it tackles 'the experience of time lived after the death of a child', an experience Riley probes with the help of her paratactic style as an 'elaborate, dynamic, silent temporal abundance, even as this is also an abundance of loss' (74). She thereby reminds us of how consoling it would be to consecrate only the writing of *dis*consolation as artistically responsible or ethically virtuous. If Riley monitors the temporal pervasiveness of loss, she also scrutinises the supposition that its formidable reach is inexpressible.

Roland Barthes advised in *A Lover's Discourse* that 'writing compensates for nothing'.[29] Riley would probably agree; no doubt Grossman, Deraniyagala, Barnes, Didion, and Crosby would too. Whether it's epic fiction bleeding horrifically into parenthood, a freak environmental disaster wreaking familial catastrophe, grief memoirs that go into intellectual combat with the social conventions of reconciliation and overcoming, or a queer theorization of disability that at once contests and replenishes writing's facility for recording the costs of learning to adapt to a life of chronic pain—however distinct in mode and context these narratives of loss and qualified survival are, they share implicitly the conviction that literature is indeed no compensation, whether one is reading or producing it. In compensation's place, they actively deliberate the challenges of living with and writing about emotional worlds that struggle for articulation, a struggle that becomes the crucible where solace is forged in all its instability within the dramatic precincts and formal textures of their prose.

What might it mean, then, to 'reconsider' what Riley calls 'the possibility of a literature of consolation'? How might literary studies begin to wonder—in the permissive, receptive, undogmatic sense of that word—what this kind of literature 'could be or what it might do' in our current moment? Lyrical as *Time Lived* is, expression is no saccharine panacea in its pages; and experimental though she certainly is, Riley has little interest in reproducing the sort of quest for redemption that has periodically been affiliated with modernist innovation. Putting grief into words, for Riley, illuminates rather than sutures the wounds loss leaves on literary form. Like many memoirists in this book, she surveys the pledges of writing when the 'very *will to tell*' grief's 'violently novel state' becomes 'sapped', when 'you feel syntax itself to be set against you' (59). The acknowledgment of this formidable challenge is an acknowledgement too of all that literature has left to do. 'Wherever is the literature' which 'deals closely' with grief's 'strange arresting of time', asks Riley—'for it *must* exist, it's needed' (61)?

The insistence alone with which Riley makes the case for this need—along with the case she makes for distinguishing literary consolation from the 'coziness' of 'sentimental' 'identification'—returns us, through its audible urgency, to matters of periodicity. Namely, would it be legitimate to regard a work like *Time Lived* as emblematic of an emerging paradigm of consolation writing, one that's specially equipped for limning the multiply overlapping 'times of great tension' that constitute the contemporary? Such a paradigm would encompass writers more concerned with language's affective potentialities than with its resigned incapacities; it would solicit in turn more critically tactful portraits of consolation's representation that dispense with the ideologically predictable view of solace as the gateway to hollow cheer, picturing it instead as integral to writers' tough and unromantic reflections on what literature does in the anticipation or aftermath of loss. A paradigm of this sort might unite the range of works included in *Discrepant Solace* not only as test cases for consolation's obstacles and controversies, but as evidence of a pervasive mode whose structures of feeling earmark a distinctive modulation in the literary present. We have yet 'to identify', claims Joseph Conte, 'what the dominant of a twenty-first-century literature will be'.[30] Nomenclatural options abound, of course.[31] And in place of a proliferation of further *isms* or escalating generic taxonomies, Conte is not alone in suggesting that 'the early millennial scene may be a phenomenological one of *affect*', even if affect's theoretical ascendancy across the humanities and social sciences no longer seems new.[32] Regardless of which labels look set to occupy the limelight in years to come, for now we have reason to appreciate how differently literature operates when it's no longer up against the 'waning of affect' that Fredric Jameson famously saw at the late-capitalist heart of postmodernity. It's not that practices of everyday postmodern life were 'utterly devoid of feeling', as he admits, but that a 'peculiar kind of euphoria' 'dominated' culture and influenced its artistic outputs. This scene of affective dilution and artistic commercialization meant rough times for what Jameson called 'personal style'. With the dissipation of affective depth, postmodernism witnessed the absorption of 'aesthetic production' into 'commodity production generally'. This resulted in the 'increasing unavailability' of styles that revolved around 'the unique and the personal', which we now see in abundance in contemporary memoir as well as in fictions that employ emotionally particularizing strategies for charting the individual's place in history.[33]

It would be tempting to look back at the authors in this book and observe them bidding a collective farewell to that particular epoch of affective evisceration and exhaustion, where style boils down to the 'wearing of a linguistic mask', in Jameson's phrase, manufacturing 'speech in a dead language'.[34] But to make that case would, in part, be to conspire with a vocabulary that arguably says more about its own narrow confines than about the artistic tendencies it names. After all, postmodern writing was never as flat, affectless, recycled, or immanently commodified as some of its classic theoretical portraits occasionally imply. Numerous figures who have sometimes found themselves sitting under the classificatory umbrella of postmodernism (Coetzee, Ishiguro, and McEwan among them) in fact produced some of their most intimately affecting and formally singular fiction through a period between the mid-1980s and early 1990s that's retrospectively considered to be postmodernity's late apogee. Moreover, accounts of postmodernism's legacies are now emerging that show how artistic responses to longing, reminiscence, and other affective postures that have periodically endured the same denigrations as consolation were not symptoms of a depthless sphere of reproduction—one capable of inspiring only hyper-stylized, unoriginal sketches of feeling—but reflexive representations of the varieties of cultural critique that nostalgia and hope might surprisingly enable.[35]

Ultimately, though, the shift I have been describing, and for which *Discrepant Solace* proposes a selective archive, isn't just a matter of reforming terminology. If the postmodern model no longer fits certain limbs of affective experience in literature now, then the understandable appetite for replacement labels seems less important than recognizing that writers' unexpected kinships possess aesthetic, philosophical, and political valences that exceed compartmentalization. Coetzee's language of the soul; Barnes's pursuit of solace in 'bleak truths'; Robinson's quest for rhetorical correlatives for worldly grace; Sebald's solemn yet restitutive syntax; Grossman's lyrical realism; and Deraniyagala's discovery of 'a better quality of agony' in detailed recollection, making for her the very labour of remembering a 'huge consolation'—these are registers of feeling that are also new registers of thinking. Modelling the means for feeling and thinking otherwise, they at once disobey the commodifying, banalizing logic of postmodern pastiche and contravene the equally flattening, bureaucratized logic of neoliberal rationality.

None of these writers deny that sorrow's visceral grammar may thwart and derail expression, that there are formidable experiences, recalled or dreaded, which indubitably defy adequate representation. But in their efforts to do some justice to inconsolable lives, they expect more from their own medium of expression than capitulation; disenchanted with deficiency, they seem disinclined to assume that literature's abstinence from what Jean-François Lyotard called 'the solace of good forms' is necessarily synonymous with rejecting consolation altogether.[36] One formal consequence of this impulse, as we've witnessed, is that the inescapable turbulences not only of grief but of terror, shame, remorse, and jeopardy are often beautifully evoked. Doubtlessly, there will be myriad counterarguments to identifying this phenomenon of aesthetic redress with what consolation means; no time like our precarious present fuels these objections more pointedly, and indeed I have tried to locate such dissent in the very contours of contemporary writing as it challenges solace without wholly abandoning it. Ultimately, it's always tough to speak of the elegant delineation of devastation or of description's facilitation of souls that 'alight inside' expressions of anguish (to borrow Riley's evocative account) without resorting to the argot of artistic exploitation, without feeling somewhat obliged to signal how vigilant we remain to what trauma's adroit rendition might claim, without reinforcing how competent we feel in keeping one incredulous step ahead of style's metamorphoses of pain. Contemporary writers open up other critical options here, as they confront psychic and material damage while bringing the hazards of its consolation into dazzling legibility. However enthralling works of discrepant solace turn out to be, they are not bribes of aesthetic pleasure; they are a reason to keep interpretive pace with what literature can do in situations that would seem to herald its inadequacy.

In agonizing, irremediable circumstances, the strenuous achievement of books like *Time Lived*, therefore, is their implication that the flipside of representational defeat is worth entertaining. For our current juncture in literary and cultural studies, there's something resonant about Riley's multi-layered invitation: to consider that the thematization of consolation's apparent unattainability isn't automatically reciprocated in negative terms by form—by syntactic fractures or structural lacunae, for instance, which could be construed as signs of compositional enervation—but may in fact spell a work's formal efflorescence; to distinguish, as this study has hopefully done, the question of what solace 'might do' for literature from the question of whether literature should comfort or therapeutically assist us; to recognize how writers can eschew the elixir of aesthetic redemption while still embracing the complexities of consolation's rhetorical and psychological manifestations. Affectively complicated, fitful, equivocal: solace serves not as an anthem to literature's dereliction or compliance but, as Riley implies, as the trigger for creative tenacity. Along these lines, the very problematics of consolation usefully spotlight the resourcefulness of contemporary writing as it acquaints conflicting feelings, capturing what Riley calls 'unassailable pathos' while capturing too through narrative development 'some feeling of futurity' (10). This motivation extends to readers, pressed as we are to think in imaginative ways about how writers deploy linguistic and generic innovations to reconfigure perceptions of literature's affective capacities—discrepant though this surge of formal positivity may feel when their works make irreparable loss seem so real.

Such is the challenge, such is the critical spur, when consolation permeates so unsettlingly and for every reader so divergently through that fold between the work and the work's expression. There it resides and from there it precariously emerges, not necessarily or always against the grain, secreted beneath the shavings pared by reading's plane. If solace remains a formal and ethical problem for contemporary writing, then it is also part of its promise. This is nowhere more apparent than when writers draw attention to the vexed effort of style itself to be a counterpoint for loss, an antagonist of despair—while refusing to guarantee the reader's comfort. In so doing, they broach the possibility of conferring value upon the venture of representing the rawest of experiences, without promoting the sense that we can tolerate distresses in melodious language that cannot be weathered in real life. Taking on material that may itself seem unspeakable, they reveal how the solace felicity imparts to suffering in the moment of its depiction by no means transmutes damage into something more bearable. A nimble double act like that suggests consolation and critique might well have a rapport after all.

Notes

INTRODUCTION

1. Sonali Deraniyagala, *Wave* (London: Virago, 2013), 3. Hereafter cited parenthetically.
2. Sonali Deraniyagala, Interview with *Indigo*, 15 March 2013: http://www.youtube.com/watch?v=aX_bb_-2uEs
3. Ibid.
4. Sonali Deraniyagala, 'A Better Quality of Agony', interview by Jeannie Macfarlane, *Hazlitt*, 2 April 2013: http://www.hazlitt.net/feature/better-quality-agony
5. Ibid.
6. Ibid.
7. Ibid.
8. Ibid.
9. Ibid.
10. Christina Crosby, *A Body, Undone: Living On After Great Pain* (New York: New York University Press, 2016), 12. Hereafter cited parenthetically.
11. Deraniyagala, 'A Better Quality of Agony'.
12. Angela Leighton, *On Form: Poetry, Aestheticism, and the Legacy of a Word* (Oxford: Oxford University Press, 2007), 221.
13. Derek Attridge, *The Work of Literature* (Oxford: Oxford University Press, 2015), 265.
14. Ibid., 269.
15. Ibid., 260.
16. Colum McCann, 'Letter to a Young Writer, Redux', *Letters to a Young Writer: Some Practical and Philosophical Advice* (London: Bloomsbury, 2018), 167, 169, 168, 167 (ebook pagn.).
17. Theodor W. Adorno, 'Commitment', *Notes to Literature: Volume II*, trans. Rolf Tiedemann (New York: Columbia University Press, 1992), 88.
18. Ibid. 88.
19. Eve Kosofsky Sedgwick, *Touching Feeling: Affect, Pedagogy, Performativity* (Durham, NC: Duke University Press, 2003), 124.
20. See Sianne Ngai's engrossing *Ugly Feelings* (Cambridge, MA: Harvard University Press, 2005); for a political reading of 'flat affects' see Lauren Berlant, 'Structures of Unfeeling: *Mysterious Skin*', *International Journal of Politics, Culture, and Society*, 28 (2015): 191–213. Ngai recommends that we regard the distinction between 'affect and emotion' as one of 'modal difference of intensity or degree, rather than a formal difference of quality or kind' (27). Rei Terada teases the categories apart when noting that 'by *emotion* we usually mean a psychological, at least minimally interpretive experience whose physiological aspect is *affect. Feeling* is a capacious term that connotes both physiological sensations (affects) and psychological states (emotions).' With these facets in mind, Terada encourages us to notice 'the common ground of the physiological and the psychological' when accounting for feeling's implications (*Feeling in Theory: Emotion after the 'Death of the Subject'* [Cambridge, MA: Harvard University Press, 2001], 4). Jonathan Flatley is also keen to differentiate rather than blend such terms: 'Where *emotion* suggests something that happens inside and tends toward outward expression,

affect indicates something relational and transformative'; as such affects 'are always amplifying, dampening, or otherwise modifying some other affect' (*Affective Mapping*: 12, 16). From her perspective as an early modernist, Katherine Ibbett posits that '[i]f an emotion is understood to belong to an individual, to usher out from an interior core, then affect work has a rather different configuration, unattached to the self' and 'instead emerging socially, extra-individually, often bodily' (*Compassion's Edge: Fellow-Feeling and Its Limits in Early Modern France* [Philadelphia, PA: University of Pennsylvania Press, 2018], 22). Throughout the coming chapters, I associate consolation with the dynamic aspects of affect that Flatley and Ibbett highlight here. Yet I also recognize that to *be* consoled—literally so, in the extra-literary sense—constitutes a distinct emotional state involving a sense of altered being or at least a modified awareness of one's own capacity to endure (though people often describe that state in terms of *feeling*: 'I felt consoled'). At the same time, one's inclination *to* console someone else suggests something closer to a feeling: to offer consolation can resemble a compulsion, an intuition, or an obligation, depending on the context in which one notices that consolation is desired and perceives how the act of giving solace might therefore be required.

21. Michel de Montaigne, 'On Diversion', *Michel de Montaigne: The Complete Essays*, trans. M. A. Screech (London: Penguin, 2003), 941.
22. Timothy Aubry, *Reading as Therapy: What Contemporary Fiction Does for Middle-Class Americans* (Iowa City, IA: University of Iowa Press, 2011), 41. In an examination of the 'social lives' of fiction as it acquires 'sacral' value and authority for different audiences, Günter Leypoldt observes that 'recent notions of cultural work come with a hermeneutically suspicious account of the pleasure of reading', one that condescendingly assumes that 'readers who are not yet aware of their most troubling issues are especially likely to enjoy fictional displacements of these issues', as though 'millions of readers engage in similar acts of symptomatic resolution or absorb similar bits of ideology' (Leypoldt, 'Degrees of Public Relevance: Walter Scott and Toni Morrison', *Modern Language Quarterly*, 77.3 [September 2016], 371, 372).
23. Steven Mullaney, *The Reformation of Emotions in the Age of Shakespeare* (Chicago, IL: University of Chicago Press, 2015), 24–5.
24. Cathy Park Hong, 'Delusions of Whiteness in the Avant-Garde', *Lana Turner: A Journal of Poetry and Opinion* 7 (Nov. 2014): https://arcade.stanford.edu/content/delusions-whiteness-avant-garde
25. Ngai, *Ugly Feelings*, 29–30. For an astute account of form's social and political 'affordances', see Caroline Levine's *Forms: Whole, Rhythm, Hierarchy, Network* (Princeton, NJ: Princeton University Press, 2015).
26. Ibbett, *Compassion's Edge*, 24.
27. Samuel Johnson, *A Dictionary of the English Language*, corrected and revised edn. (London: Thomas Tegg, 1822), 158.
28. Ibid., 735.
29. Stanley Cavell, 'The Avoidance of Love: A Reading of *King Lear*', *Must We Mean What We Say?* 2nd edn. (Cambridge: Cambridge University Press, 2002), 337.
30. Ibid., 337.
31. Carol Shields, '"Always a Book-Oriented Kid": The Early Interviews: 1988–1993', in Eleanor Wachtel, *Radom Illuminations: Conversations with Carol Shields* (New Brunswick: Goose Lane Editions, 2007), 52.
32. Carol Shields, *Unless* (2002; London: Fourth Estate, 2003), 13.
33. Primarily a student of the modern and contemporary novel, I'm aware that my sketch of opinions regarding consolation is partial thanks to its implicit periodization.

Scholarship on earlier literary-historical eras has explored the poetics and politics of solace with considerable nuance. See, for instance, the range of perspectives on offer in Catherine E. Leigla and Stephen J. Milner, eds, *The Erotics of Consolation: Desire and Distance in the Late Middle Ages* (Basingstoke: Palgrave, 2008). And also, Dorothea B. Heitsch, 'Approaching Death by Writing: Montaigne's Essays and the Literature of Consolation', *Literature and Medicine*, 19.1 (Spring 2000), 96–106. For a useful survey of new directions for the history of emotions in pre-1800 periods, see Barbara H. Rosenwein, 'Theories of Change in the History of Emotions', in *A History of Emotions, 1200–1800*, ed. Jonas Liliequist (London: Pickering and Chatto, 2012), 7–20.

34. Leo Bersani, *The Culture of Redemption* (Cambridge, MA: Harvard University Press, 1990), 97. For misgivings specifically oriented around the consolatory aspects of modernist and contemporary texts see Tammy Clewell, 'Consolation Refused: Virginia Woolf, The Great War, and Modernist Mourning', *Modern Fiction Studies*, 50.1 (Spring 2004): 197–223, and Neil Lazarus, *The Postcolonial Unconscious* (Cambridge: Cambridge University Press, 2011), whose intervention I discuss in more detail in Chapter 1.
35. Bersani, *The Culture of Redemption*, 2–3 (my emphasis).
36. Ibid., 1.
37. Ibid, 108.
38. Ibid., 22.
39. Ibid., 114.
40. Ibid., 1.
41. Attridge, *The Work of Literature*, 267.
42. Ibid., 266.
43. Cathy Caruth, *Unclaimed Experience: Trauma, Narrative, and History* (Baltimore, MD: Johns Hopkins University Press, 1996), 56.
44. Dominick LaCapra, *Writing History, Writing Trauma* (Baltimore, MD: Johns Hopkins University Press, 2001), xiv–xv.
45. Beverley Southgate, *Postmodernism in History: Fear or Freedom?* (London: Routledge, 2003), 164.
46. Anne Whitehead, *Trauma Fiction* (Edinburgh: Edinburgh University Press, 2004), 3.
47. Bersani, *The Culture of Redemption*, 35.
48. Instead of simply rehearsing the widespread praise for this novel, Paige Reynolds has shrewdly highlighted how the ethically controversial implications of representing sexual abuse coincide with the intellectual seductions of McBride's modernist experimentalism. See 'Trauma, Intimacy, and Modernist Form', *breac*, 11 Sept. 2014: https://breac.nd.edu/articles/trauma-intimacy-and-modernist-form/
49. Adam Phillips, 'The Telling of Selves: Notes on Psychoanalysis and Autobiography', *On Flirtation* (London: Faber, 1994), 74.
50. LaCapra, *Writing History, Writing Trauma*, xxiii.
51. Roger Luckhurst, *The Trauma Question* (London: Routledge, 2008), 80, 82.
52. David Watts, 'The Healing Art of Words', in *The Healing Art of Writing*, ed. Joan Baranow, Brian Dolan, and David Watts (San Francisco, CA: UC Medical Humanities Consortium, 2011), 5; Judith Lewis Herman, *Trauma and Recovery: From Domestic Abuse to Political Terror* (London: Pandora, 1994), 179. See also James W. Pennebaker, 'Telling Stories: The Health Benefits of Narrative', *Literature and Medicine*, 19.1 (2000), 3–18.
53. LaCapra, *Writing History, Writing Trauma*, 15–16.
54. As Michael S. Roth observes, while the 'traumatic cannot be contained in representation', it remains nonetheless 'too important to be left out of an attempt to make sense of the past either at the individual or collective level'. He goes on to suggest that the

so-called 'inadequacy of representation' can become too universal, when 'the process of trauma is said to illuminate the more general failure to make sense of experience'—an assumption that, in critical discourse, offers 'convenient ways for theorists to have their disruption and write about it too' (*Memory, Trauma, and History: Essays on Living with the Past* [New York: Columbia University Press, 2012], xviii, xix).

55. Suzette A. Henke, *Shattered Subjects: Trauma and Testimony in Women's Life-Writing* (London: Macmillan, 1998), xv.

56. Julian Barnes, 'Julian Barnes: The Final Interview', by Vanessa Guignery and Ryan Roberts (2007), in *Conversations with Julian Barnes*, ed. Guignery and Roberts (Jackson, MS: University of Mississippi Press, 2009), 169. Barnes's counterintuitive logic recalls, for me, Heather Love's reflections on the seemingly unlikely 'compensations' of seeing not only how things are but historiographically accounting for how bad they have been, when pursuing 'retrograde aspects of queer experience': 'If the gaze I have fixed on the past refuses the usual consolations—including the hope of redemption—it is not, for that reason, without its compensations. Backwardness can be, as Willa Cather suggests, deeply gratifying to the backward. Particularly in moment where gays and lesbians have no excuse for feeling bad, the evocation of a long history of queer suffering provides, if not solace exactly, then at least relief' (*Feeling Backward: Loss and the Politics of Queer History* [Cambridge, MA: Harvard University Press, 2007], 146).

57. Sigmund Freud, 239: To Ludwige Binswanger (11 April 1929), in *Letters of Sigmund Freud*, ed. Ernst L. Freud, trans. Tania and James Stern (London: Hogarth, 1961), 386.

58. David Constantine, *Poetry* (Oxford: Oxford University Press, 2013), 59–60.

59. Ibbett, *Compassion's Edge*, 9.

60. Ann Cvetkovich, *Depression: A Public Feeling* (Durham, NC: Duke University Press, 2012), 4, 5. Attridge offers similarly pragmatic advice, suggesting that since feeling, emotion, and affect operate 'differently in different grammatical contexts', it's 'best to employ the terms with some sense of these connotations and limitations, but otherwise not to be too particular about the distinctions one might make among them' (*The Work of Literature*, 261).

61. Ronald K. Rittgers, *The Reformation of Suffering: Pastoral Theology and Lay Piety in Late Medieval and Early Modern Germany* (Oxford: Oxford University Press, 2012), 4; George W. McClure, *Sorrow and Consolation in Italian Humanism* (Princeton, NJ: Princeton University Press, 1991), 8–9.

62. McClure, *Sorrow and Consolation in Italian Humanism*, 9, 10, 11.

63. Rittgers, *The Reformation of Suffering*, 38

64. McClure, *Sorrow and Consolation in Italian Humanism*, 165, 163, 164.

65. Melissa F. Zeiger, *Beyond Consolation: Death, Sexuality and the Changing Shapes of Elegy* (Ithaca, NY: Cornell University Press, 1997), 13, 12.

66. Rittgers, *The Reformation of Suffering*, 80, 41, 81.

67. Henry Ansgar Kelly, *Ideas and Forms of Tragedy from Aristotle to the Middle Ages* (Cambridge: Cambridge University Press, 1993), 222.

68. Paul A. Holloway, *Consolation in Philippians: Philosophical Sources and Rhetorical Strategy* (Cambridge: Cambridge University Press, 2001), 56.

69. Rachel Hewitt, *A Revolution of Feeling: The Decade that Forged the Modern Mind* (London: Granta, 2017), 7.

70. Like the rest of this book, my chapter on elegy focuses on narrative rather than poetry. There are two main reasons for this. First, I want to distinguish my intervention from the existing wealth of criticism on elegiac verse (aware as I am too that an account of

contemporary poetry in which solace plays an affective and linguistic role would justify a book-length study of its own). Second, the kind of argument I advance about consolation at the level of technique—there in Chapter 3, as in other chapters—is historically as well as aesthetically specific to transitions in fiction and in narrative modes of life-writing.

71. Julian Barnes, *Nothing to Be Frightened Of* (2008; London: Vintage, 2009), 151.
72. Clewell, 'Consolation Refused', 216.
73. Paul Ricoeur, *Oneself as Another*, trans. Kathleen Blamey (Chicago, IL: University of Chicago Press, 1992), 162.
74. Ibid., 162.
75. Andrew van der Vlies, *Present Imperfect: Contemporary South African Writing* (Oxford: Oxford University Press, 2017), 21.
76. Kazuo Ishiguro, 'Interview with Kazuo Ishiguro', by Karen Grigsby Bates (2005), in *Conversations with Kazuo Ishiguro*, ed. Brian W. Shaffer and Cynthia F. Wong (Jackson, MS: University Press of Mississippi, 2008), 202.
77. Ali Smith, *Artful* (London: Penguin, 2014), 77.
78. J. M. Coetzee, 'Samuel Beckett and the Temptations of Style', in *Doubling the Point: Essays and Interviews*, ed. David Attwell (Cambridge, MA: Harvard University Press, 1992), 47.
79. Tyrus Miller has made a compelling, if also literary-historically discrete, case for seeing the interwar period as a time for the critique and aesthetic dissolution of high modernism's formal perfectionism. See *Late Modernism: Politics, Fiction, and the Arts between the World Wars* (Berkeley, CA: University of California Press, 1999), chaps. 1 and 2.
80. Samuel Beckett, *Company* (1980), in *Company, Ill Seen Ill Said, Worstward Ho, Stirrings Still*, ed. Dirk Van Hulle (London: Faber & Faber, 2009), 30.
81. Coetzee, 'Samuel Beckett and the Temptations of Style', 47.
82. Tim Parks, *The Novel: A Survival Skill* (Oxford: Oxford University Press, 2015), 181, 180.
83. Ibid., 178, viii.
84. Ibid., 179.
85. Ibid., 180.
86. Adorno, 'Commitment', 88.
87. Fredric Jameson, *The Political Unconscious: Narrative as a Socially Symbolic Act* (London: Methuen, 1981), 214.
88. John Whittier Treat, *Writing Ground Zero: Japanese Literature and the Atomic Bomb* (Chicago, IL: University of Chicago Press, 1995), 39.
89. Jameson, *The Political Unconscious*, 20.
90. Colson Whitehead, *The Underground Railroad* (London: Fleet, 2016), 28. Hereafter cited parenthetically.
91. Anna Kornbluh, 'We Have Never Been Critical: Toward the Novel as Critique', *Novel*, 50.3 (November 2017), 406.
92. Ibid., 407.
93. Alex Preston, rev. of *The Underground Railroad*, by Colson Whitehead, *The Guardian*, 9 October 2016: https://www.theguardian.com/books/2016/oct/09/the-underground-railroad-colson-whitehead-revie-luminous-furious-wildly-inventive
94. Parks, *The Novel*, viii.
95. Ibid., 180.
96. Ellen Rooney, 'Form and Contentment', in *Reading for Form*, ed. Susan J. Wolfson and Marshall Brown (Seattle, WA: University of Washington Press, 2006), 45, 44, 43.

97. I agree with Ibbett that in light of the twentieth- and twenty-first-century orientation of work on affective forms in literary and cultural studies, there's a continued need to reengage 'the necessarily pre-modern language of affect and its disruptive potential for thinking the present'. This longer critical genealogy shows how affect can inspire 'wonder', as she puts it, across an historically capacious spectrum of genres and their social consequences, provoking us in turn to 'think outside the rigidity of national belonging, and of periodization, but still in charged relation to political dynamics' (Katherine Ibbett, '"When I do, I call it Affect"', *Paragraph*, 40.2 [2017], 252). Likewise, prefacing her inquiry into the revolutionary 'transition' in the late eighteenth century from 'affections', 'passions', and 'sentiments' to the more 'monolithic' and socially 'less approving' designation of 'emotion', Rachel Hewitt observes that '[d]ifferent communities, in different countries, at different historical moments, have entertained wildly divergent ideas about emotion: what it is, what it is for, where it originates and how it functions, which particular emotions exist and which are most important, whether and how emotions could or should be managed, and the language with which feelings are labelled and depicted' (Hewitt, *A Revolution of Feeling*, 3).
98. 'Central to the life of individuals', observes William M. Reddy, 'open to deep social influence, emotions are of the highest political significance. Any enduring political regime must establish as an essential element a normative order for emotions, an "emotional regime"' (*The Navigation of Feeling: A Framework for the History of Emotions* [Cambridge: Cambridge University Press, 2001], 124).
99. Judith Brown, 'Style', in *A New Vocabulary for Global Modernism*, ed. Eric Hayot and Rebecca L. Walkowitz (New York: Columbia University Press, 2016), 229, 230.
100. Hewitt, *A Revolution of Feeling*, 6 (my emphasis).
101. Adjusting to the temper of this moment, we're compelled 'neither to prescribe the forms that reading should take', advises Rita Felski, 'nor dictate the attitudes critics must adopt'. Rather, we must take up the opportunities that arrive when we 'steer...away from the kinds of arguments that we know how to conduct in our sleep' (*The Limits of Critique* [Chicago, IL: University of Chicago Press, 2015], 173).
102. Stephen Best and Sharon Marcus, 'Surface Reading: Surface Reading: An Introduction', *Representations*, 108.1 (Fall 2009), 18.
103. Elizabeth S. Anker and Rita Felski, 'Introduction', in *Critique and Postcritique*, ed. Anker and Felski (Durham, NC: Duke University Press, 2017), 16.
104. Jennifer L. Fleissner, 'Romancing the Real: Bruno Latour, Ian McEwan, and Postcritical Monism', in *Critique and Postcritique*, 102 (my emphasis).
105. Heather Love, 'Truth and Consequences: On Paranoid Reading and Reparative Reading', *Criticism*, 52.2 (Spring 2010): 237–8. For a bracing consideration of description as a method across disciplines, one that might change the way we think about the aims of literary analysis, see Love's 'Close Reading and Thin Description', *Public Culture*, 25.3 (Fall 2013): 401–34.
106. Lauren Berlant warns of this, when she points out the risks of 'idealizing, even implicitly, any program of better thought or reading': for how, she asks, 'would we know when the "repair" we intend is not another form of narcissism or smothering will?'. In the most scrupulously self-reflexive way, she advises that '[t]hose of us who think for a living are too well-positioned to characterize certain virtuous acts of thought as dramatically powerful and right, whether effective or futile; and we are set up to overestimate the proper clarity and destiny of an idea's effects and appropriate affects' (Lauren Berlant, *Cruel Optimism* [Durham, NC: Duke University Press, 2011], 123, 124).

107. Peter Middleton, 'Epistemological Respect', *Textual Practice* 30.7 (2016), 1182.
108. By making this argument here about how literature helps us to *think* affect not simply by representing emotional states as such but by instantiating the very conceptual and creative problematics of evoking something as potentially diffuse and ethically debatable as consolation in narratives of loss, I'm distinguishing 'literary knowledge' about affective experience from recent cognitive approaches to the way literature emotionally moves or mentally stimulates us. For a breakdown of what this rather different mode of inquiry can offer, see Paul B. Armstrong's *How Literature Plays with the Brain: The Neuroscience of Reading and Art* (Baltimore, MD: Johns Hopkins University Press, 2013).
109. Constantine, *Poetry*, 60.

CHAPTER 1

1. Philip Tomlinson, 'Thomas Hardy, Born June 2, 1840. "The Dynasts", the Book of the Moment. Poetical History with the Force of a Prophecy', *Times Literary Supplement*, Issue 2000 (1 June 1940), 266.
2. Ibid., 266.
3. Ibid., 270.
4. Sigmund Freud, 'Creative Writers and Day-Dreaming' (1908), *The Standard Edition of the Complete Works of Sigmund Freud*, vol. IX, trans. and ed. James Strachey with Anna Freud (1959; London: Vintage, 2001), 153.
5. Bersani, *The Culture of Redemption*; Andrzej Gasiorek, 'Rendering Justice to the Visible World: History, Politics, and National Identity in the Novels of Graham Greene', in *British Fiction after Modernism: The Novel at Mid-Century*, ed. Marina MacKay and Lindsey Stonebridge (Basingstoke: Palgrave, 2007), 19.
6. Dominic Head, *Ian McEwan* (Manchester: Manchester University Press, 2007), 174.
7. Ian McEwan, *Atonement* (London: Cape, 2001), 369, 359. Hereafter cited parenthetically
8. Jean-François Lyotard, *The Postmodern Condition: A Report on Knowledge*, trans. Geoff Bennington and Brian Massumi (Manchester: Manchester University Press, 1986), 81.
9. Herbert Marcuse, 'The Affirmative Character of Culture', in *Negations: Essays in Critical Theory*, trans. Jeremy J. Shapiro (London: Free Association, 1988), 102.
10. Ibid., 121, 118, 121.
11. Lazarus, *The Postcolonial Unconscious*, 31. Lazarus's enthusiasm for modernism's continued political currency for postcolonial studies departs from earlier perspectives in the field. Edward Said, for instance, argued that the encyclopedic scale of modernist fiction served a compensatory function, exemplifying 'the irony of a form that draws attention to itself as substituting art and its creations for the once-possible synthesis of the world empires' ('A Note on Modernism', in *Culture and Imperialism* [New York: Knopf, 1993], 189).
12. Lazarus, *The Postcolonial Unconscious*, 31.
13. Ibid., 32.
14. Miller, *Late Modernism*, 19.
15. Ibid., 19, 20.
16. Ibid., 20.
17. Virginia Woolf, *To the Lighthouse*, ed. Margaret Drabble (Oxford: Oxford University Press, 2000), pp. 23–4. Hereafter cited parenthetically.

18. Gillian Beer, *Virginia Woolf: The Common Ground* (Edinburgh: Edinburgh University Press, 1996), 47.
19. Elizabeth Abel, 'Spaces of Time: Virginia Woolf's Life-Writing', in *Modernism and Autobiography*, ed. Maria DiBattista and Emily O. Wittman (New York: Cambridge University Press, 2014), 56.
20. Virginia Woolf, Monday 20 July, 1925. *The Diary of Virginia Woolf: Vol. III: 1925–1930*, ed. Anne Oliver Bell (London: Hogarth, 1980), 36.
21. Virginia Woolf, Notes for Writing, *To the Lighthouse*, Berg Materials, Item 5: Woolfonline.com: Gallery: http://www.woolfonline.com/?node=content/image/gallery&project=1&parent=6&taxa=16
22. Virginia Woolf, 'A Sketch of the Past', in *Moments of Being*, ed. Jeanne Schulkind (London: Grafton, 1989), 81.
23. Virginia Woolf, 1764: To Roger Fry, 27th May 1927, *A Change of Perspective: The Letters of Virginia Woolf, Vol. III: 1923–1928*, ed. Nigel Nicolson (London: Hogarth, 1977), 385.
24. Ian McEwan, interview with Michael Silverblatt, *Bookworm*, KCRM, Santa Monica, Cal. 11 July 2002. McEwan's antagonistic relation to modernist experimentalism is well documented and I won't rehearse here the implications of his reservations toward modernism's aesthetic legacies, which I traced in greater depth in *Modernist Futures* (New York: Cambridge University Press, 2012), chapter 4, not least as I depart here from some of my own arguments there about *Atonement*'s artistic and intellectual conversations with literary history. The specifically ethical trajectory of McEwan's implied critique of 'Woolfian' modernism and the bearing this might have on our understanding of the novel's 'postmodernism' are leading concerns for some critics. Brian Finney, for example, observes that as Briony comes to acknowledge that form 'does have ethical implications', then 'the ideology of modernism (especially its prioritization of stylistic innovation)' is shown to possess 'hidden moral consequences' ('Briony's Stand against Oblivion: Ian McEwan's *Atonement*', *Journal of Modern Literature* 27.3 [Winter 2004]: 72). For Peter Boxall, *Atonement* 'is an extended examination of the ethical injunction that one must tell the truth about the past, must seek to bear witness to a historical reality even if such reality is always compromised by its dependence on the narrative forms by which we encounter it', while also offering 'a history of English prose fiction from Richardson and Fielding to Virginia Woolf, a history which is balanced around Henry James's novels *What Maisie Knew* and *The Golden Bowl*' (*Twenty-First-Century Fiction: A Critical Introduction* [New York: Cambridge University Press, 2013], 77, 71–2). See also Alistair Cormack's 'Postmodernism and the Ethics of Fiction in *Atonement*', in *Ian McEwan: Contemporary Critical Perspectives*, ed. Sebastian Groes (London: Continuum, 2009), 70–82.
25. McEwan, Green Notebook (2000–1), MS-4902, 1.9. McEwan Papers, Harry Ransom Center, University of Texas at Austin.
26. Ian McEwan, 'Interview with Ian McEwan', by Jonathan Noakes and Margaret Reynolds, in *Ian McEwan: The Essential Guide: 'Child in Time', 'Enduring Love', 'Atonement'* (London: Vintage, 2002), 19–20.
27. Interview with Daniel Zalewski, 'The Background Hum: Ian McEwan's Art of Unease', *The New Yorker*, 23 Feb. 2009. Web.
28. Laura Marcus, 'Ian McEwan's Modernist Time: *Atonement* and *Saturday*', in *Ian McEwan*, ed. Groes, 92.
29. Virginia Woolf, 'Poetry, Fiction, and the Future' (1927), in *The Essays of Virginia Woolf, Vol. IV: 1925–1928*, ed. Andrew McNeillie (London: Hogarth, 1994), 436, 438, 438–9.

30. James Wood, 'The Trick of Truth', rev. of *Atonement*, by Ian McEwan, *The New Republic*, 25 March 2002: https://newrepublic.com/article/63386/atonement-ian-mcewan-fiction
31. Boxall, *Twenty-First-Century Fiction*, 67.
32. Hermione Lee, 'If Your Memories Serve You Well', *The Observer*, 23 Sept. 2001. https://www.theguardian.com/books/2001/sep/23/fiction.bookerprize2001
33. Boxall, *Twenty-First-Century Fiction*, 67.
34. Geoff Dyer, 'Who's Afraid of Influence?', rev. of *Atonement*, by Ian McEwan, *The Guardian*, 22 Sept. 2001. https://www.theguardian.com/books/2001/sep/22/fiction.ianmcewan
35. Ian McEwan, interview with Michael Silverblatt, *Bookworm*, KCRM, Santa Monica, Cal. 11 July 2002.
36. Jesse Matz, 'Pseudo-Impressionism?', in *The Legacies of Modernism: Historicising Postwar and Contemporary Fiction*, ed. David James (Cambridge: Cambridge University Press, 2012), 116.
37. Ibid., 118, 119.
38. Cyril Connolly, *Enemies of Promise*, rev. edn. (London: Deutsch, 1988), 30.
39. Ian McEwan, 'When I Stop Believing in Fiction', *The New Republic*, 15 Feb. 2013: https://newrepublic.com/article/112374/ian-mcewan-my-uneasy-relationship-fiction
40. 'Atonement ending, first draft', 7 June 2001. MS-4902, 2.4, p. 1. McEwan Papers.
41. McEwan, interview with Michael Silverblatt.
42. Anita Brookner, 'A Morbid Procedure', rev. of *Atonement* by Ian McEwan, *Spectator*, 15 Sept. 2001, 44.
43. McEwan, Notebook (Aug. 1998–Dec. 2000). McEwan Papers.
44. Ian McEwan, 'Atonement Ending, First Draft' (7 June 2001). MS-4902, 2.4. McEwan Papers.
45. In an unpublished lecture, McEwan appears to take comfort in a poetic and intentionally enigmatic 'thought experiment', in which he pictures 'the angel-novelist hovering above an imaginary character, a character in prospect, with the aim of deciding the best manner of elaborating a mind' ('The Levers of Fiction', Graham Storey Lecture [Cambridge, 4 March 2011], 13. MS–4901, other writings, lectures [1/8]. McEwan Papers).
46. Iris Murdoch, 'Against Dryness: A Polemical Sketch', *Encounter* (January 1961), 20.
47. In place of *beat*, McEwan opted for *drain* in the early drafts. Then, in a writing note on revised segments just before the copy-editing stage, he wonders whether the combination of *waves* and *drain* constitutes a 'mixed metaphor', suggesting 'beat?' instead (MS-4902, 4.4: Writing note to *Atonement*. McEwan Papers). McEwan corrects the verb to *beat* at the proof stage (MS-4902, 4.5: *Atonement* page proofs with revisions, 2001. McEwan Papers).
48. Steve Ellis, *Virginia Woolf and the Victorians* (Cambridge: Cambridge University Press, 2007), 178.
49. Kate McLoughlin, *Authoring War: The Literary Representation of War from the Illiad to Iraq* (Cambridge: Cambridge University Press, 2011), 130–1.
50. Boxall, *Twenty-First-Century Fiction*, 73, 74.
51. '"No, not yet," and the sky said "No, not there"': E. M. Forster, *A Passage to India* (1924). In this climactic exchange between the Indian Aziz and Cyril Fielding, the phrases 'Not yet' and 'not there' not only 'apply', as Helena Gurfinkel suggests, to the 'yet-to-be-defined forms of postnational cosmopolitanism' within the context of 'Indian-British relations', but also 'to the open secret of same-sex passion that will have

to wait, until, as another Forster novel, *Maurice*, puts it in its dedication, "a happier year".' (Gurfinkel, 'Queer, Cosmopolitan', in *The Cambridge History of Gay and Lesbian Literature*, ed. E. L. McCallum and Mikko Tuhkanen [New York: Cambridge University Press, 2014], 409).
52. MS-4902, 4.3: *Atonement*, Revised fragments from Parts I–IV, 2001; McEwan adds the full phrase ('Not quite, not yet') at the proof stage. MS-4902, 4.5: *Atonement* page proofs with revisions, 2001. McEwan Papers.
53. Barnes, 'Julian Barnes: The Final Interview', 169.
54. James Wood, 'The Trick of Truth', rev. of *Atonement*, by Ian McEwan, *The New Republic*, 25 March 2002: https://newrepublic.com/article/63386/atonement-ian-mcewan-fiction
55. Iris Murdoch, 'Art and Eros', *Existentialists and Mystics: Writings on Philosophy and Literature*, ed. Peter Conradi (New York: Penguin, 1999), 491.
56. Murdoch, 'Against Dryness', 20.
57. Woolf, 'A Sketch of the Past', 111.
58. Susan Sontag, 'On Style', *Against Interpretation* (London: Vintage, 1994), 31.
59. See Jessica Berman, *Modernist Commitments: Ethics, Politics, and Transnational Modernism* (New York: Columbia University Press, 2011), Rebecca L. Walkowitz, *Cosmopolitan Style: Modernism beyond the Nation* (New York: Columbia University Press, 2006), Christopher GoGwilt, *The Passage of Literature: Genealogies of Modernism in Conrad, Rhys, and Pramoedya* (Oxford: Oxford University Press, 2011), and Urmila Seshagiri, *Race and the Modernist Imagination* (Ithaca, NY: Cornell University Press, 2009).
60. C. D. Blanton, 'Abstract in Concrete: Brutalism and the Modernist Half-Life', in *The Contemporaneity of Modernism: Literature, Media, Culture*, ed. Michael D'Arcy and Mathias Nilges (New York: Routledge, 2016), 18.
61. McEwan, Notebook (Aug. 1998–Dec. 2000), MS-4902, 1.8. McEwan Papers.
62. Blanton, 'Abstract in Concrete', 17.
63. McEwan, Notebook (Aug. 1998–Dec. 2000), MS-4902, 1.8. McEwan Papers.
64. Blanton, 'Abstract in Concrete', 18.
65. 'Unlike the truth of theory', claimed Marcuse, 'the beauty of art is compatible with the bad present, despite and within which it can afford happiness'. Only '[t]rue theory', in this account, 'recognizes the misery and lack of happiness prevailing in the established order' ('The Affirmative Character of Culture', 118).
66. One of the many roads not taken by *Discrepant Solace* follows the fuller story of what modernism's appropriations, rejections, and transnational remobilizations throughout the postwar era and beyond tell us about the matrix of politics, ethics, and literary affect. But even if texts in this book don't revisit modernist precedents quite so purposefully as McEwan does, they do nonetheless realize that distinctly modernist conviction, in Patricia Waugh's phrase, that '[a]rt must dislocate as well as console if we are to recognize ourselves through other lenses and see what we have or might become'. Turning to Kazuo Ishiguro, Waugh contends that '[a]t the centre of his fiction is the question of feeling: of whether art, in general, and the novel, in particular, can still provide a moral and political "sentimental education," an education of the heart that is deeper and more ethically resonant than mere consolation'. This amounts to a 'preoccupation with "depth" as an aesthetic exploration and expression of feeling as a vehicle for ethical understanding', which takes Ishiguro's writing 'closer to modernism than postmodernism'. Ishiguro is not alone in pursuing this preoccupation, as my corpus will hopefully make clear, a preoccupation that spans contemporary fiction and

life-writing alike. As we'll see in Chapter 6, he also provokes us to recognize how the work of consolation may have more ethical depth and resonance than an 'exercise in emotional containment undertaken as the practice of cheering oneself up' (Patricia Waugh, 'Kazuo Ishiguro's Not-Too-Late Modernism', in *Kazuo Ishiguro: New Critical Visions of the Novels*, ed. Sebastian Groes and Barry Lewis [London: Palgrave, 2011], 23, 20, 26).

CHAPTER 2

1. Cormac McCarthy, *The Road* (New York: Knopf, 2006), 180. Hereafter cited parenthetically.
2. Andrew Hoberek, 'Cormac McCarthy and the Aesthetics of Exhaustion', *American Literary History*, 23.3 (Fall 2011), 487.
3. Ibid., 497.
4. Peter Boxall, *The Value of the Novel* (New York: Cambridge University Press, 2015), 33, 61.
5. I am deeply grateful to Gerard Aching for sharing candid thoughts of his own on this question of consolation's interaction with (rather than displacement of) loss.
6. Ashley Kunsa, quoted in Hoberek, 'Cormac McCarthy and the Aesthetics of Exhaustion', 488.
7. Hoberek, 'Cormac McCarthy and the Aesthetics of Exhaustion', 492.
8. My selected examples from *The Road* may strike some readers as odd, for one could argue that they bypass moments in the novel that are more obviously—and controversially—'redemptive'. For instance, there's the 'religious sense of mission', in Michael Chabon's terms, which drives the man's faith in his son as a carrier of 'greater salvation' ('Dark Adventure: On Cormac McCarthy's *The Road*', in *Maps and Legends: Reading and Writing Along the Borderlands* [New York: Harper Perennial, 2009], 100). Survival itself contains certain consoling rhythms of its own: prosaic routine promises momentary recuperations, when 'the redemptive nature of craft', as Richard Gray observes, 'in doing a task and doing it carefully', offers the man and child 'a temporary shelter, a moment of almost ritualistic relief' (*After the Fall: American Literature since 9/11* [Oxford: Wiley-Blackwell, 2011], 42, 43). Yet perhaps my most blatant omission is the novel's wishful ending, where the boy is rescued by a couple who lead 'him back into the comforting womb of the woods and into the arms of an American form of the holy family': the consolatory implications of this salvific finale have vexed critics who share Gray's estimation that it remains 'deeply unconvincing' (47). But if the ending of *The Road* lacks anything it's that *friction* I try to pursue in this chapter between action and description, between what happens in a moment and the expressivity that moment itself generates. In McCarthy's climactic scene, style seems no longer to have any critical purchase on a scenario of such convenient redemption; the language of tough solace is overtaken by the language of sentimentality, consigning the novel's close to an implausible sequence of deliverance.
9. Sharon Marcus, Heather Love, and Stephen Best, 'Building a Better Description', *Representations*, 135.1 (Summer 2016), 1, 5.
10. Ibid., 1.
11. Georg Lukács, 'Narrate or Describe', in *Writer and Critic, and other Essays*, ed. and trans. Arthur Kahn (London: Merlin, 1970), 110.
12. Ibid., 127.
13. Ibid., 132.

14. Ibid., 139.
15. Ibid., 139.
16. Mieke Bal, 'Over-writing as Un-writing: Descriptions, World-Making, and Novelistic Time', in *A Mieke Bal Reader* (Chicago, IL: University of Chicago Press, 2006), 100; Werner Wolf and Walter Bernhart, 'Preface', in *Description in Literature and Other Media*, ed. Wolf and Bernhart (Amsterdam: Rodopi, 2007), vii.
17. Bal, 'Over-writing as Un-writing', 101.
18. For a detailed rereading of Lukács's account, showing how in fact activities of interpretation and description are (from a methodological point of view) indissolubly connected, see Cannon Schmitt, 'Interpret or Describe?', *Representations*, 135.1 (Summer 2016): 102–18. In a complementary way, Verner Wolf argues that 'descriptions are not usually an end in themselves, but are implicated in the construction of models as well as in explanations and thus in a larger explanatory and argumentative frame'. However, in the end Wolf is keener than Schmitt to preserve some distinction between describing and interpreting, summarizing that 'the point of a good description is not to explain something but to inform us about the existence of something and its specific appearance and quality, in short: to represent something vividly' ('Description as a Transmedial Mode of Representation: General Features and Possibilities of Realization in Painting, Fiction, and Music', in *Description in Literature and Other Media*, 12, 15).
19. Ruth Ronen, 'Description, Narrative and Representation', *Narrative*, 5.3 (October 1997), 274.
20. Ibid., 279.
21. Ibid., 283.
22. Chabon, 'Dark Adventure', 102.
23. As Ansgar Nünning has outlined, 'one can distinguish between different kinds of description on at least five levels of inquiry: (a) a communicative or discursive level, which focuses on the structure of narrative mediation; (b) a stylistic level, where descriptions are analysed from a linguistic point of view; (c) a structural or syntagmatic level, where analysis focuses on the internal organization of descriptions and on their relations with non-descriptive parts of a narrative; (d) a thematic and paradigmatic level; (e) a reception oriented and functional level. This allows us to distinguish between dominantly formal, stylistic, structural, and content-related subcategories of description' ('Towards a Typology, Poetics and History of Description in Fiction', in *Description in Literature and Other Media*, 102).
24. Carol Jacobs, *Sebald's Vision* (New York: Columbia University Press, 2015), 113.
25. Sebald, 'Against the Irreversible: On Jean Améry', in *On the Natural History of Destruction*, trans. Anthea Bell (London: Hamish Hamilton, 2003) 150. As Jacobs observes, the 'synoptic view' implied by narratorial omniscience is typically splintered as Sebald 'skips, with the barest of warnings, from third-person description to first-person narration and back again', because for him 'such a perspective inevitably leads to a mythification that repeats the structure of fascist ideology' (*Sebald's Vision*, 44, 88).
26. Sebald, 'Against the Irreversible', 150.
27. Luckhurst, *The Trauma Question*, 81.
28. Ibid., 83.
29. W. G. Sebald, *Austerlitz*, trans. Anthea Bell (2001; London: Penguin, 2011), 14. Hereafter cited parenthetically.
30. W. G. Sebald, 'An Attempt at Restitution', in *Campo Santo,* trans. Anthea Bell (London: Hamish Hamilton, 2005), 215.
31. Jacobs, *Sebald's Vision*, 175.

32. As readers of the German text would probably attest, fluidity isn't always the right word for Sebald's style (influenced as he was by Thomas Bernhard). So, in pursuing these remarks about tone, diction, and tempo, I'm conscious of the analytical limitations of close reading Sebald in translation. That said, critics have made the case for recognizing the translated works as a virtually distinct corpus, given how involved Sebald was in their journey from German to English. As Mark McCulloch observes, Sebald not only 'participated in the process of translation as an advisor to his translators' but was also 'keenly interested in the problem of translation, and served as the first director of the British Centre for Literary Translation' ('Introduction: Two Languages, Two Audiences: The Tandem Literary Oeuvres of W. G. Sebald', in *W. G. Sebald: History–Memory–Trauma*, ed. Scott Denham and Mark McCulloch [Berlin: Walter de Gruyter, 2006], 7).
33. As Robert Eaglestone argues, critics have tended to neglect this narrator in their preoccupation with Austerlitz's 'self-redemption', even though, rather disturbingly, this narrator positions Austerlitz as 'a "native informant" from the world of the Holocaust' in order 'to uncover his own feelings of complicity' (*The Broken Voice: Reading Post-Holocaust Literature* [Oxford: Oxford University Press, 2017], 87, 88).
34. Sebald, 'Against the Irreversible', 150.
35. J. J. Long and Anne Whitehead, 'Introduction', in *W. G. Sebald: A Critical Companion*, ed. Long and Whitehead (Edinburgh: Edinburgh University Press, 2004), 11.
36. Timothy Bewes, 'Against Exemplarity: W. G. Sebald and the Problem of Connection', *Contemporary Literature*, 55.1 (Spring 2014), 4.
37. Ibid., 19.
38. Matthew Hart and Tania Lown-Hecht, 'The Extraterritorial Poetics of W. G. Sebald', *Modern Fiction Studies*, 58.2 (Summer 2012), 219.
39. André Aciman, 'Out of Novemberland', rev. of *The Rings of Saturn*, by W. G. Sebald, *New York Review of Books*, 3 Dec. 1998, n.pag. http://www.nybooks.com/articles/1998/12/03/out-of-novemberland/
40. In a fascinating treatment of the impersonality of Sebald's prose, Torleif Persson argues that 'Sebald's work appears flat' precisely 'because of how he at once positions and undermines subjective experience as a privileged site of ethical engagement with past and present alike'. Recognizing such implications of tone also means acknowledging how models from trauma studies may not be adequate as generic or interpretive frames for Sebald, in whose view 'the past should not be "felt" in the present by means of some process of traumatic transference, but held at a distance as an object of melancholic contemplation' ('Impersonal Style and the Form of Experience in W. G. Sebald's *The Rings of Saturn*', *Studies in the Novel*, 48.2 [Summer 2016], 205, 206).
41. Regarding the status of the indescribable in *Austerlitz*, Bewes reflects that while the text 'appears to converge on the theme of the Holocaust', the Holocaust itself cannot provide or serve this thematic or exemplary function. For when treated thus, as a tropological 'element necessary to a certain literary genre or traumatic experience, the Holocaust responds by crying "obscenity"', even though it's this 'very quality' that 'makes it the supreme example, unbettered, of the category of experience known variously as the unrepeatable, the intolerable, the unrepresentable' ('Against Exemplarity', 22).
42. Sebald, 'Against the Irreversible', 161.
43. W. G. Sebald, *Die Beschreibung des Unglücks: Zur österreichischen Literatur von Stifter bis Handke* (Frankfurt: Fischer Taschenbuch Verlag, 1994), 12–13. Trans. Kevin Brazil.
44. Sebald, 'Against the Irreversible', 153, 162.
45. Ibid., 162.

46. Hart and Lown-Hecht, 'The Extraterritorial Poetics of W. G. Sebald', 225, 222.
47. Sebald, 'Air War and Literature', 58; Sebald, quoted in Jacobs, *Sebald's Vision*, 167.
48. Sebald, 'Against the Irreversible', 146.
49. Andreas Huyssen, quoted in Ruth Franklin, *A Thousand Darknesses: Lies and Truth in Holocaust Fiction* (Oxford: Oxford University Press, 2011), 194.
50. Eaglestone, *The Broken Voice*, 91.
51. Sebald, 'Air War and Literature', 70.
52. Jessica Dubow, quoted in Bewes, 'Against Exemplarity', 10n 7.
53. A. S. Byatt, quoted in Franklin, *A Thousand Darknesses*, 186.
54. Jacobs, *Sebald's Vision*, 145.
55. Ibid., 147.
56. Franklin, *A Thousand Darknesses*, 186.
57. James Wood, Introduction, *Austerlitz*, xv, xxii.
58. Bewes, 'Against Exemplarity', 3.
59. Julia Hell, 'Eyes Wide Shut: German Post-Holocaust Authorship', *New German Critique*, 88 (Winter 2003), 33–4, 35–6, 30.
60. Ibid., 34.
61. Ibid,. 36.
62. Sebald, 'Air War and Literature', 53.
63. A. O. Scott, 'A Writer Who Defied Categorization', *The New York Times*, 8 May 2012. http://www.nytimes.com/2012/05/09/movies/patience-after-sebald-a-documentary.html
64. Sebald, 'Air War and Literature', 56, 58, 59.
65. James Wood draws attention to Sebald's 'muffling' of 'extremity' in 'exquisitely courteous syntax' (Introduction, *Austerlitz*, xii).
66. Jacobs, *Sebald's Vision*, 120.
67. Ibid., x.
68. Franklin, *A Thousand Darknesses*, 196, 197.
69. W. G. Sebald, 'Between History and Natural History: On the Literary Description of Total Destruction', in *Campo Santo*, trans. Anthea Bell (London: Hamish Hamilton, 2005), 89.
70. Sebald, 'Air War and Literature', 74.
71. Sebald, 'Against the Irreversible', 150. Remarking on the figure Vera, Austerlitz's childhood carer, Jacobs observes how Vera's recounting of his past produces '[e]ighty pages of clarity in a text which…has not always been easy to follow, in which our own powers of recapitulation are rendered precarious' (*Sebald's Vision*, 105).
72. Ibid., 88.
73. See Greg Bond, 'On the Misery of Nature and the Nature of Misery: W. G. Sebald's Landscapes', *W. G. Sebald: A Critical Companion*, ed. J. J. Long and Anne Whitehead (Edinburgh: Edinburgh University Press, 2004), 31–44.
74. Wood, Introduction, xi.
75. Bal, 'Over-writing as Un-writing', 578.
76. Philippe Hamon, 'Rhetorical Status of the Descriptive', trans. Patricia Baudoin, *Yale French Studies* 61 (1981), 20, 25.
77. Luckhurst, *The Trauma Question*, 83.
78. Jesse Matz also reminds us of the analytical potential of impressions in modernist fiction. Far from imitative or concerned with surface appearances alone, 'when cultivated by James, Woolf and others, impressions undid differences between sight and knowledge, thought and feeling, appearance and reality. For they were always both – between these

opposites, synthetic acts of understanding designed to position the literary mind right between its different claims to representational value' ('Pseudo-Impressionism?', in *The Legacies of Modernism*, 117).
79. Sebald, *Die Beschreibung des Unglücks*, 13.
80. Katie Mitchell, in *Patience (After Sebald)* (2012), dir. Grant Gee, at 1:16:00–1:16:35.
81. Mitchell quoted in Isabel Sutton, 'Sebald's Apocalyptic Vision: The World Will End in 2013', *New Statesman*, 4 June 2013. http://www.newstatesman.com/culture/2013/06/w-g-sebalds-apocalyptic-vision-world-will-end-2013
82. Mitchell, in *Patience (After Sebald)*, at 16:35.

CHAPTER 3

1. Angela Leighton, *On Form: Poetry, Aestheticism, and the Legacy of a Word* (Oxford: Oxford University Press, 2007), 221.
2. This is the kind of literary-historical map Jahan Ramazani offers, whereby later elegists for the most part mock rather than model forms of comfort, converting the elegy from a curative genre into something more decidedly 'anti-therapeutic' (*Poetry of Mourning: The Modern Elegy from Hardy to Heaney* [Chicago, IL: University of Chicago Press, 1994], 17).
3. Leighton, *On Form*, 221.
4. David Kennedy, *Elegy* (London: Routledge, 2007), 2.
5. 'Sorrow', Lewis discovers, 'turns out not to be a state but a process', one that could potentially be watched and written about interminably, since '[t]here is something new to be chronicled every day' (*A Grief Observed* [London: Faber and Faber, 2013], 50). Hilary Mantel has wondered 'how to categorize' Lewis's book, given that it doesn't really belong 'under "Religion"', speaking as it does so eloquently to readers who might be 'hurtling to abandon a being who seems to have abandoned them'. And even Rowan Williams appreciates Lewis's skeptical close readings of religious solace, remarking that 'one thing you will learn in bereavement is how far you have loved someone's difference, the tang of otherness. This is a tough and not instantly consoling wisdom' (*A Grief Observed: Reader's Edition* [London: Faber and Faber, 2015], 68, 85).
6. Colm Tóibín, 'A Grief Observed', *The Guardian*, Review, Saturday 4 October 2014, 20.
7. Ramazani, *Poetry of Mourning*, 8.
8. Joseph Conrad, 'A Familiar Preface', *A Personal Record*, ed. Zdzisław Najder and J. H. Stape (Cambridge: Cambridge University Press, 2008), 11.
9. Ramazani, *Poetry of Mourning*, xi.
10. Julian Barnes, *Levels of Life* (London: Jonathan Cape, 2013), 36–7. Hereafter cited parenthetically.
11. John Paul Riquelme, 'Modernist Transformations of Life Narrative: From Wilde and Woolf to Bechdel and Rushdie', *Modern Fiction Studies*, 59.3 (Fall 2013), 472.
12. Ibid., 472.
13. Julia Jordan, '"For Recuperation": Elegy, Form, and the Aleatory in B. S. Johnson's *The Unfortunates*', *Textual Practice* 28.5 (August 2014), 747.
14. Melissa Harrison, 'An Interview with Helen Macdonald', *Caught by the River*, 1 August 2014. http://www.caughtbytheriver.net/2014/08/28622-helen-macdonald-h-is-for-hawk-melissa-harrison/ (01.12.14)
15. Stephen Moss, 'A Bird's Eye View of Love and Loss', Interview with Helen Macdonald, *The Guardian*, Wednesday 5 November 2014. http://www.theguardian.com/books/2014/nov/05/helen-macdonald-interview-winner-samuel-johnson-prize-falconry

16. Ibid.
17. Hannah Ellis-Peterson, 'Helen Macdonald's "Extraordinary" Memoir Wins Samuel Johnson Prize', *The Guardian*, Tuesday 4 November 2014. http://www.theguardian.com/books/2014/nov/04/samuel-johnson-prize-helen-macdonald-h-is-for-hawk
18. Helen Macdonald, *H is for Hawk* (London: Jonathan Cape, 2014), 135. Hereafter cited parenthetically.
19. Janette Currie, 'Walking and Manning', *Times Literary Supplement*, 31 October 2014, 8.
20. Moss, 'A Bird's Eye View of Love and Loss'.
21. Harrison, 'An Interview with Helen Macdonald'.
22. Moss, 'A Bird's Eye View of Love and Loss'.
23. Ibid.
24. David Grossman, 'Writing in the Dark', The Arthur Miller Freedom to Write Lecture (2007), in *Writing in the Dark: Essays on Literature and Politics*, trans. Jessica Cohen (London: Bloomsbury, 2008), 64.
25. Harrison, 'An Interview with Helen Macdonald'.
26. Kennedy, *Elegy*, 33 (my emphasis).
27. Currie, 'Watching and Manning', 8.
28. Harrison, 'An Interview with Helen Macdonald'.
29. Ibid.
30. Vladimir Nabokov, *Speak, Memory: An Autobiography Revisited* (London: David Campbell, 1999), 131–2.
31. Kennedy, *Elegy*, 6.
32. See the reviews of *On Elizabeth Bishop* by Lloyd Schwartz in *Arts Fuse* (5 March 2015), Dan Chiasson in the *New York Review of Books* (24 September 2015), and Joel Browner in the *New York Times Book Review* (4 September 2015).
33. Colm Tóibín, *On Elizabeth Bishop* (Princeton, NJ: Princeton University Press, 2015), 127.
34. Ibid., 35.
35. Ibid, 39–40.
36. Frances Leviston, 'Mothers and Marimbas in "The Bight": Bishop's *Danse Macabre*', *Twentieth-Century Literatre* 61.4 (December 2015), 437.
37. Tóibín, *On Elizabeth Bishop*, 37, 38.
38. Tóibín, 'A Grief Observed', 20.
39. Ibid., 20.
40. Tóibín, *On Elizabeth Bishop*, 47–8.
41. Ibid., 47.
42. Colm Tóibín, 'How I Wrote *Nora Webster*', Guardian Book Club, *The Guardian, Review* (23 Jan. 2016), 7.
43. Colm Tóibín, *Nora Webster* (London: Viking, 2014), 83. Hereafter cited parenthetically.
44. Elizabeth Bishop, Letter to Lowell, January ?29th 1958, in *Words in Air: The Complete Correspondence between Elizabeth Bishop and Robert Lowell*, ed. Thomas Travisano with Saskia Hamilton (London: Faber and Faber, 2008), 250.
45. Tóibín, *On Elizabeth Bishop*, 105.
46. Ibid., 2.
47. Ibid., 2.
48. Ibid., 14.
49. Tóibín, 'How I Wrote *Nora Webster*', 7
50. Berlant, *Cruel Optimism*, 25. In a more qualified vein, Dorothy Hale has noted that '[t]he modern novel's commitment to the creation of autonomous characters positions any act of narration as a potential encroachment on the existential freedom of that

character. The constant threat of aesthetic exploitation bolsters the novelistic aesthetics of characterological freedom, the reader's intense apprehension that fictional characters are autonomous, living beings—even to the point of seeming entitled to the rights of real people.' It's this 'understanding of the novel as caught between its social and aesthetic nature' which is 'constitutive' of Hale calls the novelistic 'aesthetics of alterity' ('*On Beauty* as Beautiful? The Problem of Novelistic Aesthetics by Way of Zadie Smith', *Contemporary Literature*, 53.4 [Winter 2012], 838).
51. Tóibín, *On Elizabeth Bishop*, 164.
52. Ibid., 47–8.
53. Ibid., 2.
54. Tóibín, 'How I Wrote *Nora Webster*', 7.
55. Tóibín, *On Elizabeth Bishop*, 19.
56. Ibid., 19–20.
57. The novel's straightforward diction and carefully paced tempo certainly weren't lost on its original reviewers. Tessa Hadley, for one, remarked that Tóibín's verbal economy poses its own challenges; apparent simplicity in the interests of linguistic transparency is as difficult to command as anything more elaborate and deliberately obfuscating. For Hadley, minimalism and maximalism coincide in this respect, as the very 'plainness' of Tóibín's 'prose has the same difficult scrupulousness as the most baroque good style; both are poles apart from the slapdash notation of a lazy shorthand'. Of course, like any style, conspicuous moderation can become its own aesthetic convention, no less prone to exhibitionism as rhetorical flamboyance might be. As Hadley admits, the novel's demonstration of 'withholding – of commentary, of explication, of any verdict, on the life he renders – is so striking that it's almost an inverted extravagance in itself'.[1] And the stylistic finesse of dealing delicately with loss connects Tóibín not only with Bishop but earlier modernists too: the fidelity to 'plainness' in *Nora Webster*, as Hadley suggests, might well make Tóibín's 'attraction to Henry James's extravagance all the more interesting' ('A Rare and Tremendous Achievement', rev. of *Nora Webster*, by Colm Tóibín, *The Guardian, Review*, Saturday 11 October http://www.theguardian.com/books/2014/oct/11/nora-webster-colm-toibin-review-rare-achievement).
58. Joyce asserts of *Dubliners*: 'I have written it for the most part in a style of scrupulous meanness and with the conviction that he is a very bold man who dares to alter in the presentment, still more to deform, whatever he has seen and heard' (Letter to Grant Richards, 5 May 1906, *Letters of James Joyce*, ed. Richard Ellmann [London: Faber & Faber, 1966], vol. II, 134). Joyce's watchfulness toward representation as interference accords with Tóibín's characterization of the intense yet unobtrusive visual quality of Bishop's work, when she stages seemingly simple scenarios of observation without commentary in poems that become the equivalent of 'modest statement', recording the perception of 'something that could not be disputed' (*On Elizabeth Bishop*, 11).
59. Tóibín, *On Elizabeth Bishop*, 59.
60. Tóibín's affirmative use of redress has something in common with Seamus Heaney's use of the term. For Heaney, the poetics of redress entails 'pressing back against the pressure of reality', and remains key to his larger claim about the transformative work of literature in the face of bald political prescriptions and ideological instrumentalism: the 'imaginative transformation of human life is the means by which we can most truly grasp and comprehend it' (*The Redress of Poetry: Oxford Lectures* [London: Faber and Faber, 1995], 1, xv).
61. Tóibín, *On Elizabeth Bishop*, 59.
62. Ibid., 61.

63. Ibid., 59.
64. Ibid., 60–1.
65. Ibid., 61.
66. Ibid., 53.
67. Ibid., 59.
68. Kennedy, *Elegy*, 146.
69. Leighton, *On Form*, 225.
70. Ibid., 222. Like Leighton, I share Derek Attridge's sentiments in his discussion of the relation between emotive content and active form, where he argues that the 'eventness of the literary work' requires that form 'be understood verbally—as "taking form", "forming", or even "losing form"'—and that ultimately, 'Form and meaning both happen, and are part of the same happening' (*The Singularity of Literature* [London: Routledge, 2004], 113, 114).
71. Tóibín, *On Elizabeth Bishop*, 7.
72. Rita Felski, 'Introduction', *New Literary History*, 45.2 (Spring 2014), v.
73. Rónán McDonald, 'After Suspicion: Surface, Method, Value', in *The Values of Literary Studies: Critical Institutions, Scholarly Agendas*, ed. McDonald (Cambridge: Cambridge University Press, 2015), 235.
74. Leighton, *On Form*, 221.
75. McDonald, 'After Suspicion', 247.
76. Tóibín, *On Elizabeth Bishop*, 127.
77. Ibid., 126.

CHAPTER 4

1. J. M. Coetzee, 'Samuel Beckett and the Temptations of Style' (1973), in *Doubling the Point: Essays and Interviews*, ed. David Attwell (Cambridge, MA: Harvard University Press, 1992), 47.
2. Gustave Flaubert, Letter to Louise Colet, 16 January 1852, *The Letters of Gustave Flaubert, Volumes 1 & II: 1830–1880*, ed. and trans. Francis Steegmuller (London: Picador, 2001), i. 213.
3. Coetzee, 'Samuel Beckett and the Temptations of Style', 47.
4. Ibid. 47
5. As one reviewer of *The Schooldays of Jesus* put it, the novel's setting is 'eerily stripped down'; relying on the most 'physically rudimentary' of descriptions, the 'scenery is so flimsily assembled that it could come straight from Ikea' (Elizabeth Lowry, 'No Passion in an Ascetic Allegory', rev. of *The Schooldays of Jesus*, by J. M. Coetzee, *The Guardian*, 18 August 2016: https://www.theguardian.com/books/2016/aug/18/the-schooldays-of-jesus-jm-coetzee-review)
6. J. M. Coetzee, 'Interview', in *Doubling the Point*, 20.
7. Coetzee, 'Samuel Beckett and the Temptations of Style', 47.
8. See David James, *Modernist Futures* (New York: Cambridge University Press, 2012), chap. 3.
9. Paul Ricoeur, *Oneself as Another*, trans. Kathleen Blamey (Chicago, IL: University of Chicago Press, 1992), 162.
10. Judith Butler, 'Afterword: After Loss, What Then?', in *Loss: The Politics of Mourning*, ed. David L. Eng and David Kazanajian (Berkeley, CA: University of California Press, 2003), 472.

11. Andrew van der Vlies, *Present Imperfect: Contemporary South African Writing* (Oxford: Oxford University Press, 2017), 21.
12. Butler, 'Afterword: After Loss, What Then?', 472.
13. J. M. Coetzee, *Age of Iron* notebook, MS-00842, 33.6: entries dated 5th Oct. and 19th Nov. 1988. J. M. Coetzee Papers, Harry Ransom Center, University of Texas at Austin.
14. J. M. Coetzee, *Age of Iron* (1990; London: Penguin, 1998), 92, 86. Hereafter cited parenthetically.
15. Kim L. Worthington, '*Age of Iron* (1990)', in *A Companion to the Works of J. M. Coetzee*, ed. Tim Mehigan (New York: Camden House, 2011), 116.
16. J. M. Coetzee, *Foe* notebook, MS-00842, 33.6. Entry dated 17 March 1984. Coetzee Papers.
17. See Timothy Bewes, *The Event of Postcolonial Shame* (Princeton, NJ: Princeton University Press, 2011), chap. 5. In his reading of *Age of Iron*, Michael Neill argues that 'sympathy offers a dangerous palliation of the shame that Elizabeth Curren's confession is designed not simply to express, but to agitate and invigorate: the expression of shame (which, unlike guilt, assumes the offender's fearful transparency) is the penance she enjoins upon herself—even if it offers no reliable promise of absolution' ('"The Language of the Heart": Confession, Metaphor and Grace in J. M. Coetzee's *Age of Iron*', in *J. M. Coetzee's Austerities*, ed. Graham Bradshaw and Michael Neill [Burlington, VA: Ashgate, 2010], 92–3).
18. David Attwell, *J. M. Coetzee and the Life of Writing: Face to Face with Time* (Oxford: Oxford University Press, 2015), 169.
19. J. M. Coetzee, *The Rule of Iron* [*Age of Iron*] draft 10. MS-00842, 16.2, 1989. Coetzee Papers.
20. J. C. Kannemeyer, *J. M. Coetzee: A Life in Writing*, trans. Michiel Heyns (Victoria: Scribe, 2012), 457.
21. Ibid., 457.
22. Andrew van der Vlies, '"[From] Whom This Writing Then?" Politics, Aesthetics, and the Personal in Coetzee's *Age of Iron*', in *Approaches to Teaching Coetzee's* Disgrace *and Other Works*, ed. Laura Wright, Elleke Boehmer, Jane Poyner (New York: MLA, 2014), 101.
23. Coetzee, *Age of Iron* notebook, 9 March 1988.
24. Ibid., 17 March 1988.
25. Derek Attridge, *J. M. Coetzee and the Ethics of Reading: Literature in the Event* (Chicago: University of Chicago Press, 2004), 93.
26. Coetzee, *Age of Iron* notebook, 20 Nov. 1988.
27. Justin Neuman, *Fiction beyond Secularism* (Evanston, IL: Northwestern University Press, 2014), 91.
28. Coetzee, *Age of Iron* notebook, 19 Nov. 1988.
29. Worthington, '*Age of Iron* (1990)', 126.
30. Jane Poyner, 'J. M. Coetzee in Conversation', in *J. M. Coetzee and the Idea of the Public Intellectual*, ed. Jane Poyner (Columbus: Ohio University Press, 2006), 21.
31. David Chidester, *Wild Religion: Tracking the Sacred in South Africa* (Berkeley: University of California Press, 2012), 77. Johann Kinghorn notes that in the 1940s the country needed a 'conceptual framework and definite policies', and 'these eventually did emerge from the fusion of the core Afrikaner values with three different currents of thought: nationalism, the neo-Calvinism of Abraham Kuyper, and racism. This fusion was mediated by the churches', as Kuyperian neo-Calvinism translated into the nationalist

cause ('Modernization and Apartheid: The Afrikaner Churches', in *Christianity in South Africa: A Political, Social and Cultural History*, ed. Richard Elphick and Rodney Davenport [Cape Town: David Philip, 1997], 142, 143). In D. G. Hart's account, the 'oldest Reformed Churches were those started for Dutch colonists in South Africa. In most cases these communions resisted evangelistic overtures to the black populations. Where Dutch Calvinists did minister to native populations the result was an order of Communion that remained separate from European bodies, an ecclesiastical version of apartheid' (*Calvinism: A History* [New Haven, CT: Yale University Press, 2013], 201).

32. Peter Walshe, 'Christianity and the Anti-Apartheid Struggle: The Prophetic Voice within Divided Churches', in *Christianity in South Africa*, 385.
33. Ibid., 388. Chidester dates the fissures between church and government earlier. In contrast to 'current formulations of religious fundamentalists as militant, violent terrorists', by the 1970s 'religious fundamentalists in Johannesburg were a "problem" because they were less militant, less racist, and less puritanical than they should have been according to the ethos of the apartheid regime' (*Wild Religion*, 76).
34. Dominic Head, *J. M. Coetzee* (Cambridge: Cambridge University Press, 1997), 143.
35. Coetzee, *Age of Iron* fragments (1 of 6), MS-00842, 14.1, dated 28 May 1987. Coetzee Papers.
36. An earlier (deleted) version of this line was more specific about the penetrative action of the letter, freighted with procreative connotations that Coetzee evidently wanted to restrain (possibly in light of Mrs Curren's ensuing reminder that 'You grew ˡⁱᵛᵉᵈ in me, once upon a time, as I grew ˡⁱᵛᵉᵈ in my mother'): 'These words are, if you like, my means of inserting myself in you for the last time and living on in you' (*Age of Iron*, MS-00842, 14.3, dated 24 September 1988. Coetzee Papers).
37. In the typed draft (FICN-37), Coetzee turns what was the original phrase 'hovering care' into the more ambivalent and multivalent 'hovering if undependable solicitude' (The Rule of Iron [*Age of Iron*] MS-00842, 10.3. Coetzee Papers).
38. The stronger nouns, *presence* and *comfort* replace the more straightforward desire for 'help', as it appears in a handwritten amendment to draft 10.3: 'I need his help, but he needs help too' (Ibid. Coetzee Papers).
39. Paul Bailey, 'Sex and Other Problems', rev. of *Disgrace*, by J. M. Coetzee, *The Independent*, 2 July 1999: http://www.independent.co.uk/arts-entertainment/books/features/sex-and-other-problems-743456.html
40. Coetzee, *Foe* note book (entry dated 5 Feb. 1985), MS-00842, 33.6 (p. 74). Coetzee Papers.
41. Jarad Zimbler, *J. M. Coetzee and the Politics of Style* (Cambridge: Cambridge University Press, 2014), 172.
42. J. M. Coetzee, *Disgrace* (1999; London: Vintage, 2000), 156. Hereafter cited parenthetically.
43. Coetzee, Casebound Notebook, Coetzee Papers, MS-00842, 35.2, entry dated 4 January 1995. Coetzee Papers.
44. Elleke Boehmer, 'J. M. Coetzee's Australian Realism', in *Strong Opinions: J. M. Coetzee and the Authority of Contemporary Fiction*, ed. Chris Danta, Sue Kossewm, and Julien Murphet (London: Bloomsbury, 2013), 9.
45. In a handwritten draft, Coetzee describes the episode as 'a scene that any of the Impressionists would have enjoyed' (Coetzee, *Disgrace*, early draft, MS-00842, 35.5 [2 of 2], dated 26 June 1998. Coetzee Papers).
46. Zimbler, *J. M. Coetzee and the Politics of Style*, 32–3.

47. Coetzee, *Disgrace* Notebook (March–August 1997), MS-00842, 35.3, entry dated 18 April 1997. Coetzee Papers.
48. Coetzee, *Disgrace*, early draft, MS-00842, 35.5 (2 of 2), dated 26 January 1998. Coetzee Papers.
49. Coetzee, *Disgrace*, 'Version 10', MS-00842, 36.7, notes labelled DISGR-NT.V10/1, dated 20 August 1997. Coetzee Papers.
50. Peter D. McDonald, 'Coetzee's Critique of Language', in *Beyond the Ancient Quarrel: Literature, Philosophy, and J. M. Coetzee*, ed. Patrick Hayes and Jan Wilm (Oxford: Oxford University Press, 2018), 173. I'm grateful both to Peter McDonald and to Patrick Hayes for generous and stimulating conversations about Coetzee's narration. The undulations I'm tracing here—what seems like a successive performance and withdrawal of free indirect style—seem to befit what McDonald calls the 'the peculiar experience of continuous composition and decomposition' throughout *Disgrace* (173).
51. Carrol Clarkson, *J. M. Coetzee: Countervoices* (Basingstoke: Palgrave, 2009), 2.
52. Gayatri Chakravorty Spivak, 'Lie Down in the Karoo: An Antidote to the Anthropocene', rev. of *The Childhood of Jesus*, by J. M. Coetzee, *Public Books*, 1 June 2014: http://www.publicbooks.org/lie-down-in-the-karoo-an-antidote-to-the-anthropocene/. For McDonald, we also learn to read ourselves: Coetzee's 'transactional' dialogue with his audience suggests that the 'implicitly desired reader...is a less professionalized, even less securely individuated and socialized figure, who is open to being taken outside her or his self' ('Coetzee's Critique of Language', 178–9).
53. Marilynne Robinson, 'Family', *The Death of Adam* (London: Picador, 1998), 90.
54. Ibid., 90.
55. Ibid., 90.
56. Marilynne Robinson, *Gilead* (2004; London: Virago, 2006), 231. Hereafter cited parenthetically.
57. Amy Hungerford, *Postmodern Belief: American Literature and Religion since 1960* (Princeton: Princeton University Press, 2010), 114.
58. Laura E. Tanner, '"Looking Back from the Grave": Sensory Perception and the Anticipation of Absence in Marilynne Robinson's *Gilead*', *Contemporary Literature*, 48.2 (Summer 2007), 231–2.
59. Robinson, 'Facing Reality', *The Death of Adam*, 83.
60. Tanner, '"Looking Back from the Grave"', 241.
61. Ibid., 242.
62. Robinson, 'The Art of Fiction No. 198', *The Paris Review*, 186 (Fall 2008). Web.
63. Robinson, 'Open Thy Hand Wide: Moses and the Origins of American Liberalism', *When I was a Child I Read Books* (London: Virago, 2012), 81.
64. Ibid., 78; John Calvin quoted in Robinson, 'Open Thy Hand Wide', 76.
65. Ibid., 68.
66. Robinson, 'The Art of Fiction'.
67. Marilynne Robinson, 'Reformation', *The Givenness of Things* (London: Virago, 2015), 28.
68. Thomas Gardner, 'Interview with Marilynne Robinson', quoted in Gardner, *A Door Ajar: Contemporary Writers and Emily Dickinson* (New York: Oxford University Press, 2006), 48.
69. Ibid., 55.
70. Tanner, '"Looking Back from the Grave"', 250.
71. Ibid., 250. Extensive commentary on aspects of Robinson's style isn't Tanner's primary concern, as her essay instead offers a series of characterological readings that draw explicitly on neuroscientific and phenomenological theories of perception, invoking

'cognitive paradigms which stress the intensity of perception as a form of compensation for loss' (234). Tanner thus focuses on Ames (rather than on the formal properties of his narration) as a kind of psychological case-study for how 'Imagination's power to counter future absence…rebounds to overwhelm the present with anticipated loss' (249).

72. Robinson, 'Puritans and Prigs', *The Death of Adam*, 156.
73. Robinson, 'Humanism', in *The Givenness of Things*, 14.
74. Ibid., 14.
75. Gardner, 'Interview with Marilynne Robinson', 65.
76. Marilynne Robinson, 'Grace and Beauty', *What Are We Doing Here? Essays* (London: Virago, 2018), 114.
77. Ibid., 101.
78. Marilynne Robinson, Absence of Mind: The Dispelling of Inwardness from the Modern Myth of the Self (New Haven, CT: Yale University Press, 2010), 7.
79. Dewey D. Wallace Jr, *Shapers of English Calvinism, 1660–1714: Variety, Persistence, and Transformation* (Oxford: Oxford University Press, 2011), 146.
80. Joseph Alleine, 'The Art of Dying Well', in *Remaines of that Excellent Minister of Jesus Christ, Mr Joseph Alleine. Being a Collection of Sundry Directions, Sermons, Sacrament-Speeches, and Letters, not Heretofore Published. All Tending to Promote Real Piety* (London: Peter Parker, 1674), 5.
81. Ibid., 6.
82. Gardner, 'Interview with Marilynne Robinson', 55.
83. Mark O'Connell, 'The First Church of Marilynne Robinson', *The New Yorker*, 30 May 2012. Web.
84. Robinson, 'Grace', *The Givenness of Things*, 34.
85. Gardner, 'Interview with Marilynne Robinson', 58.
86. Robert Chodat, 'That Horeb, That Kansas: Evolution and the Modernity of Marilynne Robinson', *American Literary History*, 28.2 (Summer 2016), 347. Chodat is drawing on James Wood's review of *Gilead*, where he argues that 'Robinson's novel teaches us how to read it, suggests how we might slow down to walk at its own processional pace, and how we might learn to coddle its many fine details' (Wood, '*Gilead*: Acts of Devotion', *The New York Times*, 28 Nov. 2004: http://www.nytimes.com/2004/11/28/books/review/28coverwood.html).
87. Chodat, 'That Horeb, That Kansas', 349.
88. Wood, '*Gilead*: Acts of Devotion'.
89. Thomas Schaub, 'Interview with Marilynne Robinson', *Contemporary Literature*, 35.2 (Summer 1994), 240–1.
90. Robinson, *When I Was a Child I Read Books*, 19–20.
91. Robinson, 'Humanism', *The Givenness of Things*, 13 (Robinson's emphasis).
92. Coetzee, Interview in *Doubling the Point*, 250.
93. Coetzee, *Age of Iron* notebook, dated 18 Nov. 1988.
94. Ibid., dated 19 Nov. 1988.
95. Coetzee, *Age of Iron*, MS-00842, 14.3, dated 28 Feb. 1989. Coetzee Papers.
96. Tim Parks picks up on a similar logic of disclosure through denials or diffusions of standpoint or generic affiliation, when observing that 'it's precisely because Coetzee does not do autobiography that he doesn't do anything but. Which is to say: it's because he is unable or unwilling to settle on a position for himself that he has to keep on worrying around the question, so much so that the writing itself becomes the place where Coetzee most convincingly is' ('In Some Sense True', *London Review of Books*, 21 January 2016, 28).

97. Coetzee, *Disgrace*, early draft, MS-00842, 35.5 (2 of 2), dated 5 December 1996. Coetzee Papers.
98. Kinghorn, 'Modernization and Apartheid: The Afrikaner Churches', 143.
99. In his sixth handwritten draft of *Age of Iron*, Coetzee's syntax isn't as paratactic, with the phrase about the embrace's transportive efficacy set off in a sentence of its own: 'We embrace our children to be folded in the arms of the future, to pass ourselves on beyond death. To be transported' (*Age of Iron*, MS-00842, 14.3, dated 11 March 1988. Coetzee Papers).
100. Calvin, sermon on Deut. 15, quoted in Robinson, 'Open Thy Hand Wide', 83.
101. Head, *J. M. Coetzee*, 137.
102. Ibid., 137.
103. Jared Zimbler, *J. M. Coetzee and the Politics of Style* (Cambridge: Cambridge University Press, 2014), 172.
104. Worthington, '*Age of Iron* (1990)', 124.
105. Neil, '"The Language of the Heart"', 102.
106. Robinson, 'Grace and Beauty', 112.
107. In Rachel Sykes's attentive reading, the apparent 'atemporality' of those novels in Robinson's Gilead series 'is the product of a quiet aesthetic that removes contemporary noise from the character's experience of the present', an aesthetic that 'has the potential to act as a "balm" for contemporary readers when it maintains the usefulness of reflection against the rush of society'. But this detachment possibly places Robinson's work in an even more 'ambiguous present in which the political and cultural "now" is vague scenery to the emotional landscape of the characters' (*The Quiet Contemporary American Novel* [Manchester University Press, 2017], 92, 91, 92–3). In a collection that hosts political scientists' responses to Robinson's fiction and essays, contributors applaud her work's pertinence 'to contemporary political theoretical discussions about racial justice'. For Alex Zamalin and Daniel Skinner, *Gilead* and *Home* show that the 'call to action—rooted in positions taken freely and articulated in public spaces—must be central to our fictionalized depictions of American racial history to adequately provide readers of those fictionalizations with an operationalizable sense of "what is to be done"' ('*Gilead*'s Two Models of Action against Racial Injustice', in *A Political Companion to Marilynne Robinson*, ed. Shannon L. Mariotti and Joseph H. Lane Jr (Lexington, KY: University Press of Kentucky, 2016), 108.
108. Coetzee, *Age of Iron* Notebook, entry dated 29 April 1989.
109. Joseph Lane and Shannon Mariotti, 'Merism and the Mermaid in a Ship's Captain: A Conversation with Marilynne Robinson', in *A Political Companion to Marilynne Robinson*, 283.
110. Ibid., 274.
111. Paul Ricoeur, *Oneself as Another*, trans. Kathleen Blamey (Chicago, IL: University of Chicago Press, 1992), 162.
112. Atul Gawande, *Being Mortal: Illness, Medicine, and What Matters in the End* (London: Profile, 2014), 1.
113. Elisabeth Kübler-Ross, ed., *Death: The Final Stage of Life* (New York: Simon and Schuster, 1975), 5.
114. Ibid., 8.
115. Ibid., 118.
116. Philippe Ariès, *The Hour of Our Death*, trans. Helen Weaver (London: Allen Lane, 1981), 300, 614, 300.

117. Ibid., 300.
118. Kübler-Ross, *Death*, 73.
119. David Foster Wallace, 'Fictional Futures and the Conspicuously Young', *Review of Contemporary Fiction*, 8.3 (Fall 1988), 43.
120. Gawande, *Being Mortal*, 238, 243.
121. Ricoeur, *Oneself as Another*, 162.
122. Claire Messud, rev. of *All at Sea*, by Decca Aitkenhead, *The Guardian, Review*, 7 May 2016, 7.
123. Ricoeur, *Oneself as Another*, 162.
124. Robinson quoted by Wyatt Mason, 'The Revelations of Marilynne Robinson', *New York Times, Magazine*, 1 October 2014. Web.
125. Ricoeur, *Oneself as Another*, 162.
126. Frank Kermode, *The Sense of an Ending* (Oxford: Oxford University Press, 2000), 144, 130
127. Ibid., 164.
128. Ibid., 179.
129. Marilynne Robinson, *Lila* (London: Virago, 2014), 240, 74.

CHAPTER 5

1. Marilynne Robinson, *Home* (2008; London: Virago, 2009), 338.
2. Mariylnne Robinson, 'The Art of Fiction, No. 198', *The Paris Review*, 186 (Fall 2008). Web.
3. Marilynne Robinson, 'Family', *The Death of Adam* (London: Picador, 1998), 90.
4. Pamela Thurschwell, *Literature, Technology and Magical Thinking, 1880–1920* (Cambridge: Cambridge University Press, 2001), 6, 7.
5. Doris Lessing, 'The Capacity to Look a Situation Coolly' (1972), interview by Josephine Hendin, in *Putting the Questions Differently: Interviews with Doris Lessing, 1964–1994*, ed. Earl G. Ingersoll (London: Flamingo, 1996), 47.
6. Lessing, 'Describing this Beautiful and Nasty Planet' (1994), interview by Earl G. Ingersol, *Putting the Questions Differently*, 232.
7. Blake Morrison, 'The Righting of Lives', *The Guardian, Review*, Saturday 17 May 2008. Web.
8. Doris Lessing, 'Impertinent Daughters' (1984), in *A Small Personal Voice: Essays, Reviews, Interviews* (London: Fontana, 1994), 101.
9. Ibid., 121.
10. Lessing, 'Writing as Time Runs Out' (1980), interview with Michael Dean, *Putting the Questions Differently*, 87.
11. Lessing, 'The Small Personal Voice' (1957), in *A Small Personal Voice*, 10.
12. Lessing, 'Acknowledging a New Frontier', interview by Eve Bertelsen, in *Putting the Questions Differently*, 131; Lessing, 'Writing as Time Runs Out' (1980), 98.
13. Lessing, 'Impertinent Daughters', 121.
14. Frank Kermode, 'The Daughter Who Hated Her', *London Review of Books*, 30.14 (17 July 2008). Web.
15. Doris Lessing, *Alfred and Emily* (London: Fourth Estate, 2008), 49. Subsequent references are cited parenthetically.
16. Lessing, 'Impertinent Daughters', 133, 134.
17. Ibid., 142.
18. Ibid., 146.

19. Ibid., 150.
20. Lessing, 'The Habit of Observing' (1985), interview by Francois-Olivier Rousseau, in *Putting the Questions Differently*, 154.
21. Lessing, 'Impertinent Daughters', 116–17, 120.
22. Heller McAlpin, Rev. of *Alfred and Emily* by Doris Lessing, *LA Times*, 27 July 2008. Web.
23. Caroline Moore, 'Doris Lessing's Writing of Her Parents' Past', *The Telegraph*, 15 May 2008. Web.
24. Susan Watkins, *Doris Lessing* (Manchester: Manchester University Press, 2010), 162.
25. Morrison, 'The Righting of Lives'.
26. John Plotz, 'Feeling Like a Stoic: Doris Lessing's Experimental Fiction', *Public Books*, 7 August 2012. Web.
27. Caryn James, 'They May Not Mean to, But They Do', Rev. of *Alfred and Emily*, by Doris Lessing, *New York Times*, 10 August 2008. Web.
28. Plotz, 'Feeling Like a Stoic'.
29. For an extended discussion of this temperament, see my 'Art Unseduced by Its Own Beauty: Toni Morrison and the Humility of Experiment', in *New Directions in the History of the Novel*, ed. Andrew Nash, Patrick Parrinder, and Nicola Wilson (Basingstoke: Palgrave Macmillan, 2014), 211–22.
30. Plotz, 'Feeling Like a Stoic'.
31. Ibid.
32. Lessing, 'The Need to Tell Stories', interview by Christopher Bigsby, in *Putting the Questions Differently*, 82.
33. Lessing, 'Describing this Beautiful and Nasty Planet', 236.
34. Joan Didion, 'Doris Lessing' (1971), *The White Album* (New York: Simon and Schuster, 1979), 119.
35. Michael LeMahieu, 'The Novel of Ideas', in *The Cambridge Companion to British Fiction since 1945*, ed. David James (New York: Cambridge University Press, 2015), 178.
36. Ibid., 177.
37. Didion, 'Doris Lessing', 120.
38. Ibid., 123.
39. Ibid., 124, 125.
40. Joan Didion, *The Year of Magical Thinking* (2005; London: Fourth Estate, 2009), 207. Hereafter cited parenthetically.
41. Joan Didion, Interview by Emma Brockes, *The Guardian*, Friday 16 December 2005. Web.
42. Hilton Als, interviewed for Griffin Dunne's documentary, *Joan Didion: The Center Will Not Hold* (Netflix, October 2017).
43. Sandra M. Gilbert highlights this tension, remarking that 'Didion appears to be unaware that hers is one in a rich and poignant tradition of modern and contemporary grief memoirs'. More speculatively, Gilbert suggests that while 'Didion's is not a project in literary criticism', nonetheless 'her obliviousness (or repression) of such memoirs may be in some way associated with a more striking lacuna in her own memoir, namely, her "refusal" (or more accurately, her repression) of mourning for Quintana', whose death following Dunne's (though before *The Year*'s release in 2005) remained a loss unincorporated in the book's later events (Rev. of *The Year of Magical Thinking*, by Joan Didion, *Literature and Medicine*, 25.2 [Fall 2006], 555, 556).
44. Ibid., 553.
45. Ibid., 555.

46. Christopher Nealon, 'The Price of Value', in *The Values of Literary Studies: Critical Institutions, Scholarly Agendas*, ed. Rónán McDonald (New York: Cambridge University Press, 2015), 101.
47. Esther Schor, *Bearing the Dead: The British Culture of Mourning from the Enlightenment to Victoria* (Princeton: Princeton University Press, 1994), 15.
48. Sebald, *Die Beschreibung des Unglücks*, 12.
49. Deborah Nelson, *Tough Enough: Arbus, Arendt, Didion, McCarthy, Sontag, Weil* (Chicago, IL: University of Chicago Press, 2017), 170, 8, 10, 164, 170.
50. Joan Didion, 'The Art of Nonfiction, No. 1', interview by Hilton Als, *The Paris Review*, 48.176 (Spring 2006), 66.
51. About the composition of *The Year*, Didion recalls that she deliberately set out 'to write it fast so it would be raw, because I had the feeling that that was the texture it ought to have' ('When Everything Changes', Interview by Jonathan Van Meter, 20 October 2005, *New York* Magazine, Web). And yet this rawness, while undeniably moving for being so candid, coexists in Didion's prose with a consistent level of tonal and lexical restraint.
52. Jesse Matz, *Lasting Impressions: The Legacies of Impressionism in Contemporary Culture* (New York: Columbia University Press, 2017), 230.
53. Didion, 'The Art of Nonfiction, No. 1', 68.
54. Matz, *Lasting Impressions*, 230.
55. Didion, 'The White Album', *The White Album*, 11.
56. Joan Didion, *Blue Nights* (London: Fourth Estate, 2011), 17.
57. Lessing, 'Unexamined Mental Attitudes Left Behind By Communism' (1992), interview by Edith Kurzweil, in *Putting the Questions Differently*, 208.
58. Anne Enright, *The Gathering* (2007; London: Vintage, 2008), 2.
59. Fredric Jameson, 'In Hyperspace', *London Review of Books*, 37.17, 10 Sept. 2015, 20.

CHAPTER 6

1. Emily Dickinson, 341: 'After great pain, a formal feeling comes –', l.1, in *Emily Dickinson: The Complete Poems*, ed. Thomas H. Johnson (London: Faber and Faber, 2016), 162. I'm grateful to Angus Brown for pointing me to this particular poem.
2. Ibid., l.13.
3. Graham Swift, 'Half a Loaf', *England and Other Stories* (London: Simon & Schuster, 2014), 75. Hereafter cited parenthetically.
4. David Grossman, 'Writing in the Dark' (2007), in *Writing in the Dark: Essays on Literature and Politics*, translated from the Hebrew by Jessica Cohen (Bloomsbury, 2007), 67.
5. Janice M. Morse, Joan L. Bottorff, and Sally Hutchinson, 'The Phenomenology of Comfort', *Journal of Advanced Nursing*, 20.1 (1994), 190, 191, 190. In her extensive work elsewhere on the ethics of defining and administering comfort, Morse insists that the solace that comes with comforting 'isn't about pillow fluffing'; instead of projecting upon the patient in or anticipating distress a preconceived idea of comfort, it should be 'driven by the patient' themselves (Janice M. Morse, 'On Comfort and Comforting', *American Journal of Nursing*, 100.9 [2000], 34, 35).
6. Birgit H. Rasmussen, Lilian Jansson, and Astrid Norberg, 'Striving for Becoming At-Home in the Midst of Dying', *American Journal of Hospice and Palliative Care*, 17.1 (2000), 38.
7. Ibid., 40.

8. Astrid Norberg, Monica Bergsten, and Berit Lundman, 'A Model of Consolation', *Nursing Ethics*, 8.6 (2001), 551.
9. Rasmussen, Jansson, and Norberg, 'Striving for Becoming At-Home in the Midst of Dying', 40.
10. Morse, 'On Comfort and Comforting', 35.
11. Elizabeth Tutton and Kate Seers, 'An Exploration of the Concept of Comfort', *Journal of Clinical Nursing*, 12 (2003), 694.
12. Morse, Bottorff, and Hutchinson, 'The Phenomenology of Comfort', 190.
13. Kazuo Ishiguro, *Never Let Me Go*: Rough Papers, MS-05377, 3.3. Ishiguro Papers, Harry Ransom Center, University of Texas at Austin.
14. Salman Rushdie, 'Kazuo Ishiguro', *Imaginary Homelands: Essays and Criticism 1981–91* (London: Granta, 1992), 244.
15. John Mullan argues that the novel 'is written at a tangent to this genre, recently favoured by many literary novelists', primarily because Ishiguro 'does not imagine a future world at all' and seems not to 'bother about the grounds for the unsettling reality' he evokes. 'If this were either a work of science-fiction novel or a dystopian fable', reckons Mullan, 'the central character would rebel, but here there is never any question of that' ('Afterword: On First Reading *Never Let Me Go*', in *Kazuo Ishiguro: Contemporary Critical Perspectives*, ed. Sebastian Groes and Sean Matthews [London: Continuum, 2009], 104–105).
16. Ishiguro, *Never Let Me Go*: Rough Papers, MS-05377, 3.3. Ishiguro Papers.
17. Rasmussen, Jansson, and Norberg, 'Striving for Becoming At-Home in the Midst of Dying', 32.
18. Norberg, Bergsten, and Lundman, 'A Model of Consolation', 545.
19. Kazuo Ishiguro, *Never Let Me Go* (London: Faber and Faber, 2005), 258. Hereafter cited parenthetically.
20. Mark Currie, 'Controlling Time: *Never Let Me Go*', in *Kazuo Ishiguro*, 93.
21. Of this sense of enclosure, Currie remarks that 'one of the principal characteristics of the novel is a kind of timelessness, achieved in part by the scarcity of historical locators and specific temporal references'. Indeed, the novel pulls away from an identifiable notion of the 'present' in two directions: 'There is, on one hand, a sense of the future, which inheres in the novel's interest in cloning; and on the other hand a sense of the past, in the form of a kind of public school memoir, or a recollection of a childhood apparently isolated from the forces of history' ('Controlling Time', 93).
22. Ishiguro, *Never Let Me Go*: Editorial Notes and Correspondence. MS-05377, 10.1 (2004). Ishiguro Papers, Harry Ransom Center, University of Texas at Austin.
23. Ibid.
24. Currie, 'Controlling Time: *Never Let Me Go*', 95.
25. Ibid., 98.
26. Ibid., 97.
27. Ibid., 103.
28. Bruce Robbins, *Upward Mobility and the Common Good: Toward a Literary History of the Welfare State* (Princeton, NJ: Princeton University Press, 2007), 200.
29. Currie, 'Controlling Time', 98.
30. Ishiguro, *Never Let Me Go*: 'First Rough Draft', Notebook: 'Clones' (2000–2001). MS-05377, 5.6. Ishiguro Papers.
31. Ishiguro, '*Never Let Me Go*: A Profile of Kazuo Ishiguro' (2005), by John Freeman, in *Conversations with Kazuo Ishiguro*, 197.
32. Robbins, *Upward Mobility and the Common Good*, 203.

33. In some 2004 notes, Ishiguro observes that 'you could say there's a "dystopian" or "sci-fi" dimension. I think of it more as an "alternative history" conceit' (MS-05377, *Never Let Me Go*, editorial notes and correspondence, 10.1 [2004]. Ishiguro Papers).
34. Kazuo Ishiguro, 'Interview with Kazuo Ishiguro', by Karen Grigsby Bates (2005), in *Conversations with Kazuo Ishiguro*, 202.
35. Robbins, *Upward Mobility and the Common Good*, 201.
36. Ishiguro, 'Interview with Kazuo Ishiguro', by Bates (2005), 202.
37. Robbins, *Upward Mobility and the Common Good*, 203.
38. Kazuo Ishiguro, 'A Conversation about Life and Art with Kazuo Ishiguro', by Cynthia F. Wong and Grace Crummett (2008), in *Conversations with Kazuo Ishiguro*, 220.
39. Kazuo Ishiguro, 'Never Let Me Go: A Profile of Kazuo Ishiguro', by John Freeman (2005), *Conversations with Kazuo Ishiguro*, 197.
40. The concept is recorded by Åsa Roxberg, Katie Eriksson, Arne Rehnsfeldt, and Bengt Fridlund in 'The Meaning of Consolation as Experienced by Nurses in a Home-Care Setting', *Journal of Clinical Nursing*, 17.8 (2008), 1079–87. Drawing on interviews with nurses they define a variety of 'consolation that protected the sufferer from being overwhelmed by the suffering', achieved by '"portioning out" the suffering, which in turn sustained the sufferer's emotional balance' (1083, 1084).
41. Ibid., 1083.
42. Anne Whitehead, 'Writing with Care: Kazuo Ishiguro's *Never Let Me Go*', *Contemporary Literature*, 52.1 (Spring 2011), 60–1.
43. Ibid., 75.
44. Ibid., 73.
45. Ibid., 67.
46. Mullan, 'Afterword', 106.
47. Rebecca L. Walkowitz, *Born Translated: The Contemporary Novel in an Age of World Literature* (New York: Columbia University Press, 2015), 103.
48. Mullan, 'Afterword', 106.
49. Robbins, *Upward Mobility and the Common Good*, 205. Ishiguro's 'sentence structure', as Robbins notes, 'seems engineered to guarantee that the best will always be made of a bad situation, with no acknowledgement that the situation will always be bad because the same system has begotten it' (205).
50. Kazuo Ishiguro, 'Kazuo Ishguro with Maya Jaggi' (1995), in *Conversations with Kazuo Ishiguro*, 116.
51. Kazuo Ishiguro, 'An Interview with Kazuo Ishiguro' by Allan Vorda and Kim Herzinger (1990), in *Conversations with Kazuo Ishiguro*, 85.
52. Nancy Armstrong, 'The Affective Turn in Contemporary Fiction', *Contemporary Literature*, 55.3 (Fall 2014), 457.
53. Kazuo Ishiguro, '"I'm Sorry I Can't Say More": An Interview with Kazuo Ishiguro', by Sean Matthews, in *Kazuo Ishiguro*, 124.
54. Ishiguro, Note dated 22 August 1995, *When We Were Orphans*: 'Notes for Novel 5', MS-05377, 26.1. Ishiguro Papers.
55. Ishiguro, *Never Let Me Go*: 'First Rough Draft', Notebook: 'Clones 7 – Section 3 Centre', MS-05377, 6.5. Ishiguro Papers.
56. Whitehead, 'Writing with Care', 58.
57. David Grossman, 'Books that Have Read Me' (2002), in *Writing in the Dark: Essays on Literature and Politics*, trans. Jessica Cohen (London: Bloomsbury, 2008), 12.
58. Ishiguro, 'An Interview with Kazuo Ishiguro', by Vora and Herzinger, 85.
59. Grossman, 'Books that Have Read Me', 12–13.

CHAPTER 7

1. David Grossman, 'Writing in the Dark,' The Arthur Miller Freedom to Write Lecture (2007), in *Writing in the Dark: Essays on Literature and Politics*, trans. Jessica Cohen (London: Bloomsbury, 2007), 64.
2. Ibid., 63.
3. Ibid., 64.
4. Linda Grant, Rev. of *To the End of the Land*, by David Grossman, *The Independent*, 27 August 2010. https://www.independent.co.uk/arts-entertainment/books/reviews/to-the-end-of-the-land-by-david-grossman-trans-jessica-cohen-2063011.html.
5. David Grossman, *To the End of the Land*, trans. Jessica Cohen (London: Cape, 2010), 79. Hereafter cited parenthetically.
6. David Grossman, 'The Desire to Be Gisella' (2006), in *Writing in the Dark*, 36.
7. David Grossman, 'Contemplations on Peace' (2004), in *Writing in the Dark*, 93.
8. Ibid., 93–4 (Grossman's emphases).
9. David Grossman, 'Individual Language and Mass Language' (2007), in *Writing in the Dark*, 85, 84.
10. David Grossman, Interview by Jonathan Freedland, *The Guardian*, podcast, 8 September 2010. http://www.theguardian.com/books/audio/2010/sep/08/david-grossman-israel-lofty-idea-worth-fighting-for
11. Grossman, 'The Desire to Be Gisella', 44.
12. Grossman, 'Contemplations on Peace', 118.
13. David Grossman, Interview by Rachel Cooke, *The Observer*, 29 August 2010. http://www.theguardian.com/books/2010/aug/29/david-grossman-israel-hezbollah-interview
14. David Grossman, 'Leave Lebanon Now' (2000), in *Death as a Way of Life: Dispatches from Jerusalem*, trans. Haim Watzman (London: Bloomsbury, 2003), 55.
15. David Grossman, 'Beware, Opportunity Ahead' (1999), in *Death as a Way of Life*, 46.
16. Grossman, 'Writing in the Dark', 61.
17. Grossman, 'Individual Language and Mass Language', 83–4.
18. Grossman, 'The Desire to Be Gisella', 46, 49, 47.
19. Ibid., 49, 51.
20. Grossman, 'Individual Language and Mass Language', 85.
21. Ibid., 85.
22. Grossman, Interview by Freedland.
23. Ibid.
24. Grossman, 'Writing in the Dark', 61.
25. Ibid., 67.
26. Grossman, Interview by Ethan Bronner, *The New York Times*, 16 Nov. 2010. http://www.nytimes.com/2010/11/17/books/17grossman.html
27. Alan Mintz, 'Ora's Tale: The Narrative Ambitions of David Grossman's *To the End of the Land*', *Hebrew Studies*, 54 (2013), 339.
28. Iris Milner, 'Sacrifice and Redemption in *To the End of the Land*', *Hebrew Studies*, 54 (2013), 328. In a reading with vocal misgivings, Todd Hasak-Lowry expresses frustration with how 'Ofer's fate in the present has been substituted with Avram's rehabilitation from the past', insofar as Ora 'had given herself (or been given) the task of saving Avram as a consolation for her inability to protect Ofer'. While I'm not entirely convinced that Grossman's progressively deepening descriptions are as explicitly 'redemptive' as Milner suggests (though the hike is undeniably rehabilitative in all sorts of ways for Ora and Avram alike), this seems a more satisfactory starting point for reading the affective work of form in this novel than Hasak-Lowry's dismissal of Ora's 'need to

speak about Ofer' as a superficial substitution, yielding ultimately a 'cold comfort, a small consolation' ('Grossman After 2000: An Ambivalent Complaint in Nine Parts', *Hebrew Studies*, 54 [2013], 307, 305).

29. David Grossman, 'Introduction' (2002), *Death as a Way of Life*, ix.
30. I'm borrowing the phrase from Raymond Williams, who develops the notion of 'militant particularism' in *Resources of Hope* (1989). It was subsequently taken up by David Harvey in *Justice, Nature and the Geography of Difference* (Oxford: Blackwell, 1996), see chap. 1.
31. Grossman, 'Books that Have Read Me' (2002), *Writing in the Dark*, 22.
32. Jacqueline Rose, 'Failed State', *London Review of Books*, 18 March 2004: http://www.lrb.co.uk/v26/n06/jacqueline-rose/failed-state
33. David Grossman, 'Two Years of Intifada' (2002), in *Death as a Way Life*, 178.
34. Tóibín, Rev. of *To the End of the Land*, by David Grossman, *New York Times Book Review*, 115.39 (2010): http://www.nytimes.com/2010/09/26/books/review/Toibin-t.html.
35. David J. Denby, *Sentimental Narrative and the Social Order in France, 1760–1820* (Cambridge: Cambridge University Press, 1994), 75, 76.
36. Ibid., 79.
37. David Grossman, 'On Hope and Despair in the Middle East', trans. Anne Harstein Pace, *Haaretz*, 8 July 2014. http://www.haaretz.com/on-hope-and-despair-1.5253853
38. Ibid.
39. Ibid.
40. Ibid.
41. Grossman, 'Individual Language and Mass Language', 85; 'Writing in the Dark', 62; Grossman, Interview with Jonathan Freedland, 8 Sept. 2010. Podcast. http://www.theguardian.com/books/audio/2010/sep/08/david-grossman-israel-lofty-idea-worth-fighting-for
42. Grossman, 'Introduction', *Death as a Way of Life*, viii–ix.
43. Ibid.,, x–xi.
44. Grossman, Interview with Freedland.
45. Grossman, Author's Note, *To the End of the Land*, 577.
46. Grossman, Interview with Freedland.
47. Grossman, Author's Note, *To the End of the Land*, 577.
48. Grossman, Interview with Freedland.
49. Jacqueline Rose, rev. of *To the End of the Land*, by David Grossman, *The Guardian*, 18 Sept. 2010. http://www.theguardian.com/books/2010/sep/18/david-grossman-end-of-the-land
50. Grossman, Interview with Freedland; Grossman, Interview by Rachel Cooke.
51. Grossman, Interview by Cooke.
52. Grossman, 'Writing in the Dark', 64.
53. Ibid., 64, 65.
54. Ibid., 67, 65.
55. Ibid., 65.
56. David Grossman, *Falling Out of Time*, trans. Jessica Cohen (London: Cape, 2014), 59. Hereafter cited parenthetically.
57. Grossman, 'Writing in the Dark', 85.
58. Coetzee, *Doubling the Point*, 250.
59. David Grossman, Interview with Natalie Haynes, Southbank Centre, London, 7 July 2018.
60. Grossman, 'On Hope and Despair in the Middle East'.

61. Mark Seltzer, 'The Official World', *Critical Inquiry*, 37.4 (Summer 2011), 727, 728.
62. Matthew L. Jockers, *Macroanalysis: Digital Methods and Literary History* (Urbana: University of Illinois Press, 2013), 9.

EPILOGUE

1. Boethius, *The Consolations of Philosophy*, trans. P. G. Walsh (Oxford: Oxford University Press, 2008), 4.
2. Sigmund Freud, 'Creative Writers and Day-Dreaming' (1908), *The Standard Edition of the Complete Works of Sigmund Freud*, vol. IX, trans. and ed. James Strachey with Anna Freud (1959; London: Vintage, 2001), 153. I'm grateful to Heather Love for pointing out the relevance here of Freud's notion of literary form as a bribe.
3. Ibid. 153.
4. Ibid. 153.
5. Ibid. 153.
6. Adorno, 'Commitment', 88.
7. Lennard J. Davis, *Resisting Novels: Ideology and Fiction* (New York: Methuen, 1987), 2, 5, 11.
8. Ibid., 2.
9. Ibid., 231.
10. See David James, 'The Novel as Encyclopedia', in *The Cambridge Companion to the Novel*, ed. Eric Bulson (New York: Cambridge University Press, 2018), 74–90; and Heather Houser, *Environmental Culture of the Infowhelm* (New York: Columbia University Press, 2020).
11. Davis, *Resisting Novels*, 22.
12. Kazuo Ishiguro, *Never Let Me Go*: 'First Rough Draft', Notebook: 'Clones' (2000–2001), MS-05377, 5.6. Ishiguro Papers.
13. Daniel Worden, 'The Memoir in the Age of Neoliberal Individualism', in *Neoliberalism and Contemporary Literary Culture*, ed. Mitchum Heuhls and Rachel Greenwald Smith (Baltimore, MD: Johns Hopkins University Press, 2017), 161.
14. Ibid., 164, 166.
15. Wendy Brown, *Undoing the Demos: Neoliberalism's Stealth Revolution* (Cambridge, MA: Zone Books, 2015), 13, 201.
16. Worden, 'The Memoir in the Age of Neoliberal Individualism', 167.
17. Derek Attridge, 'Literary Experience and the Value of Criticism', in *The Values of Literary Studies: Critical Institutions, Scholarly Agendas*, ed. Rónán McDonald (New York: Cambridge University Press, 2015), 251, 254.
18. Carolyn Lesjak, 'Reading Dialectically', *Criticism*, 55.2 (Spring 2013), 247.
19. Ibid., 249
20. Ibid., 247.
21. Berlant is recalling Eve Sedgwick's account of the critic who 'mistakes his act of negation for a performance of his seriousness', and in doing so 'elevates his thought by disclaiming anything that emanates a scent of therapy, reparation, or utopianism' (*Cruel Optimism*, 123). This foible shapes critiques of consolation that couple it with aesthetic redemption. Little room is left there for imagining a 'critical encounter', as Timothy Bewes shrewdly observes, that can acknowledge 'the notion of critical distance' as 'no longer' a 'given'; or indeed for perceiving how qualms about consolation might themselves be prone to 'a melancholic register of critical self-enclosure', whereby any 'undertaking' that seeks to read for the aesthetics of affective representation only

ever succeeds 'by reference to its limitations' ('Reading with the Grain: A New World in Literary Criticism', *differences*, 21.3 [Fall 2010], 2).
22. Best and Marcus, 'Surface Reading', 17.
23. Ibid., 17.
24. Denise Riley, 'A Part Song', *Say Something Back* (London: Picador, 2016), 8.
25. Jenefer Robinson, *Deeper than Reason: Emotion and Its Role in Literature, Music, and Art* (Oxford: Oxford University Press, 2005), 207 (emphases removed).
26. Riley, 'And Another Thing', *Say Something Back*, 37.
27. Riley, 'Listening for Lost People', *Say Something Back*, 34
28. Denise Riley, *Time Lived, Without Its Flow* (London: Capsule Editions, 2012), 8. Hereafter cited parenthetically.
29. Roland Barthes, *A Lover's Discourse: Fragments*, trans. Richard Howard (London: Penguin, 1990), 100.
30. Joseph Conte, rev. of *Postmodern/Postwar–and After*, ed. Jason Gladstone, Andrew Hoberek, and Daniel Worden, *Twentieth-Century Literature*, 64.1 (March 2017), 126.
31. Lee Konstantinou points to the fact '[t]here's no critical consensus on what to call postmodernism's successor. Strong candidates include *globalisation, cosmodernism, metamodernism, altermodernism, digimodernism, performatism, postpositivist realism, the New Sincerity*, or, for more lexically austere analysts, *the contemporary*.' And he admits that such 'terms refer to as many domains as *postmodernism* itself once did: to a new form of socioeconomic organization, a new kind of style, a new configuration of affects, and a new relation of persons to the world, time, and experience' ('Periodizing the Present', *Contemporary Literature*, 54.2 [Summer 2013], 411).
32. Conte, rev. of *Postmodern/Postwar–and After*, 126 (Conte's emphasis). For a sobering survey of affect's multidisciplinary rise, see Ruth Leys's *The Ascent of Affect: Genealogy and Critique* (Chicago: University of Chicago Press, 2017). In literary studies, the use of affect to distinguish writers' recent aesthetic preoccupations still has a good deal of critical purchase in discussions of the contemporary. In describing metamodernism's emergence as a prominent 'structure of feeling' for postmillennial culture, Robin van den Akker and Timotheus Vermeulen prefer to align it not with any one 'stylistic register' but with a constellation of affects 'shot through with productive contradictions, simmering tensions' and 'constant oscillation' ('Periodising the 2000s, or, the Emergence of Metamodernism', in *Metamodernism: Historicity, Affect, and Depth after Postmodernism*, ed. Robin van den Akker, Alison Gibbons, and Timotheus Vermeulen [London: Rowman and Littlefield, 2017], 5–6).
33. Fredric Jameson, *Postmodernism, or, The Cultural Logic of Late Capitalism* (Durham, NC: Duke University Press, 1991), 16, 4, 16, 15.
34. Ibid., 17.
35. See especially Nicola Sayers, *The Promise of Nostalgia: Reminiscence, Longing, and Hope in Contemporary American Literature and Culture* (London: Routledge, 2020), and the interventions collected in Jason Gladstone, Andrew Hoberek, and Daniel Worden, eds, *Postmodern/Postwar–and After: Rethinking American Literature* (Iowa City, IA: University of Iowa Press, 2016).
36. Jean-François Lyotard, *The Postmodern Condition: A Report on Knowledge*, trans. Geoff Bennington and Brian Massumi (Manchester: Manchester University Press, 1986), 81.

Bibliography

Abel, Elizabeth. 'Spaces of Time: Virginia Woolf's Life-Writing', in *Modernism and Autobiography*, ed. Maria DiBattista and Emily O. Wittman. New York: Cambridge University Press, 2014. 55–66.
Aciman, André. 'Out of Novemberland', rev. of *The Rings of Saturn*, by W. G. Sebald, *New York Review of Books*, 3 Dec. 1998, n.pag. http://www.nybooks.com/articles/1998/12/03/out-of-novemberland/
Adorno, Theodor W. *Notes to Literature: Volume II*, trans. Rolf Tiedemann. New York: Columbia University Press, 1992.
Alleine, Joseph. *Remaines of that Excellent Minister of Jesus Christ, Mr Joseph Alleine. Being a Collection of Sundry Directions, Sermons, Sacrament-Speeches, and Letters, not Heretofore Published. All Tending to Promote Real Piety*. London: Peter Parker, 1674.
Anker, Elizabeth S., and Rita Felski. 'Introduction', in *Critique and Postcritique*, ed. Anker and Felski. Durham, NC: Duke University Press, 2017, 1–28.
Ariès, Philippe. *The Hour of Our Death*, trans. Helen Weaver. London: Allen Lane, 1981.
Armstrong, Nancy. 'The Affective Turn in Contemporary Fiction'. *Contemporary Literature*, 55.3 (Fall 2014): 441–65.
Armstrong, Paul B. *How Literature Plays with the Brain: The Neuroscience of Reading and Art*. Baltimore, MD: Johns Hopkins University Press, 2013.
Attridge, Derek. *J. M. Coetzee and the Ethics of Reading: Literature in the Event*. Chicago, IL: University of Chicago Press, 2004.
Attridge, Derek. *The Singularity of Literature*. London: Routledge, 2004.
Attridge, Derek. 'Literary Experience and the Value of Criticism', in *The Values of Literary Studies: Critical Institutions, Scholarly Agendas*, ed. Rónán McDonald. New York: Cambridge University Press, 2015. 249–62.
Attridge, Derek. *The Work of Literature*. Oxford: Oxford University Press, 2015.
Attwell, David. *J. M. Coetzee and the Life of Writing: Face to Face with Time*. Oxford: Oxford University Press, 2015.
Aubry, Timothy. *Reading as Therapy: What Contemporary Fiction Does for Middle-Class Americans*. Iowa City, IA: University of Iowa Press, 2011.
Bailey, Paul. 'Sex and Other Problems', rev. of *Disgrace*, by J. M. Coetzee, *The Independent*, 2 July 1999: http://www.independent.co.uk/arts-entertainment/books/features/sex-and-other-problems-743456.html
Bal, Mieke. 'Over-writing as Un-writing: Descriptions, World-Making, and Novelistic Time', in *A Mieke Bal Reader*. Chicago, IL: University of Chicago Press, 2006. 96–145.
Baranow, Joan, Brian Dolan, and David Watts, eds. *The Healing Art of Writing*. San Francisco, CA: UC Medical Humanities Consortium, 2011.
Barnes, Julian. *Nothing to Be Frightened Of*. London: Vintage, 2009.
Barnes, Julian. *Levels of Life*. London: Jonathan Cape, 2013.
Barthes, Roland. *A Lover's Discourse: Fragments*, trans. Richard Howard. London: Penguin, 1990.
Beckett, Samuel. *Company, Ill Seen Ill Said, Worstward Ho, Stirrings Still*, ed. Dirk Van Hulle. London: Faber & Faber, 2009.
Beer, Gillian. *Virginia Woolf: The Common Ground*. Edinburgh: Edinburgh University Press, 1996.

Berlant, Lauren. *Cruel Optimism*. Durham, NC: Duke University Press, 2011.
Berlant, Lauren. 'Structures of Unfeeling: *Mysterious Skin*', *International Journal of Politics, Culture, and Society*, 28 (2015): 191–213.
Berman, Jessica. *Modernist Commitments: Ethics, Politics, and Transnational Modernism*. New York: Columbia University Press, 2011.
Bersani, Leo. *The Culture of Redemption*. Cambridge, MA: Harvard University Press, 1990.
Best, Stephen, and Sharon Marcus. 'Surface Reading: An Introduction', *Representations*, 108.1 (Fall 2009): 1–21.
Bewes, Timothy. 'Reading with the Grain: A New World in Literary Criticism', *differences*, 21.3 (Fall 2010): 1–33.
Bewes, Timothy. *The Event of Postcolonial Shame*. Princeton, NJ: Princeton University Press, 2011.
Bewes, Timothy. 'Against Exemplarity: W. G. Sebald and the Problem of Connection', *Contemporary Literature*, 55.1 (Spring 2014): 1–31.
Blanton, C. D. 'Abstract in Concrete: Brutalism and the Modernist Half-Life', in *The Contemporaneity of Modernism: Literature, Media, Culture*, ed. Michael D'Arcy and Mathias Nilges. New York: Routledge, 2016. 17–30.
Boehmer, Elleke. 'J. M. Coetzee's Australian Realism', in *Strong Opinions: J. M. Coetzee and the Authority of Contemporary Fiction*, ed. Chris Danta, Sue Kossewm, and Julien Murphet. London: Bloomsbury, 2013. 3–18.
Boethius, *The Consolations of Philosophy*, trans. P. G. Walsh. Oxford: Oxford University Press, 2008.
Boxall, Peter. *Twenty-First-Century Fiction: A Critical Introduction*. New York: Cambridge University Press, 2013.
Boxall, Peter. *The Value of the Novel*. New York: Cambridge University Press, 2015.
Brookner, Anita. 'A Morbid Procedure', rev. of *Atonement* by Ian McEwan, *Spectator*, 15 Sept. 2001. 44.
Brown, Judith. 'Style', in *A New Vocabulary for Global Modernism*, ed. Eric Hayot and Rebecca L. Walkowitz. New York: Columbia University Press, 2016. 214–32.
Brown, Wendy. *Undoing the Demos: Neoliberalism's Stealth Revolution*. Cambridge, MA: Zone Books, 2015.
Butler, Judith. 'Afterword: After Loss, What Then?', in *Loss: The Politics of Mourning*, ed. David L. Eng and David Kazanajian. Berkeley, CA: University of California Press, 2003. 467–74.
Caruth, Cathy. *Unclaimed Experience: Trauma, Narrative, and History*. Baltimore, MD: Johns Hopkins University Press, 1996.
Cavell, Stanley. *Must We Mean What We Say?* 2nd edn. Cambridge: Cambridge University Press, 2002.
Chabon, Michael. *Maps and Legends: Reading and Writing Along the Boderlands*. New York: Harper Perennial, 2009.
Chidester, David. *Wild Religion: Tracking the Sacred in South Africa*. Berkeley, CA: University of California Press, 2012.
Chodat, Robert. 'That Horeb, That Kansas: Evolution and the Modernity of Marilynne Robinson', *American Literary History*, 28.2 (Summer 2016): 328–61.
Clarkson, Carrol. *J. M. Coetzee: Countervoices*. Basingstoke: Palgrave, 2009.
Clewell, Tammy. 'Consolation Refused: Virginia Woolf, The Great War, and Modernist Mourning', *Modern Fiction Studies*, 50.1 (Spring 2004): 197–223.
Coetzee, J. M. *Doubling the Point: Essays and Interviews*, ed. David Attwell. Cambridge, MA: Harvard University Press, 1992.

Coetzee, J. M. *Age of Iron*. 1990; London: Penguin, 1998.
Coetzee, J. M. *Disgrace*. 1999; London: Vintage, 2000.
Coetzee, J. M. J. M. Coetzee Papers. Harry Ransom Center, University of Texas at Austin.
Connolly, Cyril. *Enemies of Promise*, rev. edn. London: Deutsch, 1988.
Conrad, Joseph. *A Personal Record*, ed. Zdzisław Najder and J. H. Stape. Cambridge: Cambridge University Press, 2008.
Constantine, David. *Poetry*. Oxford: Oxford University Press, 2013.
Conte, Joseph. Rev. of *Postmodern/Postwar–and After*, ed. Jason Gladstone, Andrew Hoberek, and Daniel Worden, *Twentieth-Century Literature*, 64.1 (March 2017): 120–7.
Cormack, Alistair. 'Postmodernism and the Ethics of Fiction in *Atonement*', in *Ian McEwan: Contemporary Critical Perspectives*, ed. Sebastian Groes. London: Continuum, 2009. 70–82.
Crosby, Christina. *A Body, Undone: Living On After Great Pain*. New York: New York University Press, 2016.
Currie, Janette. 'Walking and Manning'. *Times Literary Supplement*, 31 October 2014. 8.
Cvetkovich, Ann. *Depression: A Public Feeling*. Durham, NC: Duke University Press, 2012.
Davis, Leonard J. *Resisting Novels: Ideology and Fiction*. New York: Methuen, 1987.
Denby, David J. *Sentimental Narrative and the Social Order in France, 1760–1820*. Cambridge: Cambridge University Press, 1994.
Deraniyagala, Sonali. 'A Better Quality of Agony', interview by Jeannie Macfarlane, *Hazlitt*, 2 April 2013: http://www.hazlitt.net/feature/better-quality-agony
Deraniyagala, Sonali. Interview with *Indigo*, 15 March 2013: http://www.youtube.com/watch?v=aX_bb_-2uEs
Deraniyagala, Sonali. *Wave*. London: Virago, 2013.
Dickinson, Emily. *The Complete Poems*, ed. Thomas H. Johnson. London: Faber and Faber, 2016.
Didion, Joan. *The White Album*. New York: Simon and Schuster, 1979.
Didion, Joan. Interview by Emma Brockes, *The Guardian*, Friday 16 December 2005. https://www.theguardian.com/film/2005/dec/16/biography.features
Didion, Joan. 'The Art of Nonfiction, No. 1', interview by Hilton Als, *The Paris Review*, 48.176 (Spring 2006). 59–86.
Didion, Joan. *The Year of Magical Thinking*. 2005; London: Fourth Estate, 2009.
Didion, Joan. *Blue Nights*. London: Fourth Estate, 2011.
Dyer, Geoff. 'Who's Afraid of Influence?', rev. of *Atonement*, by Ian McEwan, *The Guardian*, 22 Sept. 2001. https://www.theguardian.com/books/2001/sep/22/fiction.ianmcewan
Eaglestone, Robert. *The Broken Voice: Reading Post-Holocaust Literature*. Oxford: Oxford University Press, 2017.
Ellis, Steve. *Virginia Woolf and the Victorians*. Cambridge: Cambridge University Press, 2007.
Ellis-Peterson, Hannah. 'Helen Macdonald's "Extraordinary" Memoir Wins Samuel Johnson Prize', *The Guardian*, Tuesday 4 November 2014. http://www.theguardian.com/books/2014/nov/04/samuel-johnson-prize-helen-macdonald-h-is-for-hawk
Enright, Anne. *The Gathering*. 2007; London: Vintage, 2008.
Felski, Rita. 'Introduction', *New Literary History*, 45.2 (2014): v–xi.
Felski, Rita. *The Limits of Critique*. Chicago, IL: University of Chicago Press, 2015.
Finney, Brian. 'Briony's Stand against Oblivion: Ian McEwan's *Atonement*', *Journal of Modern Literature* 27.3 (Winter 2004): 68–82.
Flatley, Jonathan. *Affective Mapping: Melancholia and the Politics of Modernism*. Cambridge, MA: Harvard University Press, 2008.
Flaubert, Gustave. *The Letters of Gustave Flaubert, Volumes 1 & II: 1830–1880*, ed. and trans. Francis Steegmuller. London: Picador, 2001.

Fleissner, Jennifer L. 'Romancing the Real: Bruno Latour, Ian McEwan, and Postcritical Monism', in *Critique and Postcritique*, 99–126.

Franklin, Ruth. *A Thousand Darknesses: Lies and Truth in Holocaust Fiction*. Oxford: Oxford University Press, 2011.

Freud, Sigmund. *Letters of Sigmund Freud*, ed. Ernst L. Freud, trans. Tania and James Stern. London: Hogarth, 1961.

Freud, Sigmund. *The Standard Edition of the Complete Works of Sigmund Freud*, vol. IX, trans. and ed. James Strachey with Anna Freud. London: Vintage, 2001.

Gardner, Thomas. *A Door Ajar: Contemporary Writers and Emily Dickinson*. New York: Oxford University Press, 2006.

Gasiorek, Andrzej. 'Rendering Justice to the Visible World: History, Politics, and National Identity in the Novels of Graham Greene', in *British Fiction after Modernism: The Novel at Mid-Century*, ed. Marina MacKay and Lindsey Stonebridge. Basingstoke: Palgrave, 2007. 17–32.

Gawande, Atul. *Being Mortal: Illness, Medicine, and What Matters in the End*. London: Profile, 2014.

Gilbert, Sandra M. Rev. of *The Year of Magical Thinking*, by Joan Didion, *Literature and Medicine*, 25.2 (Fall 2006): 553–7.

Gladstone, Jason, Andrew Hoberek, and Daniel Worden, eds. *Postmodern/Postwar–and After: Rethinking American Literature*. Iowa City, IA: University of Iowa Press, 2016.

GoGwilt, Christopher. *The Passage of Literature: Genealogies of Modernism in Conrad, Rhys, and Pramoedya*. Oxford: Oxford University Press, 2011.

Grant, Linda. Rev. of *To the End of the Land*, by David Grossman, *The Independent*, 27 August 2010. https://www.independent.co.uk/arts-entertainment/books/reviews/to-the-end-of-the-land-by-david-grossman-trans-jessica-cohen-2063011.html.

Gray, Richard. *After the Fall: American Literature since 9/11*. Oxford: Wiley-Blackwell, 2011.

Groes, Sebastian, and Sean Matthews, eds. *Kazuo Ishiguro: Contemporary Critical Perspectives*. London: Continuum, 2009.

Grossman, David. *Death as a Way of Life: Dispatches from Jerusalem*, trans. Haim Watzman. London: Bloomsbury, 2003.

Grossman, David. *Writing in the Dark: Essays on Literature and Politics*, trans. Jessica Cohen. London: Bloomsbury, 2008.

Grossman, David. Interview by Rachel Cooke, *The Observer*, 29 August 2010. http://www.theguardian.com/books/2010/aug/29/david-grossman-israel-hezbollah-interview

Grossman, David. Interview by Jonathan Freedland, *The Guardian*, podcast, 8 September 2010. http://www.theguardian.com/books/audio/2010/sep/08/david-grossman-israel-lofty-idea-worth-fighting-for

Grossman, David. Interview by Ethan Bronner, *The New York Times*, 16 Nov. 2010. http://www.nytimes.com/2010/11/17/books/17grossman.html

Grossman, David. *To the End of the Land*, trans. Jessica Cohen. London: Cape, 2010.

Grossman, David. 'On Hope and Despair in the Middle East', trans. Anne Harstein Pace, *Haaretz*, 8 July 2014. http://www.haaretz.com/on-hope-and-despair-1.5253853

Grossman, David. *Falling Out of Time*, trans. Jessica Cohen. London: Cape, 2014.

Guignery, Vanessa, and Ryan Roberts, eds. *Conversations with Julian Barnes*. Jackson, MS: University of Mississippi Press, 2009.

Gurfinkel, Helena. 'Queer, Cosmopolitan', in *The Cambridge History of Gay and Lesbian Literature*, ed. E. L. McCallum and Mikko Tuhkanen. New York: Cambridge University Press, 2014. 402–18.

Hadley, Tessa. 'A Rare and Tremendous Achievement', rev. of *Nora Webster*, by Colm Tóibín, *The Guardian, Review*, Saturday 11 October http://www.theguardian.com/books/2014/oct/11/nora-webster-colm-toibin-review-rare-achievement).
Hale, Dorothy J. '*On Beauty* as Beautiful? The Problem of Novelistic Aesthetics by Way of Zadie Smith', *Contemporary Literature*, 53.4 (Winter 2012): 814–44.
Hamon, Philippe. 'Rhetorical Status of the Descriptive', trans. Patricia Baudoin, *Yale French Studies* 61 (1981): 1–26.
Harrison, Melissa. 'An Interview with Helen Macdonald', *Caught by the River*, 1 August 2014. http://www.caughtbytheriver.net/2014/08/28622-helen-macdonald-h-is-for-hawk-melissa-harrison/
Hart. D. G. *Calvinism: A History*. New Haven, CT: Yale University Press, 2013.
Hart, Matthew and Tania Lown-Hecht, 'The Extraterritorial Poetics of W. G. Sebald', *Modern Fiction Studies*, 58.2 (Summer 2012): 214–38.
Harvey, David. *Justice, Nature and the Geography of Difference*. Oxford: Blackwell, 1996.
Hasak-Lowry, Todd. 'Grossman After 2000: An Ambivalent Complaint in Nine Parts', *Hebrew Studies*, 54 (2013): 299–309.
Head, Dominic. *J. M. Coetzee*. Cambridge: Cambridge University Press, 1997.
Head, Dominic. *Ian McEwan*. Manchester: Manchester University Press, 2007.
Heaney, Seamus. *The Redress of Poetry: Oxford Lectures*. London: Faber and Faber, 1995.
Heitsch, Dorothea B. 'Approaching Death by Writing: Montaigne's Essays and the Literature of Consolation', *Literature and Medicine*, 19.1 (Spring 2000), 96–106.
Hell, Julia. 'Eyes Wide Shut: German Post-Holocaust Authorship', *New German Critique*, 88 (2003): 9–36
Henke, Suzette A. *Shattered Subjects: Trauma and Testimony in Women's Life-Writing*. London: Macmillan, 1998.
Herman, Judith Lewis. *Trauma and Recovery: From Domestic Abuse to Political Terror*. London: Pandora, 1994.
Hewitt, Rachel. *A Revolution of Feeling: The Decade that Forged the Modern Mind*. London: Granta, 2017.
Hoberek, Andrew. 'Cormac McCarthy and the Aesthetics of Exhaustion', *American Literary History*, 23.3 (Fall 2011): 483–99.
Holloway, Paul A. *Consolation in Philippians: Philosophical Sources and Rhetorical Strategy*. Cambridge: Cambridge University Press, 2001.
Hong, Cathy Park. 'Delusions of Whiteness in the Avant-Garde', *Lana Turner: A Journal of Poetry and Opinion* 7 (Nov. 2014): https://arcade.stanford.edu/content/delusions-whiteness-avant-garde
Houser, Heather. *Environmental Culture of the Infowhelm*. New York: Columbia University Press, 2020.
Hungerford, Amy. *Postmodern Belief: American Literature and Religion since 1960*. Princeton, NJ: Princeton University Press, 2010.
Ibbett, Katherine. '"When I do, I call it Affect"', *Paragraph*, 40.2 (2017): 244–53.
Ibbett, Katherine. *Compassion's Edge: Fellow-Feeling and Its Limits in Early Modern France*. Philadelphia, PA: University of Pennsylvania Press, 2018.
Ingersoll, Earl G. *Putting the Questions Differently: Interviews with Doris Lessing, 1964–1994*. London: Flamingo, 1996.
Ishiguro, Kazuo. *The Unconsoled*. London: Faber and Faber, 1995.
Ishiguro, Kazuo. *Never Let Me Go*. London: Faber and Faber, 2005.
Ishiguro, Kazuo. Kazuo Ishiguro Papers, Harry Ransom Center, University of Texas at Austin.

Jacobs, Carol. *Sebald's Vision*. New York: Columbia University Press, 2015.
James, Caryn. 'They May Not Mean to, But They Do', Rev. of *Alfred and Emily*, by Doris Lessing, *New York Times*, 10 August 2008. https://www.nytimes.com/2008/08/10/books/review/James-t.html
James, David. *Modernist Futures: Innovation and Inheritance in the Contemporary Novel*. New York: Cambridge University Press, 2012.
James, David. 'The Novel as Encyclopedia', in *The Cambridge Companion to the Novel*, ed. Eric Bulson. New York: Cambridge University Press, 2018. 74–90.
Jameson, Fredric. *The Political Unconscious: Narrative as a Socially Symbolic Act*. London: Methuen, 1981.
Jameson, Fredric. *Postmodernism, or, The Cultural Logic of Late Capitalism*. Durham, NC: Duke University Press, 1991.
Jameson, Fredric. 'In Hyperspace'. *London Review of Books*, 10 September 2015. 17–22.
Jockers, Matthew L. *Macroanalysis: Digital Methods and Literary History*. Urbana, IL: University of Illinois Press, 2013.
Johnson, Samuel. *A Dictionary of the English Language*, corrected and revised edn. London: Thomas Tegg, 1822.
Jordan, Julia. '"For Recuperation": Elegy, Form, and the Aleatory in B. S. Johnson's *The Unfortunates*', *Textual Practice*, 28.5 (2014): 745–61.
Joyce, James. *Letters of James Joyce*, vol. II, ed. Richard Ellmann. London: Faber & Faber, 1966.
Kannemeyer, J. C. *J. M. Coetzee: A Life in Writing*, trans. Michiel Heyns. Victoria: Scribe, 2012.
Kelly, Henry Ansgar. *Ideas and Forms of Tragedy from Aristotle to the Middle Ages*. Cambridge: Cambridge University Press, 1993.
Kennedy, David. *Elegy*. London: Routledge, 2007.
Kermode, Frank. *The Sense of an Ending*. Oxford: Oxford University Press, 2000.
Kermode, Frank. 'The Daughter Who Hated Her', rev. of *Alfred and Emily*, by Doris Lessing. *London Review of Books*, 17 July 2008. https://www.lrb.co.uk/v30/n14/frank-kermode/the-daughter-who-hated-her
Kinghorn, Johann. 'Modernization and Apartheid: The Afrikaner Churches', in *Christianity in South Africa: A Political, Social and Cultural History*, ed. Richard Elphick and Rodney Davenpor. Cape Town: David Philip, 1997. 135–54.
Konstantinou, Lee. 'Periodizing the Present'. *Contemporary Literature*, 54.2 (Summer 2013): 411–23.
Kornbluh, Anna. 'We Have Never Been Critical: Toward the Novel as Critique', *Novel*, 50.3 (November 2017): 397–408.
Kübler-Ross, Elisabeth, ed. *Death: The Final Stage of Life*. New York: Simon and Schuster, 1975.
LaCapra, Dominick. *Writing History, Writing Trauma*. Baltimore, MD: Johns Hopkins University Press, 2001.
Lazarus, Neil. *The Postcolonial Unconscious*. Cambridge: Cambridge University Press, 2011.
Lee, Hermione. 'If Your Memories Serve You Well', *The Observer*, 23 Sept. 2001. https://www.theguardian.com/books/2001/sep/23/fiction.bookerprize2001
Leighton, Angela. *On Form: Poetry, Aestheticism, and the Legacy of a Word*. Oxford: Oxford University Press, 2007.
Leigla, Catherine E., and Stephen J. Milner, eds. *The Erotics of Consolation: Desire and Distance in the Late Middle Ages*. Basingstoke: Palgrave, 2008.
LeMahieu, Michael. 'The Novel of Ideas', in *The Cambridge Companion to British Fiction since 1945*, ed. David James. New York: Cambridge University Press, 2015. 177–91.

Lesjak, Carolyn. 'Reading Dialectically', *Criticism*, 55.2 (2013): 233–77.
Lessing, Doris. *A Small Personal Voice: Essays, Reviews, Interviews*. London: Fontana, 1994.
Lessing, Doris. *Alfred and Emily*. London: Fourth Estate, 2008.
Levine, Caroline. *Forms: Whole, Rhythm, Hierarchy, Network*. Princeton, NJ: Princeton University Press, 2015.
Leviston, Frances. 'Mothers and Marimbas in "The Bight": Bishop's *Danse Macabre*', *Twentieth-Century Literature*, 61.4 (December 2015): 436–59.
Lewis, C. S. *A Grief Observed*. London: Faber and Faber, 2013.
Lewis, C. S. *A Grief Observed: Reader's Edition*. London: Faber and Faber, 2015.
Leypoldt, Günter. 'Degrees of Public Relevance: Walter Scott and Toni Morrison', *Modern Language Quarterly*, 77.3 (September 2016): 369–93.
Leys, Ruth. *The Ascent of Affect: Genealogy and Critique*. Chicago, IL: University of Chicago Press, 2017.
Long, J. J., and Anne Whitehead, eds. *W. G. Sebald: A Critical Companion*. Edinburgh: Edinburgh University Press, 2004.
Love, Heather. *Feeling Backward: Loss and the Politics of Queer History*. Cambridge, MA: Harvard University Press, 2007.
Love, Heather. 'Truth and Consequences: On Paranoid Reading and Reparative Reading', *Criticism*, 52.2 (Spring 2010): 237–8.
Love, Heather. 'Close Reading and Thin Description', *Public Culture*, 25.3 (Fall 2013): 401–34.
Lowry, Elizabeth. 'No Passion in an Ascetic Allegory', rev. of *The Schooldays of Jesus*, by J. M. Coetzee, The Guardian, 18 August 2016: https://www.theguardian.com/books/2016/aug/18/the-schooldays-of-jesus-jm-coetzee-review
Luckhurst, Roger. *The Trauma Question*. London: Routledge, 2008.
Lukács, Georg. *Writer and Critic, and other Essays*, ed. and trans. Arthur Kahn. London: Merlin, 1970.
Lyotard, Jean-François. *The Postmodern Condition: A Report on Knowledge*, trans. Geoff Bennington and Brian Massumi. Manchester: Manchester University Press, 1986.
Macdonald, Helen. *H is for Hawk*. London: Cape, 2014.
Marcus, Laura. 'Ian McEwan's Modernist Time: *Atonement* and *Saturday*', in *Ian McEwan*. 83–98.
Marcus, Sharon, Heather Love, and Stephen Best. 'Building a Better Description', *Representations*, 135.1 (Summer 2016): 1–21.
Marcuse, Herbert. *Negations: Essays in Critical Theory*, trans. Jeremy J. Shapiro. London: Free Association, 1988.
Mariotti, Shannon and Joseph H. Lane Jr, eds. *A Political Companion to Marilynne Robinson*. Lexington, KY: University Press of Kentucky, 2016.
Mason, Wyatt. 'The Revelations of Marilynne Robinson', *New York Times, Magazine*, 1 October 2014. https://www.nytimes.com/2014/10/05/magazine/the-revelations-of-marilynne-robinson.html
Matz, Jesse. 'Pseudo-Impressionism?', in *The Legacies of Modernism: Historicising Postwar and Contemporary Fiction*, ed. David James. Cambridge: Cambridge University Press, 2012. 114–32.
Matz, Jesse. *Lasting Impressions: The Legacies of Impressionism in Contemporary Culture*. New York: Columbia University Press, 2017.
McAlpin, Heller. Rev. of *Alfred and Emily* by Doris Lessing, *LA Times*, 27 July 2008. www.latimes.com/style/la-bk-lessing27-2008jul27-story.html
McClure, George W. *Sorrow and Consolation in Italian Humanism*. Princeton, NJ: Princeton University Press, 1991.

McCann, Colum. *Letters to a Young Writer: Some Practical and Philosophical Advice*. London: Bloomsbury, 2018. Ebook.

McCarthy, Cormac. *The Road*. New York: Knopf, 2006.

McCulloch, Mark. 'Introduction: Two Languages, Two Audiences: The Tandem Literary Oeuvres of W. G. Sebald', in *W. G. Sebald: History–Memory–Trauma*, ed. Scott Denham and Mark McCulloch. Berlin: Walter de Gruyter, 2006. 7–20.

McDonald, Peter D. 'Coetzee's Critique of Language', in *Beyond the Ancient Quarrel: Literature, Philosophy, and J. M. Coetzee*, ed. Patrick Hayes and Jan Wilm. Oxford: Oxford University Press, 2018. 160–79.

McDonald, Rónán. 'After Suspicion: Surface, Method, Value', in *The Values of Literary Studies*. 235–48.

McEwan, Ian. *Atonement*. London: Cape, 2001.

McEwan, Ian. Interview with Daniel Zalewski, 'The Background Hum: Ian McEwan's Art of Unease', *The New Yorker*, 23 Feb. 2009.

McEwan, Ian. 'When I Stop Believing in Fiction', *The New Republic*, 15 Feb. 2013: https://newrepublic.com/article/112374/ian-mcewan-my-uneasy-relationship-fiction

McEwan, Ian. Ian McEwan Papers. Harry Ransom Center, University of Texas at Austin.

McLoughlin, Kate. *Authoring War: The Literary Representation of War from the Illiad to Iraq*. Cambridge: Cambridge University Press, 2011.

Messud, Claire. Rev. of *All at Sea*, by Decca Aitkenhead, *The Guardian, Review*, 7 May 2016, 7.

Middleton, Peter. 'Epistemological Respect', *Textual Practice* 30.7 (2016): 1182.

Milner, Iris. 'Sacrifice and Redemption in *To the End of the Land*', *Hebrew Studies*, 54 (2013): 319–14.

Miller, Tyrus. *Late Modernism: Politics, Fiction, and the Arts between the World Wars*. Berkeley, CA: University of California Press, 1999.

Mintz, Alan. 'Ora's Tale: The Narrative Ambitions of David Grossman's *To the End of the Land*', *Hebrew Studies*, 54 (2013): 335–44.

Montaigne, Michel de. *The Complete Essays*, trans. M. A. Screech. London: Penguin, 2003.

Moore, Caroline. 'Doris Lessing's Writing of Her Parents' Past', *The Telegraph*, 15 May 2008. https://www.telegraph.co.uk/culture/books/fictionreviews/3673291/Doris-Lessings-rewriting-of-her-parents-past.html

Morrison, Blake. 'The Righting of Lives', *The Guardian, Review*, Saturday 17 May 2008. https://www.theguardian.com/books/2008/may/17/fiction.dorislessing

Morse, Janice M. 'On Comfort and Comforting', *American Journal of Nursing*, 100.9 (2000): 34–8.

Morse, Janice M., Joan L. Bottorff, and Sally Hutchinson, 'The Phenomenology of Comfort', *Journal of Advanced Nursing*, 20.1 (1994): 189–95.

Moss, Stephen. 'A Bird's Eye View of Love and Loss', Interview with Helen Macdonald, *The Guardian*, Wednesday 5 November 2014. http://www.theguardian.com/books/2014/nov/05/helen-macdonald-interview-winner-samuel-johnson-prize-falconry

Mullaney, Steven. *The Reformation of Emotions in the Age of Shakespeare*. Chicago, IL: University of Chicago Press, 2015.

Murdoch, Iris. 'Against Dryness: A Polemical Sketch', *Encounter* (January 1961): 16–20.

Murdoch, Iris. *Existentialists and Mystics: Writings on Philosophy and Literature*, ed. Peter Conradi. New York: Penguin, 1999.

Nabokov, Vladimir. *Speak, Memory: An Autobiography Revisited*. London: David Campbell, 1999.

Nealon, Christopher. 'The Price of Value', in *The Values of Literary Studies*. 91–104.

Neill, Michael. '"The Language of the Heart": Confession, Metaphor and Grace in J. M. Coetzee's *Age of Iron*', in *J. M. Coetzee's Austerities*, ed. Graham Bradshaw and Michael Neill. Burlington, VA: Ashgate, 2010. 79–106.

Nelson, Deborah. *Tough Enough: Arbus, Arendt, Didion, McCarthy, Sontag, Weil*. Chicago, IL: University of Chicago Press, 2017.

Neuman, Justin. *Fiction beyond Secularism*. Evanston, IL: Northwestern University Press, 2014.

Ngai, Sianne. *Ugly Feelings*. Cambridge, MA: Harvard University Press, 2005.

Noakes, Jonathan, and Margaret Reynolds, *Ian McEwan: The Essential Guide: Child in Time, Enduring Love, Atonement*. London: Vintage, 2002.

Norberg, Astrid, Monica Bergsten, and Berit Lundman, 'A Model of Consolation', *Nursing Ethics*, 8.6 (2001): 544–53.

O'Connell, Mark. 'The First Church of Marilynne Robinson', *The New Yorker*, 30 May 2012. https://www.newyorker.com/books/page-turner/the-first-church-of-marilynne-robinson

Parks, Tim. *The Novel: A Survival Skill*. Oxford: Oxford University Press, 2015.

Parks, Tim. 'In Some Sense True'. *London Review of Books*, 21 January 2016. 25–8.

Pennebaker, James W. 'Telling Stories: The Health Benefits of Narrative', *Literature and Medicine*, 19.1 (2000): 3–18.

Persson, Torleif. 'Impersonal Style and the Form of Experience in W. G. Sebald's *The Rings of Saturn*', *Studies in the Novel*, 48.2 (Summer 2016): 205–22.

Phillips, Adam. *On Flirtation*. London: Faber, 1994.

Plotz, John. 'Feeling Like a Stoic: Doris Lessing's Experimental Fiction', *Public Books*, 7 August 2012. http://www.publicbooks.org/feeling-like-a-stoic-doris-lessings-experimental-fiction/

Poyner, Jane. 'J. M. Coetzee in Conversation', in *J. M. Coetzee and the Idea of the Public Intellectual*, ed. Jane Poyner. Columbus, OH: Ohio University Press, 2006. 21–4.

Preston, Alex. Rev. of *The Underground Railroad*, by Colson Whitehead, *The Guardian*, 9 October 2016: https://www.theguardian.com/books/2016/oct/09/the-underground-railroad-colson-whitehead-revie-luminous-furious-wildly-inventive

Ramazani, Jahan. *Poetry of Mourning: The Modern Elegy from Hardy to Heaney*. Chicago, IL: University of Chicago Press, 1994.

Rasmussen, Birgit H., Lilian Jansson, and Astrid Norberg, 'Striving for Becoming At-Home in the Midst of Dying', *American Journal of Hospice and Palliative Care*, 17.1 (2000): 31–43.

Reddy, William M. *The Navigation of Feeling: A Framework for the History of Emotions*. Cambridge: Cambridge University Press, 2001.

Reynolds, Paige. 'Trauma, Intimacy, and Modernist Form', *breac*, 11 Sept. 2014: https://breac.nd.edu/articles/trauma-intimacy-and-modernist-form/

Ricoeur, Paul. *Oneself as Another*, trans. Kathleen Blamey. Chicago, IL: University of Chicago Press, 1992.

Riley, Denise. *Time Lived, Without Its Flow*. London: Capsule Editions, 2012.

Riley, Denise. *Say Something Back*. London: Picador, 2016.

Riquelme, John Paul, 'Modernist Transformations of Life Narrative: From Wilde and Woolf to Bechdel and Rushdie', *Modern Fiction Studies*, 59.3 (Fall 2013): 461–79.

Rittgers, Ronald K. *The Reformation of Suffering: Pastoral Theology and Lay Piety in Late Medieval and Early Modern Germany*. Oxford: Oxford University Press, 2012.

Robbins, Bruce. *Upward Mobility and the Common Good: Toward a Literary History of the Welfare State*. Princeton, NJ: Princeton University Press, 2007.

Robinson, Jenefer. *Deeper than Reason: Emotion and Its Role in Literature, Music, and Art*. Oxford: Oxford University Press, 2005.

Robinson, Marilynne. *The Death of Adam*. London: Picador, 1998.

Robinson, Marilynne. *Gilead*. 2004; London: Virago, 2006.
Robinson, Marilynne. *Home*. 2008; London: Virago, 2009.
Robinson, Marilynne. 'The Art of Fiction No. 198', *The Paris Review*, 186 (Fall 2008). https://www.theparisreview.org/interviews/5863/marilynne-robinson-the-art-of-fiction-no-198-marilynne-robinson
Robinson, Marilynne. *Absence of Mind: The Dispelling of Inwardness from the Modern Myth of the Self*. New Haven, CT: Yale University Press, 2010.
Robinson, Marilynne. *When I was a Child I Read Books*. London: Virago, 2012.
Robinson, Marilynne. *Lila*. London: Virago, 2014.
Robinson, Marilynne. *The Givenness of Things*. London: Virago, 2015.
Robinson, Marilynne. *What Are We Doing Here? Essays*. London: Virago, 2018.
Rooney, Ellen. 'Form and Contentment', in *Reading for Form*, ed. Susan J. Wolfson and Marshall Brown. Seattle, CA: University of Washington Press, 2006. 25–48.
Rose, Jacqueline. 'Failed State', *London Review of Books*, 18 March 2004: http://www.lrb.co.uk/v26/n06/jacqueline-rose/failed-state
Rose, Jacqueline. Rev. of *To the End of the Land*, by David Grossman, *The Guardian*, 18 Sept. 2010. http://www.theguardian.com/books/2010/sep/18/david-grossman-end-of-the-land
Rosenwein, Barbara H. 'Theories of Change in the History of Emotions', in *A History of Emotions, 1200–1800*, ed. Jonas Liliequist. London: Pickering and Chatto, 2012. 7–20.
Roth, Michael S. *Memory, Trauma, and History: Essays on Living with the Past*. New York: Columbia University Press, 2012.
Roxberg, Åsa, Katie Eriksson, Arne Rehnsfeldt, and Bengt Fridlund, 'The Meaning of Consolation as Experienced by Nurses in a Home-Care Setting', *Journal of Clinical Nursing*, 17.8 (2008): 1079–87.
Rushdie, Salman. *Imaginary Homelands: Essays and Criticism 1981–91*. London: Granta, 1992.
Said, Edward. *Culture and Imperialism*. New York: Knopf, 1993.
Sayers, Nicola. *The Promise of Nostalgia: Reminiscence, Longing, and Hope in Contemporary American Literature and Culture*. London: Routledge, 2019.
Schmitt, Cannon. 'Interpret or Describe?', *Representations*, 135.1 (Summer 2016): 102–18.
Schor, Esther. *Bearing the Dead: The British Culture of Mourning from the Enlightenment to Victoria*. Princeton, NJ: Princeton University Press, 1994.
Scott, A. O. 'A Writer Who Defied Categorization', *The New York Times*, 8 May 2012. http://www.nytimes.com/2012/05/09/movies/patience-after-sebald-a-documentary.html
Sebald, W. G. *Die Beschreibung des Unglücks: zur österreichischen Literatur von Stifter bis Handke*. Frankfurt: Fischer Taschenbuch Verlag, 1994.
Sebald, W. G. *On the Natural History of Destruction*, trans. Anthea Bell. London: Hamish Hamilton, 2003.
Sebald, W. G. *Campo Santo*, trans. Anthea Bell. London: Hamish Hamilton, 2005.
Sebald, W. G. *Austerlitz*, trans. Anthea Bell. 2001; London: Penguin, 2011.
Sebald, W. G. *The Rings of Saturn*. Trans. Michael Hulse. London Vintage, 2013.
Schaub, Thomas. 'Interview with Marilynne Robinson'. *Contemporary Literature*, 35.2 (Summer 1994): 231–51.
Sedgwick, Eve Kosofsky. *Touching Feeling: Affect, Pedagogy, Performativity*. Durham, NC: Duke University Press, 2003.
Seltzer, Mark. 'The Official World', *Critical Inquiry*, 37.4 (Summer 2011): 724–53.
Seshagiri, Urmila. *Race and the Modernist Imagination*. Ithaca, NY: Cornell University Press, 2009.

Shaffer, Brian W., and Cynthia F. Wong, eds. *Conversations with Kazuo Ishiguro*. Jackson, MS: University Press of Mississippi, 2008.
Shields, Carol. *Unless*. 2002; London: Fourth Estate, 2003.
Smith, Ali. *Artful*. London: Penguin, 2014.
Sontag, Susan. *Against Interpretation*. London: Vintage, 1994.
Southgate, Beverley. *Postmodernism in History: Fear or Freedom?* London: Routledge, 2003.
Spivak, Gayatri Chakravorty. 'Lie Down in the Karoo: An Antidote to the Anthropocene', rev. of *The Childhood of Jesus*, by J. M. Coetzee, *Public Books*, 1 June 2014: http://www.publicbooks.org/lie-down-in-the-karoo-an-antidote-to-the-anthropocene/.
Sutton, Isabel. 'Sebald's Apocalyptic Vision: The World Will End in 2013', *New Statesman*, 4 June 2013. http://www.newstatesman.com/culture/2013/06/w-g-sebalds-apocalyptic-vision-world-will-end-2013
Swift, Graham. *England and Other Stories*. London: Simon & Schuster, 2014.
Sykes, Rachel. *The Quiet Contemporary American Novel*. Manchester: Manchester University Press, 2017.
Tanner, Laura E. '"Looking Back from the Grave": Sensory Perception and the Anticipation of Absence in Marilynne Robinson's *Gilead*', *Contemporary Literature*, 48.2 (Summer 2007): 227–52.
Terada, Rei. *Feeling in Theory: Emotion after the 'Death of the Subject'*. Cambridge, MA: Harvard University Press, 2001.
Thurschwell, Pamela. *Literature, Technology and Magical Thinking, 1880–1920*. Cambridge: Cambridge University Press, 2001.
Tóibín, Colm. Tóibín, Rev. of *To the End of the Land*, by David Grossman, *New York Times Book Review*, 115.39 (2010): http://www.nytimes.com/2010/09/26/books/review/Toibin-t.html.
Tóibín, Colm. 'A Grief Observed', *The Guardian, Review*, Saturday 4 October 2014, 20.
Tóibín, Colm. *Nora Webster*. London: Viking, 2014.
Tóibín, Colm. *On Elizabeth Bishop*. Princeton, NJ: Princeton University Press, 2015.
Tóibín, Colm. 'How I Wrote *Nora Webster*', *The Guardian, Review*, 23 January 2016, 7.
Tomlinson, Philip. 'Thomas Hardy, Born June 2, 1840. "The Dynasts", the Book of the Moment. Poetical History with the Force of a Prophecy', *Times Literary Supplement*, Issue 2000 (1 June 1940). 266–70.
Travisano, Thomas with Saskia Hamilton, eds. *Words in Air: The Complete Correspondence between Elizabeth Bishop and Robert Lowell*. London: Faber and Faber, 2008.
Treat, John Whittier. *Writing Ground Zero: Japanese Literature and the Atomic Bomb*. Chicago, IL: University of Chicago Press, 1995.
Tutton, Elizabeth, and Kate Seers, 'An Exploration of the Concept of Comfort', *Journal of Clinical Nursing*, 12 (2003): 689–96.
van den Akker, Robin, and Timotheus Vermeulen, 'Periodising the 2000s, or, the Emergence of Metamodernism', in *Metamodernism: Historicity, Affect, and Depth after Postmodernism*, ed. van den Akker, Alison Gibbons, and Vermeulen. London: Rowman and Littlefield, 2017. 1–20.
van der Vlies, Andrew. '"[From] Whom This Writing Then?" Politics, Aesthetics, and the Personal in Coetzee's *Age of Iron*', in *Approaches to Teaching Coetzee's* Disgrace *and Other Works*, ed. Laura Wright, Elleke Boehmer, Jane Poyner. New York: MLA, 2014. 96–104.
van der Vlies, Andrew. *Present Imperfect: Contemporary South African Writing*. Oxford: Oxford University Press, 2017.
Wachtel, Eleanor. *Radom Illuminations: Conversations with Carol Shields*. New Brunswick: Goose Lane Editions, 2007.

Walkowitz, Rebecca L. *Cosmopolitan Style: Modernism beyond the Nation*. New York: Columbia University Press, 2006.

Walkowitz, Rebecca L. *Born Translated: The Contemporary Novel in an Age of World Literature*. New York: Columbia University Press, 2015.

Wallace, David Foster. 'Fictional Futures and the Conspicuously Young', *Review of Contemporary Fiction*, 8.3 (1988), repr. in *Both Flesh and Not: Essays*. London: Hamish Hamilton, 2012. 37–72.

Wallace, Dewey D., *Shapers of English Calvinism, 1660–1714: Variety, Persistence, and Transformation*. Oxford: Oxford University Press, 2011.

Walshe, Peter. 'Christianity and the Anti-Apartheid Struggle: The Prophetic Voice within Divided Churches', in *Christianity in South Africa*, 383–99.

Watkins, Susan. *Doris Lessing*. Manchester: Manchester University Press, 2010.

Waugh, Patricia. 'Kazuo Ishiguro's Not-Too-Late Modernism', in *Kazuo Ishiguro: New Critical Visions of the Novels*, ed. Sebastian Groes and Barry Lewis. London: Palgrave, 2011. 13–30.

Whitehead, Anne. *Trauma Fiction*. Edinburgh: Edinburgh University Press, 2004.

Whitehead, Anne. 'Writing with Care: Kazuo Ishiguro's *Never Let Me Go*', *Contemporary Literature*, 52.1 (Spring 2011): 54–83.

Whitehead, Colson. *The Underground Railroad*. London: Fleet, 2016.

Williams, Raymond. *Resources of Hope*. London: Verso, 1988.

Wolf, Werner and Walter Bernhart, eds. *Description in Literature and Other Media*. Amsterdam: Rodopi, 2007.

Wood, James. 'The Trick of Truth', rev. of *Atonement*, by Ian McEwan, *The New Republic*, 25 March 2002: https://newrepublic.com/article/63386/atonement-ian-mcewan-fiction

Wood, James. '*Gilead*: Acts of Devotion', *The New York Times*, 28 Nov. 2004: http://www.nytimes.com/2004/11/28/books/review/28coverwood.html

Woolf, Virginia. *A Change of Perspective: The Letters of Virginia Woolf, Vol. III: 1923–1928*, ed. Nigel Nicolson. London: Hogarth, 1977.

Woolf, Virginia. *The Diary of Virginia Woolf: Vol. III: 1925–1930*, ed. Anne Oliver Bell. London: Hogarth, 1980.

Woolf, Virginia. *Moments of Being*, ed. Jeanne Schulkind. London: Grafton, 1989.

Woolf, Virginia. *The Essays of Virginia Wool, Vol. IV: 1925–1928*, ed. Andrew McNeillie. London: Hogarth, 1994.

Woolf, Virginia. *To the Lighthouse*, ed. Margaret Drabble. 1927; Oxford: Oxford University Press, 2000.

Woolf, Virginia. Notes for Writing, *To the Lighthouse*, Berg Materials, Item 5: Woolfonline.com: Gallery:http://www.woolfonline.com/?node=content/image/gallery&project=1&parent=6&taxa=16

Worden, Daniel. 'The Memoir in the Age of Neoliberal Individualism', in *Neoliberalism and Contemporary Literary Culture*, ed. Mitchum Heuhls and Rachel Greenwald Smith. Baltimore, MD: Johns Hopkins University Press, 2017. 160–77.

Worthington, Kim L. '*Age of Iron* (1990)', in *A Companion to the Works of J. M. Coetzee*, ed. Tim Mehigan. New York: Camden House, 2011. 113–31.

Zeiger, Melissa F. *Beyond Consolation: Death, Sexuality and the Changing Shapes of Elegy*. Ithaca, NY: Cornell University Press, 1997.

Zimbler, Jarad. *J. M. Coetzee and the Politics of Style*. Cambridge: Cambridge University Press, 2014.

Index

Abel, Elizabeth 47
Adorno, Theodor W. 8, 29, 214
aesthetics 6–11, 24, 28, 47–8, 63, 128, 138–9, 153, 155, 172, 257n.21
  of elegy 90–1
  and pleasure 213–14
  and the reading experience 11, 34–6, 218–19, 221–2
  of trauma fiction 18, 72–3
  unsentimental 153, 155, 169
  and violence 45–6, 49–50, 53–4, 81, 85–6
  see also form; modernism
affect 2–3, 5–7, 12–13, 33–6, 39–40, 42–5, 66–7, 72, 88, 97, 101, 103, 122, 157–8, 167–8, 178–80, 198, 205–7, 225
  and genre 20–1, 89–90, 100, 153, 170
  historical accounts of 21–3, 62–4, 223–4
  and neoliberalism 216
  in postmodernity 224
  theorizing the literary representation of 6–7, 10–15, 67–70, 72–3, 84–5, 116–17, 144–5, 163, 186, 223
  taxonomies of 21
  temporalities of 20, 135–6, 144–5
  and withdrawal 76, 83, 95–6, 195–6, 205
affect studies 8, 21
affective criticism 36–7, 112–13, 127–8, 191, 212, 225–6
Alleine, Joseph 134
Als, Hilton 162
Améry, Jean 74–5
Anker, Elizabeth S. 35–6
Ariès, Philippe 145
Armstrong, Nancy 189
Attridge, Derek 6, 15, 118–19, 216, 230n.60
Attwell, David 117
Aubry, Timothy 9–10

Bailey, Paul 122
Bal, Mieke 70, 84
Barnes, Julian 18–19, 24–5, 61, 90–1, 96, 100–1
  Levels of Life 91–4
Barthes, Roland 222
Bates, Karen Grigsby 183–4
Beckett, Samuel 28, 114
Beer, Gillian 47
Bergsten, Monica 181
Berlant, Lauren 107, 219, 232n.106, 257n.21
Bernhart, Walter 70
Bersani, Leo 14–15, 17

Best, Stephen 35, 69, 219
Bewes, Timothy 74, 239n.41, 257n.21
Bishop, Elizabeth 103, 107–10, 112
Blanton, C. D. 63
Boehmer, Elleke 124
Boethius 213
Bottorff, Joan 178–9
Boxall, Peter 60, 68, 234n.24
Brookner, Anita 57
Brown, Judith 35
Brown, Wendy 216
Butler, Judith 116
Byatt, A. S. 77

care 178–88
Caruth, Cathy 16
Cavell, Stanley 12–13
Chabon, Michael 71, 237n.8
Chidester, David 120, 246n.33
Chodat, Robert 138–9
Clarkson, Carrol 128
close reading 33–4, 102–3, 107–8, 112, 211–12
Coetzee, J. M. 25, 27–8, 115–28, 210
  Age of Iron 116–23
  Disgrace 116, 122–8
compassion 1–2, 21, 127, 150–1, 169, 188, 191, 221
consolation, *passim*
  in relation to comfort 1, 5–7, 9, 12, 15–18, 23, 33, 39–40, 58–9, 62, 66–8, 82–3, 94, 111–12, 122, 129–32, 134, 140–3, 146–8, 150, 159–60, 169, 178–82, 184, 187, 202–4, 208–9, 219–20
  definitions of 8–11
  as formal affordance of narrative, *see* form, style
  and gender 123–4, 151–2, 156–9, 169, 174
  histories of 12–13, 21–4
  theological valences of 21–3, 120, 131–2, 140–3
  See also solace, redemption
Connolly, Cyril 56–7
Conrad, Joseph 90
Constantine, David 20, 37
Conte, Joseph 223
critique 13–14, 33–6, 45, 70, 76–7, 191, 219, 225–6, 257n.21
Crosby, Christina 4–5
  A Body, Undone 4–5, 7–8
Currie, Janet 95, 99
Currie, Mark 182–3, 253n.21
Cvetkovich, Ann 21

Index

Davis, Lennard J. 214
Denby, David J. 206
Deraniyagala, Sonali 2–4
  Wave 2–4, 7–8, 37–9
description 2–4, 10–11, 31–2, 46–8, 52–6,
    63–87, 104–5, 111–13, 123–4, 132–3,
    139–40, 158–9, 181–3, 211–12
  and detail 37–9, 94, 107–8, 135–7, 196–9
  metrical elements of 66–7, 71
  as refuge 189–90, 196–7, 199–202, 207–8
  and tableau 206–7
  theories of 69–70, 84–5
  See also form, style
descriptive reading 36, 67–8, 112–13, 219
Dickinson, Emily 175
Didion, Joan 25–6, 161–74, 252n.51
  Blue Nights 173
  The Year of Magical Thinking 161–73, 222
Dubow, Jessica 76–7
Dyer, Geoff 53

Eaglestone, Robert 76, 239n.33
elegy 22–6, 86, 88–113, 117–18, 144, 207–9
Ellis, Steve 59
emotion, histories of 12, 21–4, 34–5
Enright, Anne 174
  The Gathering 174
Eriksson, Katie 184
eulogy 52–3, 86, 118–20, 130, 160,
    200–1, 209

Felski, Rita 35–6, 112, 232n.101
Finney, Brian 234n.24
Flatley, Jonathan 227n.20
Flaubert, Gustave 114
Fleissner, Jennifer L. 36
form 2–3, 5–8, 10–17, 20–5, 27, 33–4, 67–70,
    100, 109–10, 119–20, 129, 138–43, 146,
    150, 153, 157–8, 160–1, 167–8, 197,
    213–14, 216–17, 219–20
  and modernist aesthetics 14–15, 28, 41–54
  politics of 8, 14, 27, 29–30, 32, 35–7, 58–9,
    62, 116–17, 128, 143–4, 202–3, 206–7,
    216, 224–5
  reparative 8, 13–14, 24, 39, 42, 119–20,
    149–50, 159
  and trauma 16–19, 71–6, 80–2
  See also description, free indirect
    discourse, style
Forster, E. M. 60
Franklin, Ruth 79, 82
free indirect discourse 107–8, 110–11, 122–3,
    125–8
Freud, Sigmund 19, 42, 213
Fridlund, Bengt 184

Gąsiorek, Andrzej 42
Gawande, Atul 144–5
  Being Mortal 145
Gee, Grant 85–6
  Patience (After Sebald) 85–6

Gilbert, Sandra M. 163–4, 251n.43
Grant, Linda 193
Gray, Richard 237n.8
Grossman, David 26–7, 96, 178, 193–211,
    221–2
  Falling Out of Time 209–11
  To the End of the Land 193–209
grief 2–4, 19, 21–5, 38–9, 89–99, 102–6,
    110–11, 116–17, 129, 132, 134–9,
    145–6, 161–73, 176, 189, 193, 195,
    203–4, 208–11, 213, 219–23
  See also mourning
Gurfinkel, Helena 235n.51

Hadley, Tessa 243n.57
Hale, Dorothy J. 242n.50
Hamon, Philippe 84
Hardy, Thomas 41
Hart, D. G. 245n.31
Hart, Matthew 74–5
Harvey, David 256n.30
Hasak-Lowry, Todd 255n.28
Head, Dominic 42, 120, 142
Heaney, Seamus 243n.60
Hell, Julia 80
Henke, Suzette 18
Herman, Judith Lewis 18
Hewitt, Rachel 23–4, 232n.97
Hoberek, Andrew 65, 68–9
Hong, Cathy Park 11
Houser, Heather 214
Hungerford, Amy 130
Hutchinson, Sally 179
Huyssen, Andreas 76

Ibbett, Katherine 11, 21, 227n.20, 232n.97
Ishiguro, Kazuo 26, 178, 180–92
  Never Let Me Go 180–91
  The Remains of the Day 181

Jacobs, Carol 72–3, 78, 82, 238n.25
James, Caryn 153
Jameson, Fredric 29–30, 174, 223–4
Jansson, Lilian 179
Jockers, Matthew L. 212
Johnson, Samuel 12, 220
Jordan, Julia 94
Joyce, James 108–10, 243n.58

Kannemeyer, J. C. 118
Kelly, Henry Ansgar 23
Kennedy, David 89, 100, 110
Kermode, Frank 146, 151
Kinghorn, Johann 245n.31
Konstantinou, Lee 258n.32
Kornbluh, Anna 31–2
Kübler-Ross, Elisabeth 144–5

LaCapra, Dominick 16, 18
Lazarus, Neil 44
Lee, Hermione 52

Leighton, Angela 5–6, 88–9, 110, 112
LeMahieu, Michael 161
Lesjak, Carolyn 218–19
Lessing, Doris 25–6, 150–61, 173–4
  Alfred and Emily 151–61
  The Golden Notebook 161
Levine, Caroline 228n.25
Lewis, C. S. 89
  A Grief Observed 89, 241n.5
Leypoldt, Günter 228n.22
loss, *passim*; *see also* grief, mourning
Love, Heather 36, 69, 230n.56
Lown-Hecht 74–5
Luckhurst, Roger 18, 73, 85
Lukács, Georg 69–70
Lundman, Berit 180–1
Lyotard, Jean-François 43–4, 224–5

Macdonald, Helen 24–5, 90–1, 100–1
  H is for Hawk 95–100
  on nature writing 100
Mantel, Hilary 241n.5
Marcus, Laura 50
Marcus, Sharon 35, 69
Marcuse, Herbert 44, 63, 236n.65
Matz, Jesse 54–5, 171–2, 240n.78
McAlpin, Heller 152
McBride, Eimear 17
McCann, Colum 6
McCarthy, Cormac 65–9, 84, 202
  The Road 65–72, 84
McClure, George W. 22
McCulloch, Mark 239n.32
McDonald, Peter D. 126, 247nn.50, 52
McDonald, Rónán 112–13
McEwan, Ian 24, 63–4, 235n.45
  Atonement 42–4, 49–63
McLoughlin, Kate 60
Messud, Claire 146
Middleton, Peter 36–7
Miller, Tyrus 45
Milner, Iris 202
Mintz, Alan 202
Mitchell, Katie 85
modernism 14–15, 24–5, 28–9, 41–51, 62–4, 93, 124–5
  and the legacies of literary impressionism 52–6
  and life-writing 47–8, 93
  and postcoloniality 44
Montaigne, Michel de 9
Moore, Caroline 152
Morrison, Blake 151
Morse, Janice 179–80, 252n.5
mourning 19, 25, 88–9, 94–5, 97–8, 107, 111–15, 133, 137, 162–4, 167–73, 176, 178, 209–11
  see also grief
Mullan, John 186, 253n.15
Mullaney, Steven 10
Murdoch, Iris 58–9, 62

Nabokov, Vladimir 100
Nealon, Christopher 166
Neil, Michael 123, 245n.17
Nelson, Deborah 169
Ngai, Sianne 11
Neuman, Justin 119
Norberg, Astrid 179–81
Nünning, Ansgar 238n.23

O'Connell, Mark 135

Parks, Tim 28, 32–3, 248n.96
Persson, Torleif 239n.40
Phillips, Adam 17
Plotz, John 153, 158
postmodernism 24, 43–4, 61–2, 214, 223–4
Preston, Alex 32

queer theory 21, 222
  and critical archives of affect 21
  and histories of suffering 230n.56

race 30–2, 120, 129–30, 143–4, 148–9, 249n.107
Ramazani, Jahan 90
Rasmussen, Birgit H. 179
Reddy, William M. 232n.98
redemption 13–16, 27, 29–30, 42–4, 47–51, 108, 114–15, 128, 140–1, 198–9
Rehnsfeldt, Arne 184
restitution 71–4, 77–8, 81–2, 155–6
Reynolds, Paige 229n.48
Ricoeur, Paul 25, 114–15, 144–6
Riley, Denise 219–25
  Say Something Back 219–22
  Time Lived, Without Its Flow 220–5
Riquelme, John Paul 93
Rittgers, Ronald K. 22–3
Robbins, Bruce 183–4, 188
Robinson, Jenefer 219–20
Robinson, Marilynne 25, 114–15, 128–47
  Gilead 129–40, 143–4
  Home 129–30, 148–50
  Lila 146–7
Ronen, Ruth 70
Rooney, Ellen 33–4
Rose, Jacqueline 203, 208
Roth, Michael S. 229n.54
Roxberg, Åsa 184
Rushdie, Salman 181

Said, Edward 233n.11
Schor, Esther 168
Scott, A. O. 81
Sebald, W. G. 17, 71–87, 201
  Austerlitz 72–84
  The Rings of Saturn 85–6
Sedgwick, Eve Kosofsky 8
Seltzer, Mark 211–12

Shields, Carol 13
  Unless 13
Silverblatt, Michael 57
Skinner, Daniel 249n.107
Smith, Ali 27
Sontag, Susan 62
solace: *passim*
  and critical practice 8–12, 213, 224–6
  discrepant meanings of 5–11
  and narrative structure 13–14, 47–8, 72–3, 91, 97, 152, 172–3, 212
  see also consolation, redemption
Southgate, Beverley 16
Spivak, Gayatri Chakravorty 128
stoicism 150–3, 169, 177
style 3–4, 6, 10, 13–14, 17–18, 24–5, 34, 38–9, 42–3, 49, 53, 55–6, 58–9, 62–3, 65–71, 77, 84–7, 91, 93–6, 100, 107, 113–37, 140–2, 150, 152, 154–5, 162–5, 173–4, 186–7, 189–91, 205–7, 216–17, 224–6
  as argument 44–8, 62, 158, 174, 217
  commodification of 223
  ethical implications of 23–4, 27–33, 50, 52–3, 81–3, 128, 169–70, 222
  free indirect, *see* free indirect discourse
  historical treatment of 34–5, 56–7, 63–4, 216
  and impersonality 74, 95–6, 108, 126, 155, 161, 169, 205, 239n.40
  and the syntax of amelioration 3–4, 38–9, 93–5, 184–8
  and the work of grief 167, 221–2
  See also description, form
Sykes, Rachel 249n.107
Swift, Graham 176–8
  'Half a Loaf' (*England and Other Stories*) 176–7

Tanner, Laura E. 131–2
Terada, Rei 227n.20
Thurschwell, Pamela 150
Toíbín, Colm 24–5, 28, 89–90, 205–6
  Nora Webster 101–8, 110–12
Tomalin, Claire 95
Tomlinson, Philip 41–2
Tonkin, Boyd 77
trauma studies 16–18, 71–3, 239n.40
Treat, John Whittier 29

van den Akker, Robin 258n.32
van der Vlies, Andrew 25, 116, 118
Vermeulen, Timotheus 258n.32

Walkowitz, Rebecca L. 186–7
Wallace, David Foster 145
Walshe, Peter 120
Watkins, Susan 152
Watts, David 18
Waugh, Patricia 236n.66
Whitehead, Anne 17, 185–6, 191
Whitehead, Colson 30–3
  The Underground Railroad 30–2
Williams, Raymond 256n.30
Williams, Rowan 241n.5
Wolf, Werner 70, 238n.18
Wood, James 52, 62, 80, 83
Woolf, Virginia 24, 43–4, 48–51, 54–6, 67–8
  'A Sketch of the Past' 48–9
  To the Lighthouse 45–9, 56–7, 62
Worden, Daniel 216
Worthington, Kim 116–17

Zamalin, Alex 249n.107
Zeiger, Melissa F. 22
Zimbler, Jarad 123, 125, 142